# Awareness and Control in Sociolinguistic Research

The topic of awareness and control is an elephant in the room in sociolinguistic research. To what extent are speakers aware of sociolinguistic variables? Are there different types or levels of awareness? Is "control" of these variables a conscious or unconscious process, or is it some combination or the two? Are the variables we are aware of necessarily those we control, and vice versa? The extent to which speakers are aware of sociolinguistic information and use it strategically may drastically affect our understanding of the role that sociolinguistic cues play in the development of structural categories. This volume constitutes the first concerted effort to understand the nature of awareness and control using all the methodological and theoretical tools at our disposal. The contributors employ a variety of perspectives to address the relationship between awareness and control in sociolinguistic research.

ANNA M. BABEL is an Assistant Professor of Hispanic Linguistics at the Ohio State University.

# Awareness and Control in Sociolinguistic Research

*Edited by*

Anna M. Babel

CAMBRIDGE
UNIVERSITY PRESS

# CAMBRIDGE
## UNIVERSITY PRESS

University Printing House, Cambridge CB2 8BS, United Kingdom

Cambridge University Press is part of the University of Cambridge.

It furthers the University's mission by disseminating knowledge in the pursuit of education, learning and research at the highest international levels of excellence.

www.cambridge.org
Information on this title: www.cambridge.org/9781107072381

© Cambridge University Press 2016

First published 2016

*A catalogue record for this publication is available from the British Library*

*Library of Congress Cataloguing in Publication data*
Names: Babel, Anna M., editor.
Title: Awareness and control in sociolinguistic research / edited by Anna M. Babel.
Description: Cambridge : Cambridge University Press, [2016]
Identifiers: LCCN 2016007901 | ISBN 9781107072381 (Hardback)
Subjects: LCSH: Sociolinguistics–Research–Methodology. | Sociolinguistics–Data processing. | Qualitative research. | BISAC: LANGUAGE ARTS & DISCIPLINES / Linguistics / General.
Classification: LCC P40.3 .A937 2016 | DDC 306.44072–dc23 LC record available at https://lccn.loc.gov/2016007901

ISBN 978-1-107-07238-1 Hardback

# Contents

# Figures

# Maps

# Tables

# Contributors

ANNA M. BABEL, The Ohio State University

ERICA BECK, Independent Scholar

KATHRYN CAMPBELL-KIBLER, The Ohio State University

KATIE CARMICHAEL, Virginia Polytechnic Institute and State University

NISHAANT CHOKSI, Kyoto University

KATIE DRAGER, University of Hawai'i at Mānoa

M. JOELLE KIRTLEY, University of Hawai'i at Mānoa

KEVIN B. MCGOWAN, University of Kentucky

BARBRA A. MEEK, University of Michigan

JENNIFER NYCZ, Georgetown University

DENNIS R. PRESTON, Oklahoma State University

LAUREN SQUIRES, The Ohio State University

LAL ZIMMAN, University of California, Santa Barbara

# Foreword

Forty-five years ago, Bickerton (1971:467, fn. 9) expressed the view that:

> The sociolinguistics of the future will surely be based on surreptitious recordings by trained participant-observers or by remote-control devices at present available only to government and industrial spies and divorce peepers.

From the viewpoint of today, this prediction was clearly wrong. Not just because surreptitious recordings have long been eschewed as sociolinguistic data-gathering techniques on ethical and other grounds, but also because it is clear that we need to do more than record how speakers talk when the effects of observation are minimized. Half a century of theorizing and empirical research has taught us that in order to come to grips with perception as well as production, to pursue newer interests like social meaning and the limits of agency, and to settle older debates about speech community, communicative competence, and salience, we also need to understand what people know and are aware of, as they use language. And to do *that*, we need to ask them about their competence and performance (if you will), run experiments, read in allied fields like Anthropology and Psychology, and be better thinkers, ethnographers, socio-phoneticians, socio-grammarians, and so on. These are the kinds of activities in which the contributors to this book are engaged – vastly different from the vision of a researcher armed only with a telescope and a remote listening device. But they indeed represent the vibrant present and future of sociolinguistics.

In order to illustrate why I consider this book so important, let me enlarge upon the central point of the preceding paragraph. Back in the 1970s, when I was doing my dissertation research in Guyana, I did extensive sociolinguistic interviews and conversational recordings with dozens of people in the village of Cane Walk. The group included two weeders in the sugar cane fields, Irene and Rose, who never used the acrolectal or English pronoun variants in several singular pronoun subcategories, despite having numerous opportunities to do so. For third-person singular pronoun objects, for instance, they never used *him* or *her*, always basilectal *am* or mesolectal *he, she*: *mi sii am/ii* "I saw him~her." In this respect, they appeared to operate at the same (deep creole) level of the creole continuum, and to be similar kinds of sociolinguistic personas. But after

I had finished with my informal or spontaneous recordings, I went back to all of the speakers with controlled interviews, in which, among other things, I asked them to translate or correct sample sentences from Creole to English and vice versa. Here, a dramatic difference between Rose and Irene emerged. Rose *never* supplied the acrolectal or English variant in those two (or several other) pronoun subcategories, sometimes supplying only the mesolectal variant (*he* or *she* for object forms *him* and *her*) and asking whether *ii ga ingglish moo dan dat*? "Is there anything closer to English than that?" But Irene always did, readily deploying forms like *him* and *her* that she had never attested in her spontaneous recordings (see Rickford 1987:164–5). For Irene, therefore, her non-English usage in the spontaneous recordings can be considered an act of choice or identity. For Rose, her non-English usage seems less so, and more a reflection of a competence circumscribed by her networks, education, and exposure. Sociolinguists who depend only on long-range devices and surreptitious record-ings would see no difference between these individuals, and would therefore miss a distinction in control and awareness that a community member, an attentive ethnographer, or a contributor to this book would recognize.

Anna Babel, known for her fine contributions to Bolivian sociolinguistics and contact linguistics (e.g. Babel 2009, 2011, 2014) has provided an invalu-able service to sociolinguistics and linguistics more generally by conceiving, assembling, and editing this book. It is the outgrowth of a session on "Aware-ness and Control" that she organized at the Linguistic Society of America's 2013 annual meeting. That session featured papers by *five* scholars, most with recent or newly minted PhDs, together covering a variety of topics, methods, and emphases.

*Babel*'s own paper provided a good introduction to awareness and control, outlining three primary methods of studying it (experiments, as in sociopho-netics; ethnographic observations of linguistic variation/style shifting; and elicitations of language attitudes and ideologies), and emphasizing the import-ance of considering the larger social and cultural environment. Drawing on ethnographic data from Bolivia, she demonstrated that women's reluctance or refusal to participate in the formal male-dominated *oratoria* style at meetings and to shift the genre to discourse styles in which they feel more comfortable doesn't represent "lack of control" in the strict sense, but "a different kind of monitoring" and activism.

*Carmichael* used Matched Guise and other experimental tasks with sixty-one Ohio State undergrads to gauge their reactions to speakers said to be from Columbus, New York City, or Birmingham (although they were actually from other cities in Southern, Midlands, Western, and Mid-Atlantic dialect areas). Their ratings of these speakers on Status, Solidarity, Accentedness and City-Country dimensions revealed a deterministic role of place expectations and awareness based on personal experience and impressions from TV and the movies. The relevance of popular media in her paper (as in Drager and Kirtley's and McGowan's) suggests that we should pay more attention to these as potential influences on the production and perception of sociolinguistic variation than we normally do.

In *McGowan's* perception experiment with eighty-seven undergrads, more experienced listeners were better than less experienced listeners at distinguishing authentic speakers of Mandarin English from monolingual English speakers imitating Chinese accents, suggesting that the two groups of listeners drew on different forms of linguistic/social knowledge. But the stereotypes used by less experienced listeners helped them perform "better than chance," and in a separate production experiment, five English-speaking actors imitating Chinese-sounding English didn't restrict themselves to "highly salient, stereotypical features" of Mandarin-accented English, but variably used features associated with a broader "pan-Asian" accent.

*Nycz* examined the relation between awareness and control in the English of seventeen speakers of Canadian English who lived in the New York City area from one to thirty years (one for forty-four years), and found that high awareness of a feature (as with Canadian Raising) did not automatically lead to high control, and that good control did not require high awareness (as with Low Back Merger). This finding counters claims that in order to be acquired, the features of a second dialect $(D_2)$ must be noticed and/or be salient to first dialect $(D_1)$ speakers, and it also supports to some extent Labov's (1966) contention (see Labov 1972:104) that awareness and agency have limits when it comes to production, at least for adult speakers.

In the only paper dealing with morphosyntactic/socio-grammatical variation, *Squires* reported on participants' reactions to *standard* plural, *standard* singular, *nonstandard*, and *uncommon* variants of test sentences ("After eating, the turtle(s) *don't/doesn't* walk very fast") embedded in filler sentences. *Perceiving* was measured by reading time/speed (slowest in uncommon condition; fastest in standard; intermediate in nonstandard); and *awareness* by post-experiment metalinguistic comments. Results over three different experiments were consistent enough to confirm that *perceiving and noticing are separate cognitive processes.*

In addition to these five initial conference papers, Babel sought out six more for the book, and they add considerably to the novelty and variety of situations and variables covered in this publication, and to its theoretical heft.

*Beck* reports on experiments with young children, a segment of the population relatively understudied in sociolinguistics, especially in relation to language perception. She shows that 5- and 6-year-olds in a town near Philadelphia can discriminate between familiar and unfamiliar regional accents on an Awareness Task, although "insiders" (at least one parent speaks the local dialect) do better than "outsiders" (no parents speak the local dialect).

On an ABX discrimination task, however, both "insider" and "outsider" children performed quite well, without significant inter-group differences, suggesting that children at this age "are not heavily influenced by social knowledge in perception of regional accents."

Anthropologists *Choksi and Meek* focus on salience via orthographic representations of indigenous minority languages – a topic rare in sociolinguistics, but commoner in their subfield. Salience for them is "that which is susceptible to being noticed but not merely as a property of perception or language ... [but] also or mutually as a result of the socio-cultural context ..." Examples come from Native American languages in Yukon, Canada, and Santali in eastern India. Santals place great store on writing their language with Murmu's distinct 1925 "Ol-Chiki" script, or with modifications of Roman or other scripts that preserve their distinctive mid-central vowel. Ideologically, this is a salient symbol of their political and linguistic distinctness from Bengali and other non-indigenous neighbors, and of their aspirations for statehood.

*Zimman* takes us to another area insufficiently considered by sociolinguists – transgender individuals and the role of agency, power, and ideology in their transitions. Drawing on two years of ethnographic work with fifteen trans men ("female-to-male-trans people"), whose trans voices are more easily changed by hormone therapy than trans women, but who are also less studied, he encounters some apparent paradoxes. Confident that testosterone will eventually lower their vocal pitch, without inhibiting their "true, inner self," they reject attempts to "pass" as men by agentive means like avoiding upward inflections, while claiming agency in other respects. Given these complexities, Zimman suggests we look more critically at how agency, awareness, and control work for speakers in other situations.

Although virtually every paper in this volume includes some theoretical component, or at least a discussion of the broader implications of its ideas or findings, three of the new papers are devoted almost entirely to larger theoretical questions about awareness and control and how to model them in sociolinguistics.

*Campbell-Kibler* argues that Labov *et al.*'s (2001) "Sociolinguistic Monitor" [SLM] is too limited to socioeconomic class and standard vs. non-standard speech, and needs updating to represent variation by local group, sexual orientation, persona, stance, and other dimensions revealed by Third Wave and other sociolinguistic research, while incorporating insights from work in language processing, cognition, neuroscience, and social psychology. After summarizing some of the key ideas and findings from such work, she outlines what should be in an updated model of socio-linguistic cognition. Her list includes the *grammar* itself, as in the SLM, but also a variety of social features of speech context, linked to the grammar through rapid, automatic associative indexical links, as well as slower, more effortful and conscious processes of *self-regulation*. A *person perception system* is the third key element.

*Drager and Kirtley* explain how awareness, salience, and stereotypes of sociolinguistic variables are accounted for in exemplar models of speech perception and production in (socio-)linguistics. Individual utterances of words, their meanings and phonetics are stored cognitively as Exemplar Clouds, with social, stylistic, and other information about their contexts. Because of the automatic storage of linguistic and social information in exemplar models, speakers don't need to be consciously *aware* to perceive or process sociolinguistic variation, even for stereotypes. But exemplar weights can be used to represent *salience* or heightened attention to certain exemplars, related to their frequency and recency of activation. The authors use their own and others' sociophonetic examples as illustrations, noting in closing that Exemplar models require further development and testing.

*Preston* has long been a leading figure in perceptual dialectology, the study of what, how, and why non-linguists notice and think about people's speech. In this chapter he repeats a distinction between four aspects of folk *awareness* (its Availability, Accuracy, Detail, and Control) that he first drew in Preston (1996), but he also explores the conscious-unconscious distinction and other aspects of folk linguistics and language attitude studies not in the earlier account. How people notice and classify language features, he notes, varies according to their prior beliefs and attitudes about languages and their speakers, by elicitation conditions, and other factors. He outlines the structure of attitudinal cognitoria in general, with a specific illustration of a southeastern Michigan cognitorium for "Southern," and calls for subtler techniques for teasing out beliefs and attitudes, conscious and unconscious.

I'll close this foreword with a couple of final observations.

The first is that while every chapter covers *awareness* to some extent, several of them citing Silverstein's important (1981) paper on this subject, only about nine (Babel, Campbell-Kibler, Carmichael, Choksi and Meek, Drager and Kirtley, McGowan, Nycz, Preston, and Zimman) cover *control* too. Even among those that attend to both concepts, *control* receives less attention than *awareness*. This is interesting, given than most sociolinguistic work has been on production rather than perception, but it perhaps reflects the fact that theorizing about sociolinguistic cognition has been stronger (see Labov *et al.* 2011, Campbell-Kibler in this volume) in relation to perception than production.

Secondly, while all but three papers cite Labov's (1972) distinction between linguistic variables that are *indicators*, *markers*, and *stereotypes*, representing different levels of awareness (none, some, and a lot respectively), no one comments on Bell's (1984:151–2) "audience design" derivation of *markers*, which show interspeaker and intraspeaker variation, from *indicators*, which show only inter-speaker variation. This is surely one kind of synchronic and diachronic "fact" for which a sociolinguistic cognition model of language variation and change should account. And while *stereotypes* "under extreme stigmatization … may become the overt topic of social comment" and "may become increasingly divorced from the forms actually used in speech" (Labov 1972:180), no one comments on the fact that the extent to which this is true (i.e. the gap between stereotypical characterization and reality) will vary from one variable to another. One could fruitfully investigate this in terms of Preston's (this volume) "accuracy" factor ("Does the folk account mirror the linguistic facts?") and try to develop hypotheses about the conditions under which sociolinguistic stereotypes become more or less divorced from reality.

In pointing to aspects of awareness or control like these that are under- or unrepresented, I intend no substantive critique. This book is full of many rich observations and insights that its authors do contribute, and my parting comments should be taken as representative of additional questions that the book will stimulate readers to consider, and hopefully pursue. Issues of awareness and control are central to the development of sociolinguistic theory, and it is likely that this book will shape research on sociolinguistic variation for years to come.

JOHN R. RICKFORD, STANFORD UNIVERSITY
February 2016

## REFERENCES

Babel, Anna. 2009. *Dizque*, evidentiality, and stance in Valley Spanish. *Language in Society* 38(4):487–511.

2011. Why don't all contact features act alike? Contact features as enregistered features. *Journal of Language Contact* 4:56–91.

2014. Stereotypes over experience: *Pues* variation as an index of regional identity in the Santa Cruz valleys of Bolivia. *Journal of Sociolinguistics* 18:604–33.

Bell, Allan. 1984. Language style as audience design. *Language in Society* 13(2): 145–204.

Bickerton, Derek. 1971. Inherent variability and variable rules. *Foundations of Language* 7(4):457–92.

Labov, William. 1966. *The Social Stratification of English in New York City*. Washington, DC: Center for Applied Linguistics.

1972. *Sociolinguistic Patterns*. Philadelphia, PA: University of Pennsylvania Press.

Labov, William, Sharon Ash, Maya Ravindranath, Tracey Weldon, Maciej Baranowski, and Naomi Nagy. 2011. Properties of the sociolinguistic monitor. *Journal of Sociolinguistics* 15(4):431–63.

Rickford, John R. 1987. The haves and have-nots: Sociolinguistic surveys and the assessment of speaker competence. *Language in Society* 16(2):149–77.

Silverstein, Michael. 1981. The limits of awareness. *Texas Working Papers in Linguistics* 84:1–30. (Reprinted in Alessandro Duranti (ed.), *Linguistic Anthropology: A Reader*. Malden, MA and Oxford, UK: Blackwell (2001).)

# Preface

Awareness and control touches on every aspect of sociolinguistic work. Although scholars often refer to awareness casually or impressionistically as a side-note to other types of analysis, the practice of systematically investigating and reporting on participants' awareness of a sociolinguistic feature should be as routine as reporting on its distribution in a community of speakers. This is important because linguistic features behave differently depending on how people perceive them: highly stereotyped features will often be used selectively and with a high degree of intentionality or consciousness, while those that are lower on the scales of awareness may escape notice until some circumstance calls attention to them. And of course, no linguistic feature acts in isolation, but rather as part of a pattern of use and meaning that may be interpreted differently in different situations or from varying points of view. A linguistic feature that is highly salient in the speech of one speaker may be unremarkable in the speech of another. Listeners, too, vary – what leaps out to one person may pass completely unnoticed for another. Our perceptions of meaningful variation are shaped by our experiences, identifications, and (inter)subjectivities. Indeed, there is little doubt that even the linguistic features that we as scholars choose to study are guided by our own patterns of awareness, including how that awareness may have been shaped by our academic training.

Awareness and control has been considered an intractable problem because for several decades the dominant theoretical models in the field have enforced a separation of linguistic and social factors. Yet we need look no further than children, who have extensive input from their parents but learn to speak like their peers, to see that people perceive and produce language through the lens of social categories. The increasing prevalence and diversity of theoretical models that question this dichotomy means that we have a new opportunity to reassess our approach to the topic.

This volume brings together work on awareness and control from many perspectives in sociolinguistic research, but more than that, it brings together the work of a group of scholars who are interested in pushing the boundaries of the discipline by working beyond and across their own subdisciplinary homes.

From sociophonetics to language processing to psycholinguistics to language acquisition to perceptual dialectology to linguistic anthropology, the contributors to this volume work with a broad variety of theoretical frameworks and a range of methodological tools. The authors largely refer to a common set of sociolinguistic literature on awareness and control, including centrally Labov (1972), Silverstein (1981), and Preston (1996). Crucially, all three of these works treat awareness and control as a complex, multidimensional phenomenon in which awareness of linguistic variation is fully integrated with systems of social relations and meaning-making. This common orientation gives the volume a theoretical coherence, and allows the contributors to speak to each other across theoretical and methodological differences.

At the same time, the contributors share a common quality that one reviewer referred to as "voraciousness" in exploring work in related disciplines. This theoretical voraciousness, perhaps even omnivorousness, is key to our ability to advance this topic now. The study of awareness and control pushes us to move beyond boundaries that we have found easy and convenient, and perhaps useful for a time – "internal" versus "external" factors, experimental versus ethnographic methodologies, theoretical versus empirical approaches. Awareness and control is a topic that will not submit to these dichotomies. It cuts across all levels of linguistic structure and types of analysis. It provides a forum in which to think broadly about the whole of language, encompassing structure and ideology. By the same token, precisely because awareness and control is complicated and context-dependent, it resists separation into distinct areas of study. We all need to work together to understand this very complex, typically human problem.

The study of awareness and control brings together not just subfields of linguistics, but also has implications for psychology, biology, cognitive science, and social theory. However, the way in which we define and measure awareness and control in different fields varies considerably. For example, while anthropologists and social theorists have treated awareness as a dimension of consciousness at a societal or intersubjective level, drawing on philosophy and Marxist theory, psychologists and cognitive scientists have approached awareness as a quality of individuals, albeit individuals conditioned by their social *milieu*, that can be studied experimentally and in isolation from interaction. This tension between the individual and the sociocultural is a persistent theme that divides cultural studies from cognitive types of approaches.

Much work remains to be done in bridging disciplinary and subdisciplinary boundaries. In particular, there is a need for more engagement between the two areas that can be broadly labeled as cognitive science and social theory. Cognitive research *is* social research, and it is imperative that we approach cognitive science with models of social interaction that are as detailed and subtle as is our understanding of linguistic structure. In the academic sphere, a popular ideology that places scientism and STEM fields in opposition to the humanities and social research seems to be reinforcing the division between these purportedly distinct orientations. Since language is a social as well as an individual phenomenon, linguists are of necessity *both* cognitive scientists and social theorists, and we must work to contest these discourses. The study of awareness and control has the potential to bridge these differences. Moreover, it has the potential to move towards a holistic understanding of human experience, joining the kaleidoscopic shards of our collective partial understandings into a single coherent image.

It is clear that a continuing commitment to methodological diversity, to epistemological tolerance, and to open communication are essential to our progress in the study of awareness and control. Given that these conditions are met, where do we go next? Here are a few ideas that have emerged from this volume that will undoubtedly lead to future work:

We speak of different "levels" of awareness and control. What are these "levels" (Squires)? Are they connected, and if so, what are the connections between them? Is this the right metaphor for the different types and qualities of awareness that we can observe through our research? Are there varying degrees or intensities of awareness? How might these be related to scales of awareness (Preston)?

How do people acquire awareness and control? How does awareness and control change over the lifespan (Beck) and through different kinds of experiences, such as migration processes (Nycz) or educational institutions? How do our expectations of typical speech affect our awareness and evaluation of particular variables (Carmichael)? Is there cross-linguistic diversity in awareness and control? How do these processes work in standard language environments versus in non-standardized languages, and how are they embedded in cultural artifacts such as systems of orthography (Choksi and Meek)? How might we model the cognitive processes that underlie our ability to perceive links between language and social categorization (Campbell-Kibler, Drager and Kirtley)? How are concepts such as agency and intentionality integrated in our perception and production of linguistic features (Zimman)?

How can we use the study of awareness and control to develop links between perception and production (Babel)? People can perceive features that they do not control, as anyone who has attempted to imitate someone else's accent can attest. People also control features of which they are not aware – bidialectal speakers are often unaware of the way in which they accommodate to different types of interlocutors, as when an adult speaks to childhood friends or relatives in a way that is distinct from her normal style of speech. Yet at some level, we *must* be aware of these features in order to control them. How does our experience with language translate into an ability to perceive and produce speech (McGowan)?

I am truly grateful to all of the contributors to this volume for their generosity with their work and their great patience with me in my editorial role. The excitement and interest that this project inspires in me has only grown as I've had the opportunity to delve deeper into these topics, and I am constantly impressed and humbled by the excellence and dedication of my fellow scholars. In conclusion, I would like to offer special thanks – from all of us – to John Rickford for his encouragement and for the idea of turning our LSA session on this topic into an edited volume. It has been a rewarding experience, and I hope that this will be a useful and thought-provoking resource for other readers in the future.

ANNA M. BABEL
February 2016

## REFERENCES

Labov, William. 1972. *Sociolinguistic Patterns*. Philadelphia, PA: University of Pennsylvania Press.

Preston, Dennis. 1996. Whaddayaknow: The modes of folk linguistic awareness. *Language Awareness* 5(1):40–74.

Silverstein, Michael. 1981. The limits of awareness. *Texas Working Papers in Linguistics* 84:1–30.

# 1     Awareness, Salience, and Stereotypes in Exemplar-Based Models of Speech Production and Perception

*Katie Drager and M. Joelle Kirtley*

The contributions to this volume discuss the degree to which awareness plays a role in how language is produced (Babel, Zimman), acquired (Nycz), and processed (Beck, Carmichael, Squires). The conclusions underscore the need for models of speech production and perception that can account for different amounts of awareness and attention. In this chapter, we seek to lay out how awareness, salience, and stereotypes are implemented within exemplar-based models of speech production and perception, reflecting on predictions that these models make in regard to awareness and salience.

Before addressing how awareness and salience might work within exemplar-based models of speech, let's talk briefly about awareness and how the term is used. Sometimes researchers use the term to refer to an awareness of a social category (e.g. Jock) or a linguistic variant (e.g. fishin'), and other times they refer to the awareness of a relationship between a social category and a linguistic variant (e.g. Midwesterners say 'pop'). These differences matter when considering if/how awareness is represented in the mind and when thinking about the cognitive processes through which awareness might influence speech. In this chapter, we focus on the last of these types of awareness: the awareness of a sociolinguistic variable.

But what do we even mean by awareness? Awareness is usually taken to mean one's consciousness of events or experiences. Some prior instance of noticing is required for awareness, but deliberate effort and instruction are not. In line with Squires (this volume) and others (Bowers 1984; Schmidt 1990), we differentiate between noticing a difference (which leads to awareness) and perceiving a difference (which, in the absence of noticing, does not). Perception without awareness is possible because many cognitive processes are automatic or reflexive, which contrast with processes that are controlled or reflective (Lieberman 2003; Schneider and Shiffrin 1977; Shastri and Ajjanagadde 1993). As Lieberman explains, "controlled processes . . . typically involve some combination of effort, intention, and awareness, tend to interfere with one another, and are usually experienced as self-generated thoughts. Automatic processes . . . typically lack effort, intention, or awareness, tend not to interfere with one another, and are usually experienced as perceptions or feelings"

(Lieberman 2003: 44). Controlled and automatic processes differ, and they have varying effects on an individual's linguistic behavior.[1] We should, therefore, expect different behavior depending on a speaker's or hearer's attention.

The necessity of the distinction between controlled processes and automatic processes in sociolinguistics finds support from the different behavior observed for markers and stereotypes in speech production (Labov 1972; Trudgill 1981)[2] and across different experimental tasks that vary in the degree of introspection they require (Hay *et al.* 2010). Both controlled and automatic processes contribute to sociolinguistic behavior and, therefore, should be accounted for within our models of speech production and perception.

In this chapter we discuss automatic processes and explore the treatment of awareness in exemplar-based models of speech production and perception. We first present what we mean by exemplar-based models. Next, we discuss how attention, salience, and stereotypes are accounted for in these models, and we step through the results from our previous work in order to make explicit how the models predict the observed behavior.

## What Is Exemplar Theory?

Exemplar Theory is a collection of cognitive models in which experiences are encoded in the mind as episodic memories, known as exemplars. The models are often (but not always) implemented computationally to test the model's predictions (e.g. Hintzman and Ludlam 1980). Exemplar models originated in psychology (Brooks 1978; Hintzman and Ludlam 1980; Schacter *et al.* 1978) and continue to be influential (e.g. Nosofsky *et al.* 2011). Highly relevant to sociolinguistics are exemplar models from social psychology that examine the perception of people. In these models, individuals have mental representations of categories which contain numerous types of information about the category; including stereotypes and beliefs about the category, values associated with the category, one's past interactions with people associated with the category, and specific category exemplars (Bern 1972; Eagly *et al.* 1994; Haddock *et al.* 1993; Nosofsky *et al.* 1994; Smith 1998). The activation of exemplars affects individual behavior and attitudes, often with no awareness of the activation of the exemplars or attitude (Lewicki 1986; Smith and Zárate 1992).

Linguists have extended and modified exemplar-based models to explain linguistic behavior (Johnson 1997; Pierrehumbert 2001). In such models, when

---

[1] It is worth noting that behavior, such as a stroke in a tennis match, can result from a combination of controlled and automatic processes. "The conscious decision about which stroke to attempt may be the result of a controlled process, whereas the actual stroking of the ball may be automatic" (Fazio 1990: 97).

[2] Labov's treatment of indicators, markers, and stereotypes is discussed in several contributions to this volume (e.g. Carmichael), so – in the interest of space – is not discussed further here.

a listener encounters someone saying *pizza*, the memory of that utterance is stored as its own representation (i.e. an exemplar) that is distinct from representations that encode other occasions when the listener heard the word *pizza*, even when those utterances were produced by the same speaker.[3] But there is clearly something similar about all of the different representations of *pizza*; they are not floating around in the mind, unrelated to one another, but instead, form what is called an exemplar cloud. Exemplar clouds are often thought of at the word level (Johnson 2005; Wedel 2006), but in the multidimensional space that is the mind, they can occur simultaneously at segmental and lexical levels (Pierrehumbert 2001), and potentially at other levels of the grammar as well.

Some researchers who work with exemplar-based models implement models that are strictly episodic (what Sherman refers to as "pure exemplar models" (1996: 1127)). Proponents of these types of exemplar models argue that any generalization that takes place occurs online without levels of representation beyond the episodic memories (Hintzman 1986; Nosofsky 1986). However, exemplar-based models of speech production and perception most commonly incorporate both episodic memories and generalized levels of representation (Goldinger 2007; Hay *et al.* 2013; Hay *et al.* 2006b; Johnson 2007; McLennan 2007; Nielsen 2011; Pierrehumbert 2006; Sherman 1996). The generalized levels are deemed to be necessary because individuals can produce and perceive words that they have not encountered before, and listeners generalize learned knowledge within natural classes and phonemes (McQueen *et al.* 2006; Norris *et al.* 2003). At the same time, episodic memories are seen to be necessary because listeners are sensitive to speaker- and utterance-specific phonetic detail (Craik and Kirsner 1974; Goldinger 1997; Palmeri *et al.* 1993), as well as phonetic cues related to affect (Gobl and Ní Chasaide 2003; Morton and Trehub 2001; Nygaard and Lunders 2002). For example, in a task where listeners identify whether or not they previously heard a word, they are more accurate when the same voice is used between trials than when it is a different voice (Craik and Kirsner 1974; Palmeri *et al.* 1993), and they remain sensitive to the speaker-specific phonetic realizations for at least a week (Goldinger 1997). Additionally, some researchers argue that sound change is linked with token frequency (Bybee 2001, 2002); such findings are consistent with exemplar-based models because frequency effects are a product of having episodic representations. It is important to note that these results are also consistent with other experience-based models that store information about the relationship between phonetic realizations and token frequency. However, because the relationship can be computed online

---

[3] People who talk about cognitive models often talk about representations of the word *cat*. We decided to mix things up and talk about *pizza* instead. Maybe we're hungry.

in an exemplar-based model (thus avoiding the need for explicit storage of the association), an exemplar-based account is an especially elegant solution.

Because of results such as those outlined above (e.g. Palmeri *et al.* 1993), it is posited that a great deal of phonetic detail is encoded in exemplars. This phonetic detail may include any number of phonetic traits, including voice onset time of plosives, nasalization of vowels, or the center of gravity of fricatives. Thus, as shown in Figure 1.1, the word *pizza* that our listener heard earlier would be stored in precise acoustic detail: encoding, for example, the duration of the aspiration in /p/, the vowel quality of /i/, and the center of gravity of the aperiodic energy in /s/. For segmental phonetic cues, each phoneme that was ultimately identified is indexed to the phonetically rich exemplar. In this chapter, we refer to the phonetically detailed representations as phonetic exemplars.

Phonetic exemplars are the main focus of our discussion since most sociolinguistic work that discusses exemplar models has focused on phone variation. However, exemplar models within variationist linguistics are not limited to phonetics, phonology, or the lexicon; there are, for example, episodic models of syntactic variation (Abbot-Smith and Tomasello 2006; Bybee and Cacoullos 2008; Erker and Guy 2012). There is also evidence that phonetic

Figure 1.1 Exemplar Cloud of the Word *Pizza*

detail is encoded in the lemma (Drager 2010, 2011a; Gahl 2008; Plug 2005), across word boundaries (Hay and Maclagan 2010), in chunks of speech that constitute two or more words (Bybee 2002), and in association with certain morpho-syntactic representations (Walker 2008). Much more work is needed to clarify the relationship of probabilistic information between different levels of the grammar.

In addition to the storage of language-specific information, other kinds of information are stored. This information includes any number of markers of an individual's identity, including broad social categories (e.g. lesbian), membership in a community of practice (e.g. Norteña), or a social practice itself (e.g. wears red heels). Because these markers include a wide range of different kinds of information and the different kinds of information are, in turn, indexed to each other, we use the intentionally vague terms "social meaning" and "social indices," and we wish to make explicit that a great deal of information is stored, detailed information that goes well beyond what might be considered traditionally linguistic information. While the term "information" may be more apt since divorcing the linguistic from the social is artificial, we feel it necessary to emphasize the presence of social information in the models given the history of linguistics and the tendency of some researchers to downplay or disregard the role of the social. In these models, socially meaningful information is indexed to linguistic exemplars, and this indexing may be direct or indirect depending on the individuals' experiences. Social indexing occurs automatically, without conscious effort by the perceiver.[4] "Thus, the exemplar model intrinsically captures the observation ... that no natural human utterance offers linguistic information without simultaneously indexing some social factor" (Foulkes and Docherty 2006: 426). An exemplar-based model with social indices not only accounts for sociolinguistic variation, it is a linguistic theory which predicts that socially conditioned variation will exist. Because utterances are stored as individual memories and these memories encode and are indexed to a great deal of information and because speech perception and production rely on these stored exemplars, variation is a natural consequence of the model.

## How Does Speech Perception Work?

Listeners encounter utterances, and these utterances are then stored. Once stored, these representations can be activated. Incoming speech activates the

---

[4] McGowan (this volume) contends that awareness is required for social indexing in exemplar-based models, but we propose that his results can be explained through perceived social information (such as perceiving the speaker as Asian or Chinese when in fact the speaker is Japanese) and through the storage of imitated speech, as outlined in this paper.

exemplars it is most similar to, and perception is biased towards the activated exemplars.[5] Thus, an incoming [p] activates exemplars of [p] more than, say, [s], [k], or even [pʰ], biasing perception towards [p]. The more closely the realization of the incoming [p] matches an exemplar, the more likely the exemplar will be activated. Other exemplars are also activated, particularly where there is a great deal of allophonic variation (Boomershine *et al.* 2005; Johnson 2006).

Activation of exemplars is gradient: one exemplar of *pizza* can be more or less activated than another exemplar of *pizza*, and those representations that are activated the most influence perception the most (Hintzman 1984). Activation spreads to exemplars that are indexed to already activated exemplars, and exemplars that are recently and frequently activated reach full activation the fastest and therefore bias perception the most. While exemplars decay over time, activation slows decay (Lacerda 1995), so exemplars that encode frequently encountered realizations resist decay.

Because stored social information is indexed to detailed linguistic information, activating linguistic exemplars activates the social information to which those exemplars are indexed. Thus, if our listener is at a café and overhears someone behind her say something about "eatin' pizza," she may infer certain things about the speaker based on people she has encountered before, as well as things she's heard about groups of people and the way they supposedly talk. A large amount of literature exists, both within linguistics and social psychology, demonstrating that listeners make judgments about speakers based on their speech, and these judgments are highly consistent across different listeners (Addington 1968; Aronovitch 1976; Harms 1961; Kirtley 2010; Carmichael, this volume). In an exemplar model, this occurs because linguistic exemplars are activated upon perception, which in turn activates associated social exemplars. This process happens automatically and, therefore, awareness of the specific linguistic variants or their association with social categories or traits is not necessary.

However, the process is not as simple as an incoming utterance activating a phonetic exemplar which in turn activates one and only one social meaning; we know that the social meaning of a linguistic variant shifts depending on contextual factors, including characteristics attributed to the speaker (Campbell-Kibler 2007) and other linguistic cues in the signal (Levon 2011). In the exemplar-based model proposed by Drager (2009), patterns of activated exemplars are indexed to personal styles (Drager 2009: 184) and may, in some cases, make up the styles themselves, in which case there is no abstract representation of the style. These patterns of activation may be over any

---

[5] In Nosofsky's (1992) model, activation relies on a combination of the exemplar's strength in memory, its similarity to the incoming utterance, and random noise (Nosofsky 1992: 386).

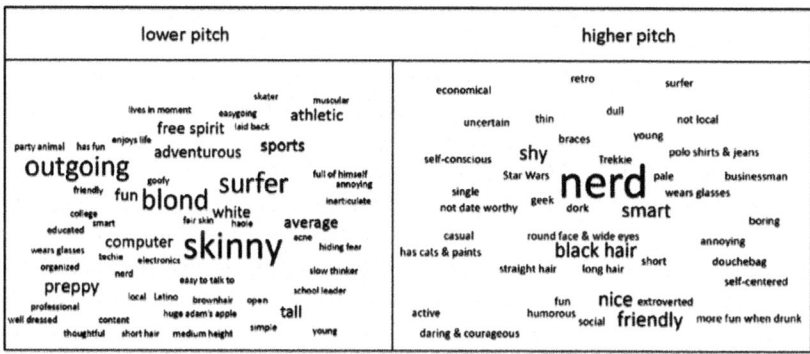

Figure 1.2 Perceived Traits for a Male Voice with Lower Pitch and Higher Pitch

number of stylistic components, including different linguistic variants. If the speaker who was talking about "eatin' pizza" also produces monophthongal /ɑɪ/, we expect our listener to attribute different social characteristics upon hearing "eatin' pizza" than were the speaker to produce diphthongal /ɑɪ/ (cf. Campbell-Kibler 2007). According to the exemplar-based model proposed by Drager (2009), this happens as a result of activation patterns that include these realizations, and social characteristics such as "educated" are primed via the activated style. The model also predicts that activation can spread to and/or from other stylistic components (e.g. hairstyle) that the listener associates with the style.

To help demonstrate how components of styles are activated in this model, Figure 1.2 shows two tag clouds from a matched guise experiment during which American-English-speaking participants responded to the open-ended question: *What do you think this speaker is like?*[6] Across the two guises, voice and content were controlled and mean pitch was manipulated. Responses are shown in Figure 1.2, with larger text indicating a larger number of participants who responded with that word or phrase. The difference in pitch seems to be related to a difference in style, ranging from what might be called a "sporty professional" style in the lower pitch guise to a "nice nerd" style in the higher pitch guise. Many participants who took part in this experiment responded with traits associated with a style rather than a label for the style itself. In the model outlined above, this happens when the incoming utterance activates phonetic exemplars to which it is most similar. Because pitch is included in the phonetic exemplars, exemplars that closely match in pitch are activated, and those that encode other phonetic

---

[6] This experiment was reported by Drager *et al.* (2010b).

information similar to that found in the incoming utterance are activated the most. The activation then spreads from the activated phonetic exemplars to indexed social information. The styles are perceived within the context of other social information attributed to the speaker (e.g. male, heterosexual) because this information, too, is activated and can serve to spread activation to social information with which it is indexed.

Exemplar-based models with social indexing also predict that listeners' perception of linguistic variants will be biased as a result of contextual factors. For example, our listener's surroundings – including the visible clientele of the café – influence her expectations about the speech she's about to hear. If our listener sees a stranger, the stored social exemplars of people who look most similar to that stranger are activated and her perception would be biased as a result. In fact, there is mounting evidence to support the prediction that social information attributed to a speaker influences how a listener will perceive their speech (Hay *et al.* 2006a; Hay *et al.* 2006b; Koops *et al.* 2008; Niedzielski 1999; Strand 1999). So, if the stranger in the café produces a linguistic variant that differs from the linguistic exemplars that are indexed to the activated social exemplars, our listener's speech processing will be slower than if it is similar (cf. Staum Casasanto 2008), and if the stranger produces an ambiguous word (e.g. does the cat sleep in the *litterbox* or *letterbox*?[7]) the listener's perception will be biased towards the speech of people deemed to be similar to the stranger (cf. Hay *et al.* 2006a). The evidence suggests that the flow of activation goes both ways: from the linguistic to the social and from the social to the linguistic. This is important to consider when thinking about how linguistic information is stored in the mind. Most models of speech perception would not predict these results because processing is strictly bottom-up (e.g. Klatt 1979) or because social information is not considered in the models (e.g. McClelland and Elman 1986).

### How Does Speech Production Work?

Stored exemplars also influence speech production. Activated linguistic exemplars bias production towards the variants they encode. As with perception, activation is fastest for recently and frequently activated exemplars, and social and contextual information can activate phonetic exemplars to which it is indexed. This can account for a wide variety of work in variationist sociolinguistics, including effects of topic (Rickford and McNair-Knox 1994), context

---

[7] Katie once misinterpreted a friend from New Zealand as saying that her cat sleeps in the litterbox. The priming of social information failed Katie that day, probably because other primes (i.e. cat → litterbox) were stronger than the social primes, and *letterbox* is not a lexical item that is found in Katie's native dialect.

(Bell 1984; Coupland 1980; Podesva 2008), and stance-taking (Johnstone 2009; Kiesling 2009).

Of course, attitudes also play a role in both speech production and perception. For example, a speaker's attitude towards an interlocutor influences the direction and amount of speech accommodation (Babel 2010; Bourhis and Giles 1977; Giles 1973; Giles *et al.* 1991). In an exemplar-based model, positive attitudes towards a person or group may activate linguistic exemplars associated with that person or group, resulting in speech convergence (Drager *et al.* 2010a: 31).[8] To account for effects of negative attitudes, Drager *et al.* (2010) offer two possibilities. The first is that negative attitudes towards a social group could influence production and perception by activating alternative social exemplars that encode social information about which the speaker-hearer has positive associations. The second explanation is that activation is inhibited by negative attitudes. In models that allow inhibition (e.g. Pierrehumbert 2001), production is biased away from variants encoded by the inhibited exemplars. Teasing apart these two interpretations remains a task for future work, and it is quite possible that both mechanisms exist and can occur simultaneously or are relied upon at different times, such as during different kinds of tasks.

Taken together, the exemplar-based models presented thus far predict that individuals will have so-called "knowledge" of sociolinguistic variation that they are not aware of. If speech is stored in the mind as socially indexed and phonetically rich episodic memories, an individual's speech production and perception can be influenced by patterns present across the exemplars even when they don't notice the patterns.[9] This contrasts with Labov's argument that variables below a speaker's conscious awareness "could hardly ... be the direct objects of social affect" (Labov 1972: 40). This conclusion is unavoidable if we assume that to be socially meaningful or have social effect is, by definition, an awareness of a relationship between social factors and language use. However, we argue that individuals do not need to be aware of variation in order for that variation to be socially meaningful. In the model outlined above, stored social information can be activated during the construction of a speaker's identity: a speaker activates social representations (e.g. intelligent, laidback, feminine) and, by doing so, activation inadvertently spreads to indexed linguistic information. It is possible, therefore, that production can be biased towards certain linguistic variants and that the bias can be socially motivated, while the speaker remains unaware of the association.

---

[8] How (or even whether) attitudes are stored remains underspecified in exemplar-based models.

[9] Docherty and Foulkes refer to associations that arise in this way as awareness, albeit implicit (Docherty and Foulkes 2014: 47). This contrasts with the treatment of awareness in this chapter which necessitates consciousness.

In order to demonstrate how sociolinguistic variation arises in an exemplar-based model even when speakers are unaware of the sociolinguistic variation, we briefly step through results from a study conducted at an all girls' high school, referred to as Selwyn Girls' High. The production data consist of recorded conversations and are reported in more detail in Drager (2011a). While there were many different social cliques observed at the school, the cliques were categorized depending on whether or not they ate lunch in the Common Room. Girls in Common Room groups (e.g. The PCs) set and perpetuated the school's norms of dress, behavior, and beliefs, and girls in most of the non-Common Room groups (e.g. The Goths) actively rejected these norms. The results indicate a number of phonetic differences across the social groups and the functions of *like*; here we focus on realizations of quotative *like* (e.g. I was like "turn that stupid thing off!") across Common Room and non-Common Room groups.

Common Room girls produced longer /l/ durations and more monophthongal vowels in quotative *like* than did non-Common Room girls. Although the girls were not aware of the phonetic differences, the differences are believed to be a result of identity construction (Drager 2011a). This is possible in an exemplar-based model with social indexing because identity construction occurs through activating social exemplars, and activation spreads from social exemplars to phonetic exemplars. Activation of social exemplars is related to an individual's attitudes towards social groups and characteristics. As examples, we discuss two speakers from two different non-Common Room groups: Holly, a member of Sonia's Group who idealized members of The PCs (a popular and powerful Common Room group), and Santra, a member of The Goths who consciously and outspokenly took part in practices that differed from girls in Common Room groups.[10] Holly produced realizations of quotative *like* that were similar to those produced by Common Room girls, whereas Santra produced realizations that were very different from those produced by Common Room girls (Drager and Hay 2012). In an exemplar-based model, the difference in realizations arose because of the social representations that were activated when Holly and Santra spoke; social representations associated with The PCs were activated when Holly talked because of Holly's alignment with The PCs, and activation then spread to indexed phonetic exemplars.[11]

---

[10] Sonia's Group was classified as a non-Common Room group because they did not eat lunch in the Common Room. However, their style of dress, weekend activities, and topics of conversation were similar to those of Common Room groups.

[11] For simplicity, we discuss the activation of exemplars at the social group level (e.g. The PCs) rather than social characteristics (e.g. bossy) or individual speakers, and we treat attitudes as categorical (i.e. positive or negative). Of course, the process of identity construction (and therefore the activation of social exemplars) is more complicated than this implies. Simultaneous activation of a wide variety of possibly conflicting information is possible in an exemplar-based model.

Because The PCs had a tendency to produce a short /l/ and monophthongal vowel in the word *like* and because Holly had encountered and stored these utterances, the phonetic exemplars encoding these realizations were triggered via activation of the social exemplars, biasing Holly's production towards variants most commonly produced by The PCs. In contrast with Holly's positive attitudes, Santra (The Goths) had negative attitudes towards Common Room groups (and The PCs especially) and had positive attitudes towards other members of The Goths. Consequently, social exemplars encoding information about The Goths were activated, biasing production towards her group's realizations. In a model that allows for inhibition of exemplars, social exemplars encoding information about The PCs would also be inhibited, biasing production away from variants of *like* produced by The PCs. The difference between Holly's and Santra's realizations arises without any need for awareness of the sociolinguistic variables because activation automatically spreads to phonetic exemplars from activated social exemplars.

### Awareness and Salience in an Exemplar-Based Model

Thus far, we have focused on demonstrating how sociolinguistic variation in production and perception is predicted by exemplar-based models in a way that does not necessitate awareness of the variation. However, awareness can influence the linguistic forms used by speakers (Labov 1972, 2001). When aware of associations between a linguistic variant and their language variety, speakers of stigmatized varieties produce the variant to differing degrees depending on context (Foster 1995) and speakers may intentionally alter their speech to avoid association with a particular dialect or community (Bucholtz 1995; Prince 1988). People also intentionally shift the way that they speak in different situations in order to match the formality of the situation, with more attention being paid to their speech as situations become more formal (Labov 1972). Alternatively, speakers' awareness of an out-group variant can lead them to adopt that variant for social purposes (Babel 2010; Bucholtz 1999; Kristiansen and Jørgensen 2005; Zhang 2005), and whether convergence is observed for a particular variable seems to be linked with awareness of the variable (Yaeger-Dror 1993; Babel 2010).

Awareness has also been shown to influence speech perception (Hay *et al.* 2006a; Niedzielski 1999). Listeners' perceptions of sounds are influenced by incoming social information, but effects are greater if listeners are aware of the sociolinguisitic variable (Niedzielski 1999) and for lexical items that are overtly associated with sociophonetic variables (Hay *et al.* 2006a). Taken together, these results suggest that awareness of sociolinguistic variables influences both the production and perception of those variables; the effect of social information on speech perception is stronger when listeners are aware of a relationship, and the effect on speech production can be even more extreme. Are these effects of awareness predicted by an exemplar-based model? In the following sections, we discuss the ways in which two concepts that are closely related to awareness – salience and attention – have been treated in exemplar-based models and discuss a way in which awareness may be incorporated into such models.

### Attention, Salience, and Awareness

Representationally, it is not entirely clear what awareness is; scholars working on exemplar-based models have instead focused on the related topic of selective attention (Nosofsky 1992). Attention and awareness are closely linked, so much so that some scholars treat them as identical (O'Regan and Noë 2001). However, a growing number of researchers posit that awareness is different from attention (Lamme 2003):[12] attention can lead to awareness, and awareness can increase the likelihood that an item will be attended to, but items can be attended to without conscious awareness and just because someone is aware of something doesn't mean they will attend to it all the time. Shifts in attention can be the result of motivations internal to the individual speaker-hearer, such as believing that a particular social category is relevant for the topic being discussed. Alternatively, shifts in attention can result from salience.

The word *salience* means different things to different researchers. In sociolinguistics, salience is tied with both noticeability and awareness of sociolinguistic variables (Labov 1972, 1974; Labov *et al.* 2011). Noticeability has been credited to a variant's distinctness or "localizedness" (Fridland *et al.* 2004; Honeybone and Watson 2013; Podesva 2011), its linguistic prominence due to volume, pitch, prosody, and position (Yaeger-Dror 1993; Podesva 2011), and its unexpectedness (Racz 2013; Preston 2010). Salience is determined by context because forms are evaluated situationally (Levon 2011; Preston 2010, 2011). In all of these accounts, salience is the degree to which something stands out relative to other, neighboring items (Hogg and Vaughan 2008: 61) and the more salient something is, the more likely it is that an individual will attend to it and become aware of it. Salience is not the same as relevance, which Pattabhiraman and Cercone (1990) argue is related to an individual's goals and motivations. Instead, they argue that salience pertains to properties of factors external to the speaker (Pattabhiraman and Cercone 1990: 80). The properties include anything that makes the object exceptional, such as its bigness, its loudness, its commonness, its rarity, or even its smallness (if in the context of big things). Such external factors include previously

---

[12] These researchers work on visual awareness and attention, but many of their arguments hold for auditory perception.

encountered items and expectations; an external factor needn't be external in the immediate environment. This means that, in an exemplar-based model, an item can stand out in relation to exemplars of related items (known as neighbors).

Items deemed salient during perception are attended to more than less salient items and, as a result, may be stored differently, affecting subsequent speech processing differently from their less salient counterparts. In the next section, we explore salience from this perspective, ascribing to the view that salience is gradient (Honeybone and Watson 2013: 311) and that it attracts attention. For the discussion, we rely on exemplar weights, which, for his mathematical implementations of the model, Nosofsky defines as the strength with which an exemplar is stored in memory (Nosofsky 1991: 135).

### Attention and Exemplar Weights

We stated earlier that recency and frequency of activation result in a greater activation of exemplars. In formalized models, this is implemented through varying exemplar weights. Attention weights, which are flexible and allow for different selective attention strategies across different tasks, work in the same way (Nosofsky 1992: 385): greater weight results in greater activation of an exemplar.[13] When something is salient (i.e. it stands out), it receives greater attention, and when the memory is stored, it is stored with greater weight.

In addition to weights on exemplars, weights may also be present on indices between a phonetic exemplar and a social representation (Drager 2011b). When attention is drawn to a relationship (through standing out or through motivations internal to the individual), it receives more weight. When a social exemplar is activated, activation spreads most quickly to phonetic exemplars for which the index has the greatest weights, and vice versa. This differential attention weighting across indices predicts that listeners' perceptions of vowels will be most influenced by incoming social information in words associated with sociophonetic variation (cf. Hay et al. 2006a) and that listeners who pay more attention to sociophonetic variation or who have more experience with the variation will be most influenced by social primes in their perception of sounds (cf. Drager 2011b). Exemplars with more weight are also more readily available for involvement in controlled processes; an exemplar model predicts that if a speaker wishes to imitate a non-native variety, the non-native exemplars that will be most activated will be variants that the speaker has attended to most in the past and/or those that the speaker consciously focuses on at the time of the production.

---

[13] Don't think attention is important? Think again! And check out *The Invisible Gorilla* (Chabris and Simons 2009).

*The Acquisition and Representation of Awareness*

An individual's awareness of a sociolinguistic variable can arise in several different ways. The first is through attention to salient items: an individual's attention is more likely to be drawn to a salient item, which increases the chances that the individual will become aware of the item. Because of this we suggest that awareness may be an activation threshold, one that is above that for perception.[14] When an object stands out in the context of its immediate environment or when perception relies on a relatively small number of exemplars that are dissimilar to neighboring exemplars, the incoming utterance is more likely to be salient (unless it is perceived as a mistake[15]) and more likely to receive attention. Sumner, Kim, King, and McGowan (2014) argue that salience influences encoding, where items that are more salient are more strongly encoded. In an exemplar-based model, this could be implemented by salient items being stored with greater exemplar weights, making the representations of these items more readily available during both production and perception by increasing their activation levels.[16]

But how well does this possibility play out in regard to other ways an item can reach awareness? Another way that awareness of a sociolinguistic variable can arise is through metalinguistic commentary; if Kainoa tells Cheri that English speakers in Hawai'i produce the GOAT vowel as monophthongal,[17] both episodic and abstract mental representations associated with this information would become highly activated, beyond the awareness threshold (i.e. Cheri becomes aware of it). It is even possible that Cheri would form an abstract representation of the relationship as a result of Kainoa's statement, possibly depending on the degree to which she has experience with Hawai'i English. This possibility brings us to a discussion of stereotypes and how they are treated in exemplar-based models of speech production and perception.

## Stereotypes and Sociolinguistic Variation

We draw on the concept of the stereotype as it is defined in the social psychology literature: "a cognitive structure that contains the perceiver's

---

[14] An alternative possibility is that awareness of an item is the abstract representation of the item, and attention is directed to/from the abstract representation.

[15] When incoming utterances are perceived as mistakes, they are subsumed under a pre-existing category.

[16] We remain uncommitted to this possibility because there is currently no mechanism in place that would alter the weights (if necessary) when a highly salient item becomes frequent and (as a result) less salient.

[17] The monophthongal realization of this vowel in Hawai'i English is something that most speakers from Hawai'i are not aware of.

knowledge, beliefs, and expectations about a human group" (Hamilton and Trolier 1986: 133). People can be aware of stereotypes or not (Greenwald and Banaji 1995) and, depending on the amount of experience with a group, there is evidence that stereotypes about the group may be represented as abstract representations or emerge over episodic memories (Sherman 1996).

To explore how stereotypes could emerge over episodic memories, we consider the results from a recent experiment conducted by the second author. Using a matched guise rating task, Kirtley (2010) investigated how listeners' previous exposure to a particular speech style (military speech) can affect how they categorize novel talkers. Auditory clips of speech were manipulated so that there were two guises that varied according to different phonetic cues. Two of these were GOOSE frontness and PRICE monophthongization, both of which are found in Southern varieties. Degree of exposure was coded according to a three-way distinction of military involvement: those who had spent time in the military, those who had family members who had been in the military, and those who had not served and whose immediate family had not served.

The results show that perceptions of military involvement were not uniform across participants; a listener's perception of a voice depended on their degree of exposure to military speech. Talkers in the Southern guise were most likely to be identified as servicemen by listeners who had not been in the military, but there was no such trend among listeners from the military. These results suggest that people who have not served in the military – and therefore have less exposure to military speech – use a stereotype of military speech (i.e. soldiers come from the South) to identify novel talkers as members of the military.

How might these results be predicted by the model we have discussed thus far? The first thing we need to consider is that, in an exemplar-based model, all utterances are stored. This means that inauthentic imitations of speech can be stored, and some individuals may even index these representations with information about the imitated style rather than the imitator (Drager 2005: 166). This is consistent with research that has shown that media portrayals can affect subsequent social judgments (Busselle 2003; Greenberg *et al.* 2002; Shapiro 1991; Zillmann and Brosius 2000). The second thing we need to consider is that many performed instances of military speech (such as the drill sergeant in Kubrick's film "Full Metal Jacket") include Southern features, such as monophthongal PRICE and fronted GOOSE. The entertainment industry uses stereotypical or archetypal characters as short-cuts to engender images without full descriptions (Busby 1976), and one American soldier stereotype is of the Southerner. Through exposure to these media, many people who have little contact with anyone in the military have stored phonetic exemplars that encode features of Southern speech and that are indexed with the label "military." Finally, the last thing we need to consider is that, in reality, people from all over the United States serve in the military; there are a wide range of backgrounds and regional accents. Therefore, people who have served in the military would have access to (and representations of) a wide range of phonetic variants, all of which are indexed with the label "military."

What does this mean for person perception? Incoming auditory information activates exemplars that encode similar information, and if enough exemplars within the category being considered receive sufficient activation, the voice is identified as belonging to that category. Perception depends on exposure, so for people with little exposure to people in the category, they must rely heavily on imitated performances of people from that category. For the participants in this experiment, this would mean that listeners with few to no ties to the military would perceive tokens in the Southern guise as having been produced by soldiers, whereas listeners who were past or active members of the military would perceive voices in both guises as soldiers, which is precisely what Kirtley (2010) observed.

While we believe that stereotypical imitations of speech influence subsequent speech perception, we also argue that stereotypes can be represented as abstract representations that are indexed to phonetic exemplars. This could mean that there is an abstract representation of the entire stereotype ("Military people are Southern people") or that the concepts form separate representations ("military" and "Southern") that are indexed to one another.[18] It is also possible that both types of representation exist; they are not mutually exclusive. We assume that such representations can form with explicit metalinguistic discussion about the relationship or from noticing a relationship. We suggest that while implicit stereotypes emerge through bottom-up processes (from exemplars), explicit stereotypes (those which the speaker-hearer is aware of) influence speech through top-down processes (from abstract representations).

When abstract representations of stereotypes are activated, this activates episodic memories that conform to those stereotypes. The episodic memories, the representation of the stereotype, and the link between them resist decay when they are activated. As a result, frequently activated stereotypes should have the strongest effect on speech perception.[19] When exceptions to the stereotype are encountered, the perception of the item may be biased so that it is perceived as conforming to the stereotype, or the exception may not be perceived as representative of the category so that it isn't integrated into the abstract representation and the stereotype remains the same (Smith and Zárate 1992).

---

[18] In Hay *et al.* (2006a) and Hay and Drager (2010), we provide some evidence for the former: an extra-large effect of the social prime was observed for a lexical item associated with a social group, but only when listeners were primed with the social category ("Australian") as opposed to the concept of the place ("Australia").

[19] As far as we know, this has not been tested explicitly.

To demonstrate how abstract representations may affect speech perception, we discuss Hay *et al.*'s (2006a) interpretation of Niedzielski's (1999) influential work on perception of the MOUTH vowel in Detroit. To explain the effect observed by Niedzielski (1999), who found that listeners shifted in their perception of MOUTH when primed with "Canada" but not "Michigan," Hay *et al.* (2006a) rely on abstracted social information indexed to phonetic exemplars. They argue that stereotypes influence which social information gets activated (and therefore which linguistic exemplars receive activation as a result). Because Detroiters believe that they speak the standard variety of American English, Hay *et al.* (2006a) argue that "Detroit" or "Michigan" may initially be stored in the mind as social categories, but that their representations rapidly decay because they are not seen as relevant to speech. Instead, exemplars from Michigan speakers are indexed as "Standard American," which means that exemplars from other regions influence perception when the concept of "Michigan" is invoked (Hay *et al.* 2006a: 372). Another possibility not discussed by Hay *et al.* is that the link between the social representation ("Michigan") and the phonetic exemplars ("raised variants of MOUTH") decays, weakening the weight of the index between the social category and the phonetic exemplars. That way, the category "Michigan" would only weakly prime raised variants produced by people from Michigan, but the category would still remain intact, making it accessible as a relevant category for other contexts (Go Blue!).

**Conclusion**

In this chapter, we outline the ways in which salience, attention, and stereotypes are treated in exemplar-based models of speech production and perception, stepping through various sets of experimental results to demonstrate our points. In these models, salience is stored as attention weights at the time of perception, where a greater weight results in a greater amount of activation. As a result, exemplars that encode salient information influence speech production and perception most strongly. When attention is paid to an item during storage, the exemplar receives greater weight, but – because the activation of exemplars and indexed social information is an automatic process – awareness and attention are not required for the production of socially meaningful variation. Nor are they required for stereotypes to affect behavior. Stereotypes can emerge over episodic memories (bottom-up processing) which can be automatic and unconscious, and stereotypes can also be stored as abstract mental representations, which could involve top-down processing.

Exemplar-based models can account for a great deal of variationist and experimental sociolinguistic work, but the models require further development and, in some places, the models' predictions still require a great deal more testing. For instance, what is the representational nature of attitudes? And what are the implications of the different implementations of negative attitudes that we describe? And, finally, what is the nature of sociolinguistic awareness in exemplar-based models? In this chapter, we propose that awareness is an activation threshold, but this possibility requires further exploration. Attention, on the other hand, is a concept which is not only closely related to both salience and awareness, but is already included in formal mathematical models. It is possible that many of the differences in linguistic behavior that have been attributed to differences in awareness may in fact boil down to differences in attention, meaning that predictions of exemplar-based models are testable based on pre-existing sociolinguistic data and suggesting that we should consider attention and awareness as related-but-separate in our investigations of language variation and change.

## REFERENCES

Abbot-Smith, Kirsten and Michael Tomasello 2006. Exemplar-learning and schematization in a usage-based account of syntactic acquisition. *Linguistic Review* 23:275–90.

Addington, David. W. 1968. The relationship of selected vocal characteristics to personality perception. *Speech Monographs* 35:492–503.

Aronovitch, Charles D. 1976. The voice of personality: Stereotyped judgments and their relation to voice quality and sex of speaker. *Journal of Social Psychology* 99(2):207–20.

Babel, Molly 2010. Dialect divergence and convergence in New Zealand English. *Language in Society* 39(4):437–56.

Bell, Allan 1984. Language style as audience design. *Language in Society* 13(2):145–204.

Bern, Daryl J. 1972. Self-perception theory, in L. Berkowitz (ed.), *Advances in Experimental Social Psychology*, Vol. 6, pp. 1–62. San Diego, CA: Academic Press.

Boomershine, Amanda, Kathleen Currie Hall, Elizabeth Hume, and Keith Johnson 2005. The impact of allophony versus contrast on speech perception, in P. Avery, B. E. Dresher, and K. Rice (eds.), *Contrast in Phonology: Theory, Perception, Acquisition*. Berlin: Mouton de Gruyter.

Bourhis, Richard Y. and Howard Giles 1977. The language of intergroup distinctiveness, in H. Giles (ed.), *Language, Ethnicity and Intergroup Relations*, pp. 119–35. London: Academic.

Bowers, Kenneth 1984. On being unconsciously influenced and informed, in K. S. Bowers and D. Meichenbaum (eds.), *The Unconscious Reconsidered*, pp. 227–72. New York: Wiley.

Brooks, Lee R. 1978. Nonanalytic concept formation and memory for instances, in E. Rosch and B. B. Lloyd (eds.), *Cognition and Concepts*, pp. 169–211. Hillsdale, NJ: Erlbaum.

Bucholtz, Mary 1995. From Mulatta to Mestiza: Passing and the linguistic reshaping of ethnic identity, in K. Hall and M. Bucholtz (eds.), *Gender Articulated: Language and Socially Constructed Self*, pp. 351–74. New York: Routledge.

1999. "Why be normal?": Language and identity practices in a community of nerd girls. *Language in Society* 28(2):203–23.

Busby, Linda. J. 1976. Myths, symbols, stereotypes: The artist and the mass media. Paper presented at the national meeting of the Speech Communication Association. San Francisco, CA.

Busselle, Rick W. 2003. Television exposure, parents' precautionary warnings, and young adults' perceptions of crime. *Communication Research* 30(5):530–56.

Bybee, Joan 2001. *Phonology and Language Use.* Cambridge University Press.
    2002. Word frequency and context of use in the lexical diffusion of phonetically conditioned sound change. *Language Variation and Change* 14:261–90.

Bybee, Joan and Rena Torres Cacoullos 2008. Phonological and grammatical variation in exemplar models. *Studies in Hispanic and Lusophone Linguistics* 1(2): 399–413.

Campbell-Kibler, Kathryn 2007. Accent, (ING), and the social logic of listener perceptions. *American Speech* 82:32–64.

Chabris, Christopher and Daniel Simons 2009. *The Invisible Gorilla: And Other Ways Our Intuitions Deceive Us.* New York: Crown Publishing Group.

Coupland, Nikolas 1980. Style-shifting in a Cardiff work-setting. *Language in Society* 9(1):1–12.

Craik, Fergus I. M. and Kim Kirsner 1974. The effect of speaker's voice on word recognition. *Quarterly Journal of Experimental Psychology* 26(2):274–84.

Docherty, Gerard J. and Paul Foulkes 2014. An evaluation of usage-based approaches to the modelling of sociophonetic variability. *Lingua* 142:42–56.

Drager, Katie 2005. The influence of social characteristics on speech perception. Unpublished MA thesis. University of Canterbury.
    2009. A sociophonetic ethnography of Selwyn Girls' High. Unpublished PhD dissertation. University of Canterbury.
    2010. Sensitivity to grammatical and sociophonetic variability in perception. *Laboratory Phonology* 1(1):93–120.
    2011a. Sociophonetic variation and the lemma. *Journal of Phonetics* 39(4):694–707.
    2011b. Speaker age and vowel perception. *Language and Speech* 54(1):99–121.

Drager, Katie and Jennifer Hay 2012. Exploiting random intercepts: Two case studies in Sociophonetics. *Language Variation and Change* 24(1):59–78.

Drager, Katie, Jennifer Hay, and Abby Walker 2010a. Pronounced rivalries: Attitudes and speech production. *Te Reo* 53:27–53.

Drager, Katie, Carly Salter, and Megan Macinkowicz 2010b. Perceived style, sexuality, and pitch: An experimental approach. Paper presented at New Ways of Analyzing Variation (NWAV) 39. San Antonio, TX.

Eagly, Alice H., Antonio Mladinic, and Stacey Otto 1994. Cognitive and affective bases of attitudes toward social groups and social policies. *Journal of Experimental Social Psychology* 30:113–37.

Erker, Daniel and Gregory R. Guy 2012. The role of lexical frequency in syntactic variability: Variable subject personal pronoun expression in Spanish. *Language* 88(3):526–57.

Fazio, Russell H. 1990. Multiple processes by which attitudes guide behavior: The MODE model as an integrative framework, in M. P. Zanna (ed.), *Advances in Experimental Social Psychology*, Vol. 23, pp. 75–109. New York: Academic Press.

Foster, Michele 1995. "Are you with me?": Power and solidarity in the discourse of African American women, in K. Hall and M. Bucholtz (eds.), *Gender Articulated: Language and the Socially Constructed Self*, pp. 329–50. New York: Routledge.

Foulkes, Paul and Gerard Docherty 2006. The social life of phonetics and phonology. *Journal of Phonetics* 34(4):409–38.

Fridland, Valerie, Kathryn Bartlett, and Roger Kreuz 2004. Do you hear what I hear? Experimental measurement of the perceptual salience of acoustically manipulated vowel variants by Southern speakers in Memphis, TN. *Language Variation and Change* 16:1–16.

Gahl, Susanne 2008. "Time" and "thyme" are not homophones: The effect of lemma frequency on word durations in a corpus of spontaneous speech. *Language* 84(3):474–96.

Giles, Howard 1973. Accent mobility: A model and some data. *Anthropological Linguistics* 15:87–105.

Giles, Howard, Nikolas Coupland, and Justine Coupland 1991. Accomodation theory: Communication, context, and consequence, in H. Giles, N. Coupland, and J. Coupland (eds.), *Contexts of Accommodation: Developments in Applied Sociolinguistics*. Cambridge University Press.

Gobl, Christer and Ailbhe Ní Chasaide 2003. The role of voice quality in communicating emotion, mood and attitude. *Speech Communication* 40(1):189–212.

Goldinger, Stephen D. 1997. Words and voices: Perception and production in an episodic lexicon, in K. Johnson and J. W. Mullennix (eds.), *Talker Variability in Speech Processing*, pp. 33–66. San Diego, CA: Academic Press.

2007. A complementary-systems approach to abstract and episodic speech perception. Proceedings of the 16th International Congress of Phonetic Sciences.

Greenberg, Bradley S., Dana Mastro, and Jeffrey E. Brand 2002. Minorities and the mass media: Television into the 21st century, in B. Jennings and D. Zillmann (eds.), *Media Effects: Advances in Theory and Research*, pp. 333–51. 2nd edn. Hillsdale, NJ: Lawrence Erlbaum Associates.

Greenwald, Anthony G. and Mahzarin R. Banaji 1995. Implicit social cognition: Attitudes, self-esteem, and stereotypes. *Psychological Review* 102(1):4–27.

Haddock, Geoffrey, Mark P. Zanna, and Victoria M. Esses 1993. Assessing the structure of prejudicial attitudes: The case of attitudes toward homosexuals. *Journal of Personality and Social Psychology* 65:1105–18.

Hamilton, David L. and Tina K. Trolier 1986. Stereotypes and stereotyping: An overview of the cognitive approach, in S. L. Gaerner and J. F. Dovidio (eds.), *Prejudice, Discrimination, and Racism*, pp. 127–57. New York: Academic Press.

Harms, L. Stanley 1961. Listener judgments of status cues in speech. *Quarterly Journal of Speech* 47(2):164–8.

Hay, Jennifer and Katie Drager 2010. Stuffed toys and speech perception. *Linguistics* 48(4):865–92.

Hay, Jennifer, Katie Drager, and Brynmor Thomas 2013. Using nonsense words to investigate vowel merger. *English Language and Linguistics* 17(2):241–69.

Hay, Jennifer, Katie Drager, and Paul Warren 2010. Short-term exposure to one dialect affects processing of another. *Language and Speech* 53(4):447–71.

Hay, Jennifer and Margaret Maclagan 2010. Social and phonetic conditioners on the frequency and degree of "intrusive/r/" in New Zealand English, in D. R. Preston and N. A. Niedzielski (eds.), *A Reader in Sociophonetics*, pp. 41–70. New York: Mouton de Gruyter.

Hay, Jennifer, Aaron Nolan, and Katie Drager 2006a. From fush to feesh: Exemplar priming in speech perception. *Linguistic Review* 23(3):351–79.

Hay, Jennifer, Paul Warren, and Katie Drager 2006b. Factors influencing speech perception in the context of a merger-in-progress. *Journal of Phonetics* 34(4):458–84.

Hintzman, Douglas L. 1984. MINERVA 2: A simulation model of human memory. *Behavior Research Methods, Instruments, & Computers* 16(2):96–101.

1986. "Schema abstraction" in a multiple-trace memory model. *Psychological Review* 93:411–28.

Hintzman, Douglas L. and Genevieve Ludlam 1980. Differential forgetting of prototypes and old instances: Simulation by an exemplar-based classification model. *Memory & Cognition* 8(4):378–82.

Hogg, Michael and Graham Vaughan 2008. *Social Psychology*. 5th edn. Harlow: Pearson Education.

Honeybone, Patrick and Kevin Watson 2013. Salience and the sociolinguistics of Scouse spelling. *English World-Wide* 34(3):305–40.

Johnson, Keith 1997. Speech perception without speaker normalization: An exemplar approach, in K. Johnson and J. W. Mullennix (eds.), *Talker Variability in Speech Processing*, pp. 145–66. San Diego, CA: Academic Press.

2005. Speaker normalization, in R. E. Remez and D. B. Pisoni (eds.), *The Handbook of Speech Perception*, pp. 363–89. Malden, MA: Blackwell Publishing.

2006. Resonance in an exemplar-based lexicon: The emergence of social identity and phonology. *Journal of Phonetics* 34(4):485–99.

2007. Decisions and mechanisms in exemplar-based phonology, in M.-J. Sole, P. Beddor, and M. Ohala (eds.), *Experimental Approaches to Phonology. In Honor of John Ohala*. pp. 25–40. Oxford University Press.

Johnstone, Barbara 2009. Stance, style, and the linguistic individual, in A. Jaffe (ed.), *Stance: Sociolinguistic Perspectives*, pp. 29–52. Oxford University Press.

Kiesling, Scott 2009. Style as stance: Can stance be the primary explanation for patterns of sociolinguistic variation?, in A. Jaffe (ed.), *Stance: Sociolinguistic Perspectives*, pp. 171–94. Oxford University Press.

Kirtley, M. Joelle 2010. Speech in the US military: A sociophonetic perception approach to identity and meaning. MA thesis. University of Hawai'i at Mānoa.

Klatt, Dennis H. 1979. Speech perception: A model of acoustic-phonetic analysis and lexical access. *Journal of Phonetics* 7(312):1–26.

Koops, Christian, Elizabeth Gentry, and Andrew Pantos 2008. The effect of perceived speaker age on the perception of PIN and PEN vowels in Houston, Texas. *University of Pennsylvania Working Papers in Linguistics* 34(2): 93–101.

Kristiansen, Tore and Jens Normann Jørgensen 2005. Subjective factors in dialect convergence and divergence, in P. Auer, F. Hinskens, and P. Kerswill (eds.), *Dialect Change: Convergence and Divergence in European Languages*, pp. 287–302. Cambridge University Press.

Labov, William 1966. *The Social Stratification of English in New York City*. Washington, DC: Center for Applied linguistics.

1972. *Sociolinguistic Patterns*. Pittsburg, PA: University of Pennsylvania Press.

1974. Linguistic change as a form of communication, in A. Silverstein (ed.), *Human Communication: Theoretical Explorations*, pp. 221–56. Hillsdale, NJ: Lawrence Erlbaum Associates.

2001. *Principles of Linguistic Change: Social factors*. Oxford, UK: Blackwell.

Labov, William, Sharon Ash, Maya Ravindranath, Tracey Weldon, Maciej Baranowski, and Naomi Nagy 2011. Properties of the sociolinguistic monitor. *Journal of Sociolinguistics* 15:431–63.

Lacerda, Francisco 1995. The perceptual-magnet effect: An emergent consequence of exemplar-based phonetic memory. Proceedings of the 13th International Congress of Phonetic Sciences 2.

Lamme, Victor A. F. 2003. Why visual attention and awareness are different. *Trends in Cognitive Sciences* 7(1):12–18.

Levon, Erez 2011. Teasing apart to bring together: Gender and sexuality in variationist research. *American Speech* 86(1):69–84.

Lewicki, Pawel 1986. *Nonconscious Social Information Processing*. San Diego, CA: Academic Press.

Lieberman, Matthew D. 2003. Reflexive and reflective judgment processes: A social cognitive neuroscience approach, in J. P. Forgas, K. D. Williams, and W. von Hippel (eds.), *Social Judgments: Implicit and Explicit Processes*, pp. 1–34. Cambridge University Press.

McClelland, James L. and Jeffrey L. Elman 1986. The TRACE model of speech perception. *Cognitive Psychology* 18(1):1–86.

McLennan, Conor. T. 2007. Challenges facing a complementary-systems approach to abstract and episodic speech perception. Proceedings of the 16th International Congress of Phonetic Sciences, pp. 67–70. Saarbrücken, Germany.

McQueen, James M., Anne Cutler, and Dennis Norris 2006. Phonological abstraction in the mental lexicon. *Cognitive Science* 30(6):1113–26.

Morton, J. Bruce and Sandra E. Trehub 2001. Children's understanding of emotion in speech. *Child Development* 72(3):834–43.

Niedzielski, Nancy 1999. The effect of social information on the perception of sociolinguistic variables. *Journal of Language and Social Psychology* 18(1):62–85.

Nielsen, Kuniko 2011. Specificity and abstractness of VOT imitation. *Journal of Phonetics* 39(2):132–42.

Norris, Dennis, James M. McQueen, and Anne Cutler 2003. Perceptual learning in speech. *Cognitive Psychology* 47(2):204–38.

Nosofsky, Robert M. 1986. Attention, similarity, and identification- categorization relationship. *Journal of Experimental Psychology* 115(1):39–57.

1991. Stimulus bias, asymmetric similarity, and classification. *Cognitive Psychology* 23:94–140.

1992. Exemplars, prototypes, and similarity rules, in A. F. Healy and S. M. Kosslyn (eds.), *Essays in Honor of William K. Estes, Vol. 1: From Learning Theory to Connectionist Theory; Vol. 2: From Learning Processes to Cognitive Processes*, pp. 149–67. Hillsdale, NJ: Lawrence Erlbaum Associates.

Nosofsky, Robert M., Daniel R. Little, Christopher Donkin, and Mario Fific 2011. Short-term memory scanning viewed as exemplar-based categorization. *Psychological Review* 118(2):280–315.

Nosofsky, Robert M., Thomas J. Palmeri, and Stephen C. McKinley 1994. Rule-plus-exception model of classification learning. *Psychological Review* 101(1):53–79.

Nygaard, Lynne C. and Erin R. Lunders 2002. Resolution of lexical ambiguity by emotional tone of voice. *Memory and Cognition* 30(4):583–93.

O'Regan, J. Kevin and Alva Noë 2001. A sensorimotor account of vision and visual consciousness. *Behavioral and Brain Sciences* 24:939–1031.

Palmeri, Thomas J., Stephen D. Goldinger, and David B. Pisoni 1993. Episodic encoding of voice attributes and recognition memory for spoken words. *Journal of Experimental Psychology: Learning, Memory, and Cognition* 19(2):309–28.

Pierrehumbert, Janet 2001. Exemplar dynamics: Word frequency, lenition and contrast, in J. Bybee and P. Hopper (eds.), *Frequency Effects and Emergent Grammar*, pp. 137–58. Amsterdam: John Benjamins.

2006. The next toolkit. *Journal of Phonetics* 34(6):516–30.

Pattabhiraman, Thiyagarajasarma and Nick Cercone 1990. Selection: Salience, relevance and the coupling between domain-level tasks and text planning, in K. McKeown, J. Moore, and S. Nierenburg (eds.), *Proceedings of the 5th International Workshop on Natural Language Generation*, pp. 79–86. Dawson, PA: Association for Computational Linguistics.

Plug, Leendert 2005. Phonetic reduction and categorisation in exemplar-based representation. Proceedings of ConSOLE 13, pp. 287–311.

Podesva, Robert 2008. Three sources of stylistic meaning, in T. Edwards, K. Shaw, S. Wagner, and E. Yasui (eds.), *Proceedings of SALSA15. Texas Linguistic Forum 51*. Austin, TX: University of Texas.

2011. Salience and the social meaning of declarative contours: Three case studies of gay professionals. *Journal of English Linguistics* 39(3):233–64.

Preston, Dennis 2010. Variation in language regard, in P. Gilles, I. Scharloth, and E. Zeigler (eds.), *Empirische Evidenzen und theoretische Passungen sprachlicher Variation*, pp. 7–27. Frankfurt am Main: Peter Lang.

2011. The power of language regard: Discrimination, classification, comprehension and production. *Dialectologia* Special Issue II:9–33.

Prince, Ellen F. 1988. Accommodation theory and dialect shift: A case study from Yiddish. *Language and Communication* 8(3):307–20.

Racz, Peter 2013. *Salience in Sociolinguistics: A Quantitative Approach*. Berlin: De Gruyter.

Rickford, John and Faye McNair-Knox 1994. Addressee- and topic-influenced style shift: A quantitative sociolinguistic study, in D. Biber and E. Finegan (eds.), *Sociolinguistic Perspectives on Register*, pp. 235–76. Oxford University Press.

Schacter, Daniel L., James Eric Eich, and Endel Tulving 1978. Richard Semon's theory of memory. *Journal of Verbal Learning and Verbal Behavior* 17(6):721–43.

Schmidt, Richard W. 1990. The role of consciousness in second language learning. *Applied Linguistics* 11(2):129–58.

Schneider, Walter and Richard M. Shiffrin 1977. Controlled and automatic human information processing: Detection, search, and attention. *Psychological Review* 84(1):127–90.

Shapiro, Michael A. 1991. Memory and decision processes in the construction of social reality. *Communication Research* 18(1):3–24.

Shastri, Lokendra and Venkat Ajjanagadde 1993. From simple associations to systematic reasoning: A connectionist representation of rules, variables and dynamic bindings using temporal synchrony. *Behavioral and Brain Sciences* 16(3):417–51.

Sherman, Jeffrey W. 1996. Development and mental representation of stereotypes. *Journal of Personality and Social Psychology* 70(6):1126–41.

Smith, Eliot R. 1998. Mental representation and memory, in D. T. Gilbert, S. T. Fiske, and G. Lindzey (eds.), *Handbook of Social Psychology*, Vol. 1, pp. 391–445. New York: McGraw-Hill.

Smith, Eliot R. and Michael A. Zárate 1992. Exemplar-based model of social judgement. *Psychological Review* 99(1):3–21.

Staum Casasanto, Laura 2008. Does social information influence sentence processing? 30th Annual Meeting of the Cognitive Science Society. Washington, DC.

Strand, Elizabeth 1999. Uncovering the role of gender stereotypes in speech perception. *Journal of Language and Social Psychology* 18(1):86–99.

Sumner, Meghan, Seung Kyung Kim, Ed King, and Kevin McGowan 2014. The socially weighted encoding of spoken words: A dual-route approach to speech perception. *Frontiers in Psychology* 4:1015. doi: 10.3389/fpsyg.2013.01015.

Trudgill, Peter 1981. Linguistic accommodation: Sociolinguistic observations on a sociopsychological theory, in C. S. Masek, R. A. Hendrick, and M. F. Miller (eds.), *Papers from the Parasession on Language and Behavior*, pp. 218–37. Chicago, IL: Chicago Linguistic Society.

Walker, Abby 2008. Phonetic detail and grammaticality judgments. Unpublished MA thesis. University of Canterbury.

Wedel, Andrew B. 2006. Exemplar models, evolution and language change. *Linguistic Review* 23(3):247–74.

Yaeger-Dror, Malcah 1993. Linguistic analysis of dialect "correction" and its interaction with cognitive salience. *Language Variation and Change* 5:189–224.

Zhang, Qing 2005. A Chinese yuppie in Beijing: Phonological variation and the construction of a new professional identity. *Language in Society* 34(3):431–66.

Zillmann, Dolf and Hans-Bernd Brosius 2000. Exemplification in communication. *Zeitschrift für Medien-psychologie* 13(3):155–6.

# 2 Sounding Chinese and Listening Chinese: Awareness and Knowledge in the Laboratory

*Kevin B. McGowan*

### Perception, Variation, and Awareness

Perception is the use of knowledge to make sense of – to impose structure upon – the signals relayed to the brain from our peripheral sense organs. For speech perception, this has been construed as using our knowledge of language to impose linguistic structure upon primarily auditory, but also visual (McGurk and MacDonald 1976) and haptic (Gick and Derrick 2009), sensations. The study of speech perception, then, can be framed as the quest to understand the process by which listeners perform this mapping from sensory events to subjective experiences of those events. An important component of this investigation is understanding the knowledge, and the sensory cues to that knowledge, that listeners bring to bear on shaping the sensory events of speech. A theoretical assumption made early in the history of this research was the separation of the speech stream into linguistic[1] cues, useful in lexical access and retrieval, and social cues, useful in obtaining information about the speaker.

  Much work on speech perception and word recognition has assumed this separation and taken the linguistic cues, whether acoustic or articulatory, to be both the primary object of research and the primary source of information for listeners. But speech is highly variable, both within and across talkers, so a long-standing puzzle for speech perception researchers has been how listeners could possibly map such highly variable acoustic input onto such apparently consistent subjective experiences of those inputs. This is known explicitly as the "lack of invariance" problem because there appear to exist no sensory cues that map one-to-one to listeners' subjective experience of particular linguistic units. Lisker (1986), for example, identifies no fewer than sixteen cues sufficient to invoke a subjective experience of voicing in English; none of which is necessary for that percept. Even when not stated explicitly, the notion that invariance really *should* exist at some level commonly emerges

---

[1] "Linguistic" is a loaded term as it embraces the assumption that social cues are *not* linguistic, but I will use it throughout this chapter as it remains the standard term for referring to sub-phonemic, phonemic, and lexical forms.

in descriptions of variation as a daunting challenge that listeners must some-how overcome in perception.

However, the dual linguistic and social aspects of speech are inescapably conveyed by means of a single acoustic signal. The same phonetic cues that have been long documented as carrying distinctive linguistic meaning simul-taneously carry the distinctive social meanings that link a voice to speaker attributes ranging from age to race to sexual orientation (e.g. Foulkes and Docherty 2006; Eckert 2008; Johnstone and Kiesling 2008; Campbell-Kibler 2009; Munson 2010). It seems likely, therefore, that listeners would use not only linguistic but also social knowledge to impose structure upon the sensory events of speech. Perhaps the probability of mapping a particular auditory event to a particular subjective experience of that event is conditional upon the social categories that are contextually salient (Sumner *et al.* 2014).

Indeed, facilitated by the introduction of exemplar models of perception into linguistics (Johnson 1997; Drager 2010, Drager and Kirtley, this volume), sociophonetics and speech perception researchers have consistently found that perception of particular phonetic cues can be altered in response to primed social categories. Listeners appear to dynamically alter the attentional weights associated with particular phonetic cues in response to manipulated social expectations (Pierrehumbert 2002). This alteration has been shown to occur both with cues that reflect actual usage (e.g. Schulman 1983; Niedzielski 1999; Hay *et al.* 2006) and with stereotypical usage (e.g. Mack and Munson 2012, Carmichael, this volume). Socially cued perception effects suggest that speech perception proceeds not by winnowing away noise to arrive at a core, intended signal, but by exploiting listeners' knowledge of real patterns of informative variation to impose structure upon auditory sensations. These findings place speech perception researchers in the unexpected position of needing to quan-tify and understand not only listeners' linguistic knowledge, but also their social knowledge.

It is typically assumed, following the model offered by Johnson (2006), that listeners whose percepts can be altered by social information necessarily have knowledge both of the socially meaningful phonetic variation itself and of the covarying social category information. In this work, it has seemed methodo-logically intractable to assess and quantify this knowledge so the argument becomes circular – listeners whose behavior is consistent with exemplar predictions of detailed experience are assumed to have detailed exemplars; listeners whose behavior is not consistent with exemplar predictions are assumed not to have the necessary experience. Escaping this circularity requires us to develop a better understanding of what it means for a listener to be more experienced, how to assess and quantify that experience, and how the accuracy and detail of one's social expectations might shape encoding and memories of linguistic experience.

We know that listeners can and do make use of patterns of socially informative variation in the speech stimulus. Furthermore, manipulating socially cued expectations can enhance, not merely alter, perception of an acoustic stimulus. Dahan *et al.* (2008) show that listeners use their knowledge of [æ]-raising before voiced velar stops, and not before voiceless velar stops, to more quickly distinguish, for example, *back* from *bag* when *bag* in the stimulus set is produced by a speaker with the raised vowel variant. Szakay *et al.* (2012) used a cross-language and cross-dialect priming task to demonstrate that variable sociophonetic cues can facilitate translation priming. Beddor *et al.* (2013) found that listeners have knowledge of informative patterns of nasal co-articulation in American English and can use these patterns to make lexical decisions as soon as evidence of nasalization is provided by the speech stream. These patterns of co-articulation are language-specific (Beddor *et al.* 2002), but also highly individual. Nevertheless, they are useful and informative to listeners. Sumner and Samuel (2009) showed that listener experience with Long Island English predicts the usefulness of semantic priming by voices with that accent. Speakers of Long-Island-accented English saw semantic priming benefits from primes spoken in this variety, while general-American listeners did not. However, Sumner and Kataoka (2013) found that general-American listeners, even those who see no benefit from non-rhotic Long-Island-accented primes, *do* see a benefit from similarly non-rhotic Southern British English primes – suggesting that simple exposure[2] to a variety is not the sole determining factor in how richly experience with that variety is encoded and stored in the lexicon.

That listeners use socially informative variation raises the important question, not normally explicitly addressed in the speech perception literature, of listener awareness. We generally assume in experimental work that speech perception occurs beneath the level of conscious awareness and is unavailable to introspection. Listeners cannot discuss or control whether they perceive consonants categorically (Liberman *et al.* 1957), perceive non-words as existing words (Ganong 1980), make use of co-articulatory evidence (Mann and Repp 1981), perceive non-native contrasts in terms of native ones (Best 1994), or any number of other classic effects. These linguistic effects occur below the level of awareness and control, so we investigate listeners' knowledge of them by designing other tasks that allow us to measure the influence of these effects indirectly. We assess the influence of semantic relatedness, for example, by measuring how long it takes listeners to decide if a target word is a real word or a non-word when the prime is semantically related or unrelated to that target.

---

[2] "Simple exposure" here appears to be identical to *perceiving* in the sense of Drager and Kirtley (this volume).

Listeners have knowledge of linguistic effects without necessarily – indeed, without typically – having awareness of that knowledge. This observation has a clear parallel in Squires's discussion (this volume) of *perceiving* and *noticing* of social variation. Although *perceiving* is probably not the ideal word, Squires has made the novel observation that there is a distinction to be made between perception that occurs when the perceiver is aware of the relationship between sensory cues and social category and perception that occurs when the perceiver is unaware of this relationship. There appear to be at least four distinct pools of knowledge language users are able to use – each with its own gradient awareness. In perception we have knowledge of phonetically cued linguistic information, but also phonetically cued social information. Similarly, for speech production we have knowledge of linguistic information conveyed by speaking, but also knowledge of social meanings conveyed by speaking. Speakers' gradient awareness of each of these four areas of knowledge has so far received very little attention in the speech perception literature.

Social knowledge has primarily received attention in sociolinguistics. For production, Labov (1972) has described the cline of social awareness as ranging from indicators – features occurring below the level of consciousness – to markers – above the level of consciousness and used to convey and infer social meaning – to stereotypes – describing features above the level of consciousness which are available for meta-linguistic, often stigmatizing, commentary. Stereotypes are strongly linked to speakers' conceptualization of a variety, but may not actually occur in that variety.[3] Preston (1996, this volume) captures this disjunction and describes clines of awareness for both production and perception by defining awareness along four independent continua: availability, accuracy, detail, and control. *Availability* is concerned with how likely a member of a speech community is to discuss a feature; features may be unavailable – never discussed – or highly available – common topics of conversation. *Accuracy* describes how closely community members' language ideologies align with linguistic reality; Michigan speakers, for example, commonly believe that their daily speech is without shibboleth and similar to, if not the definition of, supra-local standard American English (Niedzielski 1999). *Detail* describes the specificity of description community members have available to them. Detail ranges from global language ideologies without access to linguistic detail (e.g. "British people sound intelligent") to specific details (e.g. "Chinese speakers often leave out the definite article" or "Japanese speakers have trouble with r and l"). Finally, *control*, which is explicitly about production, describes whether community members can use

---

[3] These stereotypes may not occur either because they are inaccurate, such as the expectation of a gay lisp (Mack and Munson 2012), or because a change from above has led to avoidance of the stereotype, as predicted by Labov.

or perform a particular feature (although see Babel (this volume) for a model in which avoidance of a form, non-production, may also signal control).

Conceptualizing listener awareness in this way, as listeners' gradient ability to notice covarying patterns between their linguistic and social knowledges of speech, allows us to develop ways to probe and assess listeners' socially cued knowledge of speech independent of self-reported experience levels. If we suspect that listeners might bring both social and linguistic information to bear on the task of perception, or even if we simply aim to take seriously the predictions of usage-based models of speech perception (Docherty and Foulkes 2014), it becomes necessary either to control listener social experiences for the purposes of laboratory research or to quantify those experiences with tasks that transcend listener awareness of social variation. Controlling listeners' social experience in the laboratory could, in principle, be done by extending artificial language learning. Researchers would invent a language, invent a social context for that language, and train participants with varying levels of experience with those constructs. Methodologically, this route is likely to be extremely time consuming. This approach also has the shortcoming of being infelicitous for the investigation of existing sociolinguistic variables. Finally, it seems likely that participants will understand the invented language and social context in terms of their pre-existing experience with their own native language(s) and culture(s), so, even with an artificial language learning paradigm, the facts of listener experience would still need to be assessed. The alternative approach, quantifying listener experience, is still a daunting logistical challenge, but has the benefit of allowing investigation of existing sociolinguistic patterns using listeners' life experiences.

The goal of the present chapter is to explore the feasibility of assessing and quantifying listeners' accumulated linguistic and social experiences for modeling experience in laboratory research. Experiment 1 presents an accent authenticity detection task designed to indirectly measure listeners' knowledge of Chinese-accented English in terms of their ability to discriminate authentic Chinese-accented English voices from the voices of American-English speakers producing imitated Chinese accents. This task is intended to measure listener knowledge of phonetically cued social information without depending on listeners having conscious awareness of that knowledge. The explicit assumption is that one's ability to accurately discern authentic from imitated Chinese-accented English improves with increased exposure to the authentic variety. Listeners accumulate experience with covarying patterns of phonetic and social information. More experienced listeners should have a greater number of detailed experiences with patterns of phonetic variation, even those, such as Labov's indicators, below the level of conscious awareness or unavailable for introspection or commentary. Less experienced listeners, on the other hand, should have fewer detailed experiences with these patterns and may rely more heavily on patterns of variation at the level of stereotypes. These stereotypes could be derived from experience with imitated or mock varieties of the target variety (e.g. in films or by comedians), but they may also reflect experience with meta-commentary about the variety (e.g. that Boston speakers drop their [ɹ]s or that Chinese has tones).

The task of determining authenticity is analogous to the lexical decision task described above for determining semantic priming. Listeners are not asked to provide an explicit label for a voice such as "Chinese" or "not Chinese," but are asked to identify the voice as "authentic" or "not authentic". The distinction may seem subtle, but it is crucial. Listeners should be able to draw on the same linguistic and social ideologies they might use outside the laboratory when sizing up a new interlocutor or enjoying an actor's performance. Neuhauser and Simpson (2007) argue that non-native listeners and accent imitators share a surprisingly uniform cognitive prototype of what features an imitated variety should have, while true non-native speakers both produce and anticipate patterns which defy these common expectations. For example, hearing an authentic variety will present listeners with accurate variety-specific patterns of co-articulation (Beddor *et al.* 2002). Listeners with more extensive experience with the target variety should be sensitive to these patterns. Listeners with less experience, on the other hand, have no reason to expect or to prefer these patterns that exist below the level of meta-linguistic commentary. Indeed, there is some evidence that less experienced listeners will actually be more drawn to the phonetic implementation of the imitated accent. Neuhauser and Simpson (2007), for example, found that German monolingual speakers were more likely to identify German imitations of French and American accents as authentic than they were to correctly identify true non-native accents.

The German finding points to another interaction between awareness and experience that is crucial for modeling the likely exemplar representations of a listener. Specifically, some listeners will have more detailed social category representations than others. Additionally, some listeners may be capable of forming more accurate linkages between acoustic signals and social category representations (this continuum of accuracy is analogous to Preston's "detail"). In principle, these two levels of representation and encoding are independent so that one listener may be very good at linking fine phonetic detail to rather broad social categories (e.g. an acting coach), while another listener may have quite detailed social categories, but difficulty linking fine phonetic detail to those categories (e.g. Milroy and McClenaghan 1977). This claim is analogous to the observation made by Wells (1982) and cited in Agha (2003) that a working class accent may sound merely British to a Chicagoan, English to a Glaswegian, Northern to a Southerner, Liverpudlian to a Northerner, and working class to a Liverpudlian, except that this increasing complexity is not accurately described as a simple fact of one's geography. There is no reason that a Chicagoan should not, through eager attention, have quite accurate social categories for English people and accurate linkages from sociolinguistic variables to those categories. Finally, there is no reason to expect that the sheer amount of experience a Liverpudlian may have with local varieties of English will necessarily result in rich social categories and accurate linkages of fine phonetic detail to those categories. These linkages are a function of awareness of both phonetic detail and detailed social categories, attention to acoustic and contextual cues, and encoding of these cues so that the exemplar dynamics resulting from a particular degree of exposure to a variety is likely to vary from individual to individual.

In the present chapter, more experienced listeners are more accurate at both selecting the authentically Chinese-accented voice and at rejecting the imitated variety. However, less experienced listeners do perform above chance levels on authenticity detection. This finding, together with Neuhauser and Simpson's finding about German listener preferences for imitated varieties, leads to the question of what it is listeners are attending to in these imitated varieties. The second half of this chapter reports a laboratory investigation of actors' imitations of Chinese-accented English. This investigation is intended to help us to begin to understand the constellation of linguistic cues native English listeners use to perceive a particular voice as Chinese or, as we will see, as 'Asian'. The acoustic correlates of 'Chinese-ness' for less experienced listeners will be explored through a production study with a small group of American-English-speaking actors attempting to produce a percept of 'Chinese' for an American, perhaps monolingual, English-speaking audience through imitation of Chinese-accented English.

Actors were hired to perform the imitated variety rather than eliciting folk linguistic imitations (cf. Brunner 2010). This decision is motivated partially by expediency – with the assumption that actors will more successfully and consistently perform the imitated accent. More important, though, are the theoretical motivations. The actors choose to imitate some features and to ignore others with the goal of invoking a 'Chinese' character type, as defined in the expectations of their audience. It is these percepts, and the features that encourage them, that we are interested in understanding. It is presumed that perception of less successful or less consistent imitated speech will be perceived via the same mechanism and will activate the same representations, only less clearly.

### Quantifying Listeners' Experience

Quantifying listener experience with, and expectations about, language is by no means unique to questions of social experience nor indeed even to speech perception. In diverse linguistic or psychological experiments, it is often necessary to estimate, for example, the frequency of a particular lexical item in listeners' experience outside the laboratory.

The normal practice for estimating listeners' exposure to lexical frequency is to calculate these frequencies from an established corpus such as Kucera and Francis (1967) or Baayen *et al.* (1993). Although both corpora are quite dated and drawn from a mixture of print and spoken sources that are unlikely to represent the statistical patterns experienced by modern participants (Balota *et al.* 2007), these data provide an expedient and, more importantly, standard surrogate for listener experience with linguistic forms. The following section argues for the particular importance of quantifying not only listener experience, but also listeners' language ideologies in socially cued perception research.

Work in socially cued speech perception critically relies on an understanding of the identity of the listeners – their linguistic experience, how they relate to the experimenter, how they relate to the variety being studied, etc. The need to quantify listener experience is therefore likely greater than in other linguistic and psycholinguistic experimentation. Here, we have all of the same questions of frequency and patterning of linguistic forms, but with the added recognition that these forms will differ systematically by listener and social context.

It is pragmatically useful to conceive of identity as a monolithic, fixed property of an individual, but this is also a massive simplification. Identity is much better understood as a dynamic, context-sensitive construct in which interlocutors manipulate and interpret indexical forms to define their roles in a particular interaction (Bucholtz and Hall 2010). Irvine (1989) refers to "a diversity on the linguistic plane that indexes a social diversity" and recent work in sociolinguistics and linguistic anthropology has demonstrated that speakers and listeners are aware of, and exercise situational control over, these diversities. Depending on context, speakers will invoke different constellations of indexical linguistic forms – different registers – to convey the same denotational or referential meaning (Silverstein 2003). In other words, not only does one speak differently in a job interview than one speaks in casual conversation, but listeners are aware of and expect these uses of appropriate registers. Violating these expectations is possible, but this is a meaningful act.

Babel (2010) reports the use of Spanish/Quechua contact features among speakers in one Andean village. Given local ideologies that associate Quechua use with informal, rural speech, it is unsurprising that Quechua-influenced contact features in this variety of Andean Spanish are more commonly used in informal conversation than in interview or meeting contexts. However, these features are also invoked in more formal contexts as indices of the speaker's authenticity, to create intimacy, to mark one's affiliation with a particular political group, and sometimes several of these social meanings simultaneously. Individual linguistic forms may be linked to particular social meanings, but both the linkage and the meaning are highly context-dependent.

For the experimentalist, then, it is worth bearing in mind that performance on a task intended to quantify listener experience will be shaped by the formal, experimental context, by listener ideologies about the details of the language being used, and by listener ideologies about the purported speaker.

For experimental investigation of exemplar dynamics, it would be ideal to have a range of background information about each participant that it is difficult to conceive of collecting either behaviorally or through self-report. For a study like Rubin (1992) or McGowan (2015) in which listeners see an Asian or Caucasian face while listening to stimuli, this background information includes such variables as the frequency and intensity of interaction with Asian interlocutors, the probability of an Asian face accompanying a non-native English accent in the listener's experience, the distribution of facial features and L1 languages and their combination in the listeners' experience with speakers, how the listener construes the phonetic features under investigation to create meaning, how the listener self-identifies linguistically, and – critically – awareness of and attention to any acoustic cues to Asian-ness. Every aspect of stimulus presentation is potentially open to influence from listener experience and ideology.

This depth and breadth of understanding is probably impossible to achieve in the laboratory. The standard solution is to ask participants to complete a language history survey – typically in the laboratory or when registering for a subject pool. Survey instruments vary, but they generally request such information as the participants' native language(s), languages spoken at home, languages studied, places the participant has lived, etc. Experience can be inferred from such a survey instrument, but questions can necessarily only access knowledge above the level of conscious awareness.

The approach to listener experience quantification taken here adapts a task from forensic phonetics (Neuhauser and Simpson 2007) and is an attempt to assess participants' ability to correctly identify an authentic Chinese accent from a set of distractor accents. The assumption, again, is that more experienced listeners will, in the general case, have greater sensitivity to fine phonetic detail consistent with an authentic, rather than imitated, Chinese-English accent; at the same time, that less experienced listeners will be more drawn to an imitated variety. Both listener populations will apply what knowledge and stereotypes they have available to guide speech perception, but their differing levels of experience and their differing relationships to 'Chinese-ness' should be discernible via the authenticity detection task.

However, it must be noted that the generalization "Chinese accent" is so broad as to be almost offensive. The so-called "dialects" of Chinese include six separate language phyla: Sino-Tibetan, Austro-Tai, Austronesian, Altaic, Austro-Asiatic, and Indo-European. Many of these dialects are not mutually intelligible, with listener subjective ratings of mutual intelligibility closely matching performance on cross-dialectal semantic classification and speech-in-noise perception tasks (Tang and van Heuven 2009). This suggests that, although Chinese L2 English speakers may all *also* command Mandarin, or Standard, Chinese, Mandarin is itself likely to be an L2 language or spoken with the accent of a regional dialect. Additionally, different non-native English speakers from China have acquired different target Englishes. Until quite recently it has been the norm for Chinese students of English to target RP-accented British English as their normative model for acquisition. Increasingly, though, students target American English or even a contact variety known as "China English" (Qiong 2004).

## Experiment 1: Authenticity Detection Task

Experiment 1 is an accent authenticity detection task using the *yes/no* detection paradigm. The listener is presented with a single stimulus recording per trial and must press one button on a response box if the stimulus sounds like authentic Chinese-accented English and another button if the stimulus sounds like some other form of accented English. This experiment was designed to measure listeners' ability to correctly detect an authentic Chinese accent among a collection of accents that include authentic Chinese and imitated Chinese as critical stimuli, together with a set of filler accents.

One goal of this experiment was to quantify the extent to which listeners with little or no experience listening to native speakers of a target variety nevertheless use social knowledge in a systematic way during perception and to compare this performance to that of more experienced listeners. It is hoped that populations of more and less experienced listeners can be identified and their experience quantified using this method. This categorization should be particularly useful when the variety or variable in question is below the level of available, conscious awareness. It should then be possible to test the attribution of socially cued effects in speech perception to stored episodic traces of linguistic experience linked to social knowledge.

### Methods

*Stimuli*

Stimulus materials consisted of the eight sentence types listed in Table 2.1. These were all English recordings spoken by two native speakers of Mandarin Chinese and one native speaker each of Korean, Turkish, and Macedonian, all drawn from the Wildcat Corpus (Van Engen *et al.* 2010). The Wildcat Corpus includes individual words, the "Stella" passage from the Speech Accent Archive at George Mason University, the "North Wind and the Sun" from

Table 2.1 *Sentences Used in Experiment 1*

She made the bed.
Bob wore a watch on his wrist.
Dad talked about the bomb.
I wear my hat on my head.
The color of a lemon is yellow.
A racecar can go very fast.
He looked at the sleeves.
Please call Stella.

the IPA Handbook, high and low predictability sentences, and unscripted recordings from a map task. The sentence recordings from this experiment were drawn from the scripted passages and sentence recordings. These stimulus recordings were augmented with recordings of two monolingual English speakers – not trained actors – performing imitated Chinese accents.

In general, the accuracy of the imitated Chinese was poor, but as in Neuhauser and Simpson (2007) speaker manipulations were consistent. Native speakers of Midwestern American English from Michigan were asked to read, with an imitated Chinese accent, the same texts recorded by authentic Chinese-accented speakers for the Wildcat Corpus. These speakers were not presented with a model accent to imitate. The voices selected for inclusion in the study imitated the authentic backing of interdental fricatives (/ð/ → [z] and /θ/ → [s]) and the stereotypical feature /ɹ/ → [l] that is rarely, if ever, found in authentic Chinese-accented English. The American-English speakers, from southeastern Michigan, who produced the imitated Chinese consistently produced post-vocalic /ɹ/, while the authentic Chinese-accented speakers did not.

Figure 2.1 shows a spectrogram of a sample token of authentic Chinese-accented English. This male speaker has produced the word *racecar* as [ɹeɪskʰaˑ]. The word-final vowel is rhoticized for nearly its entire duration with no audible consonantal articulation. There is a pitch contour on this syllable similar to the Mandarin Chinese third tone with its characteristic dip and rise.

Figure 2.2 shows a spectrogram of a sample recording of imitated Chinese-accented English. This male speaker has produced the word *racecar* as [ʐeɪskʰaɹ]. This speaker generally replaced /ɹ/ in non-post-vocalic positions with [l]; however, in this particular token there is visible and audible frication. The post-vocalic /ɹ/ is clearly visible and audible over the last 71 ms of the token and the vowel is audibly rhoticized for 50 ms (six glottal pulses) prior to the consonantal articulation. That the imitated Chinese speakers consistently produced post-vocalic central approximants is initially surprising. The lack of post-vocalic /ɹ/ is a stereotypical feature of Chinese-accented English and one that most of the professional actors in the next section also imitated.

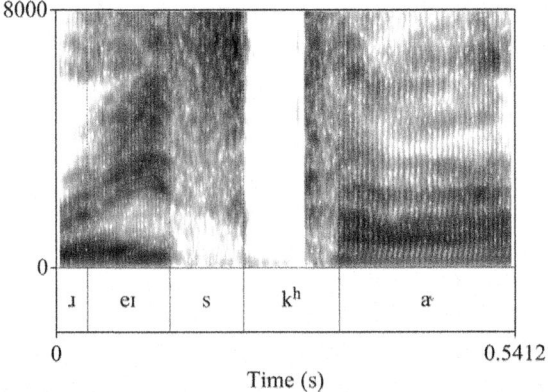

Figure 2.1 Spectrogram of Male Authentic Chinese Speaker Producing
*Racecar*
Post-vocalic /ɹ/ is clearly absent in the spectrogram.

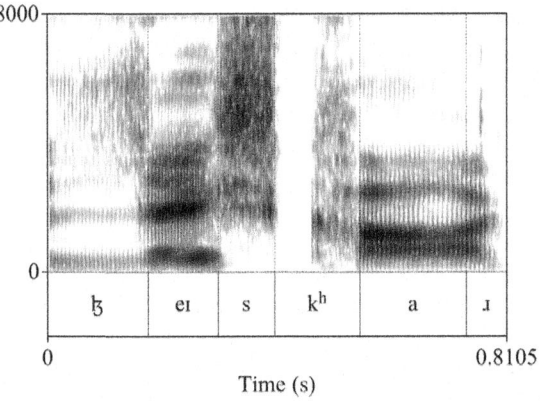

Figure 2.2 Spectrogram of Male Imitated Chinese Speaker Producing
*Racecar*
In this imitation, initial /ɹ/ has been replaced with a voiced alveolar lateral
fricative. Post-vocalic /ɹ/ is clearly visible in the spectrogram.

## Participants

Eighty-seven undergraduate students participated at one of two experiment
sites. All participants provided self-reported experience ratings (more experienced versus less experienced with Chinese-accented English) on a language
history survey. Along with questions about birthplace, places lived, languages

spoken at home, and languages spoken personally, the survey asked participants to agree or disagree, on a five-point Likert scale to statements regarding having experience listening to Chinese-accented English; having close friends who speak Chinese as a first language; having family members who speak Chinese as a first language; and a number of questions intended to ascertain listener ideologies (e.g. "It is socially acceptable to imitate a Chinese accent" or "I can distinguish a Chinese accent from a Korean or Japanese accent"). Listeners selected as "less experienced" had a mean age of 19, had lived 98 percent of their lives in the United States, were predominantly born in Michigan (51 percent) or New York (18 percent), reported having no friends or family members who spoke Chinese as a first language, and on average claimed not to have a clear idea of what a Chinese accent sounds like or to be able to distinguish Korean- or Japanese-accented English from Chinese-accented English. Listeners selected as "more experienced" had a mean age of 22, had lived 82.3 percent of their lives in the United States, were predominantly born in California (55 percent) or China (38 percent), reported having friends and/or family members who spoke Chinese as a first language, reported Mandarin as a language spoken at home, and on average claimed to have a clear idea about what a "Chinese" accent sounds like and to be able to distinguish Korean- or Japanese-accented English from Chinese-accented English. Both groups tended to agree that it is socially unacceptable to imitate a Chinese accent, with one participant writing in the margin, "unless you're Asian!".

The original intention had been to run the entire experiment at the University of Michigan research site, but locating participants who self-reported as "more experienced" at the Michigan site proved unsuccessful. For this reason, a second site was added at the University of California, Berkeley, where such a population was more readily identified.

### Michigan Listeners

Fifty-seven undergraduate students from the University of Michigan Introductory Psychology subject pool participated for partial course credit. Participants had no known hearing problems. Five participants were identified for exclusion prior to analysis for reporting experience with Mandarin Chinese – either through language study or, in four cases, for being bilingual or Heritage speakers. These participants will be included in the correspondence analysis to test the authenticity detection task's ability to accurately exclude non-representative participants, but these participants will be excluded from other statistical and visual data analysis. One participant was excluded for using Facebook and sending text messages on his smartphone during the experimental session. One additional participant was excluded from the data analysis for struggling to remain awake during the experiment and reporting the task as extremely difficult. Three data files were lost due to experimenter error.

### Berkeley Listeners

Heritage speakers with little or no proficiency in Mandarin were selected as a target population. This selection was intended to avoid the complications of interpreting the results of truly bilingual speakers for what is essentially an English language task.

Thirty Heritage Mandarin-speaking undergraduate students from the University of California, Berkeley participated in exchange for an incentive of $15.00 per participant. Two participants were removed prior to any analysis: one L1 speaker of Mandarin who had misunderstood the flier, and a second individual who misrepresented his identity. As with the excluded listeners from the Michigan group, these participants will be included in the correspondence analysis, but excluded from other statistical and visual data analysis. Time constraints limited the number of participants who could be engaged in the study at this site.

### Procedure

All listeners used Apple Macbook Computers (model 4,1; late 2008). Testing of Michigan listeners took place in an IAC sound-attenuated booth in the University of Michigan Phonetics Lab; stimuli were presented over AKG K271 mkII headphones. Responses were entered via Cedrus RB-620 low-latency response boxes with serial to USB adaptors.

UC Berkeley listeners used the same computers and software as at the Michigan site. However, these testing sessions took place in the phonology laboratory at the University of California, Berkeley. This is a quiet space dedicated to speech perception experiments, but is not a sound-attenuated booth. AKG k240 headphones and Cedrus RB-730 low-latency USB response boxes replaced the headphones and response boxes used at Michigan.

Stimuli were presented using Superlab stimulus presentation software version 4.0.8. Volume was set at a comfortable listening level. Listeners indicated their responses via button box. Listeners were instructed to press one button if the voice they heard had an authentic Chinese accent and another if the accent was not authentic Chinese. The target sentences were presented on-screen from the onset of the recording playback until the subject submitted a response. Listeners were informed that the voices would include a range of different non-native English accents, including Chinese, imitated Chinese, Korean, Turkish, and Macedonian. It was not possible to change responses or to hear recordings more than once. Listeners were encouraged to rest after each block and there were enforced breaks at the halfway point. Participants responded to eight sentences produced by seven voices in each of six blocks for 336 responses per participant.

All participants in this experiment had just completed the transcription-in-noise task reported in McGowan (2015). No voices or stimuli were repeated from that experiment.

### Predictions

The use of imitated Chinese accents was inspired by Neuhauser and Simpson (2007), who found that German monolingual speakers were more likely to identify German imitations of French and American accents as authentic than they were to correctly discriminate true non-native accents. I hypothesized that native listeners must be drawing on language ideologies concerning foreign-ness in general and the target non-native accents in particular when making discrimination judgments. This hypothesis, if supported, would have implica-tions for research in socially cued speech perception that has appealed to stored episodic traces to explain behavioral results.

It is difficult to imagine a means of differentiating between listener know-ledge gained through real communicative experience with a language variety and listener knowledge of linguistic stereotypes (again, in the sense of Labov 1972) gained through exposure to imitations of that variety or occasional brief exposure in the media. However, the Neuhauser and Simpson (2007) result suggests one possibility. If less experienced and more experienced listeners are drawing on both qualitatively and quantitatively different forms of know-ledge – in terms of both amount of experience and accuracy of linking a Chinese-accented voice to a "Chinese" social category – when detecting an authentic Chinese accent, then they should be differentially drawn to authentic and imitated stimuli.

### Results

#### *Proportion "Yes" Responses*

Figure 2.3 shows proportional "yes" responses to each non-native accent by experience level. More experienced listeners are more likely to respond "yes" to an authentic Chinese voice. More experienced listeners are also more likely than less experienced listeners to respond "yes" to an authentic Chinese accent. Less experienced listeners, by contrast, appear to be more likely than more experi-enced listeners to identify an imitated Chinese accent as "authentic." This pattern of responses suggests that more and less experienced listeners are employing different strategies when deciding whether a particular voice is "authentic."

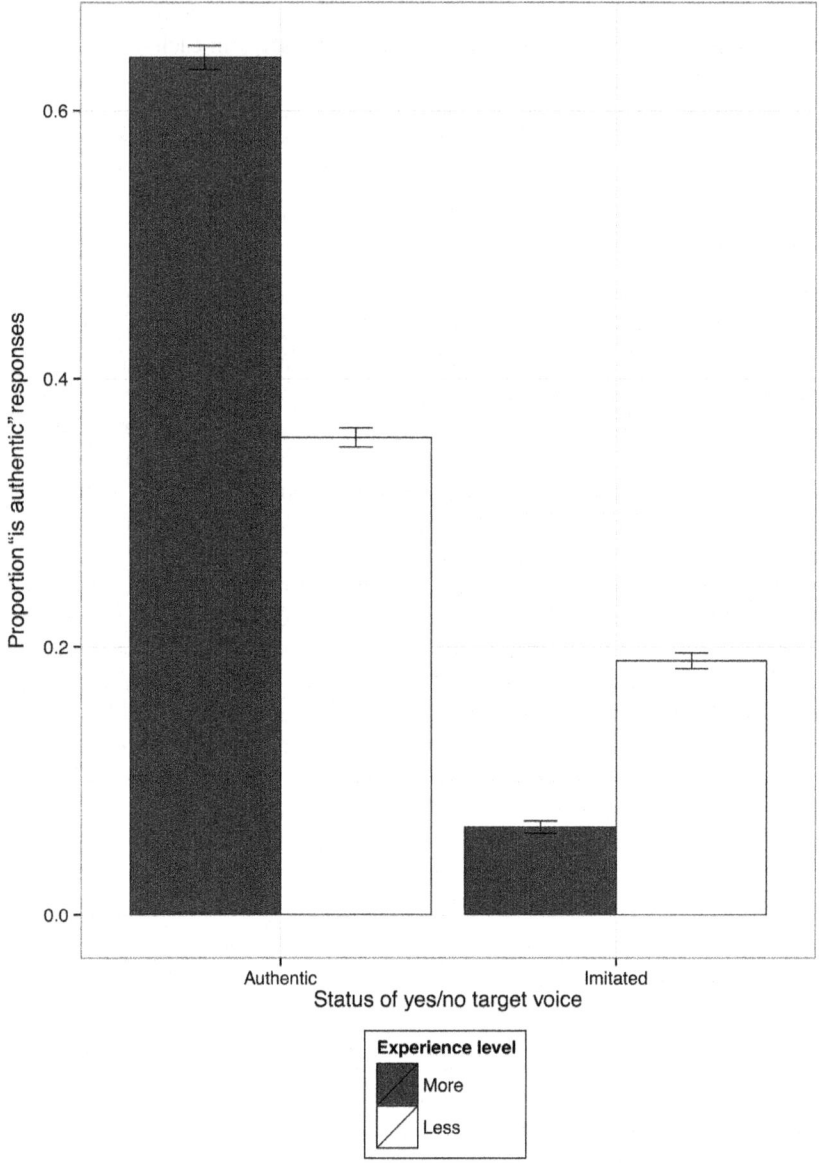

Figure 2.3 Proportion "Yes" Responses by Accent and Experience

The yes/no responses were then analyzed using the open source statistical package R (R Development Core Team 2014). The data were modeled with linear mixed-effects models, as implemented in the lme4 R package (Bates *et al.* 2014). Categorical variables were sum-coded to allow the interpretation

Table 2.2 *Fixed Effects with Coefficients and P-Values for "Yes" Responses by Accent and Experience*
*Reference levels: accent – Chinese; experience – Experienced*

| (Ref. level: experienced; Chinese) | Coef β | SE(β) | z | p |
|---|---|---|---|---|
| (Intercept) | 1.21 | 0.26 | 4.68 | <.001 |
| Accent | −1.92 | 0.05 | −37.54 | <.001 |
| Experience | −0.02 | 0.29 | −0.08 | 0.94 |
| Accent: Experience | 1.43 | 0.06 | 24.89 | <.001 |

of any lower order effects in the models as main effects rather than simple effects. Models were fitted with the maximal random effects structure justified by model comparison and the data to avoid the inflated risk of Type 1 errors in random intercept-only models (Barr *et al.* 2013). Model comparison was also used to justify the inclusion of fixed effects and interaction terms in the linear models, while statistical significance within the resulting models will be reported using Satterwate's approximations as implemented in the R package lmerTest (Kuznetsova *et al.* 2013).

The yes/no responses were analyzed with Subject and Item included as random effects with both random intercepts and random slopes for Experience. The dependent measure in this model was whether the participant responded "yes" to the stimulus ("yes" response regardless of accuracy is an indicator of the listener's belief that the stimulus is authentic Chinese). Accent and Experience were included as fixed effects. A fuller model including the interaction of Accent and Experience provided a better fit for the data than a reduced model with no interaction term ($\chi2(1) = 792.08$; $p < 0.001$). Factor levels, coefficients, standard error, z-score, and p-values for each level of these factors and interaction are reported in Table 2.2.

There is a significant main effect of Accent ($\beta = -1.92$, $p < 0.001$). Surprisingly, given the apparent differences in Figure 2.3, there is not a main effect of Experience. However, the interaction of Accent and Experience is significant, demonstrating that more and less experienced listeners are drawn differentially to the authentic and imitated Chinese accents.

### Accuracy

Table 2.3 shows percentage accuracy on the authenticity detection task by target Accent and self-reported Experience level. As anticipated, more experienced listeners appear to be more accurate when responding to either authentic Chinese or to imitated Chinese stimuli. However, accuracy results do not, on their own, necessarily reveal the listeners' ability to detect a signal such as the Chinese accent in this experiment. A listener hoping to have perfect recall on

Table 2.3 *Percent Correct Responses by Accent and Experience*

| Experience | Authentic Chinese | Imitated Chinese |
|---|---|---|
| More experienced | 64.0% | 93.5% |
| Less experienced | 35.6% | 81.1% |

Table 2.4 *Signal Detection Results Authenticity Detection Task*

| Experience | Hit rate | False alarm rate | d' | c |
|---|---|---|---|---|
| More experienced | 0.64 | 0.06 | 1.87 | 0.58 |
| Less experienced | 0.36 | 0.19 | 0.51 | 0.62 |

the Chinese-identification task could, for example, simply press the "yes" button in response to each stimulus item. Overall performance would be poor, but accuracy to the Chinese stimuli would be perfect.

A measure of response sensitivity from signal detection theory, d', represents the distance between a listener's ability to maximize hit rate (correct identifications) and minimize false rejections. Table 2.4 reports hit and false alarm rates in these results, together with d' and criterion c scores. The question addressed by these metrics is the extent to which listeners are correctly identifying authentic Chinese and rejecting other accents. The much higher d-prime score for more experienced listeners suggests that, as predicted, these listeners are much more sensitive to the differences between authentic and imitated Chinese-accented English.

The criterion measure, or c, is a measure of response bias that attempts to model the decision criterion chosen by listeners when completing a task.

$$d' = z(H) - z(F) \tag{1}$$

$$c = -0.5[z(H) + z(F)] \tag{2}$$

H represents the hit rate: correct "yes" responses divided by possible "yes" responses (equivalent to recall in information retrieval). F represents the false alarm rate: incorrect "no" responses divided by the number of potentially correct "no" responses). z() is a z-transform function (taking probabilities and returning z-scores). Positive c scores correspond to a tendency to respond "no" during the task. Both groups of listeners are biased to respond "no," but experienced listeners much more weakly so. If c = 0, the listener is unbiased; less experienced listeners have a slightly stronger "no" bias (c = 0.62) than more experienced listeners (c = 0.58). This bias to respond "no" is likely attributable to a weakness in the task's design. With three filler accents and two imitated Chinese accents, only 25 percent of the trials required a legitimate "yes" response. It is likely that a replication of this study, which removed the probably unnecessary filler accents, would not only make the task shorter and easier to administer, but also obtain even stronger d-prime results and, therefore, a more accurate predictor of group membership.

### Clustering

Figures 2.4 and 2.5 present a visualization of a correspondence analysis of the authenticity detection data, including both critical and filler trials. Correspondence analysis is an unsupervised clustering technique. From a contingency table of "yes" responses by participants to each level of the language factor, two

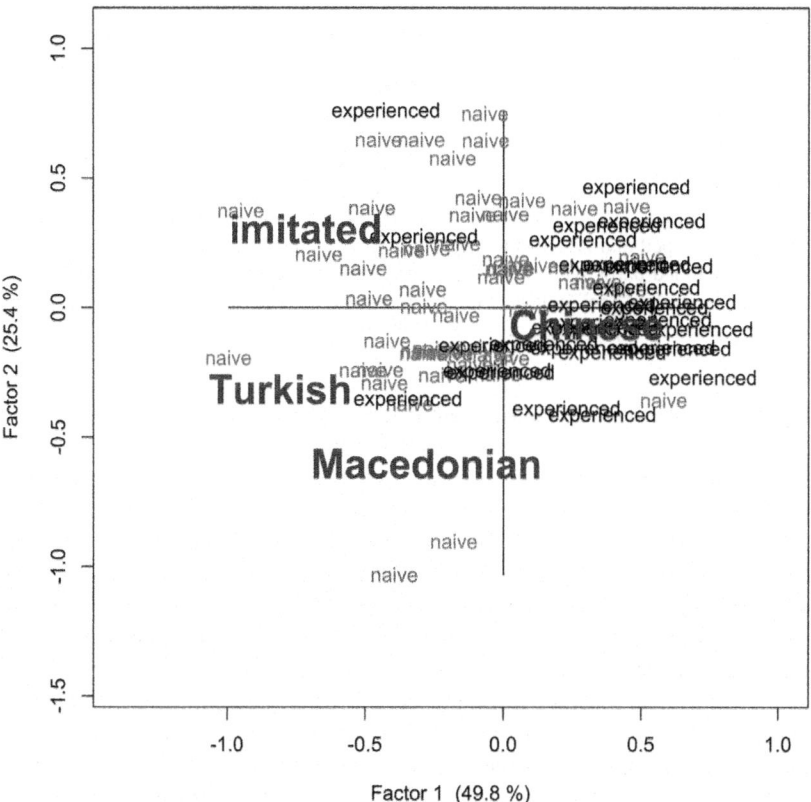

Figure 2.4 Correspondence Analysis of More and Less Experienced Listeners
More experienced listeners cluster tightly around the authentic Chinese target, while naive (less experienced) listener responses are more diffuse.

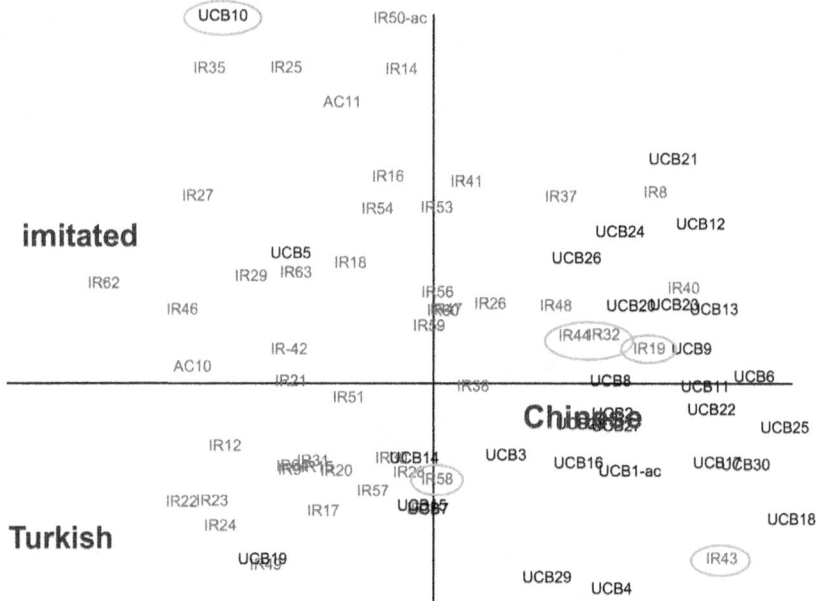

Figure 2.5 Correspondence Analysis of More and Less Experienced Listeners Cropped and Zoomed to Highlight Participant ID Detail
Circled participant IDs were independently excluded prior to further data analysis; "ucb" indicates more experienced listeners and all others are from the less experienced group.

separate square distance matrices are calculated: a row-by-row matrix (in this case, distances between participants) and a column-by-column matrix (distances between languages). The software used here, Baayen's LanguageR package for the R open source statistical environment (R Development Core Team 2014), uses a chi-squared distance metric. Like principal components analysis does for real-valued data, correspondence analysis provides a low-dimensionality map of both rows and columns in a contingency table (Baayen 2008). "Factor 1" on the x-axis represents the most informative column, authentic Chinese, with an eigenvalue rate of 0.4984 or 49.84 percent of the variance in the table. "Factor 2" on the y-axis represents the second most informative column, imitated Chinese, with an eigenvalue rate of 0.2538 or 25.38 percent of the variance in the table. This two-dimensional visualization of the data captures roughly 75.2 percent of the variance in the table; Korean contributed virtually no explanatory power to the map and has dropped out of the visualization.

Intuitively from Figure 2.4 we can see that the more experienced Heritage Mandarin participants from the University of California, Berkeley have, for the most part, clustered tightly around the Chinese label. This suggests that, as predicted, these listeners were more attracted to Chinese for responses of "authentic Chinese" than to any other language. The clustering of less experienced (here rendered as "naïve" for visual differentiation) monolingual English participants from the University of Michigan is much more diffuse. They appear to be attracted to both the imitated and authentic Chinese languages for "yes" responses, with neither cluster being a particularly good predictor of less experience.

Interestingly, all but one of the participants who were independently excluded from data analysis are outliers on this plot. Figure 2.5 is a zoomed and cropped view with the excluded participants circled. Participant UCB10 was excluded from the experienced data set for misrepresenting his identity and, reassuringly, is among the least experienced of the less experienced participants in terms of attraction to the imitated Chinese voices. Participants IR19, IR32, IR43, IR44, and IR58 were excluded from the less experienced data set for self-reporting extensive or Heritage experience with Mandarin-accented English. Of these, only IR58 does not clearly cluster with the experienced participants.

### Reaction Time

It was predicted that experienced listeners should have lower reaction time latencies overall. The question, after all, is whether the voice is authentic Chinese and these listeners have copious experience with this variety to draw upon. This prediction was not upheld. There were no predictions regarding the relative time required to respond to Authentic versus Imitated Chinese-accented stimuli, however, as shown in Figure 2.6, responses to the Authentic stimuli were 418 ms faster, on average, than responses to the Imitated stimuli. Less experienced listeners were also, on average, 155 ms faster than more experienced listeners when responding. Reaction times longer than two standard deviations above the grand mean were excluded from analysis. Even after the log transform there remain large numbers of slow outliers (visible as black circles on Figure 2.6) and this is true across listeners, across accents, and across experience levels.

### Discussion

The question posed in the authenticity detection task was whether ability to discriminate an authentic from an imitated Chinese voice might be a good predictor of listener experience level. The first prediction was that more experienced listeners would more accurately identify the authentic variety. This prediction was upheld. More experienced listeners are better able to identify

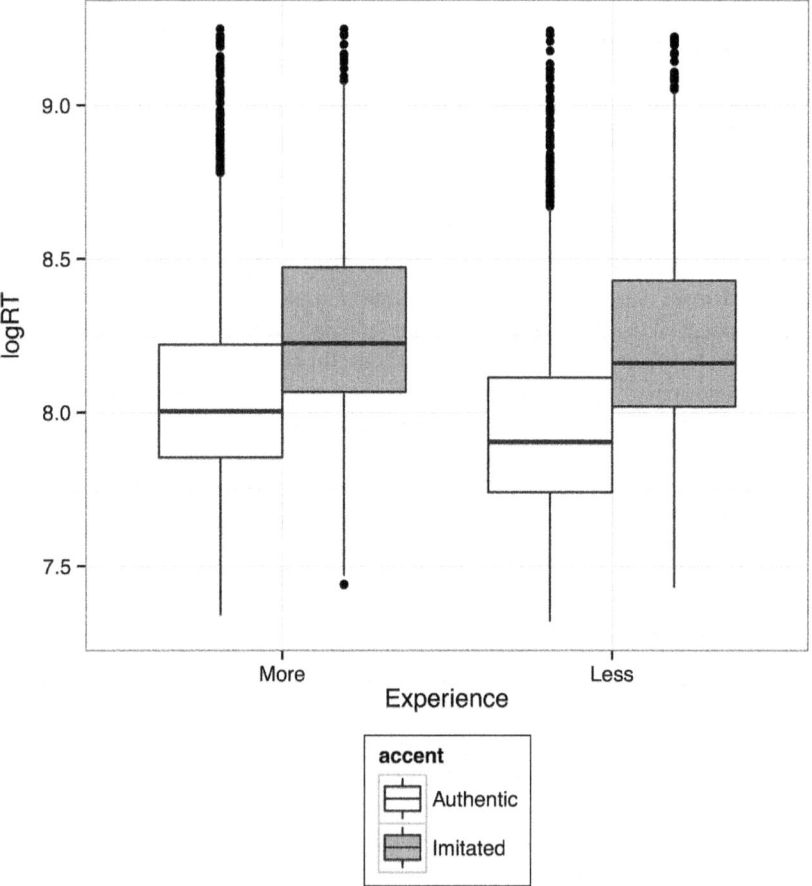

Figure 2.6 Log Transformed Reaction Times by Accent and Experience

the authentic variety (as shown by the d-prime analysis) and less likely to be charmed by the imitation, as revealed in the analysis of "yes" responses and the correspondence analysis. This result is hypothesized to be due to three factors: the accumulation of detailed episodic traces of linguistic experience; a clearer mental representation of a "Chinese" social category; and more accurate link-ages between fine phonetic detail and the social category label of "Chinese."

The second prediction was that less experienced listeners would be more drawn to the imitated variety. This prediction was also upheld with less experienced listeners being more drawn to the imitated variety, as revealed by the "yes" responses analysis, and less able to distinguish authenticity as shown by d-prime. Interestingly, while less experienced listeners are less accurate than experienced listeners at identifying an authentic Chinese voice, their performance is above chance. They are successfully drawing on *some* kind of knowledge to perform this task and this knowledge is unlikely to be a rich cloud of Chinese-accented English exemplars with accurate linkages to a well-defined "Chinese" social category. It seems likelier, given the responses on the language history survey, that these listeners are drawing on culturally available stereotypes of how Chinese-accented English sounds. This suggestion is, again, consistent with Neuhauser and Simpson's findings for German listeners hearing French and American accents.

It seems reasonable to infer, then, that more and less experienced listeners are drawing not merely on different *amounts* of knowledge, but on different *forms* of knowledge when detecting an authentic Chinese accent. This finding does not refute exemplar models, but it does suggest a need for a more nuanced understanding of the knowledge listeners use to structure speech sensory data. This more nuanced view should highlight the role of listener ideologies and listener awareness of social categories during perception. The more experienced listeners could well be drawing primarily on stored episodic traces of experience with authentic Chinese-accents, while less experienced listeners draw on stored episodic traces of comedians and actors imitating the accent. However, it should be noted that even the most experienced listener will also anticipate stereotypical features of a variety and that even in these listeners stereotype and experience must therefore interact in perception.

So, too, it should not be assumed that less experienced listeners' success on this task implies that they conceptualize "Chinese" in the same richly detailed way that the more experienced Heritage Mandarin listeners do. White Americans typically conflate all ethnicities and nationalities from East Asia into a single pan-Asian, pan-ethnic group, who, while believed to be a "model minority" are nevertheless conceptualized as perpetually foreign and essentially unassimilable (Espiritu 1992; Wong *et al.* 1998; Iwamoto and Liu 2010). For these listeners, detail about sociolinguistic features is likely to be low and the social categories to which these features are linked is likely to be coarse-grained, combining aspects of Chinese-accented English with, for example, Japanese- and Korean-accented English. These issues will be explored further in the next study, which looks at the production of imitated Chinese by less experienced, American actors.

### Usefulness as a Replacement for, or Supplement to, Self-Reported Experience

An additional goal of the authenticity detection task was to explore the usefulness of this task as a means of directly estimating participants' experience level with authentic Chinese-accented English. The *yes/no* task presented here is extremely easy to build and administer for any target variety, requiring only a fairly small set of authentic and imitated language recordings.

A task of this sort should be particularly helpful in gauging listeners' experience with language varieties for which the less experienced and more experienced populations are not so easily identified as Mandarin-accented English. It could also be helpful in assessing listeners' experience with varieties that they may have ideological reasons to disavow knowledge of (e.g. middle class African American students might wish to distance themselves from knowledge of African American Vernacular English (AAVE) – particularly in a formal context). Finally, this tool may be of use in the investigation of varieties or sociolinguistic variables that, like lexical frequency or compensation for co-articulation, are entirely below the level of listeners' conscious awareness.

This section closes with an important caution about the interpretation of the present result. Although every attempt was made to keep the experiment as consistent as possible despite the change of venues, the less experienced and more experienced listeners were, in retrospect, fundamentally not performing the same task. Although they used the same computers, were given the same instructions, heard the same stimuli, saw the same sentences, and performed the same physical task, more experienced listeners were inescapably aware of having been recruited precisely because they were Heritage speakers of Mandarin Chinese. The less experienced listeners were simply asked to identify the authenticity of a non-native accent. More experienced listeners, by virtue of their background, are not only trying to identify the authenticity of an accent, but, in a very real sense, are also striving to demonstrate and possibly even defend their own authenticity. I believe this difference alone accounts for experienced listeners' somewhat slower reaction times. Future uses of this technique will need to be more careful about keeping experienced participants naive to the role of their own experience in the experiment.

## Production of Imitated Chinese

It is difficult to discern from the results of the first experiment which features listeners were attending to when making their determination of authenticity. This task is made more difficult by the interrelatedness of the various cues that might be active at any given moment: speaking rate, pitch variability, and segmental alternations are each likely to vary in any particular word or even syllable that might be selected for presentation to a listener. This problem is, of course, not unique to the present study and numerous solutions have been used in the past to isolate the informativeness of particular acoustic features (e.g. synthesis, modification of natural speech, eye tracking, masking, etc.). However, because the subject of the present investigation is listeners' awareness and control of socially informative variation, this study moves from perception to production. Specifically, professional actors who are themselves native Michigan-English speakers and who self-identified as inexperienced with authentic Chinese-accented English were hired to perform scripted materials with an imitated Chinese accent.

It is hypothesized that, in order to create a percept of *Chinese* for an English-speaking audience, these actors will perform the same stereotypical features that less experienced listeners drew upon in Experiment 1 to make their identification decisions. Actors use imperfect imitations of "dialects" to create characters. Successful actors achieve this quickly and efficiently. This experiment is, again, inspired by Neuhauser and Simpson (2007), whose native German listeners were more likely to identify a French or American accent performed by a fellow German as authentic than truly authentic French- or American-accented speech. Actors train in many different vocal and speech traditions, but will generally only alter a specific subset of their productions which are intended to be the characteristic speech sounds of the target dialect or variety. Blumenfeld (2002), for example, provides the aspiring actor with a wide range of accents and lists of the "most important sounds" required to perform the target accent. By manipulating these stereotypical aspects of their speech, though, the actor constructs with the listener an idealized representation of the target variety. Authenticity, for a less experienced listener, may well be measured not only by how consistently the actor makes these substitutions and how well aligned these substitutions are with the listener's own stereotypical expectations, but also, in some sense, by how comfortable and familiar the non-stereotypical aspects of the voice remain.

### Chinese-Accented English

To establish a baseline for the particular features the actors are likely to imitate (and thus guide the phonetic analysis), it may be useful to compare the perceptions of Chinese-accented English made by linguists to language ideologies held by less experienced listeners.

I interviewed a linguist employed at the University of Michigan's English Language Institute, which offers English language instruction, counseling, and testing to members of the University of Michigan community. This linguist provided the following list of features that typically prove challenging for L1 Mandarin speakers seeking English proficiency through the Institute.

| | |
|---|---|
| /b/ /d/ /g/ | devoiced in final position (lab/lap, mob/mop, bed/bet, mad/mat, hard/hot, lag/lack, dog/dock) |
| /v/ | realized as [w] or sometimes [b] (vision, vet/wet, vine/wine, provide, university, overseas, involve) |

| | |
|---|---|
| /θ/ /ð/ | tongue tip is closer to the alveolar ridge than to a dental or interdental articulation resulting in [s] or [z]voiceless: (thing/ sing, thank/sank, faith/face, math/mass, method) and voiced (the, mother, either, weather, etc.) |
| /ð/ | for some speakers (this may be regional or related to an L1 other than Mandarin), /ð/ is realized as /d/ |
| /ʃ/ | more palatalized than English [ʃ] |
| /ʒ/ | realized as [w], [j] depending on vowel context or as a voiced palato-alveolar affricate [dʒ] (e.g. usual [juwəl], vision [vɪjən]) |
| /dʒ/ | occasionally realized as [ʒ] word-medially (virgin/version, ledger/leisure) |
| [ɾ] | realized as [t] / [d] (water, party, kitty, city, ladder) |
| [ʔ] | realized as [t] / [d] (mountain, kitten, fantasy) |
| /m/ | sometimes alveolar in final position (some/sun, rum/run). Rare? |
| /n/ | consonant deleted (nasalization seems to be moved to vowel) (untie, inside, romantic, human, tradition) |
| /ŋ/ | realized as [n] or deleted (with Ṽ) (thing, long, length) |
| /l/ | realized as [oʊ], [w], or deleted word finally (cold/code, fault/ fought, dull/dough, call/caw, all/awe, social, people) |
| /ɹ/ | deleted word finally for some speakers (not Beijing) (far, order, error, turn/ton, bird/bud, work/walk, mark/mock) |
| **consonant clusters** | simplified; often partially or wholly deleted – even across syllable contact boundaries (coul(d), ou(t)side, pra(c)tice, remi(nd)) |

### Folk Observations

Lindemann (2005) asked American-English listeners to label maps with descriptions of English as spoken by international students. These students provided largely negative evaluations of Chinese-accented English with, Lindemann notes, "a surprising amount of agreement" in their qualitative descriptions of the salient features of Chinese-accented English. Lindemann's data is summarized in Table 2.5.

Lindemann's respondents chiefly focus on Chinese speakers' confusion of /ɹ/ and /l/ – a feature notably absent from the linguists' description.

### Method

Five English-speaking actors, all natives of southeastern Michigan, were hired to perform a set of scripted materials. These materials included the Stella passage, "The North Wind and the Sun," and the same thirty pairs of high and low predictability sentences from Bradlow and Alexander (2007) used in Experiment 1.

Table 2.5 *Folk Features of Chinese-Accented English (from Lindemann (2005)*

Speak quickly
Pronounce L's as R's.
Voices rise when cursing
Choppy speech
High toned/high pitched English
Missing verbs (copula)
Forget to add plural "-s"
Difficult to understand

All five actors self-identified as inexperienced with Chinese-accented English – apart from their preparation for this performance. Each actor was asked to read the scripted materials twice. First they read in their normal speaking voice (which, without exception, was a performed stage version of their normal voice) and an attempted imitation of Chinese-accented English. The actors were specifically asked to perform a Mandarin-Chinese accent. Although this request is obviously quite vague, it is typical of the level at which specific accents are discussed in materials for dialect courses and actor preparation for dialect performance (e.g. Blumenfeld 2002). Three of the actors – Emma, Matt, and Sango – had been students of the same acting coach at the University of Michigan. For their preparation, these actors used materials like Blumenfeld's lists to identify the important sounds that needed to change and then modified their scripted materials by adding IPA transcriptions of the affected words or, in most cases, individual sounds, they wished to alter. As can be seen below, these actors did not arrive at the same set of features, but, for the most part, were quite consistent in their alternations. Susie prepared for the role in this project by listening to and imitating recordings of Chinese-accented speech; in particular, she listened to recordings from the George Mason University speech accent archive, which provides accurate geographic information for each accented voice. Finally, Leo prepared for this role by listening to and imitating other actors. Indeed, Leo's performance was at times reminiscent of Mickey Rooney's portrayal of I. Y. Yunioshi in the 1961 film "Breakfast at Tiffany's."

One clear limitation of this study is the use of scripted materials. The actors' performances of Chinese-accented English contain none of the elided copulas or determiners that are both characteristic of authentic Chinese-accented English and present in Lindemann's description of folk linguistic ideologies. The actors focused instead on manipulations of pitch, duration, rhythm, and specific segmental alternations – as will my analysis. Actor-specific subsections in the results section will detail the suprasegmental and segmental alternations made by each actor; however, results are likely to be quite different given a more improvizational task.

My prediction is that actors need only control features of Chinese-accented English that are socially informative to English-native listeners. To the extent that folk linguistic descriptions of an accent represent the linkages listeners have between social category and phonetic detail, the majority of actor manipulations should reflect Lindemann's respondents' folk descriptions, which were fairly low on both the Detail and Accuracy continua.

### Results

The first folk prediction is that Chinese-accented English is spoken quickly. If this feature is important for a native-English percept of "Chinese," then all of the actors are unsuccessful at producing it. Sentence durations were, on average, much longer (1,550 ms) for the actors in the Chinese condition than in their normal speaking voices (1,066 ms). Not all actors manipulated speaking rate, however. The actors identified here as Sango and Leo showed manipulation of speaking rate, while the actor identified as Emma spoke much more slowly.

Another folk prediction is that Chinese-accented English will be overall higher in pitch than English that is not Chinese-accented. A related prediction, not specifically tested with these materials, is that Chinese-accented English will rise in pitch when the speaker is cursing. There are no taboo words in these recordings and there was no request for particularly emotional speech. However, if we take these two predictions together as an expectation of both higher general F0 and more variable F0, we can evaluate them in light of the collected materials. Surprisingly, there was no average or actor-specific manipulation of pitch in the creation of a Chinese-accented guise. Averaging mean F0 for each sentence in the corpus, actors used a mean F0 of 202 Hz in the Chinese Condition and 200 Hz in the normal speaking voice condition. The results are similar for the differences between minimum and maximum F0 except for one actor, "Matt," who had a maximum pitch of nearly 400 Hz in his Chinese utterances, but only 210 Hz in his normal speaking voice.

### Segmental Alternations

Each actor performed at least a few consistent segmental alternations in their Chinese-accented guise. This is unsurprising given that these types of alternations are typically the primary focus in theatrical dialect training. The following subsections document each of the systematic segment-level consonant replacements by each actor. One slight departure from normal convention is in the use of bracketing. In the following alternations, the slashes normally used for phonemic representations are used to present the actor's own normal productions, while the square brackets represent phonetic transcriptions of the segmental realization under the Chinese-accented condition.

### Susie

| /ð/ | → | [d] | | | |
|-----|---|-----|---|---|---|
| /θ/ | → | [tʰ] | | | |
| /t/ | → | { [tʰ] | / | V__V | e.g. water |
| | | [tʰ] | / | __# | e.g. feet |
| /ɹ/ | → | ∅ | / | V____ | only in her and bird |

Susie's aspiration of intervocalic and word-final [t] is correct insofar as it accurately reflects genuine difficulties L1 Mandarin speakers have with English (as described in the section entitled "Chinese-accented English," above). Susie's alternation of the interdental fricatives with their alveolar stop counterparts accurately recapitulates authentic Chinese-accented speech to the extent that L1 Mandarin speakers have difficulty with these fricatives. However, the more common alternation for authentic Chinese-accented speech is between the interdental and alveolar fricatives. Alternation with the stops does occur (indeed, it occurs in many varieties of foreign-accented English), but is more typical of, for example, Cantonese speech than Mandarin.

### Emma

| /ð/ | → | [z] | | | |
|-----|---|-----|---|---|---|
| /l/ | → | [w] | | | |
| /t/ | → | [tʰ] | / | V____V | e.g. water |
| /C#/ | → | [Cə] | | (optionally) | |
| /CC/ | → | [CəC] | | | |

Emma alternates the voiced interdental fricative with its alveolar counterpart in much the way that native L1 Mandarin speakers do. Her performance also faithfully recapitulates alternation between the alveolar lateral and the labio-velar approximant found in authentic speech, but she does this globally for all occurrences of /l/, whereas native L1 Mandarin speakers typically have this alternation only in word-final position. Finally, her aspiration of intervocalic [t] is correct in both alternation and environment. One striking way in which Emma's performance diverged from authentic Chinese-accented English was the frequent insertion of epenthetic schwa both as a means of cluster simplification and word-finally. This feature is not typical of L1 Mandarin-accented English, which simplifies by consonant deletion, but, like Susie's alternation of the interdental fricatives with alveolar stops, is characteristic of other foreign-accented English varieties (e.g. Japanese, Cantonese, and Korean).

### Matt

| | | | | | |
|---|---|---|---|---|---|
| /l/ | → | [w] | | | |
| /ɹ/ | → | [w] | | | only in are |
| /t/ | → | [tʰ] | / | V_____V | e.g. water |

Matt, the only actor to manipulate mean pitch to any recognizable extent, employed the fewest segmental alternations of any actor. He accurately aspirated [t] inter-vocalically. Like Emma, Matt alternated the alveolar lateral approximant with the labio-velar approximant, but, again, more uniformly than this is done in authentically Chinese-accented speech. Interestingly, Matt alternated the alveolar central approximant with the labio-velar approximant in the lexical item 'are'. This may reflect Matt's awareness of native difficulty with this approximant post-vocalically, although he did not make this substitution more generally, nor did he delete post-vocalically.

### Sango

| | | | | | |
|---|---|---|---|---|---|
| /ð/ | → | [d] | | | (optionally) |
| /θ/ | → | [s] or [tʰ] | | | |
| /s/ | → | [s] | / | [+voice]_____# | e.g. falls, days, leaves, trees |
| /C#/ | → | [Cʰ] | / | ___# | e.g. feet, fast, week |
| /ɹ/ | → | ∅ | / | V_____ | e.g. dessert, her, sport, shirt, etc. |
| /dʒ/ | → | [ʒ] | / | V_____V | e.g. pigeon |

Sango's alternations were the most variable of any actor recorded for this study. Like other actors, Sango alternated the voiced interdental fricative with its alveolar stop counterpart. Like Leo, Sango consistently voiced the alveolar fricative word-finally – a pattern inconsistent with authentic Chinese-accented English and also, perhaps, incompatible with the authentic accent feature of word final devoicing of obstruents. However, several of her alternations were strikingly authentic. In particular, Sango was the only actor to lenite the voiced post-alveolar affricate to its fricative counterpart. She was also the only actor to delete /ɹ/ post-vocalically both in consonant clusters and when it is alone in coda position in her unaccented voice. Aspects of her other alternations touch on authentic features of Chinese-accented English, but the distributions are either too narrow or too wide. The voiceless interdental fricative, for example, was often realized as an authentic voiceless alveolar fricative and, somewhat less often, as an aspirated voiceless alveolar stop. Authentic aspiration of inter-vocalic [t] was represented in Sango's performance, to a certain extent, by general word-final aspiration of voiceless stops.

*Leo*

| /ð/ | → | [d] | | | |
|-----|---|-----|---|---|---|
| /θ/ | → | [tʰ] | | | |
| /s/ | → | [s] | / | [+voice]___# | e.g. days, leaves, sleeves, trees |
| /t/ | → | { [tʰ] | / | V___V | e.g. water |
| | | { ∅ | / | C___# | e.g. wrist, fast |
| /d/ | → | [t] | / | ___# | e.g. head |
| /ɹ/ | → | ∅ | / | V___ | e.g. her, water, sport |

Leo's performance, while not intended in any way to be comedic or mocking, is clearly a blend of stereotypical Japanese- and Cantonese-accented English, not entirely dissimilar to the broad, comedic variety performed by actor Mickey Rooney in the film "Breakfast at Tiffany's" as "Japanese." Like several other actors, Leo stops the interdental fricatives and, like Sango, consistently voiced the alveolar fricative word-finally. His /t/ was either aspirated inter-vocalically or deleted word-finally to simplify consonant clusters. This last feature is consistent with authentic Chinese-accented English, as were Leo's use of devoicing for word-final alveolar stops and post-vocalic deletion of the central approximant.

## Discussion

The prediction was that actors would perform primarily the highly salient, stereotypical features of a variety. Instead, the actors demonstrated surprising availability and control of a range of features which, while lacking significant overlap among them, shared many features in common, either with reported features of authentic L1 Mandarin-accented English or with aspects of those authentic alternations. Only one actor, Leo, imitated an accent clearly divergent from the requested Mandarin goal, and this accent was the result of studying other actors' performances of "Chinese." However, all actors produced imitated features suggestive of influence from Japanese, Cantonese, or Korean – suggesting a pan-ethnic Asian, rather than particularly Mandarin Chinese, set of social category representations. Perhaps, then, the level of awareness required to imitate a variety of foreign-accented English need only be consistent with the level of awareness one's audience is likely to have had during previous experience of that variety. Under normal circumstances, whether experiencing authentic Chinese-accented English or performed Asian/Chinese-accented English, it is unlikely that listeners are consciously aware of the precise national identity of the speaker. Actors not only reflect and appeal to these pan-ethnic social category representations, but create and reinforce them at the same time.

Neither the detailed, nor the general, folk predictions are well represented in these imitations. But one must wonder why actors might perform features of an accent that are not required to invoke an accented percept for less experienced listeners. One possible answer is that, in fact, these listeners possess more detailed representations of Chinese-accented English than a map-labeling task can reveal. This interpretation is certainly supported by the results of Experiment 1, in which less experienced listeners performed better than chance when identifying authentically Chinese-accented English.

The results reported here suggest that less experienced listeners have a set of surprisingly detailed phonetic expectations linked to a pan-Asian social category. This knowledge is available for use during speech perception. Listeners may acquire this awareness of at least highly salient non-native phonological features through experience with imitated varieties, suggesting an important role for imitation and stereotype in listeners' use of the complex and informative patterns of variation available in the speech stream. Finally, this experiment offers further support for previous findings that listeners arrive at expectations of non-native features by drawing phonological analogies across social boundaries (e.g. Lindemann 2003).

## Conclusions

Speech perception is the use of linguistic knowledge to impose structure upon sensory data. There is abundant evidence showing that this linguistic knowledge is richly detailed. The present study is part of another growing body of research suggesting that what we think of as "linguistic" must be expanded to include knowledge of both phonetically cued social information and social categories – directly analogous to the well-established concepts of phonetically cued segmental or sublexical information and lexical categories.

When listeners are asked to identify an accented voice as "authentically Chinese" or when an actor seeks to create a "Chinese" percept in the minds of a native English-speaking audience, they attend to or manipulate phonetic cues that are simultaneously linguistic and socially meaningful. The single speech signal carries both meanings. Particular phonetic cues within that signal activate both linguistic (sounds and words) and social (speaker attributes, social category) representations. This finding is consistent with a growing body of work in speech perception (Beddor *et al.* 2013; Sumner and Kataoka 2013), psycholinguistics (Creel and Bregman 2011), and Sociolinguistics (Szakay *et al.* 2012), in which variation in speech – even quite dramatic variation from canonical forms – is reimagined as a source of information rather than a source of noise. Phonetic cues and social category knowledge interact to enhance the multiplex perception of referential and social indices.

In the authenticity detection task, more experienced listeners were better able to discriminate between an authentic and inauthentic variety. Less experienced listeners were more drawn to the imitated variety and, in the production task, we learned that these imitated varieties index a simplified, pan-Asian social category that appears to be linked not only to expectations consistent with authentically Chinese-accented voices, but also Japanese and Korean-accented voices. This disparity highlights that, for exemplar models in which episodic memory is linked to social category information such as Johnson (e.g. 2006), awareness is required at some point during perception to link social category representations to stored exemplars. This is not meant to imply that listeners must have conscious awareness of the relationship between speaker attributes and particular phonetic cues to form a linkage between them; indeed, there is ample evidence that listeners are sensitive to phonetically cued social information below the level of conscious awareness (Koops *et al.* 2008; Nycz, this volume). Nor, I believe, does this claim contradict Squires's position (this volume) on perceiving versus noticing. Instead, the implication is that, under Johnson's model, it is impossible to form a linkage between a voice and a social category without having some awareness that the social category is salient. The phonetic variation can be learned without awareness and social cues can be learned without awareness, but the linkage from exemplar lexicon to higher level social category must require some awareness that the social category is available for linkage – even if that awareness lacks detail and accuracy. One take-away empirical prediction from the present chapter is that even thousands of hours of experience with Chinese-accented speech should not help a listener identify a voice as authentically Chinese without some awareness that the variety being experience was in fact, or perhaps in stereo-type, "Chinese." One must not only attend to the signal, but one must attend to it as a representative signal of a particular social category.

Turning to the production study, only one actor imitated, in a limited way, the word-final obstruent devoicing which is a salient feature of authentically Chinese-accented English. This result, taken with the above, suggests that Labov's model of awareness accurately predicts even trained actors' use of the features of an imitated variant. Models of perception and representation such as Johnson (2006) or Sumner and Samuel (2009), in which accented productions or representations of accented variants are subsumed under a more general, standard representation, need to take into account Labov's model of awareness and the predictions it makes about access to these variants by speakers. The mixture of stereotypically Asian features produced by the actors in the imitated accent condition suggests that actors, and the listeners they hope to entertain, possess courser-grained social categories of national identity than "Mandarin" versus "Cantonese" or even "Chinese" versus "Japanese." These results suggest that listeners' conceptualization of this social category is much broader and all-inclusive.

The results reported here suggest that less experienced listeners have a set of surprisingly detailed, if somewhat pan-Asian, expectations available for use during speech perception. These listeners may actually acquire this awareness of at least highly salient non-native phonological features through experience with imitated varieties; suggesting an important role for imitation and stereotype in listeners' use of the complex and informative patterns of variation available in the speech stream. Experienced listeners, on the other hand, as demonstrated by the results of Experiment 1, are much more accurate in identifying an authentic Chinese voice as "Chinese" and so are clearly drawing on a more fine-grained social category representation. The behavior of this experienced group of listeners is entirely consistent with exemplar models that include a linkage between knowledge of the speech signal and knowledge of speaker attributes. An interesting question not investigated in this study concerns the potential interplay of top-down stereotypical expectations and detailed bottom-up phonetic experience in the perception of listeners with extensive experience.

Finally, the ultimate goal of the chapter as a whole was to explore the feasibility of assessing and quantifying listeners' accumulated linguistic and social experiences for modeling experience in laboratory research. The authenticity detection task offers a means of assessing listeners' experience and, at least for Chinese-accented English, correlates well with listeners' self-reported experience labels. Since simply asking participants to self-report is easier and faster than administering an additional task, this task is of dubious utility for the investigation of phenomena which participants might be aware of and able to report. Furthermore, the results reported here highlight the fact that it can be difficult to tease apart quantity of experience with a target variety, in terms of raw frequency of exposure, from quality of experience, in terms of the accuracy of linkages from fine phonetic detail to social category and the structure or complexity of the social categories themselves. While the present task shows some promise, there is much room for improvement.

## REFERENCES

Agha, A. (2003). The social life of cultural value. *Language and Communication* 23(3/4):231–73.

Baayen, R. (2008). *Analyzing Linguistic Data: A Practical Introduction to Statistics Using R*. Cambridge University Press.

Baayen, R. H., Piepenbrock, R., and Rijn, H. V. (1993). *The CELEX Lexical Data Base on CD-ROM*. Philadelphia, PA: Linguistic Data Consortium.

Babel, A. M. (2010). Contact and contrast in Valley Spanish. PhD thesis. Ann Arbor, MI: University of Michigan.

Balota, D., Yap, M., Hutchison, K., Cortese, M., Kessler, B., Loftis, B., Neely, J., Nelson, D., Simpson, G., and Treiman, R. (2007). The English lexicon project. *Behavior Research Methods* 39(3):445–59.

Barr, D. J., Levy, R., Scheepers, C., and Tily, H. J. (2013). Random effects structure for confirmatory hypothesis testing: Keep it maximal. *Journal of Memory and Language* 68(3):255–78.

Bates, D., Maechler, M., Bolker, B., and Walker, S. (2014). Fitting linear mixed-effects models using lme4. *Journal of Statistical Software* 67(1):1–48.

Beddor, P., McGowan, K., Boland, J., Coetzee, A., and Brasher, A. (2013). The time course of perception of coarticulation. *Journal of the Acoustical Society of America* 133(4):2350–66.

Beddor, P. S., Harnsberger, J., and Lindemann, S. (2002). Language-specific patterns of vowel-to-vowel coarticulation: acoustic structures and their perceptual correlates. *Journal of Phonetics* 30(4):591–627.

Best, C. T. (1994). The emergence of native-language phonological influences in infants: A perceptual assimilation model, in J. C. Goodman and H. C. Nusbaum (eds.), *The Development of Speech Perception: The Transition from Speech Sounds to Spoken Words*, pp. 167–224. Cambridge, MA: MIT Press.

Blumenfeld, R. (2002). *Accents: A Manual for Actors*. New York: Proscenium Publishers Incorporated.

Bradlow, A. and Alexander, J. (2007). Semantic-contextual and acoustic-phonetic enhancements for English sentence-in-noise recognition by native and non-native listeners. *Journal of the Acoustical Society of America* 121(4):2339–49.

Brunner, E. G. (2010). Imitation, awareness; and folk linguistic artifacts. PhD thesis. Houston, TX: Rice University.

Bucholtz, M. and Hall, K. (2010). Locating identity in language, in C. Llamas and D. Watt (eds.), *Language and Identities*, pp. 18–28. Edinburgh University Press.

Campbell-Kibler, K. (2009). The nature of sociolinguistic perception. *Language Variation and Change* 21(1):135–56.

Creel, S. and Bregman, M. (2011). How talker identity relates to language processing. *Language and Linguistics Compass* 5(5):190–204.

Dahan, D., Drucker, S. J., and Scarborough, R. A. (2008). Talker adaptation in speech perception: adjusting the signal or the representations? *Cognition* 108:710–18.

Docherty, G. J. and Foulkes, P. (2014). An evaluation of usage-based approaches to the modelling of sociophonetic variability. *Lingua* 142:42–56.

Drager, K. (2010). Sociophonetic variation in speech perception. *Language and Linguistics Compass* 4(7):473–80.

Eckert, P. (2008). Variation and the indexical field. *Journal of sociolinguistics* 12(4):453–76.

Espiritu, Y. (1992). *Asian American Panethnicity: Bridging Institutions and Identities*. Philadelphia, PA: Temple University Press.

Foulkes, P. and Docherty, G. (2006). The social life of phonetics and phonology. *Journal of Phonetics* 34:409–38.

Ganong, W. F. (1980). Phonetic categorization in auditory word perception. *Journal of Experimental Psychology: Human Perception and Performance* 6:110–25.

Gick, B. and Derrick, D. (2009). Aero-tactile integration in speech perception. *Nature* 462:502–4.

Hay, J., Warren, P., and Drager, K. (2006). Factors influencing speech perception in the context of a merger-in-progress. *Journal of Phonetics* 34:458–84.

Irvine, J. (1989). When talk isn't cheap: language and political economy. *American Ethnologist* 16(2):248–67.

Iwamoto, D. K. and Liu, W. M. (2010). The impact of racial identity, ethnic identity, Asian values, and race-related stress on Asian Americans and Asian international college students psychological well-being. *Journal of Counseling Psychology* 57(1):79.

Johnson, K. (1997). Speech perception without speaker normalization: An exemplar model, in K. Johnson and J. W. Mullennix (eds.), *Talker Variability in Speech Processing*, pp. 145–65. San Diego, CA: Academic Press.

(2006). Resonance in an exemplar-based lexicon: The emergence of social identity and phonology. *Journal of Phonetics* 34:485–99.

Johnstone, B. and Kiesling, S. F. (2008). Indexicality and experience: Exploring the meanings of/aw/-monophthongization in pittsburgh1. *Journal of Sociolinguistics* 12(1):5–33.

Koops, C., Gentry, E., and Pantos, A. (2008). The effect of perceived speaker age on the perception of pin and pen vowels in Houston, Texas. University of Pennsylvania Working Papers in Linguistics: Selected papers from NWAV 36, 14(2):91–101.

Kucera, H. and Francis, W. N. (1967). *Computational Analysis of Present-Day American English*. Providence, RI: Brown University Press.

Kuznetsova, A., Brockhoff, P., and Christensen, R. (2013). lmerTest: tests for random and fixed effects for linear mixed effect models. R package version 2.0–11.

Labov, W. (1972). *Sociolinguistic Patterns*. Philadelphia, PA: University of Pennsylvania Press.

Liberman, A. M., Harris, K. S., and Griffith, B. C. (1957). The discrimination of speech sounds within and across phoneme boundaries. *Journal of Experimental Psychology* 54:358–68.

Lindemann, S. (2003). Koreans, Chinese or Indians? Attitudes and ideologies about non-native English speakers in the United States. *Journal of Sociolinguistics* 7(3):348–64.

(2005). Who speaks "broken English"? US undergraduates' perceptions of non-native English. *International Journal of Applied Linguistics* 15(2):187–212.

Lisker, L. (1986). "Voicing" in English: A catalogue of acoustic features signaling /b/ versus /p/ in trochees. *Language and Speech* 29:3–11.

Mack, S. and Munson, B. (2012). The influence of /s/ quality on ratings of men's sexual orientation: Explicit and implicit measures of the "gay lisp" stereotype. *Journal of Phonetics* 40(1):198–212.

Mann, V. A. and Repp, B. H. (1981). Influence of preceding fricative on stop consonant perception. *Journal of the Acoustical Society of America* 69:548–58.

McGowan, K. B. (2015). Social expectation improves speech perception in noise. *Language and Speech*. 58(4):502–21.

McGurk, H. and MacDonald, J. (1976). Hearing lips and seeing voices. *Nature* 264:746–8.

Milroy, L. and McClenaghan, P. (1977). Stereotyped reactions to four educated accents in ulster. *Belfast Working Papers in Language and Linguistics* 2:1–11.

Munson, B. (2010). Levels of phonological abstraction and knowledge of socially motivated speech-sound variation: A review, a proposal, and a commentary on the papers by Clopper, Pierrehumbert, and Tamati; Drager; Foulkes; Mack; and Smith, Hall, and Munson. *Journal of Laboratory Phonology* 1:157–77.

Neuhauser, S. and Simpson, A. P. (2007). Imitated or authentic? listeners' judgements of foreign accents, in *ICPhS XVI*. Saarbrücken: International Congress of Phonetic Sciences.

Niedzielski, N. (1999). The effect of social information on the perception of sociolinguistic variables. *Journal of Language and Social Psychology* 18(1):62–85.

Pierrehumbert, J. B. (2002). Probabilistic phonology: Discrimination and robustness, in R. Bod, J. Hay, and S. Jannedy (eds.), *Probability Theory in Linguistics*. Cambrigde, MA: MIT Press.

Preston, D. R. (1996). Whaddayaknow?: The modes of folk linguistic awareness. *Language Awareness* 5(1):40–74.

Qiong, H. X. (2004). Why China English should stand alongside British, American, and the other. *English Today* 20(02):26–33.

R Development Core Team (2014). *R: A Language and Environment for Statistical Computing*. R Foundation for Statistical Computing, Vienna, Austria. ISBN 3–900051-07-0.

Rubin, D. L. (1992). Non-language factors affecting undergraduates' judgments of non-native English-speaking teaching assistants. *Research in Higher Education* 33(4):511–31.

Schulman, R. (1983). Vowel categorization by the bilingual listener. PERILUS Working Papers, III:81–99.

Silverstein, M. (2003). Indexical order and the dialectics of sociolinguistic life. *Language & Communication* 23(3–4):193–229.

Sumner, M. and Kataoka, R. (2013). Effects of phonetically-cued talker variation on semantic encoding. *Journal of the Acoustical Society of America* 134(6): EL485–91.

Sumner, M., Kim, S. K., King, E., and McGowan, K. B. (2014). The socially-weighted encoding of spoken words: A dual-route approach to speech perception. *Frontiers in Psychology* 4(1015).

Sumner, M. and Samuel, A. G. (2009). The role of experience in the processing of cross-dialectal variation. *Journal of Memory and Language* 60:487–501.

Szakay, A., Babel, M., and King, J. (2012). Sociophonetic markers facilitate translation priming: Maori English goat – a different kind of animal. *University of Pennsylvania Working Papers in Linguistics* 18(2):138–46.

Tang Tang, C. C. and van Heuven V. J. (2009). Mutual intelligibility of Chinese dialects experimentally tested. *Lingua* 119(5):709–32.

Van Engen, K. J., Baese-Berk, M., Baker, R. E., Choi, A., Kim, M., and Bradlow, A. R. (2010). The wildcat corpus of native- and foreign-accented English: Communicative efficiency across conversational dyads with varying language alignment profiles. *Language and Speech* 53(4):510–40.

Wells, J. (1982). *Accents of English*. Cambridge University Press.

Wong, P., Lai, C. F., Nagasawa, R., and Lin, T. (1998). Asian Americans as a model minority: Self-perceptions and perceptions by other racial groups. *Sociological Perspectives* 41(1):95–118.

# 3  Awareness and Acquisition of New Dialect Features

*Jennifer Nycz*[*]

## Introduction

### *Awareness, Variation, and Second Dialect Acquisition*

Moving to and settling in a region that is different from the one a person grew up in is a fairly common experience in North America. Observations that one's native region and adopted region differ in accent or dialect seem to be just as common, followed closely by claims about how one's accent has or hasn't changed as a result of spending time in the new community. Mobile adults do change some aspects of their speech after exposure to new dialects (e.g. Munro *et al.* 1999; Bowie 2000; Conn and Horesh 2002; Foreman 2003; Evans 2004; Sankoff 2004; Evans and Iverson 2007; Bigham 2010; Ziliak 2013; Walker 2014). But to what extent do such changes rely on explicit speaker awareness of dialect differences? In this chapter, I examine the relationship between awareness and acquisition of new dialect features in a study of Canadians who have moved to the New York City region, describing the extent to which these speakers have changed their use of two dialect features subject to markedly different levels of awareness. While explicit awareness may enhance or attenuate adoption of new dialect features, I argue that such awareness is not necessary for dialect change, which is likely driven by unconscious, automatic processes; moreover, awareness of a dialect feature does not imply control over the use of that feature.

Sociolinguists have long posited a link between speaker awareness of a linguistic variable and behavior with respect to that variable. Labov (1963:8) remarks that in selecting linguistic variables for sociolinguistic study, "we would like the feature to be salient, for us as well as the speaker, in order to study the direct relations of social attitudes and language behavior. But on the other hand, we value immunity from conscious distortion, which greatly

[*] Thanks to Anna Babel, John Rickford, and two anonymous reviewers for their helpful feedback on this chapter, as well as the audience of the Awareness and Control in Sociolinguistic Research Symposium at the 2013 Annual Meeting of the Linguistic Society of America in Boston.

simplifies the problem of reliability of the data."[1] The assumption is that if a feature is *too* salient, speakers are more likely to change the way they use it in erratic and generalization-muddling ways. Labov (1972a) more formally links awareness and variability, distinguishing *indicators* – variables used by a particular group which are below the level of conscious awareness and do not vary stylistically – from *markers* and *stereotypes*, which rise above the level of conscious awareness and show stylistic variation. Because they are subject to conscious awareness, markers and stereotypes may also be subject to conscious distortion if speakers become too focused on linguistic form; this point has led to the development of methods which reduce attention paid to speech and thus awareness of language form at a local conversational level, so that patterning of variables will be as unaffected by conscious processes as possible (Labov 1972b). To the extent that these methods are successful, variationists can observe systematic patterns in speech which reveal the implicit knowledge (or unconscious awareness) that speakers have about the use of sociolinguistic variables (see Squires and Preston in this volume for additional discussion of implicit vs. explicit knowledge).

Scholars interested in second dialect ($D_2$) acquisition have similarly claimed a connection between awareness of features and the likelihood that speakers will change their behavior given new dialect input. In such cases, awareness can intervene at two points: speakers may drop or modify features of their first dialect ($D_1$) or accommodate towards features of the $D_2$. Trudgill (1986) addresses both points, stating that "in contact with speakers of other language varieties, speakers modify those features of their own varieties of which they are most aware" (p. 11), and that "accommodation does indeed take place by the modification of those aspects of segmental phonology that are salient in the accent to be accommodated to" (p. 20), although he also notes that linguistic constraints and social factors may play a mediating role. For Trudgill, *awareness* means conscious awareness, while *salient* describes features which are "most prominent in the consciousness" of speakers (p. 12). For Auer *et al.* (1998), salience is a complex construct comprising objective linguistic characteristics (such as lexicalization) as well as subjective characteristics which essentially reflect conscious awareness (style differences in read vs. interview speech, representation in writing, stereotyping). Similar to Trudgill, Auer *et al.* claim that "salience is a necessary but insufficient condition for dialect loss and acquisition," as the "attitudinal polarity" of social meaning attached to a

---

[1] Salience in linguistics is a complex and often problematic notion, but many discussions of salience include speaker/listener awareness as a definitional component. See Kerswill and Williams (2002) for a review of how this term has been defined and employed as an explanatory principle in the language contact literature, Choksi and Meek (this volume) for a discussion of how salience is theorized in linguistic anthropology, and Siegel (2010) for the use of this term in second dialect acquisition studies specifically.

variable may protect it from change (p. 184). Siegel (2010) agrees, concluding that "in order to be acquired, a variant must be salient enough to be noticed." *Noticing* is a term used in second language learning research to refer to conscious awareness and subjective experience of a linguistic feature; it is a step beyond mere *perception* of a feature, where speakers may have awareness of its patterning that is "not necessarily conscious" (Schmidt 1990).[2] Although terminology varies, the focus of the work reviewed here is the same: *conscious* awareness and its role in $D_2$ acquisition. Explicit awareness of a feature is seen as prior to, and indeed a prerequisite for, change with respect to that feature. At the same time, awareness (presumably explicit?) of the feature's social meaning and the speaker's attitudes around that meaning may inhibit its maintenance or adoption.

Preston (1996) presents a more detailed discussion of the relationship between awareness and language behavior, which on one reading may seem to support this view. He outlines four "modes of awareness" which capture different aspects of how non-linguists think about and use linguistic variables. Three of these modes represent facets of the knowledge that speakers have about linguistic form. A feature may have more or less *availability* to a speaker as a topic of explicit linguistic discussion; this mode more or less maps onto the notion of awareness as discussed in the literature reviewed above. In addition, a speaker's grasp of how that feature patterns linguistically or socially may vary in its degree of *accuracy* and *detail*. The fourth mode captures the degree to which speakers consciously *control* their use of a variety or feature, reflecting differences in behavior. The modes are conceptually independent, and Preston gives concrete examples of cases in which they do not align: in one case, a speaker claims to be a proficient speaker of African-American Vernacular English (AAVE), but declines to perform the variety when prompted by her parents and an interviewer, stating that she can't really speak it unless among other AAVE speakers. This case illustrates the dissociation between availability, which in this case is high (the speaker freely talks about AAVE as a variety and even claims to use it) and control, which is low (she cannot perform this variety when asked to do so). Yet, while availability and control are not clearly correlated (one could easily imagine or even call to mind specific cases of speakers for whom AAVE is highly available and who are able to shift into the variety with ease), an implicational relationship still seems to hold: try to find a speaker who is completely oblivious to the existence of AAVE, and ask them to perform this variety. *If* dialect change

---

[2] The concept of noticing and its usefulness in the study of second language acquisition has been subject to some debate (e.g. Cross 2002; Schmidt 2010), but the issue of awareness and how it relates to the acquisition of features remains a central concern (cf. Robinson *et al.* 2012). See also Preston (this volume) for a somewhat broader definition of noticing.

is largely a matter of controlled linguistic behavior – that is, a conscious choice to jettison old features or adopt new ones – then the claim that conscious awareness (high availability) is necessary for such change seems to follow.

Revisiting his modes (this volume), Preston points out that there is much more going on under the surface with respect to both awareness and behavior. The behavior he specifically addresses is language perception – the ways in which listeners interpret speech signals in a given ostensible social context or react to particular signals (or indeed, to more abstract mentions of specific varieties). It seems clear that listeners do not consciously control their perceptions or reactions in relevant cases; moreover, the explicit post hoc rationales listeners may give for their responses likely reflect only a small portion of the complex network of ideologies and associations underlying them (see also Campbell-Kibler, this volume).[3] The same is surely true of language production: the vast majority of "decisions" that speakers make about which variant to use when in real-time speech cannot be subject to conscious reflection, and speakers' grasp of the reasons behind these decisions must be incomplete at best.[4]

There is growing evidence that accommodative processes in speech production are similarly subject to largely unconscious, automatic forces. Laboratory studies of spontaneous imitation (e.g. Goldinger 2000; Delvaux and Soquet 2007; Nielsen 2011) demonstrate that speakers alter their realizations of particular sounds to converge towards that of heard voices, even though they are not instructed to imitate those voices. That is, speakers change aspects of their accent without any indication of conscious control directing this change; moreover, they are not consciously aware of the relevant differences as they do so. Unconscious convergence of this kind is not inevitable: the tendency to converge may be reined in by social or attitudinal factors which favor accent maintenance or even divergence (Babel 2010). Such evidence suggests a different view of the role of explicit awareness in $D_2$ acquisition: it is not a prerequisite to individual dialect change, but instead may act as a filter on the unconscious accommodative processes which set dialect change in motion.

### Canadians in the New York City Region

Nycz (2011, 2013a) presents a study of dialect variation in native speakers of Canadian English (CE) who have moved as adults to the New York City area.

---

[3] The inaccessibility of the cognitive processes underlying behavior is not limited to language (e.g. Nisbett and Wilson 1977).

[4] "Why did I delete the /t/ so much in *west side*? Because we were speaking casually. Also, the preceding segment shares two features with the /t/, which is, moreover, followed by an obstruent."

This work focused on speakers' fine-grained phonetic realization of two features which distinguish their native dialect from that of their new home, but also probed awareness of and attitude about these features through qualitative means.

One of the features I examined is the quality of the diphthong /aʊ/ before voiceless consonants, in words like *about* and *mouse*. CE is characterized by so-called Canadian Raising, in which the nucleus of this allophone of /aʊ/ is raised in the vowel space compared to /aʊ/ in non-pre-voiceless position (Joos 1942). Canadian Raising occurs in both /aɪ/ and /aʊ/ and is not limited to Canada. Raising of /aɪ/ has been found in Martha's Vineyard (Labov 1963), Philadelphia (Labov 1994), the Inland North (Eckert 2000), and Ocracoke Island (Schilling-Estes 1998). Raising of /aʊ/ has also been documented in Martha's Vineyard, and in Virginia (Kurath and McDavid 1961). However, /aʊ/-raising is still largely associated with CE by non-linguists (Niedzielski 1999); the phrase *out and about*, produced with hyper-raised nuclei (*oot and aboot*) is a popular, if phonetically inaccurate, stereotype of CE. The English spoken in and around New York City (henceforth NYaE), in contrast, does not exhibit raising of either /aɪ/ or /aʊ/. Labov *et al.* (2006) note the "conservative character of New York City upgliding vowels," observing that the nuclei of /aɪ/ and /aʊ/ are no higher than those of the low vowels /æ/ and /ɑ/.

The second feature I analyzed is the structure of the low back vowel system – whether there is evidence for two vowel categories, typically transcribed /ɑ/ and /ɔ/,[5] in the low back region of the vowel space, or just a single category. The Atlas of North American English (ANAE) includes Canada within the large region which does not distinguish words such as *cot* and *caught* in perception or production (Labov *et al.* 2006), and according to Boberg (2008), "virtually all native speakers of Canada today" have this merger, which has been present in Canadian English for several generations (p. 150). In contrast, New York City is located in an area where the COT/CAUGHT distinction remains robust; here, the raised quality of the vowel in CAUGHT helps to maintain the contrast. In neighboring New Jersey, these vowels are also distinct. Coye (2009) reports, based on questionnaire data, that the merger of these vowels is "gaining a solid foothold in New Jersey;" this may be true of counties in the northwest, where around 30 percent of questionnaire respondents report that the vowels of *Don* and *Dawn* sound the same, but the responses for the majority of counties in New Jersey are overwhelmingly (>85 percent) distinct.

---

[5] In this chapter I will use COT as shorthand for the class of words transcribed with /ɑ/, corresponding to the LOT lexical set (Wells 1982), and CAUGHT for the class transcribed with /ɔ/, which comprises words in the THOUGHT and CLOTH sets. Italics will be used to indicate specific words within these sets.

These two features are subject to very different levels of awareness among speakers of English in North America.[6] Canadian Raising of /aʊ/, as a stereotype of CE, has high (or *common*) availability in Preston's terms, but generally low phonetic accuracy, as the quality of the stereotyped vowel does not reflect its actual quality in CE. Awareness with respect to detail may be incomplete: metalinguistic commentary tends to focus on the words *out, about,* and *house,* rather than the conditioning context or the vowel category.[7] Finally, there seems to be a high level of control, at least with respect to performances of the stereotype; whether this control extends to more authentic realizations is unclear.

The low back vowel system is not subject to similar levels of explicit awareness. Mergers and distinctions per se are typically below the level of conscious awareness and receive no social evaluation (Labov 1994); studies of the low back merger in particular do not contradict this conclusion (e.g. Baranowski 2013). Thus, the distinction (or lack thereof) is usually not available for commentary. The quality of the individual vowels is a different story: speakers may comment on the way that New Yorkers say *coffee,* for example, imitating a high, back, and diphthongal vowel in this word and revealing at least a limited awareness of NYaE /ɔ/.

This difference between the two features allows us to formulate some soft predictions. If explicit awareness is a prerequisite for dialect change, then we expect that the Canadian speakers in this study would show no acquisition of the $D_2$ feature of low back vowel distinction per se. If they have some explicit awareness of the quality of the vowel in specific words like *coffee,* it is possible they may alter their pronunciation of these words towards the $D_2$ realization – or pointedly not do so. Behavior with respect to Canadian Raising is harder to predict: high explicit awareness will either lead to maintenance of this $D_1$ feature (because of positive associations with Canadian identity) or its eradication (if there is a desire to assimilate).

If explicit awareness is *not* a prerequisite for dialect change, but instead functions as a filter on change, then we should find evidence of convergence towards the $D_2$ in both features. This convergence may be attenuated for Canadian Raising, depending on the attitude and desire of the individual speaker. Convergence towards the low back vowel system, meanwhile, should be unaffected, if speakers indeed lack explicit awareness of the distinction per se; however, words like *coffee* may show less convergence than words like *cot,* if speakers are aware of the stigma associated with the local production of /ɔ/.

---

[6] They also potentially differ in their formal linguistic status; see Nycz (2011) for discussion of this point.

[7] Cf. Michael Moore's film *Canadian Bacon,* in which a belligerent American warns a member of the Royal Canadian Mounted Police that "we got ways of making you pronounce the letter *o,*" revealing the screenwriters' more general grasp of the feature.

The remainder of this chapter addresses the following questions: Are the specific individuals in this study explicitly aware of either (or both) of these features? If a feature is available for comment, how do they talk about it – is the social evaluation positive or negative, and do they express a desire to change that feature? How are each of these features actually used by the speakers in this sample? Finally, what do the observed patterns tell us about the relationship between awareness and dialect change?

## Methods

The data are drawn from sociolinguistic interviews I conducted with seventeen native speakers of Canadian English in 2008. All of these speakers were born and grew up in Canada and later moved to New York City or nearby towns in New Jersey after the age of 21. The twelve women and five men hail from a variety of Canadian provinces and vary in age at time of interview and age of move (Table 3.1).[8] All but two interviews took place in New York City; the remaining two interviews were held in New Jersey, in venues near the speakers' homes. My own dialect in 2008 more or less reflected what was at the time my regional background (born and lived seventeen years in New Jersey, less than an hour's drive to New York City, followed by four years in New Hampshire and seven years in New York City) and social network structure (not very dense or multiplex): I natively produce a low back vowel distinction and a low /aʊ/ nucleus in pre-voiceless contexts, but my production varies according to audience and other contextual factors.[9] In my communication with speakers before, during, and after the interview, I presented myself as an American Canadaphile who has knowledge and appreciation of some regions (e.g. southeastern Ontario) and aspects of Canadian culture (musical and culinary) and is eager to learn more about other regions and aspects (the Western provinces; politics and national identity).

Each speaker participated in four activities. First, we engaged in a one-to-one *conversation* about their life as a Canadian in the New York region. Topics in these conversations included their hometown in Canada, their experiences growing up there, their reasons for moving to the United States, and their feelings about their home and adopted countries. Next, the speaker read words from a *word list* presented with flashcards and completed a sociolinguistic *minimal pair task*. Then the speaker completed a *minimal pair judgment task*,

---

[8] For analysis of these social factors and their effect on linguistic behavior, see Nycz (2011).

[9] I have not carried out a detailed acoustic analysis of my own speech in the interviews reported on here. However, I was surprised to hear many apparently merged low back vowel tokens in my speech from the start of these conversations; this, combined with my apparent lack of Canadian Raising, assuages my initial concerns that the speakers in this study may have simply accommodated to my dialect features in the short term of the interview.

Table 3.1 *Speakers in the Study Described by Gender, Age, Number of Years Spent in the New York City Area at Time of Interview, and Region of Origin*

| Speaker | Gender | Age | Years in NYC area | From |
|---------|--------|-----|-------------------|------|
| LC | female | 30 | 1 | Ottawa/Toronto |
| LW | female | 31 | 10 | New Brunswick |
| PW | male | 32 | <1 | Vancouver/Toronto |
| BW | male | 37 | 2 | Toronto |
| NW | female | 39 | 14 | Alberta |
| TM | female | 41 | 3 | Toronto/Manitoba/Ottawa |
| ES | male | 42 | 5 | Manitoba/Alberta |
| JF | female | 45 | 14 | Manitoba |
| LG | female | 46 | 7 | Northern Ontario/Toronto |
| JC | male | 48 | 18 | Montreal |
| EW | male | 50 | 16 | Saskatchewan |
| BK | female | 54 | 21 | Ottawa/Montreal |
| GH | male | 54 | 15 | Montreal/Toronto |
| CW | female | 54 | 28 | Montreal |
| SS | female | 54 | 27 | Montreal |
| DB | female | 58 | 11 | Halifax/Toronto |
| VJ | female | 70 | 44 | Toronto |

in which they were asked to look again at the minimal pair list and say whether they thought there were any pairs which people from the New York region would have different judgments on or pronounce differently. Finally, the conversation resumed with additional discussion of linguistic features and impressions of their native dialect and the local variety. The conversational data were phonetically analyzed[10] to determine how each speaker produced the features of interest, while the metalinguistic commentary generated by all tasks was used to assess each speaker's awareness of these features.

## Results

### Canadian Raising

*Awareness of Canadian Raising*  The results regarding awareness of Canadian Raising in /aʊ/ are easily summarized: every speaker interviewed is consciously aware of this $D_1$ feature. Many speakers mentioned raising in /aʊ/ as a feature of CE before they were even asked about language in the

---

[10] Brief descriptions of the phonetic analyses are given in relevant sections below. Further details are given in Nycz (2011, 2013b).

conversation; for the rest, raising was the first or second[11] feature they responded with when asked about features of their native dialect. In addition to high availability, participant knowledge of this feature is also characterized by a high level of accuracy and detail: while the speakers acknowledge the phonetically inaccurate American *oot and about* stereotype, they accurately perform the phonetics of this feature, can distinguish their own naturally raised productions from the stereotype, and can characterize the set of words that contain it.

While /aʊ/ is subject to high awareness among these speakers, its social evaluation is not straightforwardly positive or negative. Instead, speakers consistently note simply that it is a very *Canadian* feature, one that instantly outs them to Americans as "not from here" (1). For this reason, several speakers, assuming high amounts of control over this feature, claim to have consciously reduced their use of it since moving to the States, as JF does in (2):

(1) Honest to God I think "about" – I don't say it with a Canadian pronunciation ... except sometimes in conversation people who know Canadians will go "Aha! I caught you!" ... Sometimes apparently I will say ab[ʌʊ]t (ES, 42)

(2) I feel like *I* wanna be the one who reveals I'm Canadian, I don't want people to hear it in my speech. So that's why I'm saying "ab[aːʊ]t ... so I have changed, consciously changed ... (JF, 45)

It is important to note here that speakers are not in any way ashamed of being identified as Canadian – indeed, many expressed pride in their Canadian identity. However, they would like to have some control over how this information is revealed,[12] and claim to take this control by deliberately manipulating their use of salient dialect features. In this group of speakers, we thus have across-the-board explicit awareness of a $D_1$ feature, and in several cases a desire to attenuate it, as well as a belief that this has successfully occurred.

*Use of Canadian Raising*    Formant measurements were taken at the $F_1$ maximum of the diphthong nucleus in 1,210 /aʊ/[13] words across all speakers. An Analysis of Variance (ANOVA) using treatment contrasts was carried out for each speaker, with $F_1$ as the outcome variable and a predictor variable dividing the tokens into four groups: instances of *about*, instances of

---

[11] The discourse marker "eh" is the other feature that speakers invariably mentioned.

[12] My sense is not that speakers want (even temporarily) to keep their Canadian identity a secret – instead, they do not want to derail a conversation towards discussion of the fact that they are Canadian.

[13] In non-pre-nasal contexts only; words like *down* were excluded from analysis.

*out*, tokens of other raising context words such as *shout* or *gout*, and non-raising context words like *loud* or *how*. The non-raising group was set as the control level against which the other three raising context groups were compared. What results from each of these analyses is two pieces of information per raising context group: (1) an assessment of whether the average $F_1$ for the group is significantly different from that of the non-raising group (i.e. whether that group shows significant raising); and (2) a coefficient indicating the magnitude of this difference.

The results of these analyses are summarized in Figure 3.1, which plots the regression coefficient (in Hz) associated with each word group for each speaker. A horizontal line is drawn at −60 Hz, reflecting the threshold value used by ANAE to categorize tokens as raised or not. Seven of the speakers are consistent raisers, with each of the three groups having a significantly lower $F_1$ value than the baseline non-raising group; these differences are also all above the 60 Hz threshold. Four speakers show significant raising only in *about* and *out* (again, with both of these word classes sitting above the ANAE threshold), while their other raising context words are not

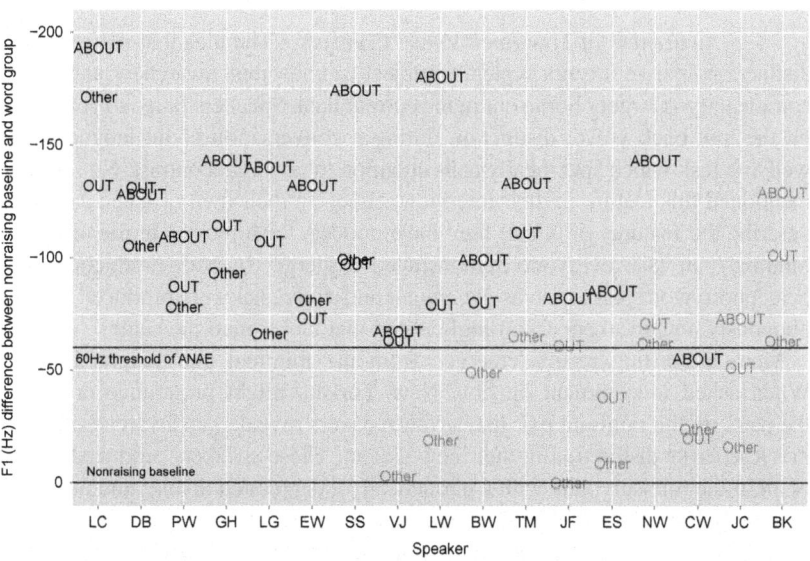

Figure 3.1 /aʊ/ Raising in *About, Out,* and *Other Raising Words* among Canadians in the New York City Area
Black type indicates a significant difference between the word group and the non-raising context baseline group.

significantly different from the non-raising baseline. Finally, four speakers show significant raising only in *about*.

A closer look at the other-raising group, however, indicates that lexical items within this group showed raising to varying extents: higher word frequency was associated with higher $F_1$, suggesting that the greater frequency of exposure to $D_2$ tokens of these items has resulted in them shifting towards $D_2$ realizations at a faster pace.

To summarize, nearly all of the speakers continue to use Canadian Raising in /aʊ/ in at least some contexts. An implicational trend can be seen: *about* is the most raised group, typically followed by *out*, then other raising-class words; this trend holds even for the two speakers who showed no significant differences between the raising groups and non-raising baseline. That is, the words which are most strongly associated with Canadian raising – via the phrase *out and about* – are also the words which most exhibit this feature, despite speakers' specific desire to attenuate it. Within the other raising-class words, higher frequency items show more convergence towards $D_2$ realizations.

### Low Back Vowels

*Awareness of Low Back Vowel Contrast*     The idea that mergers and distinctions per se are not typically subject to conscious awareness and overt commentary is largely borne out in the current data. Speakers failed to comment on the low back vowel distinction during a conversation about language, as well as a task which specifically calls attention to potential contrast. No speaker mentioned this feature in their interview, either on their own or when asked to describe the features of NYaE they have noticed.[14] Moreover, in the ordinary minimal pair task everyone demonstrated a merger in both production and perception: word pairs such as *cot/caught* and *don/dawn* were produced homophonously and speakers accordingly noted that they sound the same.

More interesting results emerged from the minimal pair judgment task. When asked to comment on how New Yorkers might pronounce or judge the pairs on the minimal pair list, seven speakers revealed an awareness of the COT/CAUGHT distinction in their new dialect. These speakers produced many or all of the relevant pairs with a phonetically exaggerated distinction, using an extremely high and often diphthongal vowel for CAUGHT words. In contrast, four other speakers showed no explicit awareness of this feature in the judgment task: they picked out other pairs as sounding different in the ambient dialect (e.g. pointing out that the words *higher* and *hire*, a distractor pair, would be produced without /r/s), but passed over the low back vowel pairs

---

[14] One speaker, TM, notes that people from Brooklyn say "dawg" [dʊəg], but neither generalizes beyond this lexical item to other CAUGHT words nor compares this realization to COT words.

without comment. The remaining six speakers showed some explicit awareness of low back vowel differences, but this awareness seemed limited to specific lexical items. VJ, for example, commented that *doll* may be produced with a more "drawn out" vowel than *tall*, but otherwise did not spot any low back differences, nor generalize to other words. The low back vowel distinction thus has low availability even for the speakers who have some explicit awareness of it, insofar as discussion of this feature can only be elicited using very targeted prompts. Moreover, the accuracy and detail of this awareness varies widely for those speakers who demonstrate it.

For those speakers who do comment on the low back vowel pairs, social evaluation focuses on the quality of the vowel in CAUGHT. For the most part, these evaluations are rather neutral – while a few speakers think the New York /ɔ/ is "grating" or "annoying," the individuals in this study are mostly amused by the difference.

Unlike Canadian Raising, then, the low back vowel system is subject to variable awareness among the expat Canadians in this study: some speakers are explicitly aware of the distinction as such, some speakers are explicitly aware of differences only in specific lexical items, and others reveal no explicit awareness of this difference.

*Use of Low Back Vowels*   Formant measurements were taken at the $F_1$ maximum of the low vowel in 3,288 tokens of COT words and 2,052 tokens of CAUGHT words across all speakers. Mixed effects linear regression was used to determine whether each speaker produced a significant distinction between these two groups in spontaneous speech. For each speaker, two analyses were run, one with $F_1$ as the dependent variable, and one with $F_2$. For each formant, a model containing phonological predictors such as following place and following manner and a random effect of word was compared to a similar model containing those same terms plus a factor coding word class. When the model including word class is found to be significantly better than the model lacking this factor, this indicates that there is variation between the word classes which cannot be attributed to phonological factors alone, and that the speaker distinguishes these word classes in production on the relevant formant dimension. The effect size associated with word class in this more complex model can be interpreted as the magnitude of this distinction.

The results of the analyses of conversational data are shown in Figure 3.2, which plots the effect size (in Hz) associated with word class obtained in the $F_2$ and $F_1$ analyses of each speaker. Eleven of the seventeen speakers produce a significant (if in some cases small) difference between COT and CAUGHT in some dimension in spontaneous speech. Yet, this behavior is not clearly related to awareness of the feature. While five of the speakers who display a contrast also have a general explicit awareness of the contrast, the other six speakers in

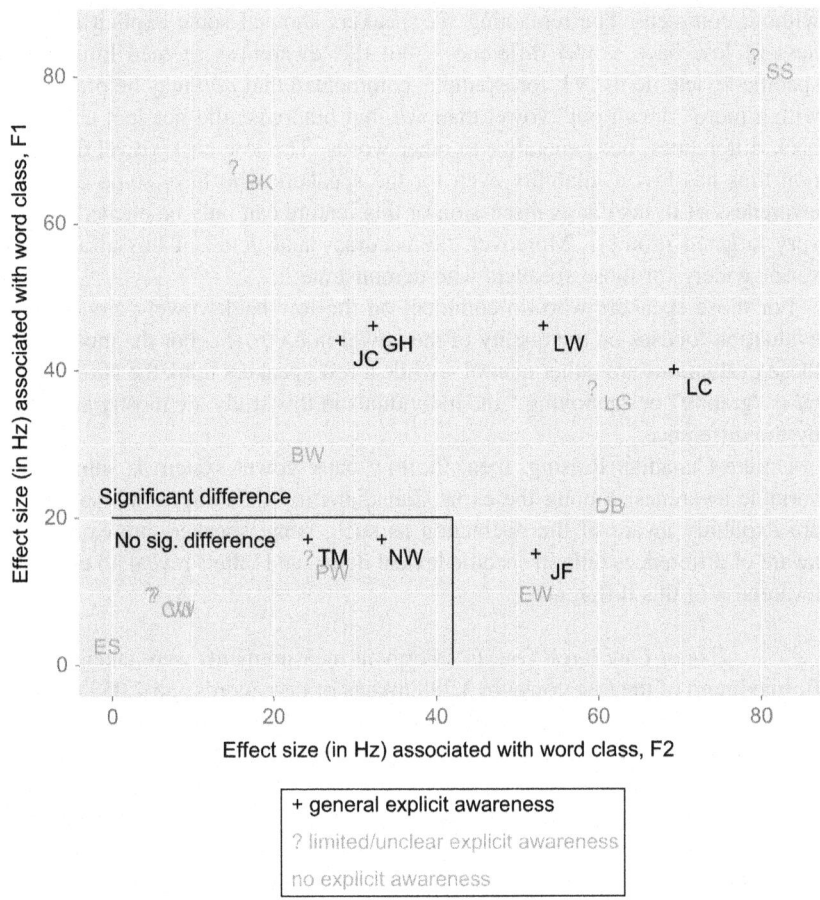

Figure 3.2 The Effect Size (in Hz) Associated with the Word Class Factor Obtained in the $F_2$ and $F_1$ Analyses of Each Speaker
Speakers with a large difference along both dimensions are plotted further away from the origin, while those with little or no difference between word classes are plotted closer to the origin.

this group appear to have acquired a distinction with limited explicit awareness or no awareness of it. Meanwhile, two speakers who have a general explicit awareness of the contrast do not exhibit a significant difference between these word classes.

There are also significant frequency effects associated with the realization of these tokens. Table 3.2 shows the results of analyses of each word class across speakers. Higher frequency cot words tend to be lower and fronter (that is,

Table 3.2 *Frequency Effects on $F_1$ and $F_2$ for Each Word Class*

|  |  | Effect (Hz/Count) | p-value |
|---|---|---|---|
| CAUGHT | $F_1$ | −0.38 | <0.05 |
|  | ($F_2$) | (−0.03) | (1) |
| COT | $F_1$ | 0.52 | <0.01 |
|  | $F_2$ | 1.72 | <0.001 |

more $D_2$-like) than lower frequency words of this class, while higher frequency CAUGHT words are higher (again, more $D_2$-like) than lower frequency CAUGHT words. These effects are not symmetrical: the frequency effects associated with the COT words are somewhat greater than and more significant than those of the CAUGHT words.

To summarize, the majority of speakers show evidence of having acquired a distinction between COT and CAUGHT words in their conversational speech, and in several cases this acquisition occurs without explicit awareness of the $D_2$ feature. In addition, higher frequency words of both classes show greater evidence of convergence towards $D_2$ realizations, although these effects are less pronounced for the CAUGHT words.

## Discussion and Conclusion

Canadian Raising in /aʊ/ and the low back vowel distinction differ greatly in the type of awareness they are subject to. The speakers in this sample, like many North Americans, are explicitly aware of Canadian Raising and its social meaning(s), and in many cases believe that they have control over this feature. Awareness with respect to the low back vowel distinction is more varied: some speakers have an explicit awareness of the distinction per se, others reveal a limited explicit awareness connected to particular lexical items or vowel qualities, and others show no evidence of explicit awareness. However, even speakers who accurately characterize this feature only do so when prompted in a particular way, so the distinction does not have high availability. As described in "Use of Canadian Raising," above, expectations about how these features should pattern will depend on whether explicit awareness is, as some scholars have claimed, a prerequisite for loss of a $D_1$ feature or acquisition of a $D_2$ feature, or rather a filter which may attenuate automatic, unconscious processes of accommodation.

Canadian Raising, the $D_1$ feature subject to high across-the-board awareness, exhibits both stability and change in the speech of these study participants. On the one hand, all speakers show robust raising in the words *out* and *about*, and several speakers continue to raise in other raising-context words. On the other hand, there is evidence of change, in that higher frequency lexical items (setting aside *out* and *about*) are realized with lower nuclei, indicating that speakers are accommodating to the $D_2$ in a patterned, lexically gradual manner. While this analysis cannot address the relationship between explicit awareness and dialect change (as speakers are uniformly aware of Canadian Raising), the data reveal a disconnect between awareness of a feature and control over that feature. If speakers are aware that this feature marks them as Canadian and want to suppress its use, then not only might we expect less raising overall, but the stereotype items *out* and *about* should be realized with the lowest nuclei rather than the highest. The patterns described here show that explicit awareness (and will to change) does not necessarily translate into control.

The stability of Canadian Raising is unexpected in both the prerequisite and the filter view of awareness, given the explicitly stated attitudes and desires of the speakers. To understand these results, the conversational context in which these data were collected must be considered. As a researcher who specifically recruited expatriate Canadians and expressed an interest in learning about each speaker's experience as a Canadian in the United States, I no doubt established a setting that was favorable to eliciting CE features; in this context, the risk of [ʌʊ]ting oneself as Canadian was a non-issue. Of course, I was still an American conducting interviews in New York or New Jersey, a context which should prevent wholesale style shifting back into the $D_1$. Indeed, total style-shifting back into $D_1$ cannot be happening for most speakers, given their decidedly non-CE realization of the low back vowel system. So while use of certain CE features like Canadian Raising might be especially favored in the data collected here, it is unlikely that this speech is qualitatively different from the speech of these speakers in everyday contexts. We might expect that in other conversational contexts, characterized by non-Canadian topics and/or less explicitly welcoming American interlocutors, the speakers in this study might suppress Canadian Raising to a larger extent. Such intraspeaker variation would indicate that explicit awareness and attitude interacts with other factors such as topic and audience to influence how features are used in particular contexts. Further research which examines topic- and audience-based variation is needed to address this issue.

The low back vowel findings are more informative. The speakers in this sample vary in their awareness of the $D_2$ low back vowel distinction, allowing a test of the idea that explicit awareness is necessary for adoption of the $D_2$ feature: if this idea is correct, those who have explicit awareness should show more acquisition of this feature (although perhaps less consistently than one might expect for a more available feature), while those with no explicit awareness should display no distinction. In the current data, this prediction fails to hold: while eleven out of seventeen speakers show evidence of having acquired a difference between the COT and CAUGHT words, three indicate no explicit awareness of this feature and three others have fairly limited explicit awareness (including the speaker who exhibits the greatest distinction between word classes!). These results indicate that explicit awareness is not a prerequisite for acquisition of this feature. Instead, automatic accommodative processes likely drive this acquisition: speakers unconsciously adjust their realizations of relevant words in the direction of those in the ambient dialect, resulting in the separation of the two word classes.

At the same time, these accommodative processes may be attenuated by awareness of a dialect feature and the evaluations that accompany it. The speakers in this study are often explicitly aware of the phonetic quality of the NYaE CAUGHT vowel and of the stigma that it carries, while the quality of COT typically goes unnoticed. The findings presented here suggest that convergence towards the $D_2$ is somewhat less advanced for CAUGHT than for COT, as frequency effects on the former are both smaller and less significant. Automatic convergence towards NYaE CAUGHT may be stunted by explicit awareness of vowel quality and its meaning, while convergence towards COT proceeds unimpeded.

REFERENCES

Auer, P., Barden, B., and Grosskopf, B. 1998. Subjective and objective parameters determining "salience" in long-term dialect accommodation. *Journal of Sociolinguistics* 2(2):163–87.
Babel, M. 2010. Dialect divergence and convergence in New Zealand English. *Language in Society* 39:437–56.
Baranowski, M. 2013. On the role of social factors in the loss of phonemic distinctions. *English Language and Linguistics* 17(Special Issue 02):271–95.
Bigham, D. S. 2010. Mechanisms of accommodation among emerging adults in a university setting. *Journal of English Linguistics* 38:193–210.
Boberg, C. 2008. English in Canada: Phonology, in E. W. Schneider (ed.), *Varieties of English: The Americas and the Caribbean*, vol. 2, pp. 144–60. Berlin: Mouton de Gruyter.
Bowie, D. 2000. The effect of geographic mobility on the retention of a local dialect. PhD thesis. University of Pennsylvania.
Conn, J. and Horesh, U. 2002. Assessing the acquisition of dialect variables by migrant adults in Philadelphia: A case study. *University of Pennsylvania Working Papers in Linguistics*, 8(3), Article 5.
Coye, D. F. 2009. Dialect boundaries in New Jersey. *American Speech* 84(4):414–52.
Cross, J. 2002. 'Noticing' in SLA: Is it a valid concept? *TESL-EJ* 6(3).
Delvaux, V. and Soquet, A. 2007. The influence of ambient speech on adult speech productions through unintentional imitation. *Phonetica* 64:145–73.
Eckert, P. 2000. *Linguistic Variation as Social Practice*. Oxford, UK: Blackwell.
Evans, B. E. 2004. The role of social network in the acquisition of local dialect norms by Appalachian migrants in Ypsilanti, Michigan. *Language Variation and Change* 1(16):153–67.

Evans, B. G. and Iverson, P. 2007. Plasticity in vowel perception and production: A study of accent change in young adults. *Journal of the Acoustical Society of America* 121(6):3814–26.

Foreman, A. 2003. Pretending to be someone you're not: A study of second dialect acquisition in Australia. PhD thesis. Monash University.

Goldinger, S. D. 2000. The role of perceptual episodes in lexical processing. *SWAP-2000*, pp. 155–8.

Joos, M. 1942. A phonological dilemma in Canadian English. *Language* 18:141–4.

Kerswill, P. and Williams, A. 2002. "Salience" as an explanatory factor in language change: Evidence from dialect levelling in urban England, in M. Jones and E. Esch (eds.), *Language Change: The Interplay of Internal, External and Extra-Linguistic Factors*, pp. 81–110. The Hague: Mouton De Gruyter.

Kurath, H. and McDavid, R. I. 1961. *The Pronunciation of English in the Atlantic States*. Ann Arbor, MI: University of Michigan Press.

Labov, W. 1963. The social motivation of a sound change. *Word* 19:273–309.

1972a. *Sociolinguistic Patterns*. Philadelphia, PA: University of Pennsylvania Press.

1972b. Some principles of linguistic methodology. *Language in Society* 1(1): 97–120.

1994. *Principles of Linguistic Change: Internal Factors*. Oxford, UK: Blackwell.

Labov, W., Ash, S., and Boberg, C. 2006. *The Atlas of North American English: Phonetics, Phonology, and Sound Change: A Multimedia Reference Tool*. Berlin: Mouton de Gruyter.

Munro, M. J., Derwing, T. M., and Flege, J. E. 1999. Canadians in Alabama: A perceptual study of dialect acquisition in adults. *Journal of Phonetics* 27:385–403.

Niedzielski, N. 1999. The effect of social information on the perception of sociolinguistic variables. *Journal of Language and Social Psychology* 18(1):62–85.

Nielsen, K. 2011. Specificity and abstractness of VOT imitation. *Journal of Phonetics* 39:132–42.

Nisbett, R. E., and Wilson, T. D. 1977. Telling more than we can know: Verbal reports on mental processes. *Psychological Review* 84(3):231–59.

Nycz, J. 2011. Second dialect acquisition: Implications for theories of phonological representation. PhD thesis. New York University.

2013a. Changing words or changing rules? Second dialect acquisition and phonological representation. *Journal of Pragmatics* 52:49–62.

2013b. New contrast acquisition: Methodological issues and theoretical implications. *English Language and Linguistics* 17(2):325–57.

Preston, D. 1996. Whaddayaknow?: The modes of folk linguistic awareness. *Language Awareness* 5(1):40–74.

Robinson, P., Mackey, A., Gass, S., and Schmidt, R. 2012. Attention and awareness in second language acquisition, in S. Gass and A. Mackey (eds.), *The Routledge Handbook of Second Language Acquisition*, pp. 247–67. Abingdon: Routledge.

Sankoff, G. 2004. Adolescents, young adults, and the critical period: Two case studies from "Seven Up," in C. Fought (ed.), *Sociolinguistic Variation: Critical Reflections.*, pp. 121–39. Oxford University Press.

Schilling-Estes, N. 1998. Investigating "self-conscious" speech: The performance register in Ocracoke English. *Language in Society* 27:53–83.

Schmidt, R. 2010. Attention, awareness, and individual differences in language learning, in W. M. Chan, S. Chi, K. N. Cin, J. Istanto, M. Nagami, J. W. Sew, T. Suthiwan, and I. Walker (eds.), *Proceedings of CLaSIC 2010*, pp. 721–37. Singapore: National University of Singapore, Centre for Language Studies.

Schmidt, R. W. 1990. The role of consciousness in second language learning. *Applied Linguistics* 11(2):129–58.

Siegel, J. 2010. *Second Dialect Acquisition*. Cambridge University Press.

Trudgill, P. 1986. *Dialects in Contact*. Oxford, UK: Blackwell.

Walker, A. 2014. Crossing oceans with voices and ears: Second dialect acquisition and topic-based shifting in production and perception. PhD thesis. Ohio State University.

Wells, J. C. 1982. *Accents of English*. Cambridge University Press.

Ziliak, Z. L. 2013. The relationship between perception and production in adult acquisition of a new dialect's phonetic system. PhD thesis. University of Florida.

# 4    Processing Grammatical Differences: Perceiving versus Noticing

*Lauren Squires*[*]

## Introduction

This chapter explores the relationship between English speakers' processing and awareness of morphosyntactic variability. Much sociolinguistic investigation has focused on speakers' explicit, metalinguistic knowledge of what linguistic differences exist and what their social meanings are. This chapter shifts the focus to how language variation is experienced in the moment in which it is encountered. I investigate this using an online experimental method to test participants' processing of grammatically variant sentences. The experiments test for both the *perceiving* of grammatical differences and the *noticing* of those differences, which I argue provide the foundation for implicit *knowledge* of variation and its social meaning.

## Theoretical and Methodological Background

Sociolinguists have long been interested in the relative degree to which the production of sociolinguistic variation is conscious or unconscious. One often-used categorization is Labov's (1972) distinction between sociolinguistic *indicators*, *markers*, and *stereotypes*. Indicators and stereotypes represent ends of a continuum of sociolinguistic awareness: indicators are linguistic features that are correlated with social properties, but they are not deployed for stylistic purposes and speakers are not aware of their social correlation; stereotypes are features subject to highly conscious discussion and social evaluation. Markers are in between, being features that both correlate with social properties and are

[*] Thank you to Anna Babel for motivating and editing this volume; thanks to Anna, two anonymous reviewers, and Kathryn Campbell-Kibler for comments on this chapter. For experimental and analytical assistance, I owe Amanda Boomershine, Damon Tutunjian, Ruth Friedman, Kelsy Hernandez, Sydney Watsek, Claire Ravenscroft, Chase Ledin, and Sarah Craycraft. I also thank Benjamin Munson, Kevin McGowan, Jen Nycz, Katie Carmichael, and John Rickford for their feedback and discussion at the 2013 LSA Annual Meeting. Finally, I'm grateful to Julie Boland and the participants in our 2013 LSA Linguistic Institute course, for valuable questions and rumination on matters related to this content. Any weaknesses of this chapter are, naturally, my responsibility.

deployed stylistically, yet speakers nonetheless may be unaware of their own stylistic uses of them (Johnstone and Kiesling 2008). Labov's categorization focuses on the relation between variation, social indexicality, and sociolinguistic awareness.

The levels of awareness articulated by the indicator/marker/stereotype categories are alternatively expressible as levels of *knowledge* held by speakers about the variation in question. I want to suggest that what *awareness* in these categories represents is the more or less *implicit versus explicit knowledge* of variation. With stereotypes, speakers *know* that the feature relates to a specific category of speaker; with indicators, speakers *do not know* that the feature relates to a specific category of speaker. Speakers have explicit knowledge of stereotypes that they can articulate and discuss (Silverstein 1981; Preston 1996), but speakers must also have some knowledge of indicators and markers to use them variably as part of their grammatical competence. But knowledge of indicators is *implicit*, not consciously articulable. This chapter begins to address the real-time processing by which speakers arrive at such states of knowledge, and by which knowledge of variation accumulates.

As used within most sociolinguistic research (as in, e.g., Silverstein 1981; Preston 1996, 2011; Mertz and Yovel 2003), *awareness* seems to be a matter of the raising of internal *knowledge* to the surface of a speaker's consciousness, with a continuum of *awareness* representing a continuum from knowledge that is implicit to explicit. The construct of knowledge is in overt focus in work by Labov (1973) and Wolfram (1982), both of whom assess the degree to which speakers are aware of – as in, the extent to which they *know* – the patterns and constraints governing dialects other than those they have productive competence in. Awareness-as-knowledge is also foregrounded in the title of Preston's (1996) now-classic piece on sociolinguistic awareness, and his contribution to this volume, which asks "Whaddaya*know*?" (my emphasis).

In contrast, we can think of a different sort of *awareness* – one that is centrally connected to subjective language experience, to in-the-moment language processing and production. One of the premises underlying this chapter is that knowledge of variation likely comes about from a process of semiosis whereby speakers are exposed to linguistic differences, notice them, and come to understand patterns of their use in connection to social facts. While much research has investigated the state of speakers' knowledge about facts of variation (e.g. Johnstone and Kiesling 2008; Campbell-Kibler 2009; Staum Casasanto 2009; Squires 2013), the process of speakers coming into that knowledge has gone relatively unexplored, particularly from a processing perspective (one recent exception is Docherty *et al.* 2013). While some beliefs about language variation may be accrued via metalinguistic stereotypes without direct experience (Carmichael, this volume; McGowan, this volume), it seems that implicit knowledge in the sense of "competence" is most likely structured from experience (see, e.g., Bresnan and Ford 2010). Explicit knowledge ("awareness") should then emerge from aggregated experiences of in-the-moment noticing of linguistic differences – and coming to understand them as linguistically and socially meaningful.

Differences within and among constructs like *knowledge, awareness,* and *noticing* have been discussed at length in the field of second language acquisition (see also Nycz, this volume, for an excellent review). Schmidt (1990) addresses the role of *consciousness* in second language learning, first determining three ways in which scholars have viewed *consciousness*: as awareness, as intention, and as knowledge. Further, three levels of awareness are distinguished: *perception, noticing,* and *understanding.* Things are frequently perceived without being noticed, Schmidt suggests, and are frequently noticed without being understood. Schmidt says:

> When reading, for example, we are normally aware of (notice) the content of what we are reading, rather than the syntactic peculiarities of the writer's style, the style of type in which the text is set, music playing on a radio in the next room, or background noise outside a window. However, we still perceive these competing stimuli and may pay attention to them if we choose (Schmidt 1990:132).

Further, Schmidt contends that noticing is requisite to understanding; there is no "subliminal" learning (although there may be subliminal perception).

If we analogize other-dialect awareness to other-language awareness, and take Schmidt's definitions seriously, then the question "How aware are speakers of sociolinguistic differences?" breaks down into three separate but related questions: How much do speakers *perceive* sociolinguistic difference? How much do speakers *notice* sociolinguistic difference? and How much do speakers *understand* sociolinguistic difference?

I want to think about these concepts as important to disentangle specifically for the burgeoning research field of "sociolinguistic perception," which investigates the relation between variation and perception (see Campbell-Kibler 2010, this volume; also Drager and Kirtley, this volume). There is a drive within sociolinguistics to more robustly understand the connection between linguistic processing and the social meaning of linguistic forms, for instance in Preston's (2011, this volume) detail of how "language regard" might influence comprehension, or in Labov *et al.*'s (2011) development of a "sociolinguistic monitor" that tracks and stores frequencies of linguistic variables. Sociolinguistic perception research holds the promise of using rigorous experimentation to explore the cognitive structuring of knowledge about variation. It is important to consider the role of awareness in producing that knowledge, in addition to the role of frequency and other linguistic factors (as many of the chapters in this volume do, notably those by Beck, Campbell-Kibler, Drager and Kirtley, McGowan, and Preston).

The present study represents an exploration into awareness by considering what happens *during the processing of language variation*. How do formal differences affect language comprehension? When are linguistic forms noticed as different? Are more-difficult-to-process forms foremost in speakers' awareness of difference? In particular, this study examines the relation between *perceiving* difference and consciously *noticing* it, positing that these processes are foundational to speakers developing *understanding* and *knowledge* of sociolinguistic variation through exposure to it.

Sociolinguistic processing *in-the-moment* is a relatively unexplored area of research (although see Loudermilk 2013), and sociolinguistic perception research has in general focused on phonological variation and phonetic variables. The present chapter extends the inquiry into the online (that is, real-time) processing of grammatical variation, attempting to measure: (a) whether speakers perceive (morpho)syntactic difference; and (b) whether they notice it. Psycholinguistic methods are well developed for measuring sentence processing (see more complete discussions in Squires 2013, 2014a, 2014b), and the method used here is self-paced reading, wherein participants move through a sentence unit by unit at their own pace. Reading speed is taken to index language processing, with more-difficult linguistic units taking longer to read than less-difficult units (Just *et al.* 1982). What is "difficult" is typically that which is unexpected, due to a violation of grammatical constraints, low probability, or both. This method has been used to show that speakers' processing is sensitive to, for instance, agreement mismatches (Pearlmutter *et al.* 1999; Breadmore *et al.* 2014), semantic anomalies (De Vicenzi *et al.* 2003), and probabilistic facts about the occurrence of structural alternatives (Bresnan and Ford 2010).

Relevant to the questions of this chapter, two prior studies have productively used self-paced reading to study the processing of regional dialect variants. Kaschak and Glenberg (2004) studied adults' "acquisition" of a novel dialect form: the [*need*+past participle] construction (e.g. *The dishes need washed*) common in the Northern Midlands dialect area of the United States. Participants, who were not speakers of the dialect, read sentences with the *need*+past participle construction more slowly than those with the standard construction (*The dishes need to be washed*). However, this effect was attenuated with multiple exposures to the pattern, and further research showed that participants were also able to generalize the construction to other structures (Kaschak 2006).

Kaschak and Glenberg's research shows that speakers are sensitive to sentence structures that are not part of their own dialect: participants perceived the "oddity" of the [*need*+past participle] construction. However, participants also became less sensitive to the construction the more they encountered it, and possibly even learned its meaning and grammatical patterning. In Schmidt's (1990) terms, they came to *understand* the form. Because Kaschak and Glenberg do not report what their subjects thought about the sentences, we cannot assess whether they metalinguistically *noticed* the construction. Yet, if Schmidt (1990) is correct, and understanding presupposes noticing, then participants should have also noticed the differences between sentences. What did participants come to understand [*need*+past participle] *as*? Did they (accurately) categorize it as a dialect form, or did they simply categorize it as an "error" and assume that the experiment involved making errorful sentences? Knowing what the participants *noticed*, and how they metalinguistically categorized what they noticed, might shed further light on the levels of awareness during the processing and acquisition of new grammatical forms.

In a study explicitly using self-paced reading to measure awareness during reading comprehension, Breadmore *et al.* (2014) consider self-paced reading times as a measure of "implicit awareness" of subject-verb agreement mismatches. To measure "explicit awareness," they used a post-experiment error correction task of the same subject-verb agreement mismatches. Comparing deaf and hearing children's performance, Breadmore *et al.* show that explicit and implicit awareness are not always aligned: deaf children did poorly at the error correction task, showing a lack of explicit awareness of agreement errors. But the deaf children's reading times *were* affected by the agreement errors, although this effect did not show up until one word later than for the hearing children.

Breadmore *et al.*'s results show that what is perceived does not always rise to consciousness, just as Schmidt (1990) suggests. Similar results have been found in recent neurolinguistic research, which has found that the brain may detect syntactic errors even when a listener does not consciously register them (Batterink and Neville 2013). On the other hand, Hanulíková *et al.* (2012) show that brain responses to grammatical errors can be modulated by sociolinguistic perceptions of the speaker: knowing that a person speaking errorfully is a non-native speaker makes the brain respond less strongly to those errors. Thus, perceiving linguistic differences might not always lead to noticing, and explicit awareness of differences – or the likelihood of them – may affect what is perceived.

The links between low-level automatic perception, conscious noticing, sociolinguistic differences, and social information are ripe for further investigation. The present chapter uses both an online behavioral measure and an offline metalinguistic task to explore the link between perception and noticing, providing a basis from which to explore further the role of sociolinguistic processing in sociolinguistic knowledge and its acquisition.

## Experiments Overview

This chapter presents the results of a series of experiments testing participants' processing of subject-verb agreement variation (Pilot Experiment, Experiment 1,

Experiment 2). The experiments tested adult English speakers' reading times in sentences containing [NP+*don't/doesn't*], where the combination of number on the subject noun and auxiliary verb form was variable. Some sentences contained standard agreement, some contained non-standard agreement, and some contained what I will call "uncommon" agreement, explained below. Participants' word-by-word reading times were measured to assess the extent to which they automatically *perceived* the variant forms, and their offline metalinguistic response to a post-experiment question was used to assess whether they had *noticed* the variant forms.

The agreement conditions are presented in (1a–d). The "non-standard" variant, [SG+*don't*], is common across varieties of English (Feature 158; often called "invariant *don't*"). In the United States, it is associated both descriptively and perceptually with lower social status (Squires 2013, 2014a). In contrast, the "uncommon" form, [PL+*doesn't*], is not known to be a dialect variant. It was included in the sentences in order to provide a point of comparison between a non-standard syntactic structure that participants would likely have encountered but probably do not use themselves, versus a structure that participants would likely not have encountered or use. This method enables probing the role of sociolinguistic experience in the perceiving and noticing of linguistic difference (see also chapters by Beck, Carmichael, Drager and Kirtley, and McGowan, this volume).

(1a) Standard (plural):    After eating, the <u>turtles</u> <u>don't</u>   <u>walk</u> <u>very</u> fast.
(1b) Standard (singular):  After eating, the <u>turtle</u>  <u>doesn't</u> <u>walk</u> <u>very</u> fast.
(1c) Non-standard:         After eating, the <u>turtle</u>  <u>don't</u>   <u>walk</u> <u>very</u> fast.
(1d) Uncommon:             After eating, the <u>turtles</u> <u>doesn't</u> <u>walk</u> <u>very</u> fast.
                                          1       2       3      4
                                         noun   don't    verb   verb+1

In each experiment, participants read sentences one word at a time through a "moving window" self-paced reading task (Just *et al.* 1982). After reading each word, they pressed a button on an experimental response box to continue to the next word. The dependent measure was word reading time, from the appearance of a word on screen to the participants' button-press to advance to the next word.

There were four critical word regions within each sentence, labelled in (1): [1] the subject noun before *don't/doesn't* (noun region); [2] *don't/doesn't* (*don't* region); [3] the main verb following *don't/doesn't* (verb region); and [4] the word following the main verb (verb+1 region). Self-paced reading studies often identify the strongest effects at the word *following* the introduction of a grammatical anomaly, with processing effects occasionally persisting even beyond (Just *et al.* 1982; Pearlmutter *et al.* 1999; Kaschak and Glenberg 2004; Kaschak 2006; Breadmore *et al.* 2014). Hence, in these experiments, the region expected to show the most consistent effect of agreement is the verb region [3]. The noun region [1] is shown in the figures below for purposes of comparison, but it is not included in the statistical analyses.

As a measure of *perceiving*, I hypothesized that participants' reading times would be fastest in the standard condition, slowest in the uncommon condition, and intermediate in the non-standard condition. Standard agreement would be the most expected in this setting (a university lab) and for this modality (written), and it was also likely to be the most-used form of agreement for the participants (who were university students). In contrast to standard agreement, non-standard agreement should also be unexpected. Yet, because it is a common (and even stereotyped) dialect variant in the United States, participants should have some knowledge of the non-standard form, and therefore its effect should be less disruptive than that of uncommon agreement.

In addition to measuring reading times, I sought to group participants in each experiment by whether they consciously *noticed* the agreement differences or not, and to investigate whether differences in noticing corresponded to differences in perceiving. Schmidt (1990:132) suggests that "noticing can be operationally defined as availability for verbal report, subject to certain conditions." I used a post-experiment questionnaire question to ask participants to report if they "noticed anything interesting about the grammar of the sentences." Participant groupings were assigned based on the following criteria: if participants mentioned either *don't*, *doesn't*, subject-verb agreement, or expressions indexing any of these specifically, I considered them to be "aware" participants. If they did not mention any of these features, they were "unaware" participants. Although this method necessarily relies on participants' metalinguistic articulation, my coding criteria for being counted as "aware" attempted to minimize the importance of terminology. To summarize the experimental method: I consider participants' perception using a quantitative measure (reading time), and their awareness using a qualitative measure (metalinguistic report); I then investigate whether awareness is a predictor of perceptual behavior (similar to Nycz, this volume).

The three experiments differed in one crucial property: the ratio of non-standard/uncommon sentences to standard sentences was decreased in each subsequent experiment. The Pilot Experiment found that the majority of participants were "aware" (discussed below). Subsequently, I sought a more balanced grouping of unaware and aware participants and hypothesized that fewer tokens of the grammatical variants would lead to fewer people noticing them. I therefore reduced the number of non-standard/uncommon sentences in Experiments 1 and 2 to attempt to increase the number of unaware participants.

## Pilot Experiment

The Pilot Experiment did not have investigating participant awareness as a main goal; rather, it was conducted to assess the processing of syntactic variation as part of a larger project, and it served as a pilot use of the "noticing" question in the post-experiment questionnaire. Full discussion of the methods and general results of this experiment appears in Squires (2014a).

Participants were exposed to sixty-four target sentences, which contained [NP+*don't/doesn't*], and sixty-four filler sentences, which were grammatically standard and did not contain *don't* or *doesn't*. After eight of the filler sentences, participants answered a yes/no comprehension question about the prior sentence, to ensure they were paying attention. The total proportion of non-standard sentences throughout the experiment was 25 percent (32 out of 128). Sentences were divided into four blocks; participants read four non-standard and four uncommon sentences, together with eight standard target sentences and sixteen filler sentences, in each block. Forty-five participants received course credit for completing the experiment; the data of two participants were removed due to experiment error.

The majority of participants – thirty-three out of forty-three – were classified as "aware" based on their post-experiment questionnaire responses. Figure 4.1 shows the mean response times (in milliseconds) across agreement conditions by both aware and unaware participants. As expected, participants' reading was slowed by both non-standard and uncommon agreement relative to standard agreement, with the largest divergence being for uncommon agreement. Additionally (and unexpectedly), the aware participants were faster at reading overall than the unaware participants. Because of this difference, and because the relation between behavior and awareness is the major question here, for this chapter I analyze and report raw reading times rather than residual reading times (in Squires 2014a, I report residual reading times). For all experiments, observations with reaction times under 30 ms and over 2,000 ms were removed as outliers prior to analysis.

To assess both agreement and awareness as predictors of reading time, I conducted statistical analysis using mixed-effects linear regression modelling with the {lmer4} package in R (Bates *et al.* 2011), estimating p-values with the {languageR} package (Baayen 2010). Reading times for each word region were analyzed independently. Every model began with two terms: experimental block as a fixed effect, since reading times decreased over the course of the experiment, and a random intercept effect for experimental item, to account for variability across sentences/words. (I did not include random effects for subjects in order to better detect an effect of awareness, which is a subject-level variable.) I then followed a model comparison procedure in which I sequentially tested the effect of agreement condition, participant

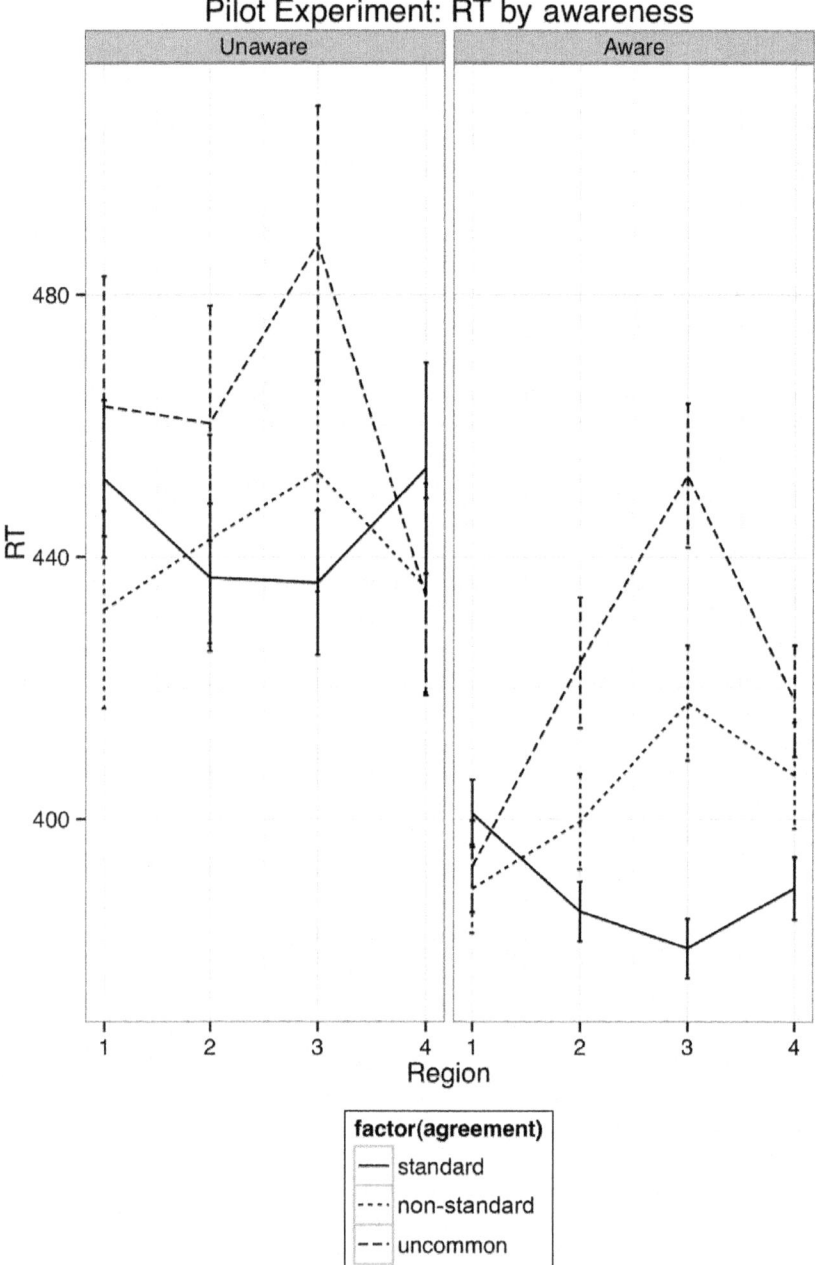

Figure 4.1 Pilot Experiment Reaction Times in Milliseconds by Agreement
and Participant Awareness, across Word Regions
(1 = noun, 2 = don't, 3 = verb, 4 = verb+1)
Error bars represent the standard error of the mean.

Table 4.1 *Pilot Experiment, Summary of Linear Regression Models*

| Word region | Factor | Estimate | SE | t value | p-level |
|---|---|---|---|---|---|
| *don't* | intercept | 525.03 | 10.99 | 47.78 | <0.001 |
| | block | −37.42 | 3.04 | −12.30 | <0.001 |
| | agreement:non-standard | 12.02 | 8.31 | 1.45 | − |
| | agreement:uncommon | 35.38 | 8.32 | 4.25 | <0.001 |
| | awareness:aware | −44.67 | 8.20 | −5.45 | <0.001 |
| verb | intercept | 546.90 | 11.81 | 46.30 | <0.001 |
| | block | −47.86 | 3.27 | −14.62 | <0.001 |
| | agreement:non-standard | 32.71 | 8.95 | 3.65 | <0.001 |
| | agreement:uncommon | 68.06 | 8.95 | 7.61 | <0.001 |
| | awareness:aware | −45.05 | 8.81 | −5.12 | <0.001 |
| verb+1 | intercept | 548.956 | 13.67 | 40.16 | <0.001 |
| | block | −38.62 | 3.15 | −12.26 | <0.001 |
| | agreement:non-standard | −16.11 | 18.34 | −0.88 | − |
| | agreement:uncommon | −18.56 | 18.41 | −1.01 | − |
| | awareness:aware | −62.58 | 11.98 | −5.23 | <0.001 |
| | agreement:non-standard x awareness:aware | 32.22 | 20.80 | 1.55 | − |
| | agreement:uncommon x awareness:aware | 46.36 | 20.86 | 2.22 | <0.05 |

Dependent variable is response time; models include random effect of items.

awareness, and the interaction of agreement and awareness. I retained a predictor when analysis of variance comparing the model with and without it showed a significant chi-square value at the $p<0.05$ level. For all three experiments, the models I present are the best-fitting models according to this procedure.

Table 4.1 summarizes the regression models for the Pilot Experiment. The parameter estimates are interpretable as predicted increases or decreases in reading time for the listed factor levels, relative to the baseline factor levels of standard (for agreement) and unaware (for awareness).

Awareness was significant as a main effect at all three word regions, with aware participants reading faster than unaware participants. Agreement showed different effects across the regions. At *don't*, uncommon sentences took longer to read than standard sentences. At the verb, both non-standard and uncommon sentences took longer to read than standard. At verb+1, there was an interaction between agreement and awareness: while there was not a main effect of agreement, for the aware participants, uncommon agreement continued to slow them down (as shown in Figure 4.1). Aware participants seemed to have a more sustained response to the agreement differences.

The finding that unaware participants were slower readers overall was surprising. It is intriguing given that much work on reading comprehension has shown correlations between poor reading skill and other cognitive and metacognitive processes, including "syntactic awareness" (Wagoner 1983;

Table 4.2 *Pilot Experiment, Supplemental Analysis of the Significance of Agreement Condition for Aware Participants (N=33) and Unaware Participants (N=10)*

| | don't | | verb | | verb+1 | |
| --- | --- | --- | --- | --- | --- | --- |
| | Non-standard | Uncommon | Non-standard | Uncommon | Non-standard | Uncommon |
| Aware | – | <0.001 | <0.001 | <0.001 | <0.01 | <0.01 |
| Unaware | – | – | – | <0.001 | – | – |

Bowey 1986; Gernsbacher 1993; Nation and Snowling 2000; Breadmore *et al.* 2014). Two unaware participants also reported having a reading disability, so there may be a relation between reading ability and sensitivity to these differences – however, these participants did no worse than others on the comprehension questions.

Because unaware participants had longer processing times overall, it seems that longer time spent processing a linguistic stimulus does not necessarily correlate with heightened awareness of that stimulus, contrary to my intuition. Moreover, the participants who did not report noticing the manipulation seem to have been less strongly affected by it, or at least less consistently affected by it, supported by the interaction effect at the verb+1 region. To investigate possible differences between the two participant groups more closely, I conducted a supplemental analysis of the two groups independently, com-paring separate regression models for the effect of agreement. Table 4.2 summarizes these results by simply reporting the significance of the agreement main effect for each group.

Agreement was a significant main effect at all word regions for the aware participants. However, for the unaware participants, agreement was only significant at the verb region, and then only in the uncommon condition. That the unaware participants did not show an effect of agreement at *don't* (the word introducing the grammatical variant) echoes Breadmore *et al.*'s (2014) findings, where subjects who were explicitly unaware were nonetheless impli-citly aware of agreement mismatches, but the effect had a later onset. The failure of agreement to more robustly predict response times for unaware participants could be due to their data having wider variance due to longer total reading times, with that variance distributed across fewer observations.

Especially given that my measure of awareness – an offline, metalinguistic self-report after the experiment – likely underestimates the number of partici-pants truly noticing the grammatical manipulation, the finding of differences between the two groups is quite compelling. Experiments 1 and 2 were designed to follow up on these initial results by investigating: (a) if the relationships between perceiving, noticing, and overall reading times could be replicated; and (b) whether fewer tokens of non-standard sentences would lessen the overall noticing of the manipulation, to create a more balanced set of unaware versus aware participants.

## Experiment 1

Experiment 1 differed from the Pilot Experiment in the proportion of non-standard and uncommon sentences throughout the experiment. Experiment 1 lowered this proportion slightly, to 19 percent from 25 percent. In each of the four blocks in the experiment, participants saw three uncommon and three non-standard sentences, together with ten standard target sentences and sixteen filler sentences (so that throughout the experiment there were twenty-four total non-standard sentences out of 128). Thirty-six participants received undergraduate course credit for their participation. Three participants' data were removed from analysis because they reported not having English as their native or most-fluent language.

Eighteen participants were coded as "aware" and fifteen were coded as "unaware." This presents a slightly more balanced grouping than in the Pilot Experiment – yet the majority of participants still reported noticing agreement differences. Figure 4.2 shows that the general results for Experiment 1 are similar to those for the Pilot Experiment. Aware participants were again faster readers overall, and the main effect of awareness was significant for all word regions, as shown by the statistical analyses summarized in Table 4.3.

At the *don't* region, uncommon agreement again led to longer reading times. At the verb, both non-standard and uncommon agreement took longer to read than standard. However, there was no main effect of agreement at the verb+1 region in this experiment, nor was there an interaction with awareness.

To probe further the differences between the groups, I again conducted a supplemental analysis treating the two participant groups independently, summarized in Table 4.4. While aware participants were affected by agreement in all three word regions, unaware participants were not affected at the verb+1 region (just as in the Pilot Experiment). And, at the verb region, only the uncommon sentences were significantly slower than standard for unaware participants, whereas for the aware participants, both non-standard and uncommon sentences were (also as in the Pilot).

Experiment 1 replicated the Pilot Experiment in three ways. First, unaware participants were slower readers than aware participants. Second, for unaware participants only, sentences in the non-standard condition never produced significantly longer reading times than those in the standard condition. Third, the difference between agreement conditions was not significant at the verb+1 region for unaware participants, but it was for aware participants. Both

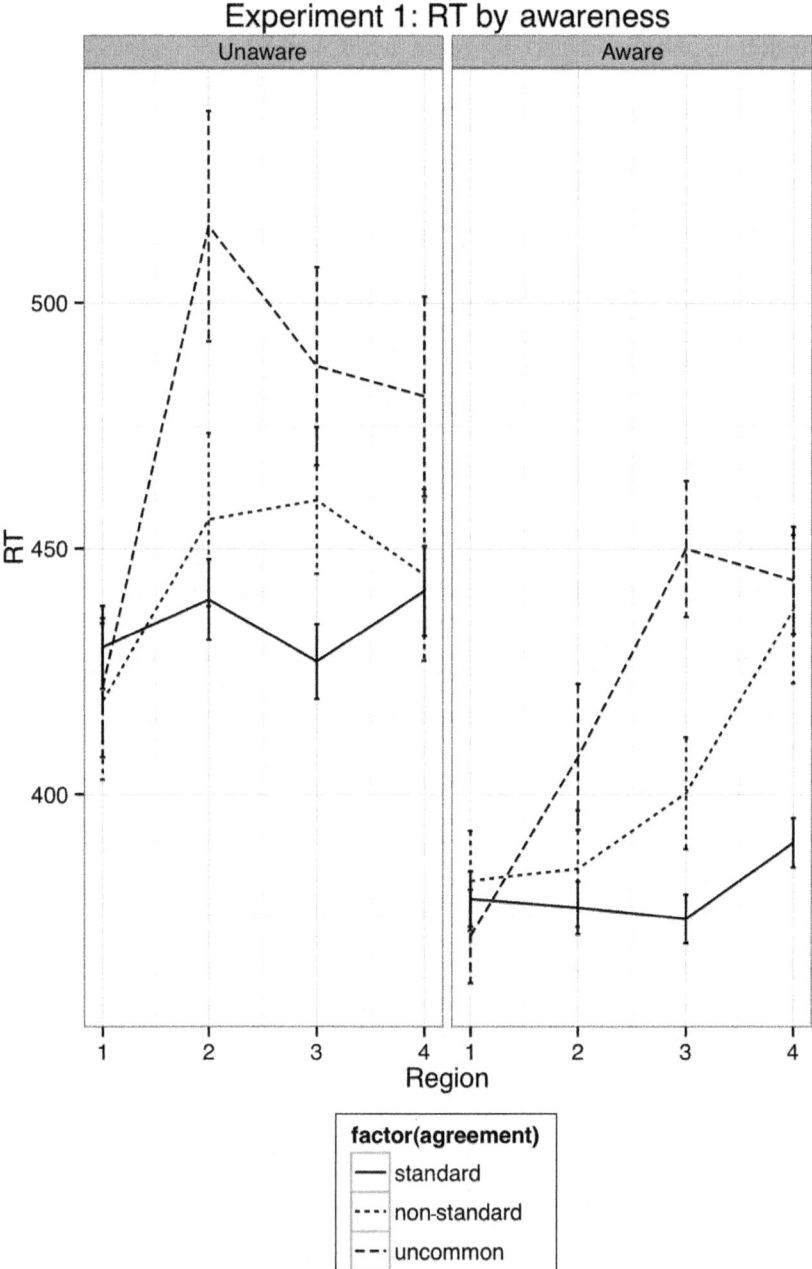

Figure 4.2 Experiment 1 Reaction Times in Milliseconds by Agreement and
Participant Awareness, across Word Regions
(1 = noun, 2 = don't, 3 = verb, 4 = verb+1)
Error bars represent the standard error of the mean.

Table 4.3 *Experiment 1, Summary of Linear Regression Models*

| Word region | Factor | Estimate | SE | t value | p-level |
|---|---|---|---|---|---|
| *don't* | intercept | 561.17 | 11.68 | 48.04 | <0.001 |
| | block | −46.40 | 3.74 | −12.41 | <0.001 |
| | agreement:non-standard | 11.72 | 11.01 | 1.06 | − |
| | agreement:uncommon | 51.64 | 11.03 | 4.68 | <0.001 |
| | awareness:aware | −72.68 | 8.40 | −8.66 | <0.001 |
| verb | intercept | 538.72 | 13.06 | 41.26 | <0.001 |
| | block | −45.00 | 4.32 | −10.42 | <0.001 |
| | agreement:non-standard | 28.84 | 12.71 | 2.27 | <0.05 |
| | agreement:uncommon | 68.36 | 12.71 | 5.38 | <0.001 |
| | awareness:aware | −50.84 | 7.50 | −6.78 | <0.001 |
| verb+1 | intercept | 533.73 | 25.38 | 21.03 | <0.001 |
| | block | −33.43 | 9.13 | −3.66 | <0.001 |
| | awareness:aware | −41.04 | 7.86 | −5.22 | <0.001 |

Dependent variable is response time; models include random effect of items.

Table 4.4 *Experiment 1, Supplemental Analysis of the Significance of Agreement Condition for Aware Participants (N=18) and Unaware Participants (N=15)*

| | don't | | verb | | verb+1 | |
|---|---|---|---|---|---|---|
| | non-standard | uncommon | non-standard | uncommon | non-standard | uncommon |
| Aware | − | <0.01 | <0.01 | <0.001 | − | <0.05 |
| Unaware | − | <0.001 | − | <0.001 | − | − |

experiments suggest some qualitative difference in the experiencing of variation between those participants who later reported noticing the manipulation and those who did not. They seem to confirm that there is a distinction between what Broadmore *et al.* (2013) call *implicit* and *explicit awareness*, or what I am calling *perceiving* and *noticing*. Both participant groups *perceived* the agreement differences, but somewhat differently; and, they did not equally *notice* it.

Importantly, for both groups of participants, the form that caused the greatest disruption was the "uncommon" form [PL+*doesn't*]. What about the non-standard pattern, which did not reach significance as different from standard for the unaware group? It could be that unaware participants did not perceive these because they had greater implicit knowledge of them − they may have been speakers of dialects who use the non-standard form. If this were the case, we might expect some consistency in the demographic make-up of the unaware participants, reflecting similar dialect backgrounds. However, to the extent that there was social heterogeneity among participants (most of whom were White, and all of whom were university students), this was no more the case for the unaware groups than the aware groups.

Unaware participants read overall more slowly than aware participants, and so perhaps sensitivity to variation is tied to more general language processing or reading comprehension skills, which vary at an individual level. For instance, because this experiment is in the reading mode, it might be the case that the unaware participants were poorer readers than the aware participants, indexed by their slower reading times. Reading skills have been linked by researchers to a variety of other cognitive abilities, including comprehension monitoring (Wagoner 1983) and syntactic awareness (Bowey 1986; Nation and Snowling 2000).

One of the factors known to affect comprehension is the ability to suppress cues that are irrelevant or contradictory to the comprehension task (Gernsbacher 1993). That is, when information is activated that "gets in the way" of comprehension, poor readers are worse at suppressing that information than good readers are, which makes comprehension more difficult. If variability in verb forms were considered a type of information that one needed to suppress in order to continue reading the sentence adeptly, we would expect poor readers to be *more* affected by agreement differences than good readers. That is, we would expect the slower readers to show more sensitivity to the agreement differences, and perhaps even more conscious awareness of them, since they would be less able to recover from the mismatches. However, it seems that the slower readers were less perceptive of the differences in the first place.

Perhaps unaware participants had a more difficult time processing the sentences in the task, and therefore had less processing energy to commit to formal differences that did not affect content (see Schmidt 1990). Or, perhaps, they were simply less likely to notice differences in general because of a lower degree of metalinguistic awareness or lower ability to monitor their own comprehension. If either of these were true, performance on the comprehension questions in the experiment should be worse for unaware than for aware participants. In the Pilot Experiment, unaware participants did average a lower percentage of correct comprehension question responses than aware participants (78 versus 87 percent), but this amounts only to a one-question difference in average accuracy between groups. In Experiment 1, average accuracy was equivalent between groups (88 percent). Generally speaking, then, failing to register awareness did not align with poor comprehension. All participants seemed to be paying attention to the task and comprehending the sentences, regardless of the degree to which they perceived or noticed the agreement differences.

Experiment 2 sought to make agreement even less salient by reducing sharply the number of non-standard/uncommon sentences during the experiment. In their investigation of the (ING) variable, Labov *et al.* (2011) suggest that the "sociolinguistic monitor" works as a logarithmic function, being extremely sensitive to the first few tokens of a socially marked variant and tapering off afterwards. Kaschak and Glenberg (2004) and Kaschak (2006) also found that participants' sensitivity to dialect structures dissipated, representing adjustment or adaptation to the initially unexpected forms. It is unclear whether speakers' tendency to register conscious awareness of what they perceive, however, is modulated by the number of variant tokens to which they are exposed during an experimental session. Experiment 1 used fewer non-standard tokens than the Pilot Experiment and had a higher proportion of unaware participants. Experiment 2 reduces the number further, attempting to further mitigate participants' noticing of the manipulation, increase the number of unaware participants, and continue probing the differences between groups described above.

## Experiment 2

Experiment 2 was identical to Experiment 1 except that only one non-standard and one uncommon sentence occurred in each experimental block, making for only eight total non-standard sentences throughout the experiment (6 percent). Thirty-six participants received extra credit for participating. Three participants' data were removed due to experiment error, and three participants' data were removed because they reported not having English as their native or most-fluent language. Even with the small amount of non-standard tokens in this experiment, a majority of participants reported noticing agreement: sixteen were coded as "aware" and fourteen were coded as "unaware."

As can be seen in Figure 4.3 and Table 4.5, the results for this experiment were somewhat different from those of the Pilot and Experiment 1. There was no main effect of awareness on reading times at any region; overall, aware participants were not faster readers than unaware participants. However, there was an interaction effect between awareness and agreement at both the *don't* and verb+1 regions.

At *don't*, there was a main effect of both non-standard and uncommon agreement, but the effect for the uncommon condition was stronger for the aware group than the unaware group. (This is visually apparent in Figure 4.2 – compare region [2] between the groups.) At the verb, both non-standard and uncommon agreement were slower than standard, and there was no interaction with awareness. At verb+1, there was a main effect of uncommon agreement, and an interaction effect such that only the aware participants were slowed by non-standard agreement.

The supplemental independent group analyses confirm different agreement effects, presented in Table 4.6. For aware participants, agreement was significant at all three regions. At *don't*, the uncommon sentences were slower than

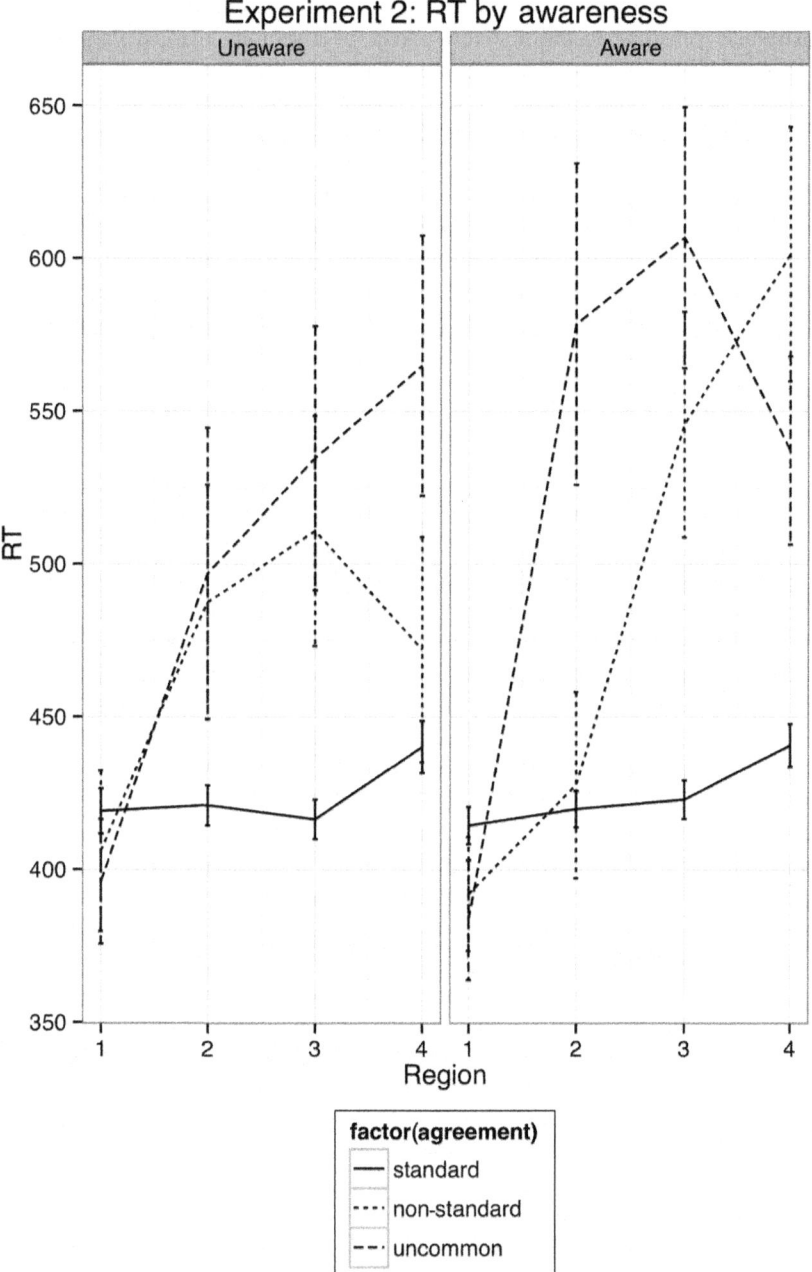

Figure 4.3 Experiment 2 Reaction Times in Milliseconds by Agreement and Participant Awareness, across Word Regions
(1 = noun, 2 = don't, 3 = verb, 4 = verb+1)
Error bars represent the standard error of the mean.

Table 4.5 *Experiment 2, Summary of Linear Regression Models*

| Word Region | Factor | Estimate | SE | t value | p-level |
|---|---|---|---|---|---|
| *don't* | intercept | 518.32 | 14.94 | 34.70 | <0.001 |
| | block | -38.92 | 5.06 | -7.70 | <0.001 |
| | agreement:non-standard | 66.61 | 30.98 | 2.15 | <0.05 |
| | agreement:uncommon | 74.49 | 30.98 | 2.40 | <0.05 |
| | awareness:aware | -1.29 | 9.70 | -0.13 | – |
| | agreement:non-standard x awareness:aware | -58.77 | 37.69 | -1.56 | – |
| | agreement:uncommon x awareness:aware | 85.76 | 37.82 | 2.27 | <0.05 |
| verb | intercept | 507.01 | 11.37 | 44.58 | <0.001 |
| | block | -34.86 | 4.10 | -8.50 | <0.001 |
| | agreement:non-standard | 109.43 | 18.95 | 5.77 | <0.001 |
| | agreement:uncommon | 154.40 | 19.10 | 8.08 | <0.001 |
| verb+1 | intercept | 520.20 | 33.51 | 15.52 | <0.001 |
| | block | -31.56 | 11.93 | -2.65 | <0.01 |
| | agreement:non-standard | 41.44 | 59.75 | 0.69 | – |
| | agreement:uncommon | 123.44 | 59.09 | 2.09 | <0.05 |
| | awareness:aware | -0.47 | 10.22 | -0.05 | – |
| | agreement:non-standard x awareness:aware | 122.15 | 40.57 | 3.01 | <0.01 |
| | agreement:uncommon x awareness:aware | -27.17 | 39.47 | -0.69 | – |

Dependent variable is response time; models include random effect of items.

Table 4.6 *Experiment 2, Supplemental Analysis of the Significance of Agreement Condition for Aware Participants (N=16) and Unaware Participants (N=14)*

| | *don't* | | verb | | verb+1 | |
|---|---|---|---|---|---|---|
| | Non-standard | uncommon | Non-standard | uncommon | Non-standard | uncommon |
| Aware | – | <0.001 | <0.001 | <0.001 | <0.01 | – |
| Unaware | <0.01 | <0.01 | <0.001 | <0.001 | – | – |

standard, and at the verb, reading was slower for both non-standard and uncommon sentences. At verb+1, aware participants were still slowed by non-standard sentences. For unaware participants, at *don't* and the verb, non-standard and uncommon sentences were slower than standard. Once again, agreement was not a significant predictor for unaware participants at the verb +1 region.

Experiment 2 did not replicate the general difference in reading times between aware and unaware participants. While there may indeed be relations between reading ability, reading skill, or comprehension skill and perception/ noticing of morphosyntactic differences, Experiment 2 did not confirm this, and more research is needed on the matter. Yet, the interaction effects do indicate some differences in processing between the groups – with aware participants affected more strongly.

Experiment 2 also sought to test whether reducing the number of non-standard sentences in the experiment would reduce the number of participants noticing the agreement differences. This did not happen: the majority of participants reported noticing the manipulation, just as in the prior experiments. With only eight non-standard tokens throughout the experiment, most participants nonetheless registered explicit awareness of the variation such that they remembered at the end of the experiment that they had encountered it. I discuss this in the section below.

### General Discussion

These experiments explored the relationship between the perceiving of linguistic variation, as measured by an online temporal measure, and the conscious noticing of that variation, as measured by participants' offline self-reports. The results are consistent enough to support the idea that perceiving and noticing are usefully considered separate cognitive processes, as suggested by second language acquisition researchers such as Schmidt (1990). That is, while participants could be divided based on their noticing of differences, both groups nonetheless showed perception of the differences; we could perhaps conclude that perception is a necessary ground for noticing. The degree of processing disruption from unexpected agreement – including its duration and magnitude – differed across groups, though. Aware participants' behavior was more consistent across experiments, whereas unaware participants' behavior was noisier, particularly on either side of the verb region (in the *don't* and verb+1 regions).

Together, the results of the experiments permit three generalizations about the processing behavior of aware versus unaware groups. First, the effect of agreement lasted longer for aware participants than unaware participants; unaware participants were never significantly affected by agreement in the verb+1 region. Second, being affected by non-standard agreement entailed also being affected by uncommon agreement, whose effect was generally larger. There was only one word region in one experiment for one participant group (Experiment 2, verb+1, aware participants) in which this generalization did not hold. Third, even very few tokens of variant grammatical patterns triggered metalinguistic awareness in the majority of participants; markedly reducing the proportion of non-standard tokens did not commensurably reduce the proportion of unaware participants (particularly from Experiment 1 to Experiment 2). The differences between groups – especially given the relatively unsophisticated method used here for measuring awareness – do suggest that perceiving and noticing are different components of sociolinguistic processing.

How do perceiving and noticing relate to knowledge? Sociolinguistic knowledge is the foundation for sociolinguistic perception: our implicit knowledge delimits our perceptual expectations and adjustments (Beck, this volume; Staum Casasanto 2009). The present study suggests that all kinds of grammatical anomalies are not equally perceived, and that this may be an outcome of the structure of participants' linguistic knowledge. I tested participants' reactions to two different kinds of grammatical "variants": one that they have likely experienced as spoken by real speakers and which is a social stereotype (SG +*don't*), and one that they are unlikely to have experienced as systematically connected to real speakers (PL+*doesn't*). As expected, across experiments, the effect of agreement was most consistent at the verb – the word immediately following the introduction of variant agreement with *don't/doesn't*. In this region, the uncommon sentences always had the longest average reading times, and these were significantly longer than those for standard sentences for both aware and unaware participants. Reading times for the non-standard sentences were slower than standard, but faster than uncommon. The logical explanation for this gradience is that participants have some experience with the "non-standard" pattern that makes it slightly less unexpected than the "uncommon" pattern, and patterns previously experienced are easier to process than patterns not experienced.

The implication is that grammatical forms that one is exposed to, even when they are different from one's own production baseline, are stored in memory – not passed over or discarded (Kaschak and Glenberg 2004; Kaschak 2006). Of course, at some level, this must logically be the case in order to explain how people make social judgments based on dialect forms that they don't themselves control. The present experiments provide empirical evidence, though, that knowledge of these forms is implicitly active during processing, rather than only activated when a task or social situation evokes overt social stereotypes (see Campbell-Kibler, this volume).

As compared to the "non-standard" pattern, exposing participants to the "uncommon" pattern is more akin to traditional sentence processing research which investigates participants' detection of syntactic errors, without considering whether these might be dialect forms or not (see discussion in Squires 2014b). Participants may have been perceiving the non-standard forms as "variants," but the uncommon forms as "errors." I think this is a central problem for sociolinguistic perception research moving forward: When linguistic differences are perceived, and even more so when they are noticed, how are they categorized? Is there a distinction between perception as *variant* and perception as *error*? If so, how do linguistic or social circumstances shift the categorization of incoming tokens? Is one more likely to lead to *noticing* and *understanding* than another? Is one more likely to be kept active in memory than another? These processes must be at the heart of the behavioral

Table 4.7 *Strings Used by*
*"Aware" Participants in*
*Describing the Sentences*

| String | Tokens |
| --- | --- |
| doesn't | 39 |
| don't | 37 |
| verb | 32 |
| correct | 29 |
| agree | 25 |
| subject | 22 |
| grammar | 13 |
| noun | 12 |
| grammatical | 11 |
| singular | 8 |
| wrong | 7 |
| plural | 7 |
| tense | 6 |
| proper | 7 |

responses we see regarding sociolinguistic experience, social evaluations not least among them.

Although the present study did not investigate these questions specifically, the qualitative responses participants gave do speak to them. When participants noticed agreement differences, how did they describe them? What exactly did they notice? In Table 4.7, I present a list of strings used by "aware" participants across all three experiments. Note that a string's number of occurrences does not necessarily line up with the number of participants who mentioned it, since some responses include the same word more than one time (especially *don't* and *doesn't*). (There are sixty-seven total aware participants.)

Immediately interesting is the fact that *don't* was mentioned almost as many times as *doesn't*. These words each appeared in equal numbers of standard and non-standard constructions across the experiments, but because the uncommon form caused the greatest degree of processing difficulty, I expected *doesn't* to be noticed more often or more strongly than *don't*. This was not the case, which perhaps speaks to the pre-existing salience of the non-standard *don't* pattern. A few participants also attempted to recreate the "incorrect" sentences in their responses. Eight of these included a SG+*don't* pattern (only half with a full NP as in the experiment; half used a singular pronoun), while only two included a PL+*doesn't* pattern (both with a full NP). Although this analysis can only be qualitative, these responses suggest that participants were applying existing knowledge of SG+*don't* during the memory task of articulating what they had noticed. These forms were more accessible because they were activated by the non-standard sentences, whereas PL+*doesn't* did not activate existing knowledge.

Although linguistic knowledge may have played a role in what participants noticed, their responses do not contain clear articulations about social meaning in the sense of stereotypes about individuals or speaker groups who might have produced these forms. As Table 4.7 shows, the strings "correct," "grammatical," "wrong," and "proper" occurred in several participants' responses. This is unsurprising given the social stigmatization of the SG+*don't* pattern and the artificiality of the PL+*doesn't* pattern. It is somewhat surprising that these terms were as close as participants came to articulating social judgments of the sentences. That is, none of their words indicate that they perceived the patterns as being dialect variants rather than as errors, although this may simply reflect the fact that in the United States, dialect variants are commonly ideologized as errors (Preston 1996). If participants perceived the non-standard sentences as forms that English speakers might plausibly produce – as sociolinguistic variants rather than errors – this was not evident in their self-reports. It is a non-trivial task for future work to understand the cognitive processing that moves one from the perception of linguistic forms to their interpretation as socially meaningful (if these can even be separated) (see also Squires 2014a).

I want to close with a few methodological comments. The experiments presented here have several limitations. First, they used written stimuli rather than spoken stimuli, which is the modality in which non-standard grammatical forms are more likely to be both experienced and expected. Writing rigidly codifies forms, perhaps making non-standard and uncommon agreement even more salient than they would be in natural spoken language (see also Meek and Choksi, this volume). The experiments did find the expected differences between the processing of the uncommon and non-standard forms, but it would be fruitful to complement this work by investigating the online perception of spoken grammatical variation. Second, the self-report method of assessing what was noticed during the experiments results in highly variable information, uncontrolled for factors related to general metalinguistic awareness, verbal ability, reading skill, etc. If nothing else, I hope to have shown that we shouldn't be satisfied to think that behaviorally sensitive experimental behavior tells the whole story: what speakers do with the information they have perceived differs, and including such information in our interpretation of results might be informative.

There is a related, more general issue of awareness within studies of sociolinguistic perception. Within sociolinguistics, there has been something of a privileging of what is "unaware," visible in the researchers' prioritizing of eliciting the most vernacular speech and the most automatic social beliefs. There is also a privileging of "unaware" processing in psycholinguistics, which takes distractor or filler items as an indispensable component of experimental methodology, and seeks the most finely tuned instruments to measure the most automatic behavioral responses or, even better, non-behavioral (neural) responses. Against this backdrop, what are we to make of the fact that the majority of the participants in my experiments reported noticing the experimental manipulation? Probing speakers' perception and knowledge of socially varying structures in particular may inevitably raise awareness, since what is perceptually salient is that which is different from what is expected – and our research questions are fundamentally about differ-ence. But in the wild, too, sociolinguistic information may be processed in just this way: by perceiving difference, taking notice of it, and figuring out where it fits in with what is already known about language and the people who speak it.

## REFERENCES

Baayen, R. H. 2010. languageR: Data sets and functions with "Analyzing Linguistic Data: A practical introduction to statistics." R package version 1.0. http://CRAN.R-project.org/package=languageR.

Bates, D., Maechler, M., and Bolker, B. 2011. lme4: Linear mixed-effects models using S4 classes. R package version 0.999375-39. http://CRAN.R-project.org/package=lme4.

Batterink, L. and Neville, H. J. 2013. The human brain processes syntax in the absence of conscious awareness. *Journal of Neuroscience* 33(19):8528–33.

Bowey, J. A. (1986). Syntactic awareness in relation to reading skill and ongoing comprehension monitoring. *Journal of Experimental Child Psychology* 41:282–99.

Breadmore, H. L., Krott, A., and Olson, A. C. 2014. Agreeing to disagree: Deaf and hearing children's awareness of subject-verb number agreement. *Quarterly Journal of Experimental Psychology* 67(3):474–98.

Bresnan, J. and Ford, M. 2010. Predicting syntax: Processing dative constructions in American and Australian varieties of English. *Language* 86(1):168–213.

Campbell-Kibler, K. 2009. The nature of sociolinguistic perception. *Language Variation and Change* 21(1):135–56.
    2010. Sociolinguistics and perception. *Language and Linguistics Compass* 4:377–89.

De Vicenzi, M., Job, R., Di Matteo, R., Angrilli, A., Penolazzi, B., Ciccarelli, L., and Vespignani, F. 2003. Differences in the perception and time course of syntactic and semantic violations. *Brain and Language* 85:280–96.

Docherty, G. J., Langstrof, C., and Foulkes, P. 2013. Listener evaluation of sociophonetic variability: Probing constraints and capabilities. *Linguistics* 51(2):355–80.

Feature 158: Invariant don't for all persons in the present tense. 2011. in B. Kortmann and K. Lunkenheimer (eds.), *The Electronic World Atlas of Varieties of English [eWAVE]*. Leipzig: Max Planck Institute for Evolutionary Anthropology. www.ewave–atlas.org/parameters/158.

Gernsbacher, M. A. 1993. Less skilled readers have less efficient suppression mechanisms. *Psychological Science* 1993(4):294–9.

Hanulíková, A., Van Alphen, P. M., Van Goch, M. M., and Weber, A. 2012. When one person's mistake is another's standard usage: The effect of foreign accent on syntactic processing. *Journal of Cognitive Neuroscience* 24(4):878–87.

Johnstone, B. and Kiesling, S. 2008. Indexicality and experience: Exploring the meanings of /aw/-monophthongization in Pittsburgh. *Journal of Sociolinguistics* 12(1):5–33.

Just, M.A., Carpenter, P.A., and Woolley, J. D. 1982. Paradigms and processes in reading comprehension. *Journal of Experimental Psychology: General* 111 (2):228–38.

Kaschak, M. P. 2006. What this construction needs is generalized. *Memory & Cognition* 34(2):368–79.

Kaschak, M. P. and Glenberg, A. M. 2004. This construction needs learned. *Journal of Experimental Psychology: General* 133:450–67.

Labov, W. 1972. *Sociolinguistic Patterns*. Philadelphia, PA: University of Pennsylvania Press.

1973. Where do grammars stop? in R. W. Shuy (ed.), *Report of the Twenty-Third Annual Round Table Meeting on Linguistics and Language Studies*, pp. 43–88. Washington, DC: Georgetown University Press.

Labov, W., Ash, S., Ravindranath, M., Weldon, T., Baranowski, M., and Nagy, N. 2011. Properties of the sociolinguistic monitor. *Journal of Sociolinguistics* 15(4):431–63.

Loudermilk, B. C. 2013. Cognitive mechanisms in the perception of sociolinguistic variation. PhD dissertation. University of California, Davis.

Mertz, E. and Yovel, J. 2003. Metalinguistic awareness, in J.-O. Ostman, J. Veschueren, J. Blommaert, and C. Bulcaen (eds.), *The Handbook of Pragmatics*, pp. 1–26. Amsterdam and Philadelphia, PA: John Benjamins.

Nation, K. and Snowling, M. J. 2000. Factors influencing syntactic awareness skills in normal and poor comprehenders. *Applied Psycholinguistics* 21:229–41.

Pearlmutter, N. J., Garnsey, S. M., and Bock, K. 1999. Agreement processes in sentence comprehension. *Journal of Memory and Language* 41:427–56.

Preston, D. 1996. Whaddayaknow: The modes of folk linguistic awareness. *Language Awareness* 5:40–74.

2011. The power of language regard – discrimination, classification, comprehension, and production. *Dialectologia* (Special Issue II):9–33.

Schmidt, R. W. 1990. The role of consciousness in second language learning. *Applied Linguistics* 11:129–58.

Silverstein, M. 1981. The limits of awareness. *Texas Working Papers in Linguistics* 84:1–30.

Squires, L. 2013. Limited bidirectionality in sociolinguistic perception. *Journal of Sociolinguistics* 17(2):200–37.

2014a. Knowledge, processing, evaluation: Testing the perception of English subject-verb agreement variation. *Journal of English Linguistics* 42(2):144–72.

2014b. Talker specificity and the perception of grammatical variation. *Language, Cognition and Neuroscience* 29(7):856–76.

Staum Casasanto, L. 2009. Experimental investigations of sociolinguistic knowledge. PhD dissertation. Stanford University, CA.

Wagoner, S. A. 1983. Comprehension monitoring: What it is and what we know about it. *Reading Research Quarterly* 18(3):328–46.

Wolfram, W. 1982. Language knowledge and other dialects. *American Speech* 57(1):3–18.

# 5     What It Means to Be an Outsider: How Exposure to Regional Variation Shapes Children's Awareness of Regional Accents in Their Native Language

*Erica Beck*

## Introduction

A regional accent is more than phonological variation in speech. It also provides social information about the speaker, first and foremost that person's place of birth or residence. How listeners perceive and interpret regional variation at different points in their lifespan has been the subject of much recent research (see Cristia *et al.* (2012) for a comprehensive review). Adults have been shown to reliably use regional variation in speech to identify a speaker's home region (Labov 1998; Clopper and Pisoni 2004; Clopper *et al.* 2012), and to make social judgments of speakers based on their regional accent (Hay *et al.* 2006; Campbell-Kibbler 2007; Staum-Casasanto 2009). However, it appears that many adults have only general representations of the differences between regional varieties (Preston 1986; Labov 1998; Clopper and Pisoni 2007; Clopper 2010), and their classification of dialects is subjective, based on how they perceive their own speech (Preston 1986; Niedzielski 2010).

One determining factor in adults' performance at identifying regional accents is early childhood experience hearing regional variation. Adult listeners who lived in multiple dialect regions as children perform better at categorizing regional accents than those with no early exposure to regional accents (Clopper and Pisoni 2004). There is evidence that exposure to regional variation also enhances discrimination ability in childhood. An accent discrimination study found that 7 year olds from multi-dialectal families in Great Britain outperformed children from families speaking only one regional variety (Girard *et al.* 2008; Floccia *et al.* 2009).

Age may mitigate the positive effects of exposure in children. A study of children's social preferences based on speaker's regional accent found that 9 and 10 year olds reliably identified regional accents, and preferred speakers from their native dialect region, whereas not all 5 and 6 year olds could identify the regional accents of their home region, or express social preferences based on a speaker's accent (Kinzler and DeJesus 2013).

The results of these studies raise the question of how exposure to regional variation affects children's ability to interpret, identify, and discriminate between regional accents. The course of development of awareness, and the factors that influence it, are not well understood. This chapter addresses this question by comparing how awareness differs between two groups of children who differ in their history of exposure to regional accents. One group is exposed predominately to the local regional accent, and the second receives input at home in a regional accent different from the local community accent. The expectation is that children who hear multiple regional varieties are more aware and better able to discriminate between regional accents. However, contrary to expectation, early exposure to multiple regional varieties does not improve children's ability to discriminate between accents and has negative correlations with awareness. This study captures a stage in development in which children's understanding of regional phonological variation is not yet fully developed, and linguistic input can clearly be seen helping to shape their interpretation of regional variation.

### Background

One model of speech perception accounts for how social information is associated with linguistic variation. Exemplar Theory (Johnson 1997; Pierre-humbert 2003; Johnson 2006) hypothesizes that tokens of speech are tagged and stored with information about the speaker's social qualities, such as gender, age, race, socio-economic status, etc. (Johnson 2006). As tokens of speech accumulate, they group together with tokens tagged as belonging to a particular social category. Eventually, the accumulated tokens are abstracted to create a representation of how that social group speaks. This abstract category allows the listener to identify new speakers belonging to that social group based on similarities between their speech and the representation created from the accumulated tokens. It also allows listeners to form expectations of speakers and their speech, as the representation of a particular variety captures the associations between the speech and social characteristics of speakers (Hay *et al.* 2006; Campbell-Kibbler 2007; Staum-Casasanto 2009).

Little work has been done exploring children's representations of social variation and the process by which they create social categories and associate them with linguistic variables. Munson (2010) hypothesizes that children's sociolinguistic representations are initially built upon interaction with specific individuals. A child creates proto-representations of social variation by associating a known individual's speech with the social characteristics attributed to that person. Thus, initially a representation of a regional accent may include only tokens of the speech from one individual the child knows. As the child's range of social interactions broadens, the speech of additional individuals will be added to the representation, eventually generalizing it from specific tokens to abstract representations of social variation.

Foulkes and Docherty (2006) expect that for children, the association of speech with social groups may proceed from the most obvious social characteristics, such as gender and age, to the least obvious, such as a person's region of origin. They also postulate that infrequent or less-obvious traits never develop the same strong links between linguistic units and social groupings, giving underspecified representations for some kinds of social variation. Regional variation is specifically mentioned as one of the more difficult sociolinguistic categories to acquire, as in many cases it has no reliable connection to appearance and is only relatively infrequently encountered. Thus, it would be expected that children would be able to identify ethnic- or gender-based variation before regional variation in speech.

Studies of young children's perception of social variation partially confirm these predictions. Children of 3 and 4 years of age in the United States were shown to correctly identify African-American and Standard English, assigning common stereotypes to speakers of those varieties (Rosenthal 1974). As far as regional variation is concerned, several studies show that 5-year-old children may not be able to accurately identify their own regional dialect, although they may express negative social evaluations of speakers of their dialect (Cremona and Bates 1977; Millar 2003). Kinzler and DeJesus (2013) found that 5 and 6 year olds from the Northern United States showed social preferences for other Northern-accented speakers, and could identify the Northern accent as the one heard in their community. In contrast, 5- and 6-year-old children from the South showed no preferences for either accent, and also were unable to reliably identify the local accent. The difference between the two groups may be that these two accents are not equally distributed across the United States; children in the South are more likely to hear Northern accents than vice versa. Hearing two regional accents may complicate identifying one as local, or assigning social preferences to them.

Ability to identify regional accents appears to improve with age. Kinzler and DeJesus (2013) also show that by age 9 to 10, children from both the North and the South are able to identify regional accents and express social evaluations of both accents, indicating that this ability develops with age. As mentioned in the introduction, although Girard, Floccia, and colleagues found that 5 year olds were unable to categorize regional accents, 7 year olds were able to successfully complete the task (Girard *et al.* 2008; Floccia *et al.* 2009).

Exposure to regional variation also appears to affect production of regional variation. Children with parents from outside the Philadelphia region were shown to acquire some regionally specific phonological variants more slowly, or less completely, than children whose parents were from the area, although the children were being raised in Philadelphia (Payne 1976; Roberts 2005).

Even more interesting was the finding that success acquiring certain regional phonological features could be predicted by whether the child had one or two parents native to the Philadelphia region (Roberts 2005).

### Children's Discrimination of Regional Variation

Three studies(Girard *et al.* 2008; Floccia *et al.* 2009; Wagner *et al.* 2013) conducted, respectively, in France, the United Kingdom, and the United States, all report children aged 5 are unable to discriminate a familiar and unfamiliar regional accent in a categorization task. Five year olds also failed using another experimental paradigm, in which they were asked to identify whether a sentence was spoken in the same accent as the sentence heard immediately prior (Girard *et al.* 2008; Floccia *et al.* 2009).

This is somewhat surprising, as infants have been shown to discriminate between regional accents (Nazzi *et al.* 2000; Kitamura *et al.* 2006; Phan and Houston 2008; Egerova 2010; Butler *et al.* 2011). Floccia and colleagues postulate that regional variation may be less salient than second language variation, as 5 and 6 year olds were successful in discriminating native and non-native accents using the same categorization tasks (Girard *et al.* 2008; Floccia *et al.* 2009). However, the difference between infants and 5 and 6 year olds may be that the 5 year olds are processing the sentence stimuli for meaning, in addition to discriminating between accents, whereas infants may only be paying attention to the phonological features of the stimuli. The additional burden of interpreting meaning in sentences may divert children's attention from the accent in which the stimuli were spoken. Given that Floccia and colleagues report that 7 year olds also participating in these studies discriminate between accents with a greater than chance accuracy (Girard *et al.* 2008; Floccia *et al.* 2009), this may be a memory or attention issue rather than an inability to hear regional differences in speech.

An attention-based explanation is supported by the findings of another study, in which 5 and 6 year olds successfully discriminated between regional accents when presented with shorter stimuli. Using an ABX task, and word-length, as opposed to sentence-length stimuli, Beck (2014) shows that 5- and 6-year-old children can reliably discriminate a familiar from an unfamiliar regional accent . Beck (2014) also finds that children can successfully discriminate between two regional accents in another experimental paradigm, in which children are asked to pick the speaker sounding most similar to themselves based on regional accent, again using only single word stimuli. Thus, it seems likely that sentence-length stimuli pose trouble for children between the ages of 5 and 6. This may be the result of either short-term memory limitations or processing constraints preventing them from focusing on the phonological content of the sentences.

A second consideration is that 5- and 6-year-old children are learning to interpret accents for social meaning, and have yet to acquire what regional accent represents. Therefore, a second objective of the Beck (2014) study was to assess whether awareness of regional accents contributed to the ability to discriminate between them. One result was the finding that children whose parents were from outside the dialect region in which the study was conducted differed from all other subjects in their awareness of regional accents. Since this finding parallels other studies in which early exposure affects children's abilities to identify regional variation, a separate analysis was conducted to isolate and examine these effects.

This chapter presents the results of that analysis. The effect of early exposure to regional variation on 5 and 6 year olds' awareness and ability to discriminate between regional accents is examined in the results of two tasks from the larger Beck (2014) study. The participants in the study were children living in a town of about 30,000 residents on the outskirts of Philadelphia, USA, and attending kindergarten at one of two public schools in the town. The performance of two sub-groups of these participants, dubbed "Insiders" and "Outsiders," are compared. Insiders are from families where at least one parent is a native of the child's hometown. Outsiders are children from families where neither parent is a native of the hometown, and therefore likely are not speakers of the local regional variety. Both Insiders and Outsiders were born and raised in the same town, and therefore have exposure to the same local regional variety. Insiders, however, have had most of their input exclusively in the local regional variety, and don't have experience with other regional accents. The Outsiders have had exposure to both the local and a non-local variety from birth.

Both Insiders and Outsiders participated in two tasks. The first assesses awareness of regional accents, asking them to identify speakers of different regional varieties, and whether they recognized regional variation as a kind of social variation. This is referred to as the Awareness Task. The second task is an ABX discrimination task, contrasting the local accent and an unfamiliar non-local accent. In addition to comparing the results of the two groups, the results of the two tasks are tested for correlations with one another using a mixed effects logistical regression model. This analysis should show whether awareness of regional variation has any influence on performance on the ABX discrimination task for either group.

## Experiment 1: Awareness Task

### Introduction

In the Awareness Task, children are asked five questions assessing their knowledge of regional variation and the geographical concepts underlying it.

No previous study, to my knowledge, has directly asked children to identify the regional accents that they are discriminating, or asked whether they understand regional variation to be a system of social variation.

As part of the Beck (2014) study, parents filled out an extensive questionnaire on the family's residential and language history, as well as demographic information about the child, such as age, ethnicity, and gender. These factors were tested for correlations with children's responses on the Awareness Task using a general linear model. Given other findings that older children perform better at identifying and categorizing regional accents (Girard *et al.* 2008; Floccia *et al.* 2009; Kinzler and DeJesus 2013), increased age was expected to correlate with better performance on this task.

The general expectation was that Outsiders would answer more questions correctly than Insiders, as they have more exposure to regional variation, and may have heard more commentary on regional variation, given that their families are from other dialect areas and may point out differences between their speech and the local community's. However, it was expected that Insider children at least would recognize the local accent, and be able to say that it was from their hometown.

### Methods

*Subjects*    Sixty-six children (thirty-five female), aged 61 to 77 months, average age 70.4 months, or 5.10, participated in this study. All subjects resided in a town near Philadelphia, USA. For the analyses in the present chapter, children who had two parents from the town in which the study was conducted were compared to children with neither parent born in that town. Only monolinguals were included in the analyses, to avoid confounds with language proficiency. All of the subjects included in this comparison were Caucasian and had no reported hearing or speech problems.

All participants in this study were recruited from two elementary schools in the same town, and had been attending Kindergarten in these schools for approximately five months when the study took place. None of the children was reported to have any contact with the non-local accent used in the study (Southern US English), and none of the Insiders was reported to have regular or prolonged contact with speakers with a different regional accent.

*Materials*    Subjects were asked five questions to assess their awareness of regional accents. Two questions asking children to identify locations on a map were included to test whether knowledge of geography or relative locations in the country improved understanding regional variation. Children were provided with a colorful map of the United States to use as an aid in answering these two questions.

The audio clips used in the Accent ID questions were single-word clips taken from the set of audio stimuli used in the discrimination experiment. A complete description of those clips and how they were recorded is given in the description of the second task below. The five questions, together with the abbreviated names by which they are referred to in this chapter, are given below:

> Can you show where we live (*while looking at a map of the United States*)? (Map ID Local Region)
> Can you show me and name any other places you know (*while looking at a map of the United States*)? (Map ID Other Region)
> Does this person sound like he lives here? (Accent ID Local)
> Does this person sound like he lives here? (Accent ID Non-Local)
> Can you guess why these two people talk differently? (Explanation)

### *Procedure*

Prior to participating in this study, subjects' parents were asked to fill out an extensive background questionnaire on the family's residential and linguistic history. The parents were not interviewed by the experimenter, so the data collected in the questionnaire are subject to parents' judgments and accuracy in reporting. Despite this, the analysis suggests that the data on exposure collected for the study participants help to explain differences in performance found between these two groups of subjects.

The subjects were tested at their elementary schools, at a table outside the classroom where they were often administered tests or given individualized instruction, making the setting familiar to them. The Awareness Task was consistently administered after the Discrimination Task, in order to avoid biasing their responses to the Discrimination Task. All children were offered a short break before between the two tasks.

*Results*   Outsider children are more accurate using a map to identify their home and other locations on a map than their Insider peers. However,

Table 5.1 *Comparison of Awareness Task Results, Insiders and Outsiders*

|  | Insiders (n=24) | Outsiders (n=13) |
|---|---|---|
| Map ID Local | 71% (17) | 85% (11) |
| Map ID Other Region | 61% (15) | 69% (9) |
| Accent ID Local | 74% (18) | 54% (7) |
| Accent ID Non-Local | 53% (13) | 31% (4) |
| Explanation | 36% (9) | 38% (5) |

they are much less proficient than Insiders at identifying local and non-local regional accents. Both groups do approximately equally well at stating that regional accent distinguishes the two sets of speakers heard in the stimuli. This question was expected to be the hardest to answer, as it requires not only knowledge of regional accent as a kind of sociolinguistic variation, but also the ability to abstract that knowledge in order to make a generalized statement about it.

Responses to the Accent ID Local item were counted as correct if the child indicated in any way that the local speakers were from their hometown; they were not required to explicitly name the town. Thus, responses such as "from here" or "from my town" were accepted as correct answers. The same is true for the Accent ID Non-Local item; any response indicating that the speaker was non-local was counted as correct. For example, some children said the non-local speaker was from another state, from "far away," or "not from here." All of these answers were counted as correct.

A general linear model was used to test for correlations between demographic factors, prior exposure to regional variation, and responses to the Awareness Task items. Because there were numerous demographic and exposure factors for which data were collected on the questionnaire, each factor was plotted against total number of correctly answered questions on the Awareness Task. Two factors patterned with performance on the Awareness Task and were thus included in the statistical model: age and Outsider status.

For three Awareness Task questions, Accent ID Local, Accent ID Non-Local, and Explanation, being an Outsider correlated negatively with correctly answering those three questions. Outsider children were less likely than Insider children to identify either accent correctly, or know that the sets of speakers differed by regional accent.

Increased age positively correlated correctly answering Map: ID Local. It also positively correlated with the Explanation item, the most abstract of the questions asked in the task. This may reflect the fact that older children have an easier time generalizing about regional variation than younger children.

*Discussion*   The results of this task show that Outsiders are at a relative disadvantage as compared to Insiders at identifying regional accents,

Table 5.2 *Can You Find and Name Where You Live on a Map?* *(Map ID Local)*

|          | Estimate | Standard error | t value | Pr(>|t|) |
|----------|----------|----------------|---------|----------|
| Age      | 0.02917  | 0.01440        | 2.025   | 0.0471   |
| Outsider | 0.15328  | 0.06564        | 2.335   | 0.0227   |

Table 5.3 *Can You Find and Name any Other Place on a Map?*
*(Map ID Non-local)*

|  | Estimate | Standard error | t value | Pr(>|t|) |
|---|---|---|---|---|
| Age | 0.017686 | 0.016606 | 1.065 | 0.291 |
| Outsider | 0.004921 | 0.075677 | 0.065 | 0.948 |

Table 5.4 *Does This Person Sound Like He Lives Here?*
*(Accent: ID Local)*

|  | Estimate | Standard error | t value | Pr(>|t|) |
|---|---|---|---|---|
| Age | 0.009886 | 0.014865 | 0.665 | 0.50843 |
| Outsider | −0.202895 | 0.067740 | −2.995 | 0.00392 |

Table 5.5 *Does This Person Sound Like He Lives Here*
*(Accent: ID Non-local)*

|  | Estimate | Standard error | t value | Pr(>|t|) |
|---|---|---|---|---|
| Age | 0.01771 | 0.01559 | 1.136 | 0.2602 |
| Outsider | −0.18056 | 0.07103 | −2.542 | 0.0135 |

Table 5.6 *Why Do These Two Speakers Talk Differently?*
*(Explanation)*

|  | Estimate | Standard error | t value | Pr(>|t|) |
|---|---|---|---|---|
| Age | 0.05157 | 0.01347 | 3.829 | 0.000299 |
| Outsider | −0.14694 | 0.06138 | −2.394 | 0.019664 |

knowing that accents mark a local/non-local distinction or recognizing regional variation in general.

In terms of geographical knowledge, Outsiders have a relative advantage over Insiders. Seventy-one percent of Insiders could correctly identify their home on a map, but 85 percent of Outsiders could do so. The reason for this difference perhaps relates to the frequency with which parents from outside the area may talk about or visit other geographical regions, making maps and geography more relevant or salient to Outsider children. These questions were included in this task to assess whether children with better understanding of geography also did better at understanding regional differences in speech. Given that Outsider children did well at identifying geographical locations but poorly at identifying accents and regional variation in general, and the Insiders showed the reverse pattern, it seems unlikely that geographical knowledge is a prerequisite for identifying regional accents.

As hypothesized, both groups of subjects show the greatest relative difficulty answering the Explanation item, which asks them to report that regional accents is the kind of variation heard in the task. It is therefore unsurprising that older children perform better at this task than younger children; their ability to formulate abstract statements should improve with age.

It was expected that increased age would correlate with correctly answering all of the questions on the Awareness Task; however, this was only the case for the Explanation and Map ID Local items. The reason for this could be that the range of participant ages was 61 to 77 months, less than 15 months' difference between the oldest and youngest participants. However, the lack of consistent correlation between age and awareness across all of the Awareness Task items indicates that age is not the only, or even chief, factor in the development of sociolinguistic competence.

The surprising result was that Outsiders were less accurate than Insiders at identifying the local and non-local accents. Outsiders were expected to have an advantage over the Insiders, given their history of exposure to regional accents. In this study, the Outsiders are less able than Insiders to identify a local regional accent, a non-local regional accent, or state why two speakers with regional accents sound different.

This parallels Kinzler and DeJesus's (2013) finding that 5 and 6 year olds in the Southern United States also have difficulty identifying the local accent and assigning common social stereotypes to those accents, and suggests that hearing two regional accents in the community complicates the process of recognizing the association between accent and geographical region.

The reason for the relative disadvantage of Outsiders may be that their input does not suggest there is only one regional variety. If they hear one regional variety at home and another in the community, they would have reason to believe there are two regional accents used in their hometown, as from the child's perspective, both accents are used by local speakers. Until they realize that the parents are not natives of the town, Outsiders would have little reason to believe the differences in accent are associated with a speaker's place of residence.

This finding also appears to support Munson's (2010) prediction that children construct a "library" of speakers, which forms the basis for their representations of sociolinguistic variation. However, the Outsiders have labeled some speakers in the "library" in a way that causes confusion when they have to draw on those representations in order to identify local accents. Many of the Insiders possibly have no other regional accent represented in their exemplar cloud, yet they can rule out the possibility that an unfamiliar accent is local. This finding raises the possibility that entire exemplar categories have to be reassigned labels as sociolinguistic sophistication increases throughout development, and possibly the lifespan, as listeners learn new social categories. How that reassignment of exemplars to newly learned categories proceeds and the interaction of labeling of exemplars on perception remain to be more closely examined.

The results of this task provide further evidence that ability to identify local and non-locals may depend on the kind of exposure children have to regional variation in early childhood. For children who hear a different regional variety in the home, the connection between a speaker's place of residence and accent may not be transparent. As a result, children who hear multiple regional varieties in their input have less awareness of regional variation than children whose input is predominately in one regional variety. Age plays less of a role in awareness than expected, showing correlations with only the most abstract question asked in this task, but not with identifying regional accents or regional variation.

## Experiment 2: ABX Discrimination Task

### Introduction

This experiment tests whether Outsiders and Insiders differ in their ability to discriminate between a familiar and unfamiliar regional accent in their native language. Although previous studies have shown that children have difficulty with regional accent discrimination using a categorization task (Girard *et al.* 2008; Floccia *et al.* 2009; Wagner *et al.* 2013), this study uses an experimental paradigm with which 5 and 6 year olds have been successful. For a detailed discussion of the methodology used in this study, consult Beck (2014). As with the previous task, Outsiders were expected to perform better than Insiders, given their greater exposure to regional variation.

### Methods

*Participants*  The same group of participants who completed the Awareness Task participated in the Discrimination Task. However, some children did not complete the Discrimination Task, and as a result, only data from the ten Outsiders and twenty Insiders who completed this task were included in the analysis.

*Materials*  Twenty-five stimulus words representing six vowel-quality differences between the Philadelphia and General Southern accents were identified and recorded (Labov *et al.* 2006; Schneider 2008). The six vowel groups are characterized by the vowels in the following words (words in block letters following Wells (1982)): *FACE, PRICE, GOAT, GOOSE, peel, and tail.* In the *peel* and *tail* class, the critical difference between the accents is the reversal of the vowel quality before /l/ in minimal pairs such as heel and hill. In Philadelphia, "peel" is pronounced [pil] and in General Southern [pɪl], whereas for the word *hill* the pronunciation in Philadelphia is generally [hɪl] and in General Southern [hil]. The same is true for the *tail* class, but the two vowels that are interchanged are [e] and [ɛ]. For the *GOOSE* class of words, the /u/ is more fronted in Southern than in Philadelphia, and often preceded by the glide /j/, such that the pronunciation of *tune* becomes [tjun], for example. The *PRICE* class has a vowel that is pronounced as a diphthong in Philadelphia, but as a monophthong in Southern [aɪ] versus [aː]. Finally, the *GOAT* class of words has a vowel quality in Philadelphia of [oʊ] that is considerably more fronted in Southern.

The stimuli for this task were created from recordings of six Caucasian male speakers, three for each regional accent, 25 to 35 years of age, and all lifelong residents of their respective hometowns. The local speakers were all from the same town as the children. The non-local speakers were all from the same town in Northern Louisiana, and speakers of General Southern American English.

In the Discrimination Task, children heard a single word spoken once in each of the two accents (referred to as the A and B tokens). Then a third token of that word was played in one of the two accents (the X token). The children then were asked to match the X token with either the A or B. The order of the trials was pseudo-randomized in one of four orders, ensuring that both Southern and Philadelphia accents were the "X" token 50 percent of the time, and that the matching token for a given word appeared equally as often in both the A and B positions across the entire experiment. This was done in order to minimize effects of order, since it is possible that a short inter-stimulus interval (ISI) between the matching tokens might facilitate matching, whereas a longer ISI might make matching tokens harder.

*Procedure*   The children were tested on the same day and in the same location as in the Awareness Task. After receiving the children's oral consent to participate in the experiment, the experimenter began by showing them a PowerPoint presentation with pictures of each of the stimuli words in the experiment. They were asked to name the picture shown on each slide. This ensured that the children knew the stimuli words, but hadn't heard them pronounced by anyone except themselves immediately prior to completing the task. If the child incorrectly named a picture, or provided a synonym for the target word, they were asked to guess again until they said the target word.

The experiment was also presented on Microsoft PowerPoint. Small pictures of radio speakers represented each token that the child heard. The speaker icon for each token on the PowerPoint slides were labeled as one of A, B, or ?. After listening to all three tokens, the child could either point to one of the icons or say "A" or "B" to indicate his or her response. Responses were recorded by the experimenter, together with any commentary on the accents made during the testing session.

The children were given three warm-up trials that did not include any of the target vowel contrasts, in order to introduce them to the format of the experiment. No feedback was given in the experimental trial, and when giving instructions, no reference was made to matching accents, regions, or any other suggestion of how children should match the speakers. This was done to test whether regional accent was a salient feature by which to match speakers, and not to bias children's responses.

*Results*    The Insiders (n=20) averaged 16.7/25 (67 percent) correct matches. The Outsiders (n=10) averaged 16.3/25 (65 percent) correct matches. The averages for the two groups were not significantly different from one another ($t= 0.296$, $p=0.7695$ in a two-tailed t-test). Both groups performed above chance (Outsiders $t= 30.268$, $p=2.294 \times 10^{-10}$ in a one-tailed t-test), Insiders ($t= 25.430$, $p=3.888 \times 10^{-16}$ in a one-tailed t-test).

Using a mixed effects logistic regression model, the Awareness Task questions were examined for correlation with performance on the Discrimination Task. This model takes into account independent variables selected by the researcher, in this case, the Awareness Task questions and subject age, as well as random effects of variation across subject and items in the task. A binomial link function was used in the model, allowing for data that are not normally distributed, such as the binary responses in the present task, to be used in the model.

As the Tables 5.7 and 5.8 show, only one correlation between Awareness Task items and performance on the Discrimination Task was found for either of these two groups. The Outsiders showed a positive correlation between ability to identify the local regional accent and discrimination between the accents. The Insiders showed no correlations between any Awareness Task items and discrimination ability.

### Discussion

In this task, both Outsiders and Insiders performed better than chance at discriminating between regional accents. The performance of both groups indicates that 5- and 6-year-old children can reliably discriminate between regional accents based solely on the acoustic differences between the accents.

Table 5.7 *Correlations with Awareness Task and Discrimination, Insiders*

|                     | Estimate | Std. error | Z value | Pr(>\|z\|) |
|---------------------|----------|------------|---------|------------|
| Map ID Local        | 0.13817  | 0.43340    | 0.319   | 0.750      |
| Map ID Other Region | 0.17877  | 0.53813    | 0.332   | 0.740      |
| Accent ID Local     | 0.37474  | 0.50739    | 0.739   | 0.460      |
| Accent ID Non-Local | –0.02486 | 0.43191    | –0.058  | 0.954      |
| Explanation         | –0.15770 | 0.50258    | –0.314  | 0.754      |
| Age                 | 0.05043  | 0.06801    | 0.742   | 0.458      |

Table 5.8 *Correlations with Awareness Task and Discrimination, Outsiders*

|                     | Estimate | Std. error | Z value | Pr(>\|z\|) |
|---------------------|----------|------------|---------|------------|
| Map ID Local        | 0.65919  | 0.53125    | 1.241   | 0.2147     |
| Map ID Other Region | 0.42077  | 0.48382    | 0.870   | 0.3845     |
| Accent ID Local     | 0.57306  | 0.27067    | 2.117   | 0.0342     |
| Accent ID Non-Local | –0.15593 | 0.43244    | –0.361  | 0.7184     |
| Explanation         | 0.07388  | 0.38086    | 0.194   | 0.8462     |
| Age                 | 0.06561  | 0.04274    | 1.535   | 0.1247     |

The average scores of the two groups were not significantly different, showing that exposure to regional variation does not enhance or degrade the ability to discriminate acoustically between regional accents for the participants in this study. This finding is in contrast to some earlier studies (Girard *et al.* 2008; Floccia *et al.* 2009; Wagner *et al.* 2013), which found that 5 year olds had difficulty discriminating between regional accents.

Subject age shows no correlations with discrimination ability. As in the Awareness Task, one possible explanation is that the range of subject ages is narrow. A second possibility is that this task was relatively easy, and as a result age does not affect performance, whereas in tasks using longer stimuli or more difficult paradigms, increased age provides an advantage.

The one correlation found in the analyses between the Awareness Task items and performance on the Discrimination Task was in the Outsiders group. Outsider children who correctly identified the local regional accent in the Awareness Task correlated with greater accuracy discriminating between regional accents.

Beck (2014) finds other participants in that study also show correlations between awareness and performance using the same discrimination task as described in the present chapter. For the African-American participant group, not included in the present analyses, but described in Beck (2014), the correlations between Awareness Task items and performance on the Discrimination Task depended on which accent was the matching accent in a given trial. Correctly identifying the local regional accent in the Awareness Task correlated positively with correctly answering Discrimination Task items in which the local speakers matched. For the Discrimination Task items in which the non-local speakers matched, there was a correlation with the Awareness Task Explanation item, which asked children to identify regional variation as the reason why the two sets of speakers sounded different. The analysis suggested that the correlations may represent strategies children used to find matching speakers, and that they used different strategies depending on which accent matched in each trial.

It is possible that the correlation between correctly identifying the local accent and correctly matching speakers also represents a strategy used by some Outsider participants to discriminate between the accents in this study. Outsiders who could identify the local accent may have used this heuristic to identify and match local speakers. Remember, however, from the Awareness Task that Outsiders performed poorly as a group at identifying the local regional accent. Thus, this correlation reflects only those few Outsiders who were aware that there was a local accent and could correctly identify it.

Interestingly, although proportionally more of the Insiders than Outsiders could correctly identify a local accent, there was no correlation between that knowledge and performance on the Discrimination Task for the Insider group. There were also no correlations between any other Awareness Task items for the Insiders, suggesting that they were not utilizing social knowledge as a heuristic for discriminating between the accents heard in the Discrimination Task.

### General Discussion

From the two tasks described here, the effect of exposure to a non-local regional variety in the home in early childhood becomes apparent. While exposure to multiple regional accents doesn't affect the ability to discriminate between two regional accents, it does affect children's awareness of regional accents between the ages of 5 and 6. Outsider children perform worse at identifying accents as local or non-local than their Insider peers, and being an Outsider negatively influences the ability to recognize regional accent as a kind of linguistic variation between speakers.

A possible explanation for the differences in awareness between these two groups is that Outsiders have not understood the association between accents and geography. Outsiders can hear the regional variation in their input, but don't understand that regional accent corresponds to the speaker's place of origin, given the distribution of regional accents in their input. Insiders, on the other hand, receive the bulk of their input in a single regional variety, shared by the majority of their community. The correspondence between a familiar accent and the hometown is more straightforward, and therefore more easily identifiable, for Insiders.

Possibly for this same reason, Insider children are also more likely than Outsiders to know that an unfamiliar regional accent is not from their hometown. Insiders' representation and understanding of the local regional accent may provide a reliable means of contrasting familiar and unfamiliar accents, allowing them to more readily identify unfamiliar accents as non-local.

Foulkes and Docherty (2006) make a prediction that regional variation may be one of the last kinds of speech variation identified by children, given that its source, the speaker's place of origin, is not as visually apparent as other social qualities, such as gender. They also predict that awareness of social variation improves with exposure to it, adding to children's difficulties with identifying it. The present study has shown that despite the lack of transparency, many 5 year olds have no trouble identifying regional variation in speech, or recognizing regional variation. Ironically, and in contradiction to Foulkes and Docherty's prediction, the children with the least amount of experience with contrasting regional varieties perform best at identifying it. The hypothesized opacity of the source of regional variation only holds for Outsiders, who must sort out the source of multiple varieties, indicating that exposure does not always entail awareness of a variety.

Munson's (2010) "library of speakers" hypothesis of sociolinguistic category formation could predict these findings. A category for a regional accent is founded on the association of the speech tokens from a familiar individual with the labels for social qualities, in this case place of origin, of that speaker. Outsiders may have labeled the speech of their parents as local. When asked to identify local speech, they access the categories labeled as local, only to find multiple, dissimilar kinds of speech. This creates a conflict when children are asked to identify other local speakers based on accent, as there is only a partial match. Insiders do not share this conflict and their library of speakers supports an identification of regional accents as local or non-local.

Presumably, as Outsiders learn about their parents' place of origin, they re-label their representations of the parents' speech, and they are able to identify regional varieties. However, this raises the question of whether representations of social categories develop independently from linguistic categories, and what role labels play in defining which categories develop. Based on the findings in the present chapter, it appears that at this stage of development there can be a disconnect between the development of social and linguistic categories under certain circumstances. Because no other social knowledge beyond labels for local and non-local speakers was addressed in this study, this remains a question for future investigations.

From the differences in awareness between the two groups, it is clear that input plays a role in forming categories for regional variation in speech. For 5 and 6 year olds in this particular context, less regional variation in the input helps to create a representation of the local accent, associated with the child's hometown. Exposure to multiple regional varieties obfuscates the link between geographical location and accent, which doesn't impede discrimination, but complicates identification of regional accents. This raises the question of how labels for linguistic varieties and social categories develop and influence linguistic representations across the course of development – a question for future studies.

## Conclusion

This comparison of 5- and 6-year-old children with different histories of exposure to regional variation shows that they can reliably discriminate between a familiar and an unfamiliar regional accent at this age, regardless of their linguistic background. However, their awareness of regional variation depends on their exposure to regional accents. Children who hear multiple regional accents at home and in their community have a harder time identifying the local variety. They also have more difficulty explaining that regional variation identifies speakers as being from different places. This is likely to be because their experience with regional varieties at home has not permitted them to associate accent with a speaker's place of origin. Despite this, they are able to discriminate between regional accents of their native language as well as children without exposure to multiple regional varieties. Children who hear predominately one regional accent in their input perform better at associating the local accent with their hometown, although this does not provide any advantage in discriminating between regional accents. The lack of effect of accent identification on discrimination suggests that the 5 year olds in this study were not heavily influenced by social knowledge in perception of regional accents, or at least in tasks that don't explicitly reference the connection between the two. More work is needed to better understand when and how social knowledge influences speech perception in children across different social contexts, and the relation between the formation of linguistic and social categories over the course of language acquisition.

REFERENCES

Beck, E. (2014). The role of socio-indexical information in regional accent perception by five to seven year old children. PhD dissertation. Department of Linguistics. Ann Arbor, MI: University of Michigan.

Butler, J., Floccia, C., Goslin, J., and Panneton, R. (2011). Infants' discrimination of familiar and unfamiliar accents in speech. *Infancy* 16(4):392–417.

Campbell-Kibbler, K. (2007). Accent, (ING), and the social logic of listener's perceptions. *American Speech* 82:34–64.

Clopper, C. (2010). Classification of regional language varieties, in D. Preston and N. Niedzielski (eds.), *A Reader in Sociophonetics*, pp. 203–21. New York: De Gruyter Mouton.

Clopper, C. and Pisoni, D. B. (2004). Homebodies and army brats: Some effects of early linguistic experience and residential history on dialect categorization. *Language Variation and Change* 16:31–48.

  (2007). Free classification of regional dialects of American English. *Journal of Phonetics* 35:421–38.

Clopper, C., Rohrbeck, K., and Wagner, L. (2012). Perception of dialect variation by young adults with High-Functioning Autism. *Journal of Autism and Developmental Disorders* 42:740–54.

Cremona, C. and Bates, E. (1977). The developmental attitudes towards dialect in Italian children. *Journal of Psycholinguistic Research* 6(3):223–32.

Cristia, A., Seidl, A., Vaughn, C., Schmale, R., Bradlow, A., and Floccia, C. (2012). Linguistic processing of accented speech across the lifespan. *Frontiers in Psychology* 3:479.

Egerova, N. (2010). Neural correlates of dialect perception in 5-month-old infants: A Near Infrared Spectroscopy study. Master's Degree dissertation. Linguistics. Groningen, the Netherlands: University of Groningen.

Floccia, C., Butler, J., Girard, F., and Goslin, J. (2009). Categorization of regional and foreign accent in 5- to 7-year old British children. *International Journal of Behavioral Development* 33(4):366–75.

Foulkes, P. and Docherty, G. (2006). The social life of phonetics and phonology. *Journal of Phonetics* 34:409–38.

Girard, F., Floccia, C., and Goslin, J. (2008). Perception and awareness of accents in young children. *British Journal of Developmental Psychology* 26:409–33.

Hay, J., Warren, P., and Drager, K. (2006). Factors influencing speech perception in the context of a merger-in-progress. *Journal of Phonetics* 34:458–84.

Johnson, K. (1997). Speech perception without speaker normalization, in K. Johnson and J. W. Mullennix (eds.), *Talker Variability in Speech Processing*, pp. 145-166. San Diego, CA: Academic Press.

  (2006). Resonance in an exemplar-based lexicon: The emergence of social identity and phonology. *Journal of Phonetics* 34:485–99.

Kinzler, K. and DeJesus, J. (2013). Northern=smart and Southern=nice; The development of accent attitudes in the United States. *Quarterly Journal of Experimental Psychology* 66(6):1146–58.

Kitamura, C., Panneton, R., Notley, A., and Best,C. (2006). Aussie-Aussie-Aussie, Oi-Oi-Oi: Infants love an Australian accent. Conference of the Journal of the Acoustical Society of America.

Labov, W. (1998). The three English dialects, in M. D. Linn (ed.), *Handbook of Dialects and Language Variation*, pp. 39–81. San Diego, CA: Academic Press.

Labov, W., Ash, S., and Boberg, C. (2006). *Atlas of North American English*. Berlin: Mouton de Gruyter.

Millar, S. (2003). Children and linguistic normativity, in D. Britain and J. Cheshire (eds.), *Social Dialectology: In Honor of Peter Trudgill*, pp. 287–97. Philadelphia, PA: John Benjamins.

Munson, B. (2010). Levels of phonological abstraction and knowledge of socially motivated speech-sound variation: A review, a proposal and a commentary on the papers by Clopper, Pierrehumbert, and Tamati; Drager, Foulkes; Mack; and Smith, Hall and Munson. *Laboratory Phonology* 1(1):157–77.

Nazzi, T., Jusczyk, P., and Johnson, E. K. (2000). Language discrimination by English-learning 5-month-olds: Effect of rhythm and familiarity. *Journal of Memory and Language* 43:1–19.

Niedzielski, N. (2010). Linguistic security, ideology and vowel perception, in D. Preston and N. Niedzielski (eds.), *A Reader in Sociophonetics*, pp. 253–64. Berlin: De Gruyter Mouton.

Payne, A. (1976). The acquisition of the phonological system of a second dialect. PhD dissertation. Philadelphia, PA: Department of Linguistics, University of Pennsylvania.

Phan, J. and Houston, D. (2008). Infant dialect discrimination. Research on Spoken Language Processing. No. 29, pp. 316–29. Bloomington, IN: Indiana University, Speech Research Laboratory.

Pierrehumbert, J. (2003). Phonetic diversity, statistical learning, acquisition of phonology. *Language and Speech* 46:115–54.

Preston, D. (1986). Five visions of America. *Language in Society* 15(2):221–40.

Roberts, J. (2005). Acquisition of sociolinguistic variation, in M. J. Ball (ed.), *Clinical Sociolinguistics*, Vol. 36, pp. 151–64. Malden, MA: Blackwell.

Rosenthal, M. (1974). The magic boxes: Pre-school children's attitudes toward Black and Standard English. *Florida FL Reporter* 12(1/2):55–62.

Schneider, E. (2008). *Varieties of English 2: The Americas and the Carribean*. Berlin: Walter de Gruyter.

Staum-Casasanto, L. (2009). What do listeners know about sociolinguistic variation? *University of Pennsylvania Working Papers in Linguistics* 15(2):40–9.

Wagner, L., Clopper, C., Pate, J. K. (2013). Children's perception of dialect variation. *Journal of Child Language* 41(5):1–23.

Wells, J. (1982). *Accents of English*. Cambridge University Press.

# 6     Towards a Cognitively Realistic Model of Meaningful Sociolinguistic Variation

*Kathryn Campbell-Kibler*

## Introduction

Linguistics has long been remarkable for its inclusion of cognitive-centered approaches which privilege the individual mind as a unit of analysis, interactional approaches that focus on the complex structures emergent in multi-person social settings, and community-based approaches that study patterns across large networks of interactions. All three approaches are crucial to full understanding, as they examine the same phenomena at different scales. In particular, advances in the one can make evident limitations in the others. Most recently, interaction- and community-focused work in the "third wave" of variation research (Eckert 2012) has documented the complexity in speakers' social engagement with language variation and in so doing has strained our existing models of sociolinguistic cognition to the breaking point. I suggest in this chapter that we need to rebuild these models in light of this third-wave evidence, in addition to work in sociophonetics and sociolinguistic cognition and related advances in language processing and social cognition.

Sociolinguistic cognition refers to the processes through which language and social structures encounter one another within the mind, not necessarily specific structures dedicated solely to sociolinguistic cognition. When it comes to cognitive theorizing, the field of sociolinguistic variation has relied overwhelmingly, implicitly or explicitly, on the model developed by Labov (1966, 1972). In these early works, the language system is distinguished from a socially oriented system (usually positioned simply as speakers themselves), which expresses and acts on social preferences for language. This model has been further developed in the form of the *sociolinguistic monitor* or SLM (Labov 1993; Labov *et al.* 2011), a deliberative module, positioned "downstream" from a grammar unit, which makes and acts on judgments regarding the social prestige of possible utterances, as well as socially judging utterances of other speakers.

In this chapter I discuss the current state of cognitive modeling in sociolinguistics and propose a new approach. In the second section, I describe the primary current model(s) of sociolinguistic cognition. The third section summarizes the sociolinguistic behavior which a model must capture. The fourth section presents findings from sociophonetics that can inform our theorizing. A summary of relevant models from language processing and social cognition is provided in the fifth section. The final section presents thoughts on a new direction for modeling building, focusing on three independently motivated constructs: a grammar with associational links to non-linguistic concepts, a person perception system, and a behavioral monitoring system.

## Existing Models

Early sociolinguistic variation research focused on the community level, deliberately challenging the primacy of the individual speaker privileged by the Chomskyan approach. But while a community-level analysis is extremely valuable, it must integrate with a model of cognition at the individual level, which provides explanations of what speakers are able to do with their language and under what circumstances. All sociolinguistic work draws on some understanding of the cognitive abilities of speakers. Much of this theorizing has been done implicitly, as researchers discuss in general terms how "aware" or "conscious" speakers are of this or that form without defining precisely what is intended by these terms, while some has been explicit. Little of it, however, has taken advantage of the advances in related fields (cognitive psychology, social cognition) which have investigated and problematized ideas like awareness and consciousness.

In the current discussion, I will focus on the challenge of modeling the cognitive processes which link features of language to other aspects of social understanding. This is to limit the scope of the chapter, not to dismiss the considerable theoretical challenge of modeling the rest of the processes through which language is produced and perceived. Variationists have much to contribute to that project and have done so repeatedly, most often taking theoretical tools from other areas of linguistics and testing their ability to treat variable data (e.g. Guy 1991). For the current work, it is the interface between those linguistic systems and the social cognition that is at issue, or in more familiar sociolinguistic terms, the cognitive modeling of the social signifi-cance, social meaning, and/or indexical meaning of language forms.

Labov (1966, 1972) posits shared community-wide evaluative norms, according to which speakers recognize prestige forms. The apparent ease with which speakers perform this evaluation "correctly" (i.e. in agreement with others in New York City) is contrasted with the difficulty they often show in recognizing and consciously manipulating their own linguistic productions. This difficulty leads to one of the key theoretical constructs of variation, that of *attention paid to speech*. In this model, language production directly from the grammar is relatively effortless, but for social reasons speakers, particularly stigmatized speakers (such as working class New Yorkers), may wish to diverge from the speech their grammar produces, via effortful language management. Labov (1966) documents multiple cases of speakers who appear unaware of their own speech patterns, typically reporting that they use the prestige norms more often than their interview data would suggest. This contrast between speakers' inability to report which forms they use even while manipulating those forms in predictable ways is an important point for any models of sociolinguistic cognition. As such, it provides a key rationale for positioning socially useful language manipulation as effortful and resource-heavy.

The sociolinguistic interview as a data-collecting tool is structured around the manipulation of attention paid to speech, intended to lure it out with standard language tasks like reading aloud on the one hand, or distract the conscious mind from monitoring with exciting speech content ("danger of death" stories) on the other. The malleability of a given variable to such tricks reveals useful information about whether and how speakers have positioned it on the prestige scale. Labov found that variables may show differential use across speech tasks even absent explicit speaker commentary about them, and suggested a three-way division of variables on this basis (Labov 1972). *Indicators* are variables which exhibit socioeconomic patterning across speakers, but no task-based shifting, suggesting that speakers' monitors do not register them as standard/non-standard. In contrast, *markers* do show such shifting; they are listed, as it were, in the monitors. Finally, *stereotypes* are variables which show both types of production patterns and additionally are culturally named and discussed (e.g. "dropping one's g's" or "dis and dat"). This tripartite division implies that the assessment and social control systems have access to some but not all linguistic objects, including some which are not available to introspection and explicit verbal description.

This idea of the grammar (producing the vernacular) on the one hand and a language-external process of monitoring on the other is further developed in Labov (1993), which introduces the sociolinguistic monitor, based on "the unobservability of linguistic structure." This phrase refers to the observation that social evaluations are typically prompted by the frequencies of specific language forms, particularly words or pronunciations of words, rather than more complex relationships between multiple elements in a grammar, such as phonological merger or splits. Labov proposes that the cognitive capacity for socially evaluating and controlling language features is restricted, either entirely or primarily, to "surface" language forms like words and sounds, while being unable to observe "deeper" aspects of language like phonological categories or syntactic structures. These limitations necessitate positioning the monitor outside the grammar.

The sociolinguistic monitor is responsible for the social evaluation of speech generally, a function which includes forming social understandings of other people based on their own speech, developing a self-reflective (often inaccurate) image of one's own speech patterns and controlling (often unsuccessfully) speech production to maximize its social appropriateness.

The SLM has received increased attention recently, beginning with the work of Labov *et al.* (2011), who examined listener responses to varying frequencies of (ING). The conceptualization of the monitor as sensitive to frequencies rather than individual tokens raises questions as to how this frequency assessment is managed, and Labov *et al.* (2011) identified three areas of interest: the length of time over which it can accumulate; the size of frequency differences to which it is able to attend; and its response pattern. They found that the impact of speech cues accumulates over a window at least a minute long and that the effect of subsequent tokens is attenuated in the face of preceding marked tokens. Wagner (2013) reports a similar curvilinear response, but Levon and Fox (2014) failed to replicate the effect with British listeners, and suggest differences in the social meaning of the variables in the two contexts as an explanation. Given the mixed results and the limited variables investigated, caution is warranted in concluding that the curvilinear response is a fundamental of perception. Nonetheless, the pattern is intriguing.

The monitor as a construct is part of a larger theory of sociolinguistic language patterns. The concept of the vernacular (Labov 1972) refers to speech produced exclusively by the grammar, with little to no interference by the monitor. Guy and Cutler (2011) expand on this claim, suggesting that the work of the monitor in helping to produce an "inauthentic" sociolinguistic self (styles based on the monitor rather than the grammar) will show distortions in the linguistic constraints of a variable.

In addition, the distinction between change from below and change from above (Labov 1966) is based on the theory that the sociolinguistic monitor operates within a relatively high level of awareness, such that it is only able to judge or alter certain speech patterns. Based on the assumption that speakers typically want to sound more prestigious rather than less prestigious, it was hypothesized that only prestigious forms ("from above" in the socioeconomic sense) could survive as incoming changes in situations where speakers knew about them ("from above" in the awareness sense). Changes from below in the former sense would be nipped in the bud by speakers' sociolinguistic monitors if they were not also from below in the latter sense, that is, invisible to the monitor.

In the time since the model was first introduced, however, critiques have emerged, forcing the reconceptualization of a number of its predictions. One such critique challenges the model's focus on the single dimension of prestige. As early as Trudgill (1974), variationists observed male speakers apparently orienting to working-class forms, in a move that was termed "covert prestige," but was not fully integrated into the model. More tellingly, Rickford (1986) pointed out the essentially consensual model of social class underlying the Labovian approach, and contrasted it with the explicitly Marxist understanding of class shown by many of the speakers in his own data from Guyana. Further complexity was introduced by Eckert (2000) and others, showing that patterned linguistic variation may be observed in response to many social attributes that are not about socioeconomic status, or not only about socio-economic status. Linguistic variation has been linked to high school social groups (Drager 2009; Eckert 2000; Moore 2011), gang affiliation and degree of engagement (Mendoza-Denton 2008), sexual orientation (Podesva 2011), and many other social structures.

This theoretical development goes beyond simply expanding the number of social constructs the monitor is concerned with, however. Third-wave variation work has drawn from linguistic and cultural anthropology to explore the semiotic relationships linking variable language forms to other constructs. While all three of Peirce's (1901) sign types are relevant for understanding the social construction of variation, the field has centrally concerned itself with indexical links (Silverstein 1976; Ochs 1992; Silverstein 2003). Speakers and listeners learn these links through observations of co-occurrence and meta-discourse, which position particular forms tied to particular meanings. These connections are made to seem natural and self-evident through their repetition and their embedding in culturally normative systems of understanding. Having learned these connections, speakers can employ the forms to try to invoke their associated social constructs, either to appropriately align with existing features of a situation or to alter a situation (Silverstein 1976). This work is a crucial tool in the construction of social structures both large and small. Linguistic features, in this view, are resources for social activity, similar to other social objects like wearable fashion, consumption practices, bodily hexis, etc. (Hebdige 1979; Bourdieu 1982; Coupland 2007).

Speakers' ability to construct any given personal style, stance, or situational feature is constrained primarily by two factors: their sociolinguistic facility with the semiotic systems in question; and the willingness of their interlocutors (at any cognitive level) to interpret the performance in the ways intended. The former includes the ability to produce the appropriate forms in the right linguistic contexts, but also to perceive existing social features of the context and produce combinations of cues that are socially coherent for the audience. This ability may be influenced by the amount and type of exposure a speaker has had to the forms in question, but also by their motivation and perhaps general variation in linguistic flexibility. Audience acceptance of intended meanings will presumably be influenced by the sociolinguistic performance itself, but by other characteristics of the speaker including demographic categories, as well as the social goals of the audience (Campbell-Kibler 2008).

In this approach, the complexity of the speaker/hearer's social abilities and responsibilities increases substantially. The meanings that they may express and understand through language variation are multidimensional and subject to constant change. To take just a single example, Zhang (2005) documents a set of variables used by young professionals in Beijing. Both the variables and the professionals can be loosely categorized within an overarching framework: the variables are generally either local, part of a Beijing-specific accent, or part of standard Mandarin and therefore placeless. The speakers Zhang interviewed were employed by either state-run businesses or multi-national corporations. These broad categories were linked, with state employees more likely to use local features. But within these broad categories, Zhang documented tremendous nuance, specific to the career trajectories of speakers and the social and characterological history of the variables. Beijing professionals developing sociolinguistic selves must not only consider whether they want to identify as a local or as a cultured and cosmopolitan international citizen. In the context of only a single variable, they must also consider their own relationship, in a given conversation, to the characterological figure of the "alley saunterer" – a shady, "in the know" man who frequents alleys and is involved in local black markets and other illegal activities and both his strengths (local knowledge, interpersonal networks) and his weaknesses (fecklessness, shady moral character).

These patterns of behavior documented in the third-wave tradition are difficult to account for the Labovian cognitive model. First, the sociolinguistic system is tasked not only with monitoring the prestige or standardness of language, but of any social meaning, the import of which can only be understood in a complex larger context filled with interactants, goals, and ideologies. The social complexity of both speaking and listening increases enormously in this framework, such that the task of tracking both the social meaning of both incoming and outgoing language with a conscious, effortful system becomes intractable. To incorporate the insights of the third wave, our cognitive model needs updating.

### What Are We Modeling?

The previous section made clear that the current state of cognitive modeling in sociolinguistics, while capturing some crucial insights, is inadequate to the task of modeling our current understanding of sociolinguistic behavior. This section will sketch some of the abilities and phenomena that a model of sociolinguistic cognition needs to account for. The sociolinguistic abilities of individuals are complex and embedded in larger, even more complex systems, but may roughly be categorized into three main types: the production of sociolinguistically meaningful forms; the comprehension (linguistic and social) of such forms; and metapragmatic behaviors which create, negotiate, and reaffirm meaning-form links. Note that in practice comprehension can only be observed through metalinguistic acts or further production, but given the disciplinary, theoretical, and methodological differences in the approaches to "perception" on the one hand and "ideologies" on the other, they are divided here for ease of explication.

As noted in the section above, the field of sociolinguistic variation has shown over the years that speakers are capable not only of producing language with coherent referential meaning, but of adapting their non-referential choices to contexts and goals. Silverstein (1976) complicates our modeling task by observing that only some of such uses may be described as *presupposing* indexical uses, in which the language forms produced share indexical links to entities (people, topics, situational dynamics) already independently present in the discourse. Many others represent *creative* uses, in which the use of the form itself introduces an entirely or partially new entity, as, for example, the first use of the French form *tu* between new acquaintances creates a bid for intimate status which may be responded to in various ways. Thus, sociolinguistic production firmly includes behavior that we might characterize as volitional, such as initiating an informal or intimate relationship with an acquaintance. Further, such volitional or agentive behavior at least some of the time involves the adjustment of forms upon which speakers are unable to comment explicitly in any detail (e.g. Labov 1963).

While there is a connection between consciously articulable goals and sociolinguistic behavior, they are not always in synchrony. Despite the evidence that speakers are able to manipulate their linguistic forms in ways that support their social goals and beliefs as they would verbally articulate them, the evidence also points to limitations on these abilities. Speech errors and self-corrections do occur (see Kitzinger 2013 for an overview), including those which revolve around indexical rather than referential meanings. Speakers require a certain level of exposure to skillfully produce language forms and the necessary level appears to vary based on, among other factors, the linguistic level of the forms. New lexical items or new uses for existing items may only require a single instance to adopt, while certain complex phonological systems may require sustained exposure, perhaps only during childhood, for speakers to produce identically to others (Payne 1980). Our model must allow speakers to learn new forms and new links between forms and social constructs, but should not predict instantaneous learning or perfect performance.

In addition to creating sociolinguistic performances, individuals are able to incorporate the speech of others into their mental understanding of the situation. Listeners are able not only to extract linguistic meaning from utterances, but to recover indexical links between the forms used by speakers and social structures, both presupposing and creative. More specifically, speakers are able to associate language forms with qualities of the speaker (Lambert *et al.* 1960), the topic (Cargile and Giles 1998), stances towards interlocutors (Ball *et al.* 1984) and others. Note, however, that the meanings recovered by listeners may not always be precisely (or even generally) those imagined by the speaker delivering the message.

When forming these social perceptions, listeners are able to take into account pre-existing information (from prior linguistic cues or other sources of information) and use them to guide perception. The contribution of language cues to the ultimate percept may differ based on the other linguistic cues available, such as regional accent (Campbell-Kibler 2007), extra-linguistic information like profession (Campbell-Kibler 2010), situational constraints such as speech task (Cargile 1997), or message content (Cargile and Giles 1998). More complex factors of stylistic structure have also been documented. Pharao *et al.* (2014) found that fronted /s/ tokens which prompt listeners to hear white Danish boys as gay-sounding become irrelevant to sexual orientation when placed in the speech of speakers of Danish "street style" associated with descendants of Turkish and other immigrants. Further, evaluations need not depend only on one speaker's performance, but can be developed in response to a speaker's positioning in relation to another, for example judging a job applicant's choice to maintain a "broad" accent differently when they are interviewed by a speaker with a "broad" vs. a "refined" accent (Ball *et al.* 1984).

Like production, listener perceptions show impressive skills, but also limitations which offer potential insight into their workings. Evaluator mood is a well-known influence on evaluations (Forgas and Moylan 1988) and evaluations of people are no exception (Forgas and Bower 1987). More intriguingly, some evidence suggests that different linguistic performances may be differently susceptible to mood effects: Campbell-Kibler (2011) found that speakers using the *-ing* form of (ING) were exempted from a mood effect of ratings of intelligence which impacted other recordings.

Although perception can occur on its own, without observable behavioral consequences, such episodes are difficult to study, meaning that all research on perception is also research on metalinguistic characterization, the last category of sociolinguistic behavior to be accounted for (Jakobson 1960; Silverstein 1976). Such characterization can take place in a wide range of ways, including explicit description, assessment of speakers, deployment of variation in response, and others. Agha (2007: 16) introduces the notion of *reflexive activity*, the "activities in which communicative signs are used to typify other perceivable signs." Through these activities, *reflexive models* are produced, transmitted, and altered, and through these models speakers and listeners make social sense of their own and others' linguistic (and other) behavior. Such activity is as much a part of sociolinguistic behavior as the utterance of sociolinguistically variable forms itself.

Sociolinguistic beliefs are embedded throughout the explicit and introspectively accessible belief systems speakers hold about their worlds and the people in them, but we do not yet know how integrated these beliefs are with the systems responsible for production and perception. Labov (1993) notes the "reflexive stigma principle" that people who use stigmatized forms are often those most inclined to criticize them. While it is not clear that this is a general principle, we do see repeated evidence that production and perception behavior often do not align with stated ideologies. Kristiansen (2009) discusses the disconnects between Danish youths' beliefs about regional varieties when explicitly asked as opposed to their social responses to actual speakers of those varieties. Most notably, regional varieties, declared the most preferred in explicit surveys, lead speakers to be ranked as least intelligent and least socially desirable. Observations like these have led to the divide between overt and covert attitudes.

Already our summary of the sociolinguistic phenomena to be captured has become multi-layered, as we observe that specific language forms and indexical links that appear to influence some types of behavior (e.g. speech choices in different speech tasks) may be invisible in other types of behavior (e.g. explicit metapragmatic discussion of forms). These fractures and disconnects provide valuable starting points for our models, because they point to joints in the systems which manage these behaviors. The next section tackles such disconnects more explicitly, by examining the small body of work which experimentally probes sociolinguistic cognitive processes.

### Where Systems Collide

One of the foundational challenges in linguistics is the question of how listeners are able to understand speech as well as they do, given the incredible amount of variability it contains. For some time, phoneticians hypothesized that the comprehension system filtered out and discarded this variability, but more recently it has become clear that much information about variable productions is retained and able to influence future perception and production processes (Goldinger 1998). Moreover, listeners appear to be able to map specific kinds of variability to external influences and adjust their learning patterns accordingly, discounting situationally triggered interference, while generalizing apparently speaker-specific cues (Kraljic et al. 2008).

Part of this tradition has explored not only idiosyncratic differences between speakers, but also structured differences linked to known social categories. This work has shown that connections between language forms and other social constructs can be accessed and maintained cognitively through processes which are not easily accessible to introspection. For example, Niedzielski (1999) showed that invoking a national or regional variety label can shift the phonetic character listeners report hearing in speech immediately after hearing it. But Hay and Drager (2010) have shown that this association need not be explicit, occurring in response to seemingly incidental exposure to stuffed toys symbolic of the varieties (in this case, New Zealand and Australia). Further, the effect appears to depend on the speakers' attitudes towards the variety invoked, seen even more clearly in a production-based follow-up study (Drager *et al.* 2010).

Relatedly, Strand (1999) demonstrated that listeners take not only the sex of the speaker (based on a photo) into account when judging the boundary between /s/ and /ʃ/, but the gender typicality, such that men's and women's faces rated by independent judges as highly masculine and feminine respectively provoked a stronger difference in /s/-/ʃ/ category boundary than did faces rated as less masculine and feminine. This suggests that the classification of phonemes may be influenced by nuanced social factors. Staum Casasanto (2008) has likewise shown that the perceived race of a face presented as the speaker influences how likely listeners are to hear a string like [mæs] as the word *mass* versus a reduced form of *mast*. The identification of vowel quality and the categorization of closely related consonants are central linguistic processes, typically seen as rapid and outside of conscious awareness. Even if the effects are triggered by conscious reflection on the nationality, gender, and/or race involved, the ability of such reflection to influence rapid, frequent, and early processes as phonological categorization requires a model of linguistic processing which integrates social information at more levels than the sociolinguistic monitor allows.

The rapid nature of sociolinguistic integration is further supported by Van Berkum *et al.* (2008), who document that the social category of a voice (young vs. old or posh vs. less posh) can influence the patterns of ERP response (Event Related Potential) associated with semantically surprising information. Brain responses within 200 to 300 milliseconds register the difference between an adult's voice saying "I have a glass of wine with dinner" (unsurprising) and a child's voice saying the same thing (surprising). For these effects to appear, our social expectations about who is speaking and thus what practices they are likely to engage in must be used quite early in the language processing stream.

Another aspect of language processing which appears to be both functional outside of introspective awareness and susceptible to social influence is that of alignment or accommodation. Accommodation has long been studied as an interactional strategy through which speakers appeal to or distance themselves from their interlocutors by manipulating their linguistic similarity (Giles and Powesland 1975). More recently, alignment has been investigated as an automatic response to linguistic input (Bock 1986; Pickering and Garrod 2004). This tradition has demonstrated that these effects emerge even in contexts where it is difficult to attribute a conscious interactional strategy to the behavior, typically because the social setting is highly impoverished (e.g. repeating words after a pre-recorded voice, as in Goldinger 1998).

Despite the apparent lack of introspective motivation or control in such research (a pre-recorded voice is not able to appreciate accommodation towards it), evidence has emerged for a social dimension to such effects. Babel (2010) has shown that New Zealanders' degree of vocalic accommodation while shadowing an Australian speaker correlated with their implicit attitudes towards Australians, although was unaffected by the (somewhat heavy-handed) manipulation of liking towards the specific speaker shadowed. Along similar lines, Yu *et al.* (2013) found that explicit liking ratings of a speaker predicted degree of convergence towards the exaggerated VOTs in his narrative. They also found an effect of their likability manipulation, but in the unexpected direction, with the less likable guise prompting greater convergence. Given the startling nature of their manipulation (the unlikable guise involved the speaker describing a blind date insultingly), it may be that memorability or attention is another key factor in accommodation patterns.

A few studies have reported similar effects for syntactic structures. Balcetis and Dale (2005) show that participants were more likely to re-use syntactic structures used by a confederate when that confederate behaved in friendly and pro-social ways as opposed to rude ways. They also found increased convergence for annoyed versus patient confederates, possibly as an interactional repairs strategy or due to the memorability or attention factor discussed for Yu *et al.* (2013). Weatherholtz *et al.* (2014) similarly found effects of social judgments on syntactic priming, this time in a less interactive task. After listening to a politically charged diatribe in one of three accents, listeners were asked to describe line drawings in an apparently unrelated task. They were more likely to adopt the dative construction (DO, *Give me the book* vs. PO, *Give the book to me*) when they rated the speaker as more standard and when they were personally inclined towards compromise in conflict situations. Two effects reflected different priming effects for the two forms (DO vs. PO): the perceived similarity between the speaker and the participant; and the perceived intelligence of the speaker. These latter interactions suggest that such priming is influenced not only by social factors solely, but by a complex interaction between social assessments and expectations, which are driven in part by previous experience of frequencies (see Jaeger and Snider 2013).

All of this work taken together shows that our cognitive models of language and social processing must allow for these systems to be integrated in a parallel manner, rather than the original model of an independent grammar which only feeds into the social system after having performed its function. What it does not do yet, however, is to tell us exactly how and where these systems are integrated and through what mechanisms. We can, however, identify some hypotheses. First, at least some of this processing is functioning in systems not dependent on introspectively available reasoning, given that they occur even when such reasoning would dismiss it as unnecessary or even counter-productive, as, for example, in Hay and Drager (2010), when incidental exposure to the concept of a variety impacted processing of a different variety. Next, expectations seem to play a key role, such that social and other types of non-linguistic reasoning may set expectations of behavior (including linguistic choices) that are used in the online processing or management of incoming stimuli.

These hypotheses leave many open questions about the nature of integration between the social and linguistic systems. Prior to tackling them directly, it seems wise to turn to the existing literatures on consciousness, memory research, social cognition, and language processing. Given the breadth of all of these domains, I will not present a thorough overview of any, but will rather focus on the elements of each most likely to be relevant for the modeling task as outlined above.

### Sociolinguistic Cognition Is a Kind of Cognition

In order to formulate a plausible model of sociolinguistic cognition, it is necessary to understand as fully as possible the larger cognitive systems within which it operates. This is a task easier said than done, given that the larger study of human cognition is a work very much in progress. Nonetheless, some progress has been made which may shed light on sociolinguistic cognition. This discussion will focus on four areas: consciousness, memory, social cognition, and language processing.

Linguists have long struggled with the idea of conscious awareness and its role in sociolinguistic processing, with some theorists dismissing the possibility of socially motivated language processing outright, based on an assumption that social reasoning is necessarily conscious. Labov documented the complex social associations of the centralization of /ay/ and /aw/ in Martha's Vineyard, then stated: "It has been noted that centralized diphthongs are not salient in the consciousness of Vineyard speakers. They can hardly therefore be the direct objects of social affect" (Labov 1972: 40). This assumption remains active in the field; Brulard and Carr (2013: 151) argue that their evidence of variable accommodation of Scottish Standard English speakers to RP could not be mediated by attitudinal factors regarding national identity, based on their belief that "sense of national or regional identity is necessarily *conscious*, and that unconscious accent accommodation falls below the level of conscious sense of identity" (emphasis in original).

While this idea seems to be common among linguists, it is not well supported by cognition research. Cognitive psychology has shown the wide range of processes which are carried out without effort, deliberation, or introspective awareness (Evans 2008), including many social cognitive

processes (Hassin *et al.* 2005). Indeed, the question of the role of consciousness as any kind of causal factor at all in human behavior is a topic of some
debate, with many researchers portraying consciousness as purely epiphenom-
enal (for a discussion, see Baumeister *et al.* 2011). In social cognition specifically, evidence has been offered for automatic elements of person perception
(Ferguson 2008; Macrae and Martin 2007), stereotype application (Galinsky
and Moskowitz 2007; Park *et al.* 2008), and social goal pursuit (Bargh *et al.*
2008; Ferguson 2008), among many others.

Dual-systems models of cognitive psychology and social cognition (for a
summary, see Evans 2008) have theorized that cognition consists of at least
two systems or types of systems, one of which is (variably across specific
models) relatively slow, available to introspection, and/or under conscious
control, while the other is fast, operates outside of awareness, and/or cannot
be prevented or can only be prevented with effort (e.g. Smith and DeCoster
2000). As Evans (2008) explains, while the evidence supporting dual systems
models is strong, a coherent single model has not yet emerged, due in part to
the many dimensions along which the system can be divided. The available
evidence suggests that the dichotomies typically invoked as signifying conscious or unconscious processes do not align consistently with each other
across specific phenomena, making the construction of an overarching dual
systems model challenging. Several researchers have proposed a move away
from dual systems models towards more complex multiple interlocking
systems without a clear automatic/controlled or conscious/unconscious divide
(e.g. Van Bavel *et al.* 2012). Despite these continued debates, what is clear and
widely understood is that many important processes, including social processes, at least occasionally occur quickly, without introspective awareness
and/or in ways apparently at odds with verbally reported or experimentally
manipulated intentions.

In addition to the complexity of consciousness versus awareness, there is
another crucial feature of the psychology literature which sociolinguists typically neglect and that is the apparent multiplicity of systems. At base, sociolinguistic systems, like many human cognitive processes, are memory systems:
speakers are exposed to forms and social constructs in particular combinations,
and they alter their future behavior on the basis of information, habits, etc.
retained from these past experiences. Debates within variation tend to assume a
single cognitive locus for such learning, but research on memory has increasingly indicated the existence of multiple overlapping and, at times, competing
memory systems, each with its own strengths, weaknesses, and ideal time
depth (for an overview, see Squire 2004). The famous case of H.M. demonstrated that the total loss of the ability to form new episodic memories (due to
surgery to treat epilepsy) left H.M. with several other types of memory
retained, including the ability to learn new physical skills and some perceptual

learning (Milner *et al.* 1968). Experiments with similar patients have shown that social learning abilities may also be retained in such cases, including developing an aversion to specific individuals in response to problematic behavior such as being stuck with a pin when shaking hands (Draaisma 2000: 198). In developing our models of sociolinguistic cognition, it may be instructive to turn to research on memory, particularly on language and memory, to better understand what systems might be contributing to the phenomena we study.

The cognitive phenomena most directly of interest to sociolinguistics are language processing and social cognition, with the latter much more poorly represented in our field. The study of social cognition is vast, with many different abilities and behaviors constituting independent subfields of research. One such subfield crucial for sociolinguistics is person perception, the processes by which individuals organize information about other people into models of that person's qualities and likely future behavior. The idea that learning about people differs substantially from learning other kinds of information dates back to Asch (1946), who observed that the order in which personality traits were presented had a striking effect on the resulting impression of the individual described. Evidence has repeatedly shown that information understood as about a person is better retained and structured differently from the same information presented as unrelated items in a list (Chartrand and Bargh 1996). Evidence of this sort has led social cognition researchers to posit an independent system for person perception, in which an individual's behavior spontaneously gives rise to inferred personality traits (Brown and Bassili 2002; Uleman *et al.* 1996) which may likewise be influenced by co-presented visual cues (Carlston and Mae 2007). How direct observations of faces and voices are integrated in learning and recognition is a related area of concern likely to be of interest to sociolinguists (Campanella and Belin 2007; Kamachi *et al.* 2003; Stevenage *et al.* 2012).

Part of the process of perceiving a person is identifying the social groups to which they belong and applying, failing to apply, or choosing not to apply the expectations and stereotypes associated with those groups to that individual (Jussim *et al.* 1996; Operario and Fiske 2004). Because of the real world effects of these processes, they have received a great deal of study in social psychology. In particular, researchers have found that a common pattern, among US college participants, is for the egalitarian nature of explicitly endorsed beliefs to be at odds with more implicit attitudes and associations (e.g. Evans 2008: 257). These conflicting forces, which can be pitted against each other experimentally (Govorun and Payne 2006; Payne and Stewart 2007), have lent support to the argument that person perception is carried out by at least two different processes, which at times prompt individuals towards divergent behaviors.

Note that the mere existence of opposing forces does not necessarily drive us to multiple systems. Even within explicit, verbally articulated domains, contradictory beliefs are commonplace. Rather, we see support for different systems in the difference in speed between the two types of responses and in their relationship. The classification of people into groups and the resultant reactions appear, at least in the case of face perception, to be very rapidly deployed. White and Black participants show differential Event Related Potential (ERP) patterning for racial in-group versus out-group faces (Ito and Bartholow 2009). This rapid reaction is still susceptible to contextual cues, however. In an approach/avoidance task in which participants are told to manipulate a joystick towards or away from themselves in response to a given category of stimulus, the task instructions create a local context (equating, for example, a Black face with "approach" for a White participant) which attenuates this neural reaction (Cunningham *et al.* 2012).

This seemingly more automatic system also appears to be associative rather than propositional in nature (Gawronski and Bodenhausen 2011), in that social constructs have been shown to prime each other (Bargh 2006) in ways that do not always enhance performance from a rational perspective. One well-documented version of this priming is known as the weapons task, in which participants are exposed to a Black or White man's face for a brief period of time, then shown a picture of a gun or a non-weapon tool such as a wrench. Participants are asked to identify the second object as a tool or a gun and either are or are not given time constraints. Immediately preceding exposure to a Black face increases errors of mistaking a tool for a gun, particularly under time pressures (Park *et al.* 2008; Payne 2001, 2005). This suggests influence from a rapid system which is susceptible to racist stereotypes linking Black men to notions of violence. This association influences participant responses despite the irrelevance of the face to the task in the experimental context.

Competing with associative, rapidly deployed perception are slower systems based on propositional reasoning, which are more able to take into account details of behavior and form a tailored understanding of an individual (Fiske and Neuberg 1990; Showers and Cantor 1985). Unlike the rapid association of concepts, which proceeds quickly and relatively effortlessly, rational consideration of individual information is mediated by the mental resources available and the motivation to think carefully about the perceptual target. For example, people's assessment of a target's behavior is more sophisticated when they believe they will be interacting with the target in the future than when the task is merely intellectual (Devine *et al.* 1989). Motivation may not only influence the rigor of the perception process, but also its direction, even to the extent of altering more general beliefs to support a socially desired assessment of an individual (Klein and Kunda 1992).

Another vast literature is that on self-regulation, through which individuals monitor their behavior and alter it as needed to pursue goals (Wagner and Heatherton 2015). Most commonly studied in the context of health-related behavioral choices like smoking and food choice, self-regulation is typically understood as a limited resource which can be depleted through use (Baumeister and Heatherton 1996). As part of the executive control system more generally (Diamond 2013), self-regulation abilities can also be worn down through other ego-depleting activities or experiences such as the Stroop task (von Hippel and Gonsalkorale 2005). Self-regulation applies to a wide range of behavior types, from blocking stereotypical assumptions to refraining from eating unhealthy foods, and, presumably, substituting socially useful language forms for less useful, but perhaps situationally triggered, forms. Little work has connected this social psychological understanding of regulation to sociolinguistic models.

One necessary precursor to managing behavior is reasoning about one's own beliefs and goals. Reasoning is similar to other mental processes in having been posited to include both automatic or associative elements and deliberative or propositional elements, although it is worth noting that these two dichotomies need not be aligned with one another. The existence of both associative and propositional systems may be seen informally in the joke question "What do cows drink?" which, particularly after other forms of priming, often prompts an initial impulse of "Milk," then followed by the accurate response of "Water." In addition to competing with each other, these systems presumably also interact with and influence one another. In order to be represented in either system, however, language forms and social constructs must be represented in the cognitive system, a mental learning process analogous to Agha's cultural-level idea of registers. These concepts, for example, *polite*, *Southern accent*, or *refined speech*, exist within a much larger structured field of concepts which constitute the set of declarative knowledge available to a given individual (see Squire 2004 for a cognitive, Deacon 2003 for a semiotic discussion).

Finally, our models must have an adequate understanding of expectation (Van Berkum 2010). Variationists have something of a love/hate relationship with the notion of salience, which repeatedly emerges as an important construct in our research, while being notoriously difficult to pin down (for a singularly cogent treatment, see Auer *et al.* 1998). One potentially useful path in tackling ideas of what is or is not salient in a given context is to engage with broader cognitive notions of expectation (see also Ráckz 2013). Expectation and surprisal have emerged as central concepts in psycholinguistics, for example in that patterns of syntactic priming may be influenced by the degree of prediction error they trigger in a comprehender (Jaeger and Snider 2013). In non-linguistic processing as well, the mind seems strongly inclined to develop expectations about upcoming events and actions, prompting increases in alertness when these expectations are violated (Bar 2007); in the words of Van Berkum (2010) "the brain is a prediction machine that cares about good and bad."

Newer models of cognition have placed increasing focus on prediction as a fundamental process, incorporated into processes from language to vision to physical movement. Most notably, Pickering and Garrod (2013) propose a model of language processing which integrates language production and perception into an interwoven single system. In this model, speaker/hearers are not only producing their own utterances and comprehending those of others, but constantly maintaining impoverished (and therefore rapid) predictive models of both their own speech and that of others. These *forward models* are continually checked against perceptions, providing an alert system for the correction of errors in one's own speech or unexpected behavior on the part of others.

This section has provided an unfortunately brief overview of some recent insights on the diversity of cognitive systems, focusing on those most likely to be relevant to sociolinguistic cognition. Space constrains our ability to explore all of the relevant cognitive systems likely to contribute to sociolinguistic processing. In addition to those already discussed, it is likely that language variation is influenced by systems of affect or emotion, which appear to be distinct from, for example, those related to stereotypical beliefs about other groups (Amodio and Devine 2006). In the next section, I will take some of these insights as a starting point for reconceptualizing our own models, with an emphasis on the ways in which concepts related to awareness and control are handled.

## A New Model

It is important to note at the outset that the approach to sociolinguistic cognition discussed here is not an exclusive system. There is little evidence to suggest that sociolinguistic processes are independent of the social cognition and linguistic processing systems. Indeed, we might think of the entire question of sociolinguistic cognition as one of interface: where, why, and how do the social and linguistic systems meet? A model which answers this question fully must necessarily be based on accurate, well-established models of those systems or families of systems. Unfortunately, such models do not exist, both areas being currently subject to hot debate along a number of dimensions. Instead, sociolinguists can draw on insights common across the changing models, while also contributing some necessary constraints on their character, by virtue of what we know of their interface.

Just as in the original monitor-based model, the language processing system forms the most basic element of our model of sociolinguistic behavior. The existence of some amount of specialized machinery for language production and comprehension is one of the most widely supported conclusions of modern linguistics (e.g. Fodor 1983) although the exact extent and nature of the language-specific portions of processing continue to be a matter of debate (e.g. Lieberman 2006). One of the key questions is the relationship between the production and perception processes. Although these are obviously linked, or language learning would not occur, they are also obviously at least partly distinct, given that speakers can understand varieties different from those they produce. As noted above, Pickering and Garrod (2013) have offered one view of an integrated production/perception system which prioritizes prediction as a key feature of both processes. This approach has many benefits, including capturing effects showing the influence of production and comprehension on one another, capturing speakers' skills at maintaining very small gaps between turns, and providing an independently motivated notion of at least one dimension of salience. This model provides a promising base on which to build a more specific understanding of sociolinguistic phenomenon.

Based on the research presented in "Where systems collide," above, our grammar must necessarily incorporate social features of the speech context, including the social identities or group affiliations of the speaker, addressee(s), and other participants; the speaker's and others' stances towards each other; the topic of conversation; the physical and conceptual setting of the speech and many other features (for one discussion of such dimensions, see Hymes 1967). While earlier models of the grammar made such inclusion essentially impossible, more recent models have allowed for it, as new evidence has emerged suggesting that quite a lot of token-level detail makes its way into language-learning, including ongoing learning by adult native speakers (see as examples Goldinger 1998; Pierrehumbert 2001). Constraint- and construction-based models of syntax may incorporate some social information (e.g. Bender 2001), but this possibility has been most thoroughly explored for models of sound variability, in the tradition of exemplar phonology (Johnson 2006; Drager and Kirtley, this volume).

In these models, social information, as well as other information like fine-grained acoustic details, is stored, with as yet unknown detail and for unknown amounts of time, at a basic level associated with, at least originally, each token heard in a speech setting (Goldinger 1998; Johnson 2006). This detail is included in a complex perceptual space, which generalized across to create abstract phonological categories (Beckman and Edwards 2000).

The grammar's use of social information has been most clearly documented in perception, where our ability to control potentially confounding factors is much greater. As noted in "Where systems collide," above, sociophonetic research motivates connections between language and social processing in systems which can contribute to language processing absent the verbally accessible awareness of the listener. Strand (1999) provides just one example: phonological boundaries between /s/ and /ʃ/ being influenced by social perceptions of the speaker. The more culturally feminine the speaker seems to be, the more "feminine" the phonological boundary assigned to their speech by listeners (ambiguous tokens more likely to be heard as "shod" than "sod"). This suggests that language perception systems not only adapt flexibly to speakers and situations (Dahan *et al.* 2008), but that this adaptation is influenced by social assessments. These social assessments must stem from relatively complex systems, given not only that gender itself is a complex social construct, but that Strand's results demonstrate within-sex-class effects of degree of femininity or masculinity.

The role of social information in production systems is less well understood, but the body of variation work to date all bears strong witness to the influence of external social factors on essentially all levels of linguistic production. This influence may be triggered by clearly speaker-external factors like interlocutor, location, and topic (Blom and Gumperz 1972; Rickford and McNair-Knox 1994), but frequently serve to support larger social goals, whether situational or ongoing projects of identity definition (Eckert 2000).

Much of the phenomena attributed to the sociolinguistic monitor and most of the phenomena documented in the third-wave tradition of variation can be handled in a model in which social information is connected to the grammar itself through associative links. Linguistic forms can be primed by interlocutors, physical locations, speech activities, and other external cues, facilitating their processing and increasing the likelihood of their production. They could also be primed by internally generated cues activated by social goals, memories of other interactions, or conscious reasoning or thoughts, accounting for volitional sociolinguistic style management. Such priming could presumably only influence forms already in the grammar, providing a natural limitation on speakers' sociolinguistic performance by virtue of the challenges of language learning more generally.

The linkage of social information to grammatical structures and stored linguistic exemplars, however, does not obviate our need for a resource-heavy, attention-based process along the lines of the sociolinguistic monitor. Some sociolinguistic shifts occur apparently independently of conscious introspection, but other sociolinguistic behavior appears effortful, poorly integrated with other linguistic structures, and/or available to verbally accessible control. At a trivial level, it is possible for speaker to speak or refrain from speech when requested, or to produce specific words, including non-words, in response to verbal instructions. In spontaneous speech, speakers are observed at times producing less socially desirable forms, particularly when under cognitive load, tired, upset, or intoxicated. The existence of indexically based self-corrections, where speakers catch themselves producing an indexically less desired form and substitute another, likewise suggest that the concept of speakers "monitoring" their speech remains a useful notion. It is less common to hear reports of monitoring of sociolinguistic perception processes, but it may occur. Individuals with a commitment to linguistic equity may find, for example, that they catch themselves drawing stereotype-based conclusions about an interlocutor and attempt to rectify those impressions after the fact.

Little work has investigated the boundaries of conscious sociolinguistic control. As a result, we have very little systematic knowledge of, for example, which forms speakers are capable of consciously controlling in production (e.g. when explicitly instructed to do so, regardless of organic social motivations). Researchers frequently note informally when variables are subject to explicit commentary in the communities of use, but this has focused on what speakers tend to talk about rather than what they are capable of discussing. Sociolinguists are often in the habit of informally noting the difficulties respondents have in articulating specific language differences, but the limits on human ability to respond to, discuss, and control variables remain poorly understood.

Despite the clear existence of socially informed speech monitoring, there is no reason to believe that such monitoring is performed by a language-specific system. There are extensive literatures on various aspects of monitoring in speech (e.g. Levelt 1983; Blackmer and Mitton 1991), including speech perception (e.g. van de Meerendonk *et al.* 2009), and on the interactional mechanisms for detecting and repairing errors (e.g. Schegloff *et al.* 1977; Kitzinger 2013), although not typically with a focus on indexical meanings of speech forms. The mechanisms for such monitoring are still very much an open question, with some theories proposing that the comprehension system itself serves as a monitor (Levelt 1983), while others suggest that an entirely distinct and less nuanced system attempts to predict behavior by both the speaker and any interlocutors (Pickering and Garrod 2013, 2014).

In the case of sociolinguistic production particularly, we might think of the object of monitoring being the speech produced by the speaker, or possibly the inner speech under preparation prior to utterance (Nooteboom 2005). This speech is produced from the grammar based on the previously learned linguistic systems and influenced by social context on an associative basis. The self-regulation system, however, applies editing to the speech to align with various social goals which might include producing grammatical speech (in both the linguistic sense of avoiding speech errors, as well as the prescriptive sense of avoiding socially stigmatized forms), but also, for example, producing specific forms appropriate to the situation such as more learned lexical items in a stressful professional setting or suppressing verbal indications of anger in a delicate conversation. Our understanding of sociolinguistic behavior would suggest that the cognitive constructs capable of being monitored for social factors are likely to be limited both in number and in formal complexity, relative to the objects manipulated by the grammar itself (Agha 2007; Labov 1993).

Alongside the grammar and a self-regulation system, another element is needed, namely the person perception system. Here I am departing from the traditional variationist model by separating the systems which evaluate the speech of other speakers and those which oversee speakers' own speech. While it is clear that individuals' actual judgments of others often bear some relation to their preferences in their own speech, this is not always the case (Labov 1966, 1993) and we have little evidence as to how closely linked the two processes are. When these systems do coincide, it is plausible that these alignments come from their shared relationship to belief and emotional systems of preference. As with self-regulation, person perception is likely not speech-specific, but rather forms part of a much larger system which also draws on visual information, content, and second-hand reports, among others. Work on the integration of visual, auditory, and semantic cues has focused primarily on the perception of emotion, but provides a useful starting point for sociolinguistic questions of information integration (e.g. de Gelder *et al.* 2002; de Gelder and Vroomen 2000; Nygaard and Queen 2008). Person perception is a complex process in which "bottom-up" information drawn from, for example, direct observation or second-hand reports is combined with "top-down" expectations, including those prompted by situational structures and social category-triggered stereotypes (for one model on how these elements interact, see Freeman and Ambady 2011). We see evidence of this interplay in sociolinguistic perception frequently, for example in Carmichael's contribution to this volume.

These three independently motivated elements, a socially linked grammar, a general self-regulation system, and a general person perception, working together provide a more complete explanation for the sociolinguistic behavior modeled by the sociolinguistic monitor. Looking at the broad spectrum of sociolinguistic behavior discussed in "What are we modeling?" above, other systems are also necessary alongside these three, including general problem solving through which speakers might reason about what the wisest linguistic choices might be, or introspective reflection which might lead to the creation, alteration, or sharing of explicit ideological beliefs. The three discussed in this section, however, represent the central backbone of sociolinguistic cognition.

## Conclusion

Work in sociolinguistic variation has recently begun to engage more closely with the sociolinguistic monitor as a theoretical construct, attempting to pin down its rates of sensitivity and time window (Labov *et al.* 2011), as well as its ability to operate on linguistic forms at varying levels of culturally established discussion or enregisterment (Levon and Fox 2014). In this chapter I have argued that a more basic level of theorizing is needed, namely a discussion of what exactly the mechanisms are that speakers use to manage their sociolinguistic business. A responsible model of these mechanisms must draw on insights from language processing and social cognition, as well as the small but exciting body of work which has united one or both of these fields with sociolinguistics. I propose that the existing cognitive models within variation be more strongly informed by not only theoretical and psycholinguistics, but social cognition and cognitive psychology more broadly.

I propose that a full model of sociolinguistic processing is best built with independently motivated constructs, not with sociolinguistic-specific machinery. The first of these is a grammar with integrated social information, in the form of associative links between linguistic objects (including stored exemplars, phonological categories, lexical items, and syntactic constructions) and social cognitive constructs (including representations of individual people, social groups, personality traits, and emotions). Our model must also include a person perception system, which integrates visual cues, linguistic and paralinguistic information, third-party information, and more.

Finally, sociolinguistic processing also involves the self-regulatory system, tasked with monitoring behavior, including speech behavior, and initiating repairs when necessary. We might as a starting point follow existing variationist tradition and hypothesize that this self-regulatory system is able to access and attempt to control linguistic objects traditionally classified by sociolinguists as "above the level of consciousness," as we also further develop our understanding of what is intended by "consciousness" in this description.

These models offer not only tools for explaining data that we have already gathered, but also guidance for future questions. Foremost among these are the points at which language processes are "visible" to social processes, including person perception and self-regulation, and/or subject to influence by them. While the evidence suggests that there exist links in both directions, we do not yet know how closely related the two directions are.

Finally, these models provide a caution for sociolinguists who are not strongly interested in issues of cognitive modeling. As the work in this volume demonstrates, there is interest in issues of awareness and control across a wide range of theoretical and methodological commitments in linguistic anthropology and sociolinguistics. It would be ideal as we engage in this work to understand precisely what we mean by terms like awareness, control, covert, overt, and salience, to name but a few, and to ground that understanding in cognitively realistic theory. Failing that Herculean accomplishment, it is important that we note where and how these terms are still poorly understood by those most involved in investigating them, so we may limit our use of such constructs to what they can comfortably support.

REFERENCES

Agha, Asif. 2007. *Language and Social Relations*. Cambridge University Press.
Amodio, David M. and Devine., Patricia G. 2006. Stereotyping and evaluation in implicit race bias: Evidence for independent constructs and unique effects on behavior. *Journal of Personality and Social Psychology* 91(4):652–61.
Asch, Solomon E. 1946. Forming impressions of personality. *Journal of Abnormal and Social Psychology* 41:258–90.
Auer, Peter, Barden, Birgit, and Grosskopf, Beate. 1998. Subjective and objective parameters determining "salience" in long-term dialect accommodation. *Journal of Sociolinguistics* 2(2):163–87.
Babel, Molly. 2010. Dialect convergence and divergence in New Zealand English. *Language in Society* 39(4):437–56.
Balcetis, Emily E. and Dale, Rick. 2005. An exploration of social modulation of syntactic priming, in *Proceedings of the 27th annual meeting of the cognitive science society*, pp. 184–9.
Ball, Peter, Giles, Howard, Byrne, Jane L., and Berechree, Philip. 1984. Situational constraints on the evaluative significance of speech accommodation: Some Australian data. *International Journal of the Sociology of Language* 46:115–29.
Bar, Moshe. 2007. The proactive brain: Using analogies and associations to generate predictions. *TRENDS in Cognitive Sciences* 11(7):280–9.
Bargh, John A. 2006. What have we been priming all these years? On the development, mechanisms, and ecology of nonconscious social behavior. *European Journal of Social Psychology* 36:147–68.
Bargh, John A., Green, Michelle, and Fitzsimons, Gráinne. 2008. The selfish goal: Unintended consequences of intended goal pursuits. *Social Cognition* 26(5):534–54.
Baumeister, Roy F. and Heatherton, Todd F.. 1996. Self-regulation failure: An overview. *Psychological Inquiry* 7(1):1–15.
Baumeister, Roy F., Masicampo, E. J., and Vohs, Kathleen D. 2011. Do conscious thoughts cause behavior? *Annual Review of Psychology* 62:331–61.
Beckman, Mary E. and Edwards, Jan. 2000. The ontogeny of phonological categories and the primacy of lexical learning in linguistic development. *Child Development* 71(1):240–9.
Bender, Emily. 2001. Syntactic variation and linguistic competence: The case of AAVE copula absence. PhD dissertation. Stanford University, CA.
Blackmer, Elizabeth R. and Mitton, Janet L. 1991. Theories of monitoring and the timing of repairs in spontaneous speech. *Cognition* 39:173–94.
Blom, Jan-Petter and Gumperz, John. 1972. Social meaning in linguistic structures: Code-switching in Norway, in John Gumperz and Dell H. Hymes (eds.), *Directions in Sociolinguistics: The Ethnography of Communication*, pp. 407–34. Oxford, UK: Blackwell.
Bock, Kathryn J. 1986. Syntactic persistence in language production. *Cognitive Psychology* 18:355–87.
Brown, Rick D. and Bassili, John N.. 2002. Spontaneous trait associations and the case of the superstitious banana. *Journal of Experimental Social Psychology* 38:87–92.
Brulard, Inès and Carr, Philip. 2013. Variability, unconscious accent adaptation and sense of identity: The case of RP influences on speakers of Standard Scottish English. *Language Sciences* 39:151–5.

Bourdieu, Pierre. 1982. *Language and Symbolic Power*. Gino Raymond and Matthew Adamson (trans.). Cambridge, MA: Harvard University Press.

Campanella, Salvatore and Belin, Pascal. 2007. Integrating face and voice in person perception. *TRENDS in Cognitive Sciences* 11(12):535–43.

Campbell-Kibler, Kathryn. 2007. Accent, (ING), and the social logic of listener perceptions. *American Speech* 82(1):32–64.

    2008. I'll be the judge of that: Diversity in social perceptions of (ING). *Language in Society* 37(5):637–59.

    2010. The effect of speaker information on attitudes toward (ING). *Journal of Language and Social Psychology* 29(2):214–23.

    2011. The sociolinguistic variant as a carrier of social meaning. *Language Variation and Change* 22(3):423–41.

Cargile, Aaron Castelan. 1997. Attitudes towards Chinese-accented speech: An investigation in two contexts. *Journal of Language and Social Psychology* 16:434–43.

Cargile, Aaron Castelan and Giles, Howard. 1998. Language attitudes toward varieties of English: An American-Japanese context. *Journal of Applied Communication Research* 26:338–56.

Carlston, Donal E. and Mae, Lynda. 2007. Posing with the flag: Trait-specific effects of symbols on person perception. *Journal of Experimental Social Psychology* 43:241–8.

Chartrand, Tanya L. and Bargh, John A. 1996. Automatic activation of impression formation and memorization goals: Nonconscious goal priming reproduces effects of explicit task instructions. *Journal of Personality and Social Psychology* 71(3):464–78.

Coupland, Nikolas. 2007. *Style: Language Variation and Identity*. Cambridge University Press.

Cunningham, William A., Van Bavel, Jay J., Arbuckle, Nathan L., Packer, Dominic J., and Waggoner, Ashley S. 2012. Rapid social perception is flexible: Approach and avoidance motivational states shape P100 responses to other-race faces. *Frontiers in Neuroscience* 6, Article 140.

Dahan, Delphine, Drucker, Sarah J., and Scarborough, Rebecca A. 2008. Talker adaptation in speech perception: Adjusting the signal or the representations? *Cognition* 108:710–18.

Deacon, T. W. 2003. Universal grammar and semiotic constraints, in M. H. Christiansen and S. Kirby (eds), *Language Evolution*, pp. 111–39. Oxford University Press.

de Gelder, Beatrice, Pourtois, Gilles, and Weiskrantz, Lawrence. 2002. Fear recognition in the voice is modulated by unconsciously recognized facial expressions but not by unconsciously recognized affective pictures. *Proceedings of the National Academy of Sciences of the USA* 99(6):4121–6.

de Gelder, Beatrice and Vroomen, Jean. 2000. The perception of emotions by ear and by eye. *Cognition and Emotion* 14(3):289–311.

Devine, Patricia G., Sedikides, Constantine, and Fuhrman, Robert W. 1989. Goals in social information processing: The case of anticipated interaction. *Journal of Personality and Social Psychology* 56(5):680–90.

Diamond, Adele. 2013. Executive functions. *Annual Review of Psychology* 64: 135–68.

Draaisma, Douwe. 2000. *Metaphors of Memory: A History of Ideas about the Mind.* Cambridge University Press.

Drager, Katie. 2009. A sociophonetic ethnography of Selwyn Girls' High. PhD dissertation. University of Canterbury.

Drager, Katie, Hay, Jennifer, and Walker, Abby. 2010. Pronounced rivalries: Attitudes and speech production. *Te Reo* 53:27–53.

Eckert, Penelope. 2000. *Linguistic Variation as Social Practice: The Linguistic Construction of Identity in Belten High.* New York: Blackwell.

　2012. Three waves of variation study: The emergence of meaning in the study of variation. *Annual Review of Anthropology* 41:87–100.

Evans, Jonathan St. B. T. 2008. Dual-processing accounts of reasoning, judgment, and social cognition. *Annual Review of Psychology* 59:255–78.

Ferguson, Melissa J. 2008. On becoming ready to pursue a goal you don't know you have: Effects of nonconscious goals on evaluative readiness. *Journal of Personality and Social Psychology* 95(6):1268–94.

Fiske, Susan T. and Neuberg, Steven L. 1990. A continuum of impression formation, from category-based to individuating processes: Influences of information and motivation on attention and interpretation. *Advances in Experimental Social Psychology* 21:1–74.

Fodor, Jerry A. 1983. *The Modularity of Mind.* Cambridge, MA: MIT Press.

Forgas, Joseph P. and Bower, Gordon H. 1987. Mood effects on person-perception judgments. *Journal of Personality and Social Psychology* 53(1):53–60.

Forgas, Joseph P. and Moylan, Stephanie. 1988. After the movies: Transient mood and social judgments. *Personality and Social Psychology Bulletin* 13(4):467–77.

Freeman, Jonathan B. and Ambady, Nalini. 2011. A dynamic interactive theory of person construal. *Psychological Review* 118(2):247–79.

Galinsky, Adam D. and Moskowitz, Gordon B. 2007. Further ironies of suppression: Stereotype and counterstereotype accessibility. *Journal of Experimental Social Psychology* 43:833–41.

Gawronski, Bertram and Bodenhausen, Galen V. 2011. The Associative–Propositional Evaluation model: Theory, evidence, and open questions. *Advances in Experimental Social Psychology* 44:59–127.

Giles, Howard and Powesland, Peter. 1975. *Speech Style and Social Evaluation.* San Francisco, CA: Academic Press.

Goldinger, Stephen D. 1998. Echoes of echoes? An episodic theory of lexical access. *Psychological Review* 105(2):251–79.

Govorun, Olesya and Keith Payne, B. 2006. Ego-depletion and prejudice: Separating automatic and controlled components. *Social Cognition* 24(2):111–36.

Guy, Gregory R. 1991. Explanation in variable phonology: An exponential model of morphological constraints. *Language Variation and Change* 3:1–22.

Guy, Gregory R. and Cutler, Cecelia. 2011. Speech style and authenticity: Quantitative evidence for the performance of identity. *Language Variation and Change* 23:139–62.

Hassin, Ran R., Uleman, James S., and Bargh, John A. (eds.). 2005. *The New Unconscious.* Oxford University Press.

Hay, Jennifer and Drager, Katie. 2010. Stuffed toys and speech perception. *Linguistics* 48(4):865–92.

Hebdige, Dick. 1979. *Subculture: The Meaning of Style.* New York: Routledge.

Hymes, Dell. 1986[1967]. Models of the interaction of language and social life, in John J. Gumperz and Dell Hymes (eds.), *Directions in Sociolinguistics: The Ethnography of Communication*, pp. 35–71. Oxford, UK: Blackwell.

Ito, Tiffany A. and Bartholow, Bruce D. 2009. The neural correlates of race. *Trends in Cognitive Sciences* 13(12):524–31.

Jaeger, T. Florian and Snider, Neal. 2013. Alignment as a consequence of expectation adaptation: Syntactic priming is affected by the prime's prediction error given both prior and recent experience. *Cognition* 127(1):57–83.

Jakobson, Roman. 1960. Linguistics and poetics, in T. A. Sebeok (ed.), *Style in Language*, pp. 350–377. Cambridge, MA: MIT Press.

Johnson, Keith. 2006. Resonance in an exemplar-based lexicon: The emergence of social identity and phonology. *Journal of Phonetics* 34:485–99.

Jussim, Lee, Fleming, Christopher J., Coleman, Lerita, and Kohberger, Cortney. 1996. The nature of stereotypes: II. a multiple-process model of evaluations. *Journal of Applied Social Psychology* 26(4):283–312.

Kamachi, Miyuki, Hill, Harold, Lander, Karen, and Vatikiotis-Bateson, Eric. 2003. "Putting the face to the voice:" Matching identity across modality. *Current Biology* 13:1709–14.

Kitzinger, Celia. 2013. Repair, in Jack Sidnell and Tanya Stivers (eds.), *The Handbook of Conversation Analysis*, pp. 229–256. Maiden, MA: Blackwell.

Klein, William M. and Kunda, Ziva. 1992. Motivated person perception: Constructing justifications for desired beliefs. *Journal of Experimental Social Psychology* 28:145–68.

Kraljic, Tanya, Samuel, Arthur G., and Brennan, Susan E. 2008. First impressions and last resorts: How listeners adjust to speaker variability. *Psychological Science* 19(4):332–8.

Kristiansen, Tore. 2009. The macro-level social meanings of late-modern Danish accents. *Acta Linguistica Hafniensia* 41:167–92.

Labov, William. 1963. The social motivation of a sound change. *Word* 19:273–309.
    1966. *The Social Stratification of English in New York City*. Washington, DC: Center for Applied Linguistics.
    1972. *Sociolinguistic Patterns*. Philadelphia, PA: University of Pennsylvania Press.
    1993. The unobservability of structure and its linguistic consequences. Paper presented at NWAV 22, University of Ottawa.

Labov, William, Ash, Sharon, Ravindranath, Maya, Weldon, Tracey, Baranowski, Maciej, and Nagy, Naomi. 2011. Properties of the sociolinguistic monitor. *Journal of Sociolinguistics* 15(4):431–63.

Lambert, Wallace E., Hodgson, R. C., Gardner, R. C., and Fillenbaum, S. 1960. Evaluational reactions to spoken languages. *Journal of Abnormal and Social Psychology* 60(1):44–51.

Levelt, Willem B. 1983. Monitoring and self-repair in speech. *Cognition* 14:41–104.

Levon, Erez and Fox, Sue. 2014. Social salience and the sociolinguistic monitor: A case study of ing and th-fronting in Britain. Unpublished manuscript.

Lieberman, Philip. 2006. *Toward an Evolutionary Biology of Language*. Cambridge, MA: Belknap Press.

Macrae, C. Neil and Martin, Douglas. 2007. A boy primed Sue: Feature-based processing and person construal. *European Journal of Social Psychology* 37:793–805.

Mendoza-Denton, Norma. 2008. *Homegirls: Language and Cultural Practice among Latina Youth Gangs*. Malden, MA: Blackwell.

Milner, Brenda, Coricin, Suzanne, and Teuber, H.-L. 1968. Further analysis of the hippocampal amnesic syndrome: 14-year follow-up study of H.M. *Neuropsychologia* 6:215–34.

Moore, Emma. 2011. Interaction between social category and social practice: Explaining was/were variation. *Language Variation and Change* 22:347–71.

Niedzielski, Nancy A. 1999. The effect of social information on the perception of sociolinguistic variables. *Journal of Language and Social Psychology* 18(1):62–85.

Nooteboom, Sieb G. 2005. Lexical bias revisited: Detecting, rejecting and repairing speech errors in inner speech. *Speech Communication* 47:43–58.

Nygaard, Lynne C. and Queen, Jennifer S. 2008. Communicating emotion: Linking affective prosody and word meaning. *Journal of Experimental Psychology* 34(4):1017–30.

Ochs, Elinor. 1992. Indexing gender, in Alessandro Duranti and Charles Goodwin (eds.), *Rethinking Context: Language as an Interactive Phenomenon*, pp. 335–58. Cambridge University Press.

Operario, Don and Fiske, Susan T. 2004. Stereotypes: Content, structures, processes, and context, in Marilynn B. Brewer and Miles Hewstone (eds.), *Social Cognition*, pp. 120–41. Malden, MA: Blackwell.

Park, Sang Hee, Glaser, Jack, and Knowles, Eric D. 2008. Implicit motivation to control prejudice moderates the effect of cognitive depletion on unintended discrimination. *Social Cognition* 26(4):401–19.

Payne, Arvilla C. 1980. Factors controlling the acquisition of the Philadelphia dialect by out-of-state children, in William Labov (ed.), *Locating Language in Time and Space*, pp. 143–78. New York: Academic Press.

Payne, B. Keith. 2001. Prejudice and perception: The role of automatic and controlled processes in misperceiving a weapon. *Journal of Personality and Social Psychology* 81:181–92.

 2005. Conceptualizing control in social cognition: How executive functioning modulates the expression of automatic stereotyping. *Journal of Personality and Social Psychology* 89(4):488–503.

Payne, B. Keith and Stewart, Brandon D. 2007. Automatic and controlled components of social cognition: A process dissociation approach, in John A. Bargh (ed.), *Social Psychology and the Unconscious: The Automaticity of Higher Mental Processes*. New York: Psychology Press.

Peirce, Charles S. 1901. Sign, in J. M. Baldwin (ed.), *Dictionary of Philosophy and Psychology*, Vol. 2, p. 527. New York: Macmillan.

Pharao, Nicolai, Maegaard, Marie, Møller, Janus S., and Kristiansen, Tore. 2014. Indexical meanings of [s+] among Copenhagen youth: Social perception of a phonetic variant in different prosodic contexts. *Language in Society* 43(1): 1–31.

Pickering, Martin J. and Garrod, Simon. 2004. Toward a mechanistic psychology of dialogue. *Behavioral and Brain Sciences* 27(2):169–89.

 2013. An integrated theory of language production and comprehension. *Behavioral and Brain Sciences* 36(4):329–92.

 2014. Self-, other-, and joint monitoring using forward models. *Frontiers in Human Neuroscience* 8(132).

Pierrehumbert, Janet. 2001. Exemplar dynamics: Word frequency, lenition and contrast, in Joan Bybee and Paul Hopper (eds.), *Frequency and the Emergence of Linguistic Structure*, pp. 137–57. Amsterdam: John Benjamins.

Podesva, Robert J. 2011. The California vowel shift and gay identity. *American Speech* 86(1):32–51.

Ráckz, Peter. 2013. *Salience in Sociolinguistics: A Quantitative Approach*. Berlin: De Gruyter.

Rickford, John R. 1986. The need for new approaches to social class analysis in sociolinguistics. *Language and Communication* 6(3):215–21.

Rickford, John R. and McNair-Knox, Faye. 1994. Addressee- and topic-influenced style shift: A quantitative sociolinguistic study, in David Biber and Edward Finegan (eds.), *Sociolinguistic Perspectives on Register*, pp. 235–76. Oxford University Press.

Schegloff, Emanuel A., Jefferson, Gail, and Sacks, Harvey. 1977. The preference for self-correction in the organization of repair in conversation. *Language* 53(2):361–82.

Showers, Carolin and Cantor, Nancy. 1985. Social cognition: A look at motivated strategies. *Annual Review of Psychology* 36:275–305.

Silverstein, Michael. 1976. Shifters, linguistic categories, and cultural description, in Keith Basso and Henry Selby (eds.), *Meaning in Anthropology*, pp. 11–55. Albuquerque, NM: University of New Mexico Press.

  2003. Indexical order and the dialectics of sociolinguistic life. *Language and Communication* 23:193–229.

Smith, Eliot R. and DeCoster, Jamie. 2000. Dual-process models in social and cognitive psychology: Conceptual integration and links to underlying memory systems. *Personality and Social Psychology Review* 4(2):108–31.

Squire, Larry R. 2004. Memory systems of the brain: A brief history and current perspective. *Neurobiology of Learning and Memory* 82:171–7.

Staum Casasanto, Laura. 2008. Does social information influence sentence processing? in 30th annual meeting of the Cognitive Science Society. Washington, DC.

Stevenage, Sarah V., Hugill, Andrew R., and Lewis, Hugh G. 2012. Integrating voice recognition into models of person perception. *Journal of Cognitive Psychology* 24(4):409–19.

Strand, Elizabeth A. 1999. Uncovering the roles of gender stereotypes in speech perception. *Journal of Language and Social Psychology* 18(1):86–99.

Trudgill, Peter. 1974. *The Social Differentiation of English in Norwich*. Cambridge University Press.

Uleman, James S., Hon, Alex, Roman, Robert J., and Moskowitz, Gordon B. 1996. On-line evidence for spontaneous trait inferences at encoding. *Personality and Social Psychology Bulletin* 22(4):377–94.

Van Bavel, Jay J., Xiao, Yi Jenny, and Cunningham, William A. 2012. Evaluation is a dynamic process: Moving beyond dual system models. *Social and Personality Psychology Compass* 6(6):438–54.

Van Berkum, Jos J. A. 2010. The brain is a prediction machine that cares about good and bad – any implications for neuropragmatics? *Italian Journal of Linguistics* 22(1):181–208.

Van Berkum, Jos J. A., van den Brink, Danielle, Tesink, Cathelijne M. J. Y., Kos, Miriam, and Hagoort, Peter. 2008. The neural integration of speaker and message. *Journal of Cognitive Neuroscience* 20(4):580–91.

van de Meerendonk, Nan, Kolk, Herman H. J., Chwilla, Dorothee J., and Vissers, Constance Th.W.M. 2009. Monitoring in language perception. *Language and Linguistics Compass* 3(5):1211–24.

von Hippel, William and Gonsalkorale, Karen. 2005. "That is bloody revolting!": Inhibitory control of thoughts better left unsaid. *Psychological Science* 16(7):497–500.

Wagner, Dylan D. and Heatherton, Todd F. 2015. Self-regulation and its failure: The seven deadly threats to self-regulation, in Mario Mikulincer, Phillip R. Shaver, Eugene Borgida, and John A. Bargh (eds.), *APA Handbook of Personality and Social Psychology*, Vol. 1: *Attitudes and Social Cognition*, pp. 805–42. Washington, DC: American Psychological Association.

Wagner, Suzanne Evans. 2013. Individual differences in social competence and attention to detail affect the sociolinguistic monitor. Paper presented at UKLVC 9.

Weatherholtz, Kodi, Campbell-Kibler, Kathryn, and Florian Jaeger, T. 2014. Syntactic alignment and social perception. *Language Variation and Change* 26(3):387–420.

Yu, Alan C. L., Abrego-Collier, Carissa, and Sonderegger, Morgan. 2013. Phonetic imitation from an individual-difference perspective: Subjective attitude, personality and "autistic" traits. *PLoS ONE* 8(9).

Zhang, Qing. 2005. A Chinese yuppie in Beijing: Phonological variation and the construction of a new professional identity. *Language in Society* 34:431–66.

# 7    Place-Linked Expectations and Listener Awareness of Regional Accents

*Katie Carmichael*

## Introduction

It has been demonstrated that listeners have distinct ideas about the relationship between regional accents and where a speaker is from (Clopper and Pisoni 2006b, 2007; Preston 1989, 1996). This knowledge represents a certain kind of sociolinguistic awareness: the awareness that there exists some link between a speaker's language practices and their home region or place of origin. Indeed, individuals share many common stereotypes about regional (place-linked) dialects, even if they have little exposure to speakers of these dialects in their day-to-day lives (Hartley and Preston 1999; Preston 1989, 1996). Likewise, when presented with linguistic stimuli, listeners form distinct social impressions in response (Callan *et al.* 1983; Luhman 1990), and listeners' reactions to speakers can sometimes depend on where they determine the speaker to be from – regardless of whether they are actually correct in that determination (Campbell-Kibler 2009; Williams 1989). However, there has been little work addressing the space between these abstract sociolinguistic stereotypes about regional accents, and speakers' in-the-moment social judgments when presented with regional speech forms. The current study seeks to fill this gap by posing the question: how do listeners make use of their sociolinguistic awareness about language and place when presented with novel linguistic input?

Multiple methodological approaches were combined in this study to examine this question: participants completed a listening task, free-listing task, perceptual dialectology map task, and follow-up interview. These tasks were designed to assess participants' social and linguistic associations with certain places, and with the dialects linked to those locales. In the listening task, I manipulated the level of accentedness and speakers' reported hometown to investigate how listeners make use of their mental schema connecting place and regional accents when presented with linguistic stimuli. In addition to examining how this awareness is used in action, this chapter discusses some of the ways in which this awareness is built, by analyzing how participants describe their reactions to the tasks, and the resources they appealed to in completing the tasks.

Responses to the four tasks suggested that participants' knowledge of given places, and the social and linguistic qualities associated with them, built up a set of expectations that was exploited in order to make sense of the linguistic input they were presented with. A number of participants implied a deterministic link between where one is from and what their accent will sound like. In effect, by treating accent as dependent entirely on where one is from, these participants denied speakers from places where accentedness is expected any level of control over non-standard, regionally linked features. Additionally, it was found that personal experience and media representations were the main resources participants used to build their sociolinguistic awareness of the relationship between regional accents and place.

The results discussed in this chapter indicate that listeners make active use of their knowledge about the connections between regional accents and the social/place-linked meanings attached to these language practices, employing this awareness when presented with new linguistic input. They also rely on assumptions about speaker control over dialectal features in order to resolve mismatches between their expectations of accentedness and what they encounter in the moment. The findings discussed here build on our understanding of how place-linked associations play into sociolinguistic awareness more generally, and answer recent calls (e.g. Becker 2009; Daleszynska 2011) for sociolinguists to complexify our conceptions of place and the role that speakers' ideas about language and place can have in the production and perception of sociolinguistic identity.

## Awareness, Control, and Regional Accents

Speakers' awareness of, and control over, linguistic variables has always been relevant to the study of sociolinguistic variation. Much of the treatment of these issues within variationist sociolinguistics has been affected by the initial assumptions of William Labov, who designed early data collection methods around the idea that the amount of attention a speaker paid to their speech would affect their realization of certain socially meaningful linguistic variants (e.g. 2006[1966], 1972, 1984). Within this approach, Labov (1972) also accounted for the fact that some linguistic variation was not socially meaningful because it was below the level of consciousness. His concepts of stereotypes, markers, and indicators (listed in order from highest level of awareness to lowest) furthermore contained assumptions about speaker control – Labov theorized that it is the features that speakers are most aware of that they have the greatest control over.

Another way Labov affected sociolinguists' conceptions of speaker awareness and control was by introducing the idea of *The Observer's Paradox*, which can be summarized as the problematic aim of observing the way people speak when they are not being observed. The idea behind this line of thinking is that if speakers are made aware of someone listening for meaningful variation in their speech, they will exert control over the forms they use, thereby producing data that is somehow disingenuous compared to the "true vernacular." And, indeed, Labov (2006[1966]: 86) identifies the vernacular as the paramount interest of sociolinguists, explaining that it is "the language first acquired by the language learner, controlled perfectly, and used primarily among intimate friends and family members." Again, the issue of control comes up, this time in a slightly different way, where it is suggested that speakers do not exert the same level of control over non-vernacular, or self-aware, forms of language. It is likely for this reason that the study of performed speech was not pursued within sociolinguistics until more recently (e.g. Schilling-Estes 1998; Johnstone 1999; Carmichael 2013), even though anthropology and folklore took a performance turn in the 1960s. It has been demonstrated since then that performed speech shows systematic patterning (Schilling-Estes 1998) and represents a useful tool for understanding the local perception of certain linguistic features (Carmichael 2013). But, as a whole, the assumptions that form the very basis of sociolinguistic inquiry – that speakers are variably aware of different linguistic features, and that if their attention is drawn towards them they may exert control over them – have remained relatively unchanged throughout the history of sociolinguistics.

That is not to say that other researchers have not theorized about speaker awareness and control. Le Page and Tabouret-Keller's (1985) "Acts of Identity" model incorporated social theory in order to capture some of the driving forces behind variation. Their model suggested that speakers must possess some level of sociolinguistic awareness, associating specific linguistic patterns with particular social groups, and that furthermore speakers must exert some amount of control over their language practices in order to emulate certain patterns or diverge from them, depending on the level of affiliation with that social group.

More recently, within the frame of sociocultural linguistics Bucholtz and Hall (2005, 2008) have pursued the role of speaker agency, or an individual's ability to make active decisions about their own social/linguistic actions, particularly as expressions of identity. Bucholtz and Hall (2005) discussed the tension between structure and agency within sociolinguistic research: how many of our linguistic choices are deliberate and purposeful, and how many of them are the result of habit? Like Le Page and Tabouret-Keller, Bucholtz and Hall attribute a high level of awareness and control to speakers.

In contrast with those studies mentioned, work on accommodation has sought to account for the sometimes automatic or unconscious linguistic shifts speakers make. Some of these theories have depended on audience (Bell 1984;

Giles *et al.* 1991), while more recent studies have focused on linguistic changes made in response to unconscious triggers (Hay and Drager 2010). These studies test the limits of awareness, showing that speakers have control over linguistic variation even in instances in which the speaker is unaware of their actions. Such mismatch between awareness and control has also been pursued in research on regional, or place-linked, linguistic features. In the city of Pittsburgh, the pronunciation of words such as "downtown" with monophthongal /aw/ ("dahntahn") has entered into many speakers' awareness of local speech patterns, and is often actively employed to index a Pittsburgh-linked identity (Johnstone *et al.* 2002; Johnstone *et al.* 2006). However, Johnstone and Kiesling (2008) found that some speakers use monophthongal /aw/ in their speech without being conscious of its social meaning, demonstrating that awareness of linguistic features and control of them do not always co-occur.

Rather than examining awareness and control in terms of an individual speaker in a specific interaction, as is done in many of the studies discussed above, the current study focuses on listeners' awareness on a broader level by examining general awareness of the relationship between place and regional accent, and how that relates to social judgments about speakers said to be from a given place. As Johnstone (2004) points out, from the beginning of variationist research, with its roots in dialect geography, place has been used as an explanatory factor for linguistic variation. But only recently have more sociolinguistic researchers been examining how individuals conceive of their relationship with certain places and the linguistic features tied to them.

Some work has been completed establishing awareness of a link between place and regional accents, with perhaps the best-known evidence for this coming from Preston's (1989, 1996, 1999) perceptual dialectology research, and the subsequent studies that followed in this thread (Bucholtz *et al.* 2007; Fought 2002; Hartley and Preston 1999; Iannàccaro and Dell'Aquila 2001). In perceptual dialectology map tasks, participants are asked to mark on a map where people "speak with an accent," or "speak most correct," and there is often a high level of agreement in terms of perceptions. Such findings demonstrate that there exist a number of agreed-upon perceptions and stereotypes about certain places and the linguistic features associated with those places.

Examining the link between places and regional accents from an experimental approach, dialect classification tasks such as those administered by Clopper and Pisoni (2006b, 2007) have demonstrated that, overall, naive listeners are quite skilled at determining a speaker's place of origin based on linguistic input alone. Moreover, this place-accent link may be manipulated in perception tasks (Niedzielski 1999; Campbell-Kibler 2009). In one of her tasks, Niedzielski presented listeners from Detroit with vowel tokens featuring varying levels of Canadian raising, asking them to identify the vowel. Half of the listeners believed the speaker was from Detroit and half believed the speaker to be Canadian. Overwhelmingly, speakers identified as Canadian were heard as featuring raised vowel variants, while vowel tokens from those believed to be from Detroit were categorized as unraised, regardless of the actual variant heard. In Campbell-Kibler's study of the sociolinguistic perception of (ING), the effect of place on social judgments was investigated by presenting audio clips of speakers from California and North Carolina in which the only difference was whether the speaker said /ɪn/ or /ɪŋ/. Regardless of variant used, Southern speakers were judged low on intelligence. For Californian stimuli, only speakers perceived as working class were down-rated when they used the alveolar variant. Campbell-Kibler interprets this patterning as a result of Southern speakers already being down-rated for their accent and thus not being able to be further down-rated for their use of alveolar (ING). This patterning of results demonstrated that where a speaker is from affects listeners' social perceptions of linguistic features.

The studies discussed above present varied perspectives on the relationship between awareness and control, and further establish that many speakers possess a general awareness of the link between place and regional accents, the relationship between which will be examined more closely throughout the rest of this chapter.

## Methodology

Participants in this study completed a matched guise listening task, a questionnaire (including free-listing task), a perceptual dialectology map task, and a follow-up interview, in groups of one to three. While the listening task, questionnaire, and perceptual dialectology map task were all completed individually, follow-up interviews were completed as a group. A total of eighty-three participants completed the tasks, but the data were discarded for twenty-two people who were either not from Ohio or did not speak English natively. Because the study dealt with sociolinguistic perceptions about US dialects as a whole, it was thought that limiting the analyzed data to native English speakers from Ohio would mitigate the effect of participants' varying experiences with different US dialects. The sample for this study thus consisted of sixty-one Ohio State undergraduates, approximately balanced across male (twenty-eight) and female (thirty-three) participants; fifty of the participants were white, with the remaining participants identifying as Black (three), Hispanic (one), Asian (six), or mixed (one). Ages ranged from 18 to 37, with a median participant age of 21 years old. Participants received class credit (if they were enrolled in linguistics classes) or $10 for their time, depending on recruitment source.

The listening task represented a modified matched guise, designed based on previous speaker evaluation studies (e.g. Lambert *et al.* 1960; Anisfeld *et al.* 1962; Milroy and McClenaghan 1977). I specify that the task was "modified" from traditional matched guise tasks in that spontaneous speech was used, thus the content of the utterances presented as stimuli was not identical. During this task, each participant was situated at a separate computer with Bose Quiet Comfort 15 acoustic noise-cancelling headphones, and stimuli were presented using eprime 2.0 software. Participants heard recordings of Southern, Midlands, Western, and Mid-Atlantic speakers from the Nationwide Speech Corpus (Clopper and Pisoni 2006a); on the top of the screen participants saw the speaker's pseudonym, age, and reported place of origin – whether Birmingham, Alabama; Columbus, Ohio; or New York, New York. These places were chosen because they represent three areas of the United States with strong social and linguistic ideologies tied to them. New York City English (New York) and Southern English (Birmingham) are both marked, stigmatized dialects within the United States, which have been shown to pattern with negative judgments about speakers (e.g. Preston 1996, 1999). In contrast, Columbus, Ohio is located within the Midwest, a more linguistically "unmarked" area which is ideologically tied to so-called standard language varieties (Bonfiglio 2002). In addition, the study took place in Columbus, Ohio, making this location all the more an unmarked baseline for many participants. In addition to indicating where speakers were "from," I included names and ages for each speaker in an attempt to make speakers' reported hometown stand out less as the variable being tested. However, participants were asked to pay special attention to the information about each speaker under the premise that they would need to give reactions to specific speakers during the follow-up interviews, lending some confidence that participants did note speakers' hometowns.

The goal of the listening task was to manipulate the pairing of regional accentedness and where listeners were told the speaker was from, such that in some cases, this information matched, but in others it did not. Although none of the speakers was actually from any of the three cities used in the current study, it was considered a perceptual "match" if the speaker was from the dialect area in which that city is located – except of course, in the case of Western speakers, who were treated as equivalent to Midlands speakers for the purposes of this study. The intended perceptual result of this manipulation was that some speakers said to be from Birmingham and New York sounded more regionally accented than others. Participants rated speakers along a visual analog scale for eleven social qualities (selected based on past speaker evaluation research, e.g. Zahn and Hopper 1985), listed below.

| Educated | – – – – – – – – – – – – – – – – – – – – – | Uneducated |
|---|---|---|
| Upper class | – – – – – – – – – – – – – – – – – – – – – | Lower class |
| Smart | – – – – – – – – – – – – – – – – – – – – | Dumb |
| Accented | – – – – – – – – – – – – – – – – – – – – | Unaccented |
| Polite | – – – – – – – – – – – – – – – – – – – – | Rude |
| Friendly | – – – – – – – – – – – – – – – – – – – – | Unfriendly |
| Pleasant | – – – – – – – – – – – – – – – – – – – – | Unpleasant |
| Honest | – – – – – – – – – – – – – – – – – – – – | Dishonest |
| Confident | – – – – – – – – – – – – – – – – – – – – | Unsure |
| City | – – – – – – – – – – – – – – – – – – – – | Country |
| Speaks well | – – – – – – – – – – – – – – – – – – – – | Speaks poorly |

After the listening task, participants filled out a questionnaire aimed at finding out socio-demographic information about each participant. The questionnaire also included a free-listing task in which participants were asked to write the first three words that came to mind when they thought of people from each place, in order to get an idea of what place-based evaluations participants came in with. Finally, the questionnaire asked participants if they believed people from the three places to be accented, and if they thought they had an accent themselves. Although the terms presented in the listening task could affect choice of terms in the free-listing task, it would likely only be in terms of breadth of descriptors; in contrast, if the free-listing task was completed before the listening task, it is possible that participants would rate speakers according to the abstract stereotypes about a given place that they had just reported, rather than in response to the linguistic stimuli presented. Since an essential goal of this study was to examine how participants reacted in the moment to linguistic input, it was crucial not to bias the listening task. In addition, since the listening task rotated the accentedness of speakers across different places – in that half of the speakers from each place were more "accented" and half were less "accented" – it was assumed that the listening task stimuli would not shift participant expectations in terms of overall accentedness linked to a given place.

For the third task in the experiment, participants were given a blank map of the United States and asked to mark where people speak with an accent and to provide descriptive labels and examples if possible. This task served to uncover the participants' ideologies about place-based linguistic variation.

Lastly, follow-up interviews provided an opportunity to ask about reactions to the listening task, clarify questionnaire responses, and discuss or refine reasoning behind markings on the perceptual dialectology maps. Participants were also asked about their experiences with each place, with the goal of obtaining richer descriptions of the ideological associations with New York, Birmingham, and Columbus.

**Results**

*Listening Task*

A detailed treatment of listening task results may be found in Carmichael (submitted), although general findings will be summarized in this section. Listening task ratings were submitted to factor analysis in order to determine the driving factors in the data, which I will refer to hereafter as status, solidarity, and accentedness. The factor I am calling status is most heavily weighted for *dumb*, *uneducated*, *speaks poorly*, and *lower class* ratings, while the factor I refer to as solidarity is most heavily weighted for *rude*, *unfriendly*, and *unpleasant*. Together, status and solidarity accounted for 40 percent of the variance in the data – perhaps unsurprising, since these two dimensions have come up frequently in past speaker evaluation studies (Callan *et al.* 1983; Luhman 1990; Edwards 1999; Milroy and Preston 1999). A third factor accounted for a further 7 percent of the variance in the data; it was most strongly (negatively) weighted for unaccented ratings, for which reason I refer to it as accentedness. Interestingly, perceived accentedness did not always coincide with the speakers who featured marked Southern or New York dialects, in that some Midlands/Western ("unmarked") speakers were also rated as accented by participants in this study. Throughout the rest of the chapter, therefore, I will refer to accentedness of speakers according to perceived accentedness that participants established based on their ratings. A final consideration that will be discussed in this section will be the variable of city-country, which came up repeatedly in the free-listing task, map task, and follow-up interviews, suggesting it is important to consider in relation to the other three factors.

Overall, speakers said to be from New York and Birmingham were rated lower along the status dimension than speakers said to be from Columbus – except in the case of speakers said to be from Columbus who were perceived as accented. In contrast with "unaccented" Columbusites, speakers said to be from Columbus who were perceived as accented generally received similarly low status ratings to speakers said to be from New York or Birmingham. This patterning recalls the effects Campbell-Kibler (2009) found in her (ING) data. She found that regardless of whether Southerners used the non-standard (ING) variant, they were down-rated in speaker evaluations, while speakers "who could be from anywhere" featured more nuanced effects, depending on perceived class of the speaker.

Solidarity ratings revealed a bias towards speakers said to be from Birmingham, who were rated high on solidarity regardless of perceived accentedness. Interestingly, speakers said to be from Birmingham were in fact up-rated if

## Movers' solidarity by accentedness mean factor scores

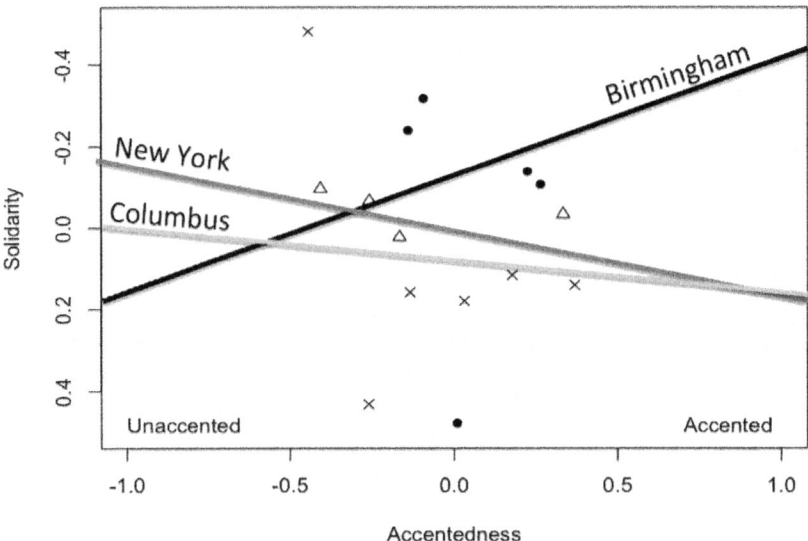

Figure 7.1 Accentedness and Solidarity Ratings for Speakers Said to Be from Birmingham, New York, and Columbus

they were perceived as accented. This differs substantially from the relationship between solidarity ratings and perceived accentedness for speakers said to be from Columbus or New York, who received lower solidarity ratings the more accented they were. Correlations between accentedness and solidarity ratings for each place may be seen in Figure 7.1, where the darkest line represents data for speakers said to be from Birmingham.

Figure 7.1 demonstrates the negative correlation between accentedness and solidarity for speakers said to be from Columbus and New York, which is all the more interesting taken in combination with city-country ratings. As expected based on past studies (e.g. Preston 1996, 1999), as well as results for the other tasks in the current study (see the following section), speakers said to be from Birmingham were overwhelmingly rated as country and those from New York were rated as city. However, speakers said to be from New York who were perceived as less accented were rated less "city" than those perceived to be accented. This interaction did not hold for Birmingham speakers, who were rated as country regardless of perceived accentedness. Those speakers said to be from Columbus featured a mixture of city/country ratings, perhaps unsurprising since Columbus is a smaller city characterized by suburban sprawl blending out into countryside. However, a closer look at which speakers were rated city and which were rated country revealed some interesting interactions with the other factors of significance. To begin with, those speakers said to be from Columbus who were rated as more "country" were also the speakers perceived as most accented. Furthermore, these same speakers took a hit on solidarity ratings, seemingly down-rated for their "country" accents. Examining the speakers said to be from Columbus who were rated more "city," we encounter a similar correlation with accentedness, in that "city" Columbusites were those perceived as least accented. Moreover, these same "city" Columbusites were up-rated along the status dimension. This patterning is particularly interesting in combination with findings for New Yorkers, for whom "cityness" was positively correlated with perceived accentedness. That is, a New Yorker who is more accented is seen as more "city," while a Columbusite who is more accented is seen as more "country." The reasons for this conflicting patterning will be examined in further detail in following sections.

To summarize, listening task results revealed interactions between the factors of status, solidarity, accentedness, and the city-country spectrum. While speakers said to be from Birmingham were rated "country" whether they were perceived as accented or not, they received higher solidarity ratings if perceived as accented. Speakers said to be from New York were consistently rated as "city," but speakers perceived as less accented were also rated as less "city." Finally, ratings for speakers said to be from Columbus were highly dependent on perceived accentedness, with those speakers perceived as accented rated more "country" and down-rated on solidarity. In contrast, Columbus speakers perceived as less accented were rated as more "city" and received higher status ratings. Table 7.1 presents these findings below.

I argue in the discussion section that this patterning of results, in combination with findings from the other tasks, reflects listeners employing their expectations about the relationship between place, regional accents, and other social qualities. In the next section, I examine data from the other tasks to

Table 7.1 *Listening Task Results*

|  | Speakers said to be from Birmingham | Speakers said to be from Columbus | Speakers said to be from New York |
|---|---|---|---|
| Speakers perceived as **more accented** | Country | Country | City |
|  | – | – | – |
|  | High Solidarity | Low Solidarity | – |
| Speakers perceived as **less accented** | Country | City | (Less) City |
|  | – | High Status | – |
|  | – | – | – |

clarify the structure of participants' sociolinguistic awareness relating to place and regional accents, while identifying some of the strategies listeners employed to reconcile new linguistic input that did not match with their mental schema entering into the experiment.

*Questionnaire, Perceptual Dialectology Map Task, and Follow-Up Interview Results*

Because results for the questionnaires, map task, and follow-up interviews presented some interactions and related patterns, they will be discussed together in this section.

Questionnaires included a free-listing task in which participants were asked to list the first three words that came to mind when thinking of Birmingham, Alabama; Columbus, Ohio; and New York, New York. To provide a visual representation of word frequency, a word cloud for each place was generated using Wordle (Feinberg 2009), the results of which are presented in Figures 7.2, 7.3, and 7.4. In these Wordle graphics, the size of the font indicates word frequency: the larger the word, the more instances of that word there were in the free-listing task. The largest words thus demonstrate a consensus among participants about the relative representativeness of that term for a given place. Moreover, a Wordle graphic with many large words – especially semantically related large words – indicates a higher level of agreement between participants.

Figure 7.2 shows that three main words showed up repeatedly in the free-listing task for Birmingham: "country," "Southern," and "accent." "Country" appeared twenty-six times, "Southern" twenty-one times, and "accent" four-teen times. Notably, 63 percent of participants who listed a word related to

Figure 7.2 Word Cloud for Birmingham

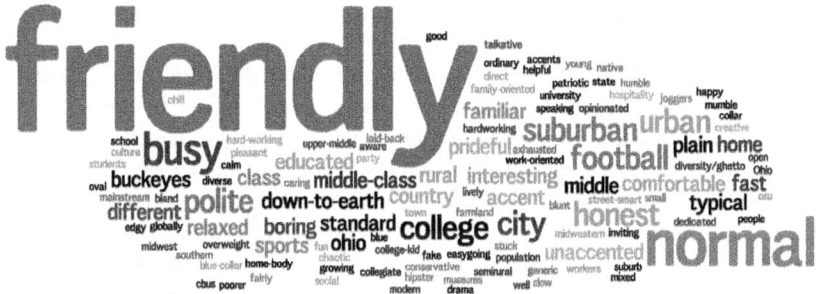

Figure 7.3 Word Cloud for Columbus

Figure 7.4 Word Cloud for New York City

"accent" (including "Southern accent" and "accented") also listed one related to "country" (including "hillbilly," "rural," and "farmers"). Furthermore, words relating to high solidarity, such as "polite," "hospitable," "friendly," "kind," and "honest" appear relatively frequently as well. This patterning mirrors the correlations in the listening task between country ratings, accentedness, and high solidarity ratings for speakers said to be from Birmingham.

Figure 7.3 presents the word cloud for Columbus, which looks very different from the word cloud for Birmingham. Rather than being occupied by a few words that were very frequent, most words consisted of single tokens – except for the word "friendly," which appeared on fifteen different questionnaires. The next most common term was "normal" (perhaps an unsurprising descriptor, given that every participant lived in Columbus or its environs at the time of the experiment), which still only featured six tokens. This complex constellation of terms may relate to participants' differing experiences with Columbus as a place or to its lack of national stereotypes; in contrast, many described Birmingham or New York in terms of stereotypes or representations in media.

The word cloud for New York City (Figure 7.4) appears to represent the middle ground between the word cloud for Columbus, which featured many single token descriptors, and that for Birmingham, which was dominated by a few frequently repeated words. Words like "city" (sixteen), "rude" (twelve), and "busy" (eighteen) appeared at the highest rates, while "accent" appeared relatively frequently as well (six – which is about half as frequent as for Birmingham, but still more than Columbus's two "accent" tokens).

Considered together, these free-listing results indicate higher expectations of accentedness for speakers from New York and Birmingham than for those from Columbus. This claim is bolstered by perceptual dialectology map results, which revealed that participants almost always marked areas including Birmingham and New York, while less than half of the participants marked an area including Columbus. Furthermore, when asked if people from Columbus have accents, survey responses overwhelmingly indicated that Columbusites are thought of as unaccented, plain, or normal.

*Do people from Columbus, Ohio have accents? If so, what do they sound like?*

> 33: They sound almost "accentless" like they are newscasters.
> 10: No – they sound like me.
> 11: People from Columbus, Ohio have typical Midwestern accents – we sound like what is typically thought of when one thinks about American English – Plain with mostly even stress.
> 31: No accents here!
> 35: Yes. I don't know I come from Central Ohio, I can't hear this accent.
> 41: Not that I can hear.
> 42: Yes, very plain sounding. A constant speed.
> 44: None that I can really hear. It seems very Midwest – like news anchors.
> 47: No, it is a very language-neutral place.
> 57: I don't notice the Midwest accent. I'm sure they sound like they have accents to people from other regions.

The concept of Midwestern accents being neutral or those adopted by news anchors carried over to the perceptual dialectology maps. For example, even when looking at the maps of participants who marked Columbus, the labels for these areas included words and phrases presented below.

- Midwestern/Midland
- Midwest accent "plain"
- Midwest, typically considered Standard American English
- Midwest, this is what I have so I can't hear the accent
- Midwest dialects that newscasters love
- non-regional diction (newscaster)
- normal accent

- normal speaking rate, clearer speech
- neutral

Many of these responses seem to acknowledge the standard, unmarked quality of Columbus, Ohio (and other Midwestern) accents. Preston (1996) found that the labels most commonly assigned to the Midwest and Inland North (Great Lakes area) were positive words such as "standard, regular, normal, and everyday" (306). Figures 7.5, 7.6, and 7.7 show some examples of these labels; in the case of Figure 7.6, "normal accent" encompasses an area that includes all of the West.

The idea of Columbus as representing a "normal" or "standard" region (in terms of language as well as social qualities) came up in follow-up interviews as well, as demonstrated below.

> 32: Where I'm from [in Northern Ohio], people are much less pleas-
> ant than people in Columbus, but I still think people in Columbus
> are like normal that's what I said [in the free-listing task].
> 31: Yeah I would say like I guess normal.
> 32: It's just normal average just –
> 31: Yeah I would say I would group the Midwest as just pretty
> average.
> . . .
> 33: I grew up here so people don't usually like comment on it
> [accents], but I've always been told that Ohio accents are kind of
> like accentless, like that's what newscasters go for?
> 32: mm-hm. I've always heard that too.
> 13: It's often looked at as a, uh, Ohio as just a neutral accent. And
> I see it often used as a reference point of "okay you – we don't
> have an accent" or what the newscasters go for.
> INTERVIEWER: So the word normal seems to have come up for
> both of you. So where do you think on your map people speak the
> most normal English?
> 14: The Midwest.
> INTERVIEWER: Anywhere in particular or just sort of generally?
> 14: Uh, I think like, Ohio, Indiana, Illinois. That kind of region
> I guess, specifically. Michigan.

In contrast, the abnormal and non-standard quality of Birmingham and New York varieties of English was frequently pointed out on maps and in interviews. For example, while labels for the Birmingham-inclusive areas usually included some version of "Southern/South" (98 percent) or "country" (14 percent), other words included more linguistic labels such as "twang," "drawl," "y'all," or a combination of all of these words. The most common linguistic commentary on New York City speech was accomplished by providing examples of r-less words such as "cah" for "car."

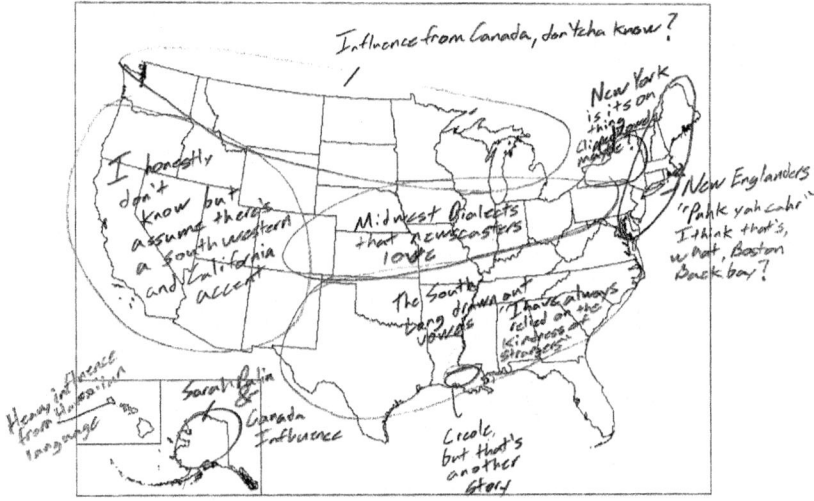

Figure 7.5 Participant 17's Perceptual Dialectology Map

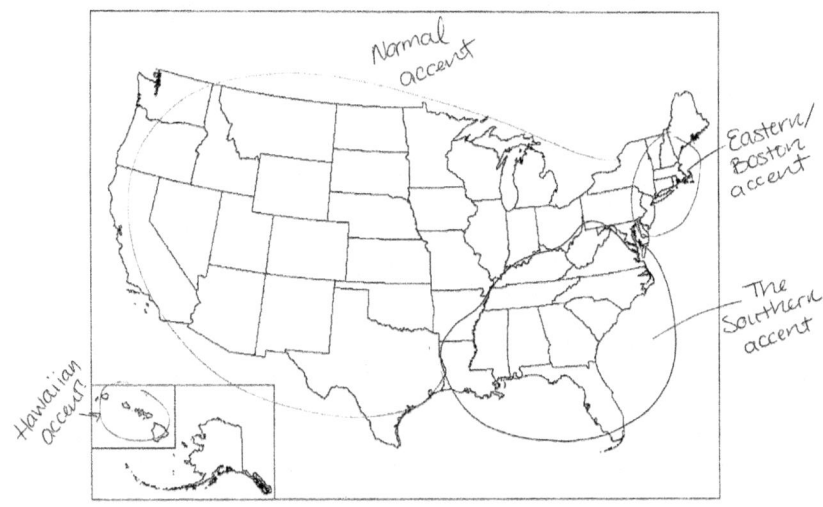

Figure 7.6 Participant 43's Perceptual Dialectology Map

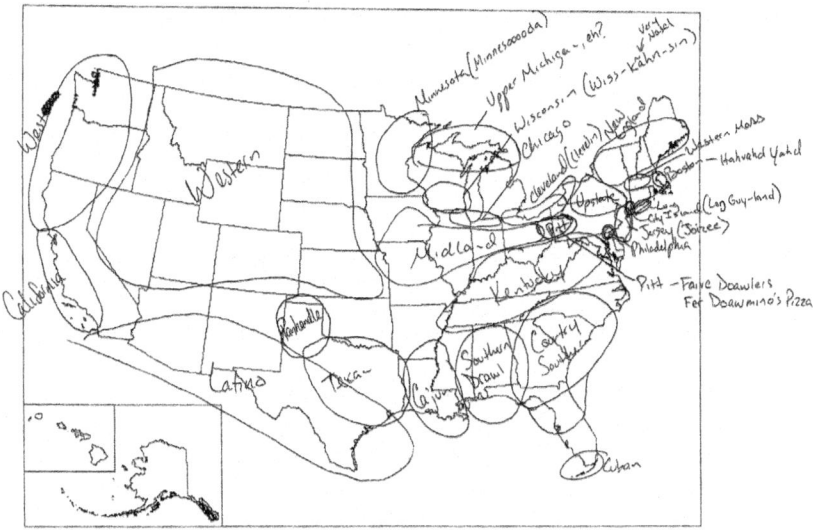

Figure 7.7 Participant 58's Perceptual Dialectology Map

On maps as well as in follow-up interviews, frequent reference was made to political figures with notable accents and/or strong ties to their home states (e.g. Sarah Palin on participant 17's map), in addition to other media figures from television and movies (participant 17's map makes reference to the television show *Jersey Shore* and includes a quote from the quintessential Southern debutante Blanche DuBois from the play *A Streetcar Named Desire*: "I have always relied on the kindness of strangers"). Below are some examples from follow-up interviews.

> 47: I felt like people from New York would have almost like an Italian-inspired accent, just because that's what pops in my head from movies and TV shows.
>
> INTERVIEWER: Any movies and TV shows in particular?
>
> 47: Like *Sopranos*? That kind of thing.
>
> INTERVIEWER: Have any of you been to Birmingham at all? No, none of you? So what were you drawing on for Birmingham speakers?
>
> 26: The movie "Sweet Home Alabama" {laughter}
>
> 27: Pretty much just media.
>
> INTERVIEWER: Media?
>
> 27: Things like that.

Some of the media references that came up in the map tasks and follow-up interviews can be seen in Table 7.2 below.

Table 7.2 *Media Representations of Birmingham, Columbus, and New York*

|  | Media representations |
|---|---|
| Birmingham, Alabama | *Sweet Home Alabama, Gone with the Wind, Divine Secrets of the Ya-Ya Sisterhood, Miss Congeniality, A Streetcar Named Desire*, The Real Housewives of Atlanta, Paula Deen from The Food Network, Jeff Foxworthy |
| Columbus, Ohio | newscasters |
| New York, New York | *Seinfeld, The Godfather, The Sopranos, Jersey Shore, NYPD Blue, Sex & The City, Will & Grace, Do the Right Thing, Law & Order, The Real Housewives of New York/New Jersey* |

Note that the only media representation of Columbus mentioned by participants was "newscaster speak." The media results from Table 7.2 mirror word cloud results, which showed a high level of consensus about stereotypical features relating to Birmingham and New York, with little agreement about Columbus. That is, participants' mental representations of Birmingham and New York appear to feature stereotypes more prominently than for Columbus – whether due to sheer availability of stereotypes (from media or otherwise), or to the fact that every participant has had personal experiences in Columbus, thereby rendering media representations a less useful tool in building sociolinguistic awareness.

## Summary and Discussion

Results from the listening task indicate that participants' ratings of social factors such as status, solidarity, and city-country associations depend heavily on the interaction between perceived accentedness and where a speaker is believed to be from. Data from the free-listing task, perceptual dialectology map task, and follow-up interviews point to strong associations of accentedness with Birmingham and New York City. In contrast, Columbus was rarely marked in the map task as a place in the United States possessing a regional accent, and was further described as specifically *not* accented in questionnaire responses. Moreover, in the free-listing task there was high agreement on a few descriptors for Birmingham and New York City, while descriptors for Columbus were significantly more varied, without much consensus. This patterning likely reflects fewer clear social stereotypes tied to Columbus, in addition to the differing personal experiences that each participant had with Columbus.

Taken all together, these results suggest that participants made use of a mental schema linking speech patterns to place. The question arises: how is this sociolinguistic awareness developed? What are the building blocks of such a schema, relating language, place, and social judgments? Responses to the free-listing and map tasks, and from follow-up interviews, suggest two main provenances. The first is personal experience. Taking, for example, the word cloud results for all three places: while the word clouds for Birmingham and New York included repeated tokens of stereotyped features, Columbus free-listing terms featured much greater diversity, with a number of singleton tokens. Perhaps unsurprisingly given the fact that all participants in the study were Ohio State undergraduates, many words to describe university life were featured, such as *college, Ohio State, sports, football, students, buckeyes, young, party, school*, and *university*. Words relating to the city-country continuum came up too, with *suburb/suburban* written down by several participants, as well as more traditionally Midwestern "small town" descriptive words like *family-oriented, down-to-earth, hardworking, blue collar, small, conservative*, and *boring*. In contrast, a number of more cosmopolitan descriptors like *busy, street-smart, social, opinionated, hipster, museums, art*, and *globally aware* were featured on Columbus free lists. These (sometimes conflicting) constellations of terms may relate to participants' differing experiences with Columbus, as one participant mentioned when the experimenter pointed out that all three participants present wrote down fairly similar terms for New York and Birmingham, but differed drastically in their free-listing of Columbus terms.

33: I think it's just maybe because we're living in Columbus so we might have a different perspective but I feel like mine definitely – I mean I feel like we all picked up on different things but I think they're all accurate representations. I think it just depends on like if you were born here, or if you lived other places.

Indeed, because all of the participants had personal experience with Columbus, being current residents of the town, they drew on their Columbus-specific experience to explain the stimuli they encountered. For example, many partici-pants expressed an expectation that within Ohio, accented speakers populate rural or "country" areas, or at the very least the outskirts of the city, which are the realm of accents. Illustrating this point, the following passages present one participant explaining that he assumed speakers he perceived as accented were not from the city, and another framing such a belief as practically universal.

11: I guess I was trying to go more by personal experience than anything else, just from people that I know, um, where they've come from, um, for example I'm from Dayton but I don't really speak like my friends who are from Bellbrook [a town 10 miles south of Dayton's city center], which is kind of the … country area. They sound more um, more like they're from maybe Kentucky or Tennessee. So if I heard any trace of an accent like that I generally said that they were accented and probably not from the city. Whereas if they talked sort of in a typical Midwestern with you know very plain speech, nothing's really stressed, I was more likely to say they were from the city.

12: We all make the judgment that people who have an accent are from the country.

The existence of an accented "country" Ohioan as an available referent for many participants may help to explain correlations between the factors of city-unaccented and country-accented in the listening task for speakers said to be from Columbus.

> INTERVIEWER: Okay, {to 27} so [in the free-listing task] you actually wrote "city" for Columbus {to 26} and you wrote neither "city" nor "country" for Columbus, so where does Columbus fall in this whole city-country thing?
>
> 26: Columbus. I would say city. Um, country would be like a little bit further out if you like drive North on [I-]71 or something.
>
> 27: Yeah.
>
> 26: And you hit just straight flat land, and you just see cows and stuff, that would be country, but if you're talking just about Columbus, there's like a lot of like buildings so I would say that is a city.
>
> INTERVIEWER: Did you, when you were doing the listening task, did Columbus people – were you rating them more city or more country do you remember?
>
> 27: I think it was a toss-up for me, they went both ways.
>
> 12: I think part of the thing that swayed my um like the way I rated people was my, um, cousins live sort of close to – they live sort of like, they live in southeast Ohio and so they sort of have accents and like, just talk, like, funny to me.
>
> 15: yeah I have a lot of friends that're from like Southern Ohio and they're like – they have some families that are like fairly unedu-cated and people from there are just like ... not to be like stereo-typical, but from some like farm area and they're a little more, um, like, just like their families in history are just a little bit less educated, so I feel like Columbus, like as a metropolitan area in general is a bit more ... educated.

This sort of commentary, taken in combination with listening task results, suggests that to be accented from Columbus – or Central Ohio more broadly – is to be country (and possibly less educated, which would follow the patterning of lower status ratings for "country," accented Columbusites in the listening task). Indeed, "country talk" has been enregistered in other communities (Hall-Lew and Stephens 2011) and there is evidence that within Ohio, country associations are linked equally to southern areas of the state, particularly Appalachia, and any rural areas, including those in the North (Campbell-Kibler 2012). Thus, "country" is both a place and a way of speaking/being. The conflation of place and accent (and even socioeconomic status) can be seen in one participant's explanation of the "Grovetucky effect," referring to a South Columbus suburb called Grove City which he identifies as "Appalachian."

10: Outside [of Columbus] is more of the Grovetucky effect that I was talking about, which in most people's minds it's very quickly an Appalachian sort of sound. Or um a socioeconomical level. Um like I said I haven't spent much time there, I drove through it once and I thought it was nice, but I was told not to go back, by people from this area [Central Columbus].

In providing these sorts of explanations, participants in the listening task were able to discredit accented speakers' claims to Columbus as a place, or at least marginalize them by placing them in liminal spaces outside of city limits, while continuing to treat place as a deterministic factor for accents.

The second main source of sociolinguistic awareness uncovered in this study consists of media representations. This is unsurprising given past findings about how certain regional and otherwise non-mainstream dialects are represented in media (e.g. Lippi-Green 1997). What is interesting here is how clear the differentiation in representation was between the three places – with stronger weighting of media representations for the New York and Birmingham dialects that also came up in the tasks as more "salient" or non-standard than Columbus. In the perceptual dialectology maps as well as during follow-up interviews, multiple and varied media representations came up for New York and Birmingham, including specific mafia (*The Godfather, The Sopranos*) and police officer (*Law & Order, NYPD Blue*) personae for New York and Southern belle (*Gone with the Wind, A Streetcar Named Desire*) and redneck (Jeff Foxworthy, *Sweet Home Alabama*) personae for Birmingham. In contrast, the only representation of Columbus dialects came from reference to "newscaster" speak – generally without even identifying an individual newscaster to stand in as the embodiment of that dialect.

The sociolinguistic awareness built up by personal experience and media representations clearly framed participants' (sometimes unmet) expectations of accents from each place, as seen in the examples below:

3: I expected the Ohio to be more like non-regional like more like my accent and I expected like the – the Alabama to be really Alabama-y.

47: Just recognizing that someone's from Birmingham and that he doesn't have the thick accent I'd think he'd have was just bizarre to me almost.

The response to these unmet expectations, interestingly, was not generally to adjust the schema – instead, they chose to view the individual as an exception to the rule, for which other explanations must be sought. Below, one participant seems to assume that unaccented New Yorkers "aren't from there" and another participant explicitly attributes transplant status to the unaccented speakers said to be from Birmingham in the experiment.

> 8: The people from Birmingham, I was a little surprised their accents were closer to mine than what I'm used to in the south.

INTERVIEWER: So what was the effect of that? What did that make you think about them?

8: It made me question whether they're from Birmingham or not ... *I think they're transplants, I think they're Northern people.*

25: Not everyone who comes from a certain area speaks a certain way. Like I've had people say "oh you're from Southern Ohio, I would've thought you would've have an accent," and I'm like, "no. Not all of us do." And just like not everybody from New Jersey has an accent, not everybody from New York has an accent. I mean it just depends on smaller than state regions.

INTERVIEWER: So what, um, sorts of things does it depend on? So what do you think when you meet someone from New Jersey who doesn't have that accent?

25: I mean *it's probably a matter of like how long they've lived in the area.*

32: I just think of New York maybe as a place where *a lot of people who aren't from there* live there you know what I mean? So you do get, you do get a little bit of that like the standard stereotypical New York accent, but you also get a lot of neutral, you get some southern, you get foreign.

Taken in combination with descriptions of "country" Columbusites as the residents of marginal areas outside city limits, explanations that appeal to a different hometown as the source of unexpected accentedness continued the trend of framing the relationship between place and accent as deterministic. Treating place as a determining factor in whether one will be accented also speaks to the issue of *perceived* speaker control, in that participants ascribed very little control over linguistic variables to speakers from places where accentedness is expected. Indeed, this helps to explain listening task results in which accented speakers from Birmingham or New York were not down-rated, and those who were unaccented from those places were simply portrayed as not being "from there." In contrast, speakers said to be from an "unaccented" place like Columbus who were perceived as accented were down-rated in the listening task, and in some cases explained away as being "country" Columbusites from the outer edges of the city.

## Conclusions

This study has made use of a variety of methods to better understand the role of regional accents and place associations in individuals' sociolinguistic awareness. Patterning in listening task results demonstrated that participants altered their social judgments about speakers depending on perceived accentedness.

For example, when presented with an accented speaker from Birmingham, listeners reacted differently in terms of their social evaluations than when they encountered a Columbusite perceived to be accented. Findings from a free-listing task, perceptual dialectology map task, and follow-up interviews suggested that these participants made use of place-linked sociolinguistic expectations when presented with novel linguistic input and place information about the speaker. Some of the strategies participants appealed to included their personal experiences, as well as media representations of people from the places of interest. Follow-up interviews furthermore indicated that some participants viewed the place-accent link as almost deterministic, developing detailed explanations for why their accentedness expectations were not always met, rather than adjusting their mental schema.

The results of these four tasks have several implications for our understanding of the ways in which listeners use their sociolinguistic awareness, and their perceptions of speaker control over linguistic variables, when presented with novel linguistic input. To begin with, I have argued in this chapter that the awareness of a link between regional accents and certain places created sociolinguistic expectations that affected participants' evaluations of the speakers in the listening task. When expectations about the accentedness of speakers from a given place went unmet, participants' reactions to the stimuli reflected this mismatch, in very specific and systematic ways. For speakers from a place where accentedness was expected, neither accented nor unaccented speakers were down-rated. In contrast, speakers perceived as accented who were from a place where accentedness was *not* expected were down-rated. These results suggest participants were making active use of their sociolinguistic awareness during the listening task. Follow-up interviews revealed that participants frequently explained away mismatches between place and accentedness, in effect treating place as a deterministic factor in whether a given person is accented. Examining listening task results through this frame, it appears that participants used this perception about speaker control by making allowances for speakers who are expected to be accented (and thus have less control over linguistic variables), but down-rating accented speakers from a place where accentedness is unexpected. That is, participants used both their sociolinguistic awareness, and their perceptions about speaker control over linguistic variables, in socially evaluating speakers.

## REFERENCES

Anisfeld, Moshe, Bogo, Norman, and Lambert, Wallace E. 1962. Evaluational reactions to accented English speech. *Journal of Abnormal and Social Psychology* 65(4):223–31.

Becker, Kara. 2009. /r/ and the construction of place identity on New York City's Lower East Side. *Journal of Sociolinguistics* 13(5):634–58.

Bell, Allan. 1984. Language style as audience design. *Language in Society* 13(2):145–204.

Bonfiglio, Thomas P. 2002. *Race and the Rise of Standard American*. Berlin: Mouton de Gruyter.

Bucholtz, Mary and Hall, Kira. 2005. Identity and interaction: A sociocultural linguistic approach. *Discourse Studies* 7(4–5):584–614.

2008. All of the above: New coalitions in sociocultural linguistics. *Journal of Sociolinguistics* 12(4):1–31.

Bucholtz, Mary, Bermudez, Nancy, Fung, Victor, Edwards, Lisa, and Vargas, Rosalva. 2007. Hella Nor Cal or totally So Cal?: The perceptual dialectology of California. *Journal of English Linguistics* 35(4):325–52.

Callan, Victor J., Gallois, Cynthia, and Forbes, Paula A. 1983. Evaluative reactions to accented English: Ethnicity, sex role, and context. *Journal of Cross-Cultural Psychology* 14:407–26.

Campbell-Kibler, Kathryn. 2009. The nature of sociolinguistic perception. *Language Variation and Change* 21:135–56.

2012. Contestation and enregisterment in Ohio's imagined dialects. *Journal of English Linguistics* 40(3):281–305.

Carmichael, Katie. 2013. The performance of Cajun English in Boudreaux and Thibodeaux jokes. *American Speech* 88(4):377–412.

Submitted. "Since when does the Midwest have an accent?": The role of regional accent and preconceived notions of place in speaker evaluations.

Clopper, Cynthia G. and Pisoni, David B. 2006a. The Nationwide Speech Project: A new corpus of American English dialects. *Speech Communication* 48:633–44.

2006b. Effects of region of origin and geographic mobility on perceptual dialect categorization. *Language Variation and Change* 18:193–221.

2007. Free classification of regional dialects of American English. *Journal of Phonetics* 25:421–38.

Daleszynska, Agata. 2011. What's gender got to do with it?: Investigating the effect of gender and place on /t,d/ deletion in Bequia. Proceedings of the Summer School of Sociolinguistics, University of Edinburgh, January 2011.

Edwards, John. 1999. Refining our understanding of language attitudes. *Journal of Language and Social Psychology* 18:101–10.

Feinberg, Jonathan. 2009. *Wordle: Beautiful Word Clouds*. www.wordle.net/

Fought, Carmen. 2002. California students' perceptions of, you know, regions and dialects? in Daniel Long (ed.), *Handbook of Perceptual Dialectology*, Vol. 2, pp. 113–34. Amsterdam: John Benjamins.

Giles, Howard, Coupland, Joustine, and Coupland, Nicholas. 1991. Accommodation theory: Communication, context, and consequence, in Howard Giles, Joustine Coupland, and Nicholas Coupland (eds.), *Contexts of Accommodation*. New York: Cambridge University Press.

Hall-Lew, Lauren and Stephens, Nola. 2011. Country talk. *Journal of English Linguistics* 40(3):256–80.

Hartley, Laura C. and Preston, Dennis. 1999. The names of US English: valley girl, cowboy, yankee, normal, nasal and ignorant, in Tony Bex and Richard J. Watts (eds.), *Standard English, The widening debate*, pp. 207–39. London and New York: Routledge.

Hay, Jennifer and Drager, Katie. 2010. Stuffed toys and speech perception. *Linguistics* 48(4):865–92.

Iannàccaro, Gabriele and Dell'Aquila, Vittorio. 2001. Mapping languages from inside: Notes on perceptual dialectology. *Social and Cultural Geography* 2(3):265–80.

Johnstone, Barbara. 1999. Uses of Southern-sounding speech by contemporary Texas women. *Journal of Sociolinguistics* 3:505–22.

2004. Place, globalization, and linguistic variation, in Carmen Fought (ed.), *Sociolinguistic Variation: Critical Reflections*, pp. 65–83. Oxford University Press.

Johnstone, Barbara, Andrus, Jennifer, and Danielson, Andrew E. 2006. Mobility, indexicality, and the enregisterment of "Pittsburghese." *Journal of English Linguistics* 34(2):77–104.

Johnstone, Barbara, Bhasin, Neeta, and Wittkofski, Denise. 2002. "Dahntahn" Pittsburgh: Monophthongal /aw/ and representations of localness in Southwestern Pennsylvania. *American Speech* 77(2):148–66.

Johnstone, Barbara and Kiesling, Scott F. 2008. Indexicality and experience: Variation and identity in Pittsburgh. *Journal of Sociolinguistics* 12:5–33.

Labov, William. 2006[1966]. *The Social Stratification of English in New York City.* Washington, DC: Center for Applied Linguistics; 2nd edn. Cambridge University Press.

1972. Some principles of linguistic methodology. *Language in Society* 1:97–120.

1984. Field methods of the project on language change and variation, in John Baugh and Joel Scherzer (eds.), *Language in Use: Readings in Sociolinguistics*, pp. 28–53. Englewood Cliffs, NJ: Prentice Hall.

Lambert, W. E., Hodgson, R. C., Gardner, R. C., and Fillenbaum, S. 1960. Evaluational reactions to spoken languages. *Journal of Abnormal and Social Psychology* 60(1):44–51.

Le Page, Robert B. and Tabouret-Keller, Andrée. 1985. *Acts of Identity: Creole-Based Approaches to Language and Ethnicity.* Cambridge University Press.

Lippi-Green, Rosina. 1997. *English with an Accent: Language, Ideology, and Discrimination in the United States.* New York: Routledge.

Luhman, Reid. 1990. Appalachian English stereotypes: Language attitudes in Kentucky. *Language in Society* 19(3):331–48.

Milroy, Lesley and McClenaghan, P. 1977. Stereotyped reactions to four educated accents in Ulster. *Belfast Working Papers in Language and Linguistics* 2(4):1–11.

Milroy, Leslie and Preston, Dennis R. 1999. Introduction to special issue on language attitudes. *Journal of Language and Social Psychology* 18:4–9.

Niedzielski, Nancy A. 1999. The effect of social information on the perception of sociolinguistic variables. *Journal of Language and Social Psychology* 18(1):62–85.

Preston, Dennis 1989. *Perceptual Dialectology: Nonlinguists' Views of Areal Linguistics.* Providence, RI: Foris Publications.

1996. Where the worst English is spoken, in Edgar Schneider (ed.), *Focus on the USA*, pp. 297–360. Amsterdam: John Benjamins.

1999. The South: The touchstone, in Cynthia Bernstein, Thomas Nunnally, and Robin Sabino (eds.), *Language Variety in the South Revisited*, pp. 311–51. Tuscaloosa, AL: University of Alabama Press.

Schilling-Estes, Natalie. 1998. Investigating self-conscious speech: The performance register in Ocracoke English. *Language in Society* 27:53–83.

Williams, R. T. 1989. The (mis)identification of regional and national accents of English: Pragmatic, cognitive and social aspects, in Ofelia García and Ricardo Otheguy (eds.), *English across Cultures, Cultures across English: A Reader in Cross-cultural Communication*, pp. 55–81. Berlin: Mouton de Gruytor.

Zahn, Christopher J. and Hopper, Robert. 1985. Measuring language attitudes: The speech evaluation instrument. *Journal of Language and Social Psychology* 4(2):113–23.

# 8    Whaddayaknow now?

*Dennis R. Preston*[*]

## Introduction

In the study of subjective responses to language attitudes, beliefs, and ideologies, a most important concern is how and why persons notice the performance of another speaker (or group), how they process what is noticed, and how they respond to the product of that processing. In this chapter I will update reflections on the first two of these questions, since the product of processing (the expression) has been a much-studied fact, although I will appeal to such research products to justify what I believe about folk noticing and processing.

## What Can Be Known and in What Way Do We Know It?

In "Whaddayaknow" (Preston 1996a), I provided a summary, explication, and evaluation of Silverstein's 1981 work on the "limits of awareness" and my own outline of the "modes" of folk[1] linguistic awareness.

Silverstein's account catalogs structural and pragmatic facts about language on the basis of their availability to the consciousness of non-linguists and, therefore, on their ability to report them. For example, discontinuous structures such as the English progressive, in which the copula is separated from '–ing'

---

[*] Several people have asked why there is a "wh" in the title of Preston 1996a (repeated here), suggesting that since the rest of the spelling indicates casual pronunciation this should be simply "W." Although the hw/w map of Labov *et al.* (2006: 50, Map 8.1) does not show the distinction in the Louisville, KY area (my home region), I assure the reader that the hw/w distinction is strong in my most casual speech and has simply disappeared among younger speakers in Louisville.

[1] By "folk" I mean, and have meant in earlier publications on folk linguistics (e.g. Niedzielski and Preston 2003: xviii), those who are not professionally trained in the field; I definitely do not mean rural, poorly educated, unsophisticated, or marginalized members of society. Both brain surgeons and rocket scientists, to choose the two most traditional areas of learned sophistication, at least for a long time in US culture before large-scale public awareness of computers, are capable of folk linguistic attitudes and beliefs. Moreover, folk beliefs are, unlike the status assigned them in the popular notion of "folklore," both those which correspond to and disagree with scientific understandings of the world; I do not mean for folk linguistics to carry the usual "false" sense in the field found in, for example, the label "folk etymology."

by the main verb, are the sorts of facts that are unlikely to be understood by folk respondents as unified (i.e. one in which the copula and '–ing' are components of a single fact). In the pragmatic world, Silverstein noted that forms with "unavoidable referentiality" are more likely to have their associated pragmatic facts overtly known to non-linguists, using as his example the deference-familiarity dichotomy embedded in many pronoun systems. Since, for example, any employment of Polish 'ty' (familiar second person singular) or 'Pan(i)' (deferential second person singular) unavoidably refers to individuals, the associated pragmatic meaning is more available to folk knowledge.

In that same article, I treated Silverstein's limitations of folk linguistic awareness under the label "Availability," but I added three more concerns:

(1) Availability – Is a linguistic fact available to the conscious awareness of a folk respondent? If so, is it a common focus in the speech community (a stereotype), an easily elicitable fact, an observation that can only be extracted from respondents after careful fieldworker explanation, or one that non-linguists simply do not have (and cannot have made) available to them for overt comment?

(2) Accuracy – Does the folk account mirror the facts (or one of the linguistic accounts of them)?

(3) Detail – Does the folk account focus on global linguistic facts (e.g. Arabic-accented English) or on detail (Arabic speakers say "b" instead of "p" when they speak English)?

(4) Control – Can folk respondents offer an imitation or performance of the linguistic elements or varieties they comment on? (Preston 1996a: 40–1)

The most important fact that this list does not take fully into account is the conscious-unconscious distinction, one of the main focuses of this volume. Not long after this 1996 article, Nancy Niedzielski and I made a rough distinction between folk linguistics and language attitude studies based at least in part on that dichotomy. We suggested that what speakers were conscious of was folk linguistics and that which did not rise to the level of conscious awareness was language attitude study, although we left an opportunity for speakers to give overt reports about how they had reacted – that is, folk linguistic characterizations of nonconsciously motivated attitudinal responses (Niedzielski and Preston 2000: esp. 25–30).

This is at least partly in line with Hoenigswald's (1966) proposal for the study of folk linguistics, which notes that ". . . we should be interested not only in (a) what goes on (language), but also in (b) how people react to what goes on . . . and in (c) what people say goes on . . ." (20). But in the details of the text he notes that "how people react" may be explicit (within the realm of awareness) or implicit, and, as regards the former, ". . . with either a correct explanation or an incorrect rationalization . . ." (19). In other words, implicit reactions are neither correct nor incorrect, presumably because they do not involve "explanation" or "rationalization." This seems odd to me; even when people react explicitly they do not necessarily accompany such a reaction with an explanation or rationalization. For example, "I don't like the way people from Louisville (Kentucky, USA) talk" is an explicit (b) – a reaction to an (a) (i.e. "what goes on"). If that person were to go on to say "Because they talk through their noses," they are probably wrong about the facts, but their (b) response is not wrong; it is their explanation or rationalization that is at fault, and that is surely a (c), but in this case it is a (c) comment on a (b) rather than on an (a). People who simply shudder (unconsciously) when they hear people from Louisville also exhibit a (b) (implicitly), but might, perhaps after many such shudders, recall all this and report as follows: "I hate it when people from Louisville talk; it makes me shudder, but I don't really know why." I take all of this to be (c): what someone has said about what went on, but, again, in these cases what went on is not about language itself (a), but about the reaction to it (b). To taxonomize somewhat differently, then, but still borrowing Hoenigs-wald's basic outline, we should be interested in (a) what goes on linguistically, (b) how people react to (a), either (i) implicitly, or (ii) explicitly, and (c) what people say about (a) and (b), both (b)(i) and (b)(ii).

Before leaving Silverstein's account of what *can* be noticed by non-linguists (1981), Sibata's notion (along with my 1996a corollary) of what is *likely* to be noticed (1971), and my catalog of *modes* or types of noticing (or at least evidence of noticing) (1996a), one particularly underexplored area should be noted. The fourth mode of folk linguistic awareness proposed in Preston (1996a) appears to be one of granularity – "3) *Detail*: A linguistic object may be characterized with great specificity or none" (41). I now believe that one cannot approach this distinction until a more general account of folk linguistic theory is taken into consideration, and there is surely some circular-ity here. A folk theory is constructed at least in part out of just such folk responses as those that reflect these levels of granularity, but we can put up with a little moving back and forth between the construction of a more general theory and the pieces of evidence for it, particularly if the growing outlines of the theory allow us to reconsider and refashion the techniques in our approaches to the evidence itself. One upshot of a folk versus linguistic theory of language is that the parallelism between levels of granularity is not at all guaranteed. Here (Table 8.1) is an admittedly incomplete look at the levels of detail that might be involved in folk and linguistic characterizations of /ɪ/-/ɛ/ conflation before nasals (a very common phenomenon in much Southern US speech).

At first glance, readers may think that Table 8.1 simply turns plain talk into fancy talk in the contrast between the folk and linguistic levels, but that is not so. Even at the most general level of comparison, real people and linguists do

Table 8.1 *Levels of Generality in Folk and Linguistic Accounts of [ɪ]/[ɛ] Conflation*

|  | Folk | Linguistic |
|---|---|---|
| Most general | has an accent | has regional pronunciation features |
|  | has a Southern accent | has Southern regional features |
|  | (Southerners say [ɪ] for [ɛ]) | Southerners conflate [ɪ] and [ɛ] before nonvelar nasals |
| Least general | "pen" sounds like "pin"; "hem" like "him"; get" like "git" | "pin" and "pen," "hem" and "him," are homophones; "get" has the vowel [ɪ] |

not always cover the same territory with their observations. When the folk say that someone has an accent, there are at least two important differences. First, for linguists, if the word "accent" is a technical term at all, it refers exclusively to the phonetic/phonological level. Folk respondents very often refer to the entire linguistic system with this word. Second, and more importantly, linguists know that everyone speaks some regional variety, even those heavily invested in removing such matters from their speech. Folk comment abounds, however, with the idea that somewhere there is "accent-free" speech; in the United States, for example, many respondents identify the Upper Midwest as "accent-free," perhaps particularly those from the area itself.

At finer levels of granularity, things are even more distinct between linguists and the folk. A folk observation that "pen" sounds like "pin" and "get" sounds like "git" might lead to the belief (at the next level up of generality) that such speakers pronounce /ɛ/ as /ɪ/ when, in fact, the conflation occurs only before nonvelar nasals, and "git" is a lexical rule.

In short, what I suggested for *Detail* (1996a and above) is fraught throughout with these distinctions, and the folk notions need to be discovered on their own, not assumed from scientific classification. McGowan (this volume) proposes similar more detailed suggestions for the category of *Control* (Preston 1996a and above).

One might object, however, that this comparison between folk and scientific beliefs is based only on the sorts of things that students are told are not true during introductory linguistics, but a value in investigating the awareness and beliefs of the folk lies in the fact that such beliefs may provide clues for scientific work. Plichta (2004), for example, took seriously the folk comment that big-city upper Midwesterners were "nasal" and went on to show that there was a positive correlation between advancement in the Upper-Midwestern US Northern Cities Vowel Shift and nasality in non-nasal environments. The folk belief led him in a direction that most linguists would not have recommended, and the utility of folk linguistics would appear to have considerable implications for professionals interested in the actual structure and variety of language.[2]

## Who Cares and Why?

Is a (b)(ii) (i.e. overt) reaction to an (a) fact the domain of language attitude study or of folk linguistics? To pursue the above example, is folk linguistics not allowed to study and account for an instance of "Louisville talk" (an (a)) that causes involuntary shuddering and is not available to consciousness – (b) (i), but given the green light to consider uses that cause an explicit remark: "Ugh, when Louisvillians talk I shudder" – a (c) description of a (b)(i or ii)?

Even more territorial perhaps is the idea that these beliefs and reactions, regardless of their implicit or explicit nature, are organized into systems of cultural behavior under the rubric "language ideology." Here is a quick (and overgeneralized) correlation of fields and subfields and their domains:

(1) Sociolinguists (and dialectologists[3]) are interested in folk linguistics (c).
(2) Social psychologists (of language[4]) are interested in language attitudes (b).
(3) Linguistic anthropologists are interested in language ideologies (not referenced in Hoenigswald's remarks).

Happily, more than a few of these people have been in touch with one another (or at least have consulted one another's' work) to reduce this insularity.

(1) Sociolinguists have learned from social psychologists how to employ careful experimentalism in their work. Graff *et al.* (1986), an early example, uses the matched guise technique to determine the salience of specific linguistic markers in awakening respondent identification of speaker ethnicity. Even more recently, sociolinguists have learned advanced techniques in uncovering implicit (or "unconscious") reactions of respondents who have been presented

---

[2] Folk linguistics is not productive for just descriptive and theoretical matters; it has obvious relevance to work in applied linguistics. It would be foolish to try to do something about someone's language without knowing what their theory of language was. These connections are outlined in some detail in Niedzielski and Preston 2009 and are the subject of an entire issue in an applied linguistics journal (Wilton-Franklin and Stegu 2010).

[3] Although there is earlier work on folk linguistics (e.g. Polle 1889), the earliest comprehensive forays were in the subfield of perceptual dialectology and were carried out in Dutch-speaking and Japanese areas by regional dialectologists, although there is one such German work in this early period (Büld 1939) that has been reviewed and commented on most recently in Twilfer (2010). Many of the early Dutch and Japanese studies are available in English translations in Preston 1999b.

[4] I must specify social psychologists *of language* since, amazingly, this subfield of the study of attitudes, influential as it has been, has apparently escaped the attention of attitude scholars in general. In a general survey (Albarracín *et al.* 2005), the names Wallace Lambert, Howard Giles, and Peter Garrett cannot be found in the references, nor is there any discussion of language as an attitude object in any of the chapters.

with speech samples for evaluation (e.g. Campbell-Kibler 2012 and this volume; Pantos and Perkins 2013).

Sociolinguists have contributed back to social psychology the fact that such detailed linguistic elements (as well as global samples) are important considerations, as shown in a number of articles in the *Journal of Language and Social Psychology* 18:1 (Milroy and Preston 1999) and many later publications, particularly in the subfield of sociophonetics.[5]

(2) Sociolinguists have also learned from recent trends in the social psychological study of attitudes that discoursal as well as experimental evidence can be important (e.g. Potter and Wetherell 1987), and have returned the favor by suggesting more linguistically oriented methods of analyzing discourses relevant to folk linguistics and the study of language attitudes (e.g. Preston 1993, 1994, 1999a, 2010a).

(3) Sociolinguists have also learned from social psychologists the importance of the cognitive underpinnings of folk and attitudinal factors, and that fact is explored more fully below.

(4) Sociolinguists have learned from linguistic anthropologists that attitudes towards and folk beliefs about language are not isolated instances, but reflect patterned and structured ideologies within cultures and speech communities. Perhaps the most influential of these has been Silverstein's notion of *indexicality* (e.g. Silverstein 2003), which places folk responses into hierarchical, derived, and transformed patterns. Sociolinguistically oriented responses to this tradition are Lippi-Green (1997: 64), Milroy and Milroy (1999: 151–6), and Preston (1998: 265–6), in all of which language ideologies are derived from careful consideration of sociolinguistic patterns and processes, as well as social attitudinal factors.

I believe that folk linguistics, language attitude study, and language ideologies have a commonality and that I can help to show this by appealing to both the procedural aspects and the underlying constructs of what I have called "language regard" (Preston 2010b). I use this term to avoid the consciousness-unconsciousness split of folk linguistics versus the social psychology of language and the implication that those two do not seek the structural organization of belief and attitude associated with anthropological investigations. I will not disregard the fact that some research has shown interesting mismatches between more and less conscious responses to linguistic stimuli and that the organizing principles of ideological studies have helped in our interpretive work, but I will focus here on the common ground. I agree with Dell Hymes:

---

[5] Clopper *et al.* (2011) is a thorough survey of experimentalism in the identification and judgment of individual linguistic elements in the sociophonetic tradition.

It should be possible to cut across this distinction between conscious and unconscious attitudes, and simply take the whole attestation of behavior with regard to language use as the subject matter for our type of description (Hymes 1971: 26).

### Cognitive Pathways

Niedzielski and Preston (2003) suggest shared characteristics for folk linguistics and language attitudes, and Figure 8.1 builds in procedural as well as static concerns.

I will explicate this triangle and its parts by attending to both the conceptual characteristics of the units and the procedural mechanisms involved.

Behind everything lies the activity that will serve as the stimulus for "Noticing." It would be a mistake, however, to say that this is always a case of (a), that is, an instance of language production, although that may be the most normal route for the triggering of regard processes. There are at least several other possibilities:

(1) A researcher may offer no speech sample at all and ask a respondent to rely on internal resources (memories and caricatures of (a), but see (3) below) in an attempt to elicit attitude or belief. In perceptual or folk dialectology, for example, respondents are asked if speakers in nearby areas sound just like

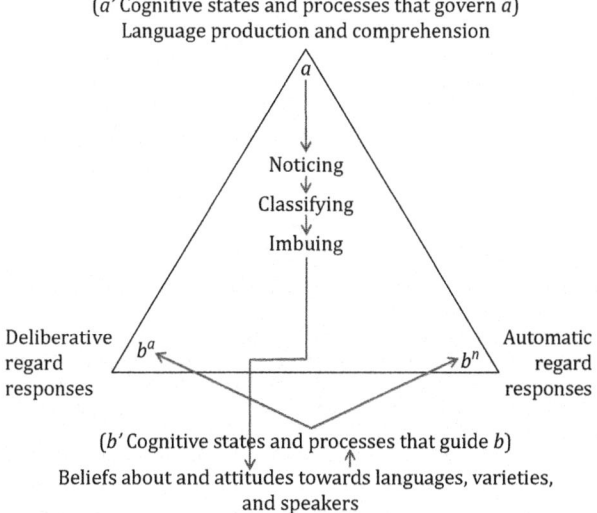

Figure 8.1 The Domains and Procedural Characteristics of Folk Linguistics and Language Attitude Studies
Adapted from Niedzielski and Preston 2003: xi.

them, a little different, or very different;[6] or respondents are asked to draw maps of larger areas where people "speak differently" and to comment on the speakers and features of their language in the areas they outlined.[7]

(2) Respondents may comment on *a*, that is, on the "Cognitive states and processes that govern *a*" of Figure 8.1. Folk respondents often discuss such matters as first and second language acquisition (e.g. Niedzielski and Preston 1997; Pasquale and Preston 2013) and outline their ideas of the cognitive requirements for and operations of such abilities. This is also surely a matter for folk, attitudinal, and ideological studies of language, but it may not be triggered by an example of an actual *a*.

(3) The most unusual cases of *a*-inspired responses are perhaps those that go awry, for they are often very strong indicators of attitudinal and ideological factors. In these cases, hearers of *a*-data misclassify the signal. One of the most dramatic illustrations of this possibility is Niedzielski (1999). Forty-two south-eastern Michigan respondents, all local native speakers whose vowel systems reflected the Northern Cities Vowel Shift (NCVS),[8] were asked to match a pronunciation of the word "last" to one of three others of the same word. The initial stimulus was one in which the F1 of the [æ] vowel was raised to roughly the height of a more typical [ɛ], a usual relocation in the NCVS. In the sample words to which this pronunciation was to be matched, three alternatives were given: the matching one (with the vowel at the same F1 height of [ɛ]), one called "canonical" (i.e. with an [æ] pronunciation), and a third with an even lower and backer vowel (i.e. [a]). The puzzling result was that, although these three pronunciations were very distinct, not one respondent got it right; in fact, four of the forty-two even identified the [a] pronunciation, a lower and backer one, as the match (Niedzielski 1999: 72).

Do Michiganders hear badly? Not at all. Niedzielski explains the results by noting that the respondents were informed that the speakers were local Michiganders, and that it was that identity that prevented their detection of any

---

[6] Early examples of such work from Dutch and Japanese dialectologists are available in Preston 1999a.

[7] The first maps of this sort that I know of are in Preston 1982.

[8] The NCVS is a rotation of the short vowels taking place (and has largely taken place) in the major urban areas around the US Great Lakes (Rochester and Buffalo, New York; Cleveland and Toledo, Ohio; Detroit, Lansing, and Grand Rapids, Michigan; Chicago, Illinois; Milwaukee and Madison, Wisconsin) and is spreading into surrounding smaller cities and towns and the countryside (e.g. Labov *et al.* 2006). It consists of the following apparently historically ordered steps:

(1) Fronting and raising of /æ/ (TRAP) to a position close to a conservative /ɛ/ or even /ɪ/
(2) Fronting and lowering of /ɑ/ (LOT) to a position close to a conservative /æ/
(3) Fronting and lowering of /ɔ/ (THOUGHT) to a position close to conservative /ɑ/
(4) Lowering and backing of /ɛ/ (DRESS) to a position close to either conservative /æ/ or /ʌ/
(5) Backing of /ʌ/ (STRUT) to a position close to conservative /ɔ/
(6) Lowering and backing of /ɪ/ (KIT) to a position close to conservative /ɛ/

linguistic element that differed from their internal characterization of the standard or correct form. Indeed, when young Michiganders are presented with NCVS details in linguistics and sociolinguistics courses and given examples, they vehemently deny that they or fellow Michiganders have such pronunciations. Niedzielski relies on other work in folk and attitudinal linguistics to confirm her suspicions that Michiganders do not hear vowels that do not conform to their notion of local correctness. In a series of articles summarized in Preston 1996b and in Niedzielski and Preston 2000 and 2003, it is shown that in a hand-drawn map task Michiganders annotate Michigan with such words as "normal" and "correct' and in an overt ranking of "correct" English in the United States, they rank Michigan as the home of the most correct English in the country. In short, their perception of their own pronunciation and of those they consider to be just like them is misdirected by their attitudinal and ideational construction of the "correct" English of the local area. Carmichael (this volume) also combines a variety of perceptual tasks in determining an array of attitudes to local as well as regionally stereotyped varieties.

Understanding, then, that the "stimulus" for a language regard response may be more complex than an *a* performance, we may look at the remaining characteristics of Figure 8.1. Regardless of the source or even the accuracy of the perception of the stimulus, a regard response (whether overtly stated or only internally realized) will not arise unless the stimulus is recognized, the step of the process called "Noticing," a characteristic that has not gone without comment in earlier work, although often with different labels and different focuses. The Japanese dialectologist and sociolinguist Takesi Sibata has suggested that "[i]t appears to be natural for forms which differ from those which one usually uses to attract one's attention" (1971: 374), and I have suggested that this includes items one "... usually uses *or expects to be used* ..." (Preston 2005: 148, emphasis in original) to cover such noticeable language events as adult talk by a child and many others.[9]

The implication in Sibata's comments is that such noticing is conscious, but it may operate at other levels. Rubin's study (1992) of the decreased ability of undergraduate students to comprehend a lecture when spoken in an unaccented US English voice but attributed (by means of a picture) to an Asian Teaching Assistant rather than to a European American TA points to the complexity I have in mind and is clearly related to the possibilities of linguistic stimuli

---

[9] Such an expectation is no doubt the source of the label "articulate," used by many to describe the speech of African Americans who do not speak African American English, regarded by many as "inarticulate." The comment is so widespread and so rightfully objected to that it has surfaced as the title of a recent book: *Articulate while Black* (Alim and Smitherman 2012). The title is actually a sarcasm built on another sarcasm. "DWI" is the label in many areas in the United States for "Driving while intoxicated." African Americans, who are more frequently stopped for alleged traffic violations or simply general suspicions, particularly if they are driving in affluent, principally European American areas, are said to be caught "DWB" – Driving while Black.

going awry outlined above. What happened in the Rubin study? The linguistic stimulus was "ready to be noticed" because of the ethnic identity seen in the picture, and, sure enough, it was, although it was not there. Not only did the respondents do less well on the comprehension test of the lecture, they also said the lecturer was "more accented" than when the priming face was European American. I do not believe that all of the attitudinally and ideologically triggered events that followed took place consciously, as I caricature them here:

(1) This is an Asian TA; she's going to have an accent.
(2) I hear that accent.
(3) Since this is hard-to-understand accented speech, I'm not even going to try to listen because I'm sure I won't understand well.

This is as implausible as Niedzielski's Michigan respondents overtly reporting that they heard non-standard speech (when the [æ] version of "last" was presented for matching) and refused to match it to anything a Michigan speaker said, although it is clear that their notion of the correctness of Michigan speech is consciously available to them (e.g. Preston 1996b; Niedzielski and Preston 2000).

Sibata's dictum and my corollary are not the only linguistic comments on noticing. Labov's distinction between *indicators*, *markers*, and *stereotypes* (1972: 314) and Trudgill's characterization of *salience* (Trudgill 1986: 10–21) within the framework of Labov's distinctions are directly relevant and should be consulted, but need not be reviewed here. Another characterization that has arisen in work on second language acquisition, however, requires further comment. I believe that *noticing*, contra Schmidt 1995, can occur consciously or unconsciously, an interpretation consistent with modern social psychological thinking, particularly perhaps in the literature that focuses on the search for *implicit* responses (e.g. Devine 1989; Fazio *et al.* 1995; Dovidio *et al.* 1997). What I mean by *noticing* is simply this: the uptake of an event such that procedural work is carried out on it. If *noticing* in second language acquisition studies refers to something else, then I have no quibble with their use.[10] The role of nonconscious factors in language attitudes is thoroughly explored in Campbell-Kibler 2010.

---

[10] I believe that a great many things that are eventually learned in a second language are not consciously noticed at all, but are certainly brought on board for processing; I will not pursue this here. See Cross (2002) for an assessment of the arguments and a review of the literature concerning the consciousness controversy as regards noticing in second language acquisition research. Squires (this volume) calls what I refer to as notice that triggers conscious awareness "noticing" and that which does not "perceiving," and Drager and Kirtley (this volume) also point out the distinction. I believe any differences in our views are only terminological, for I certainly mean to distinguish between these two modes.

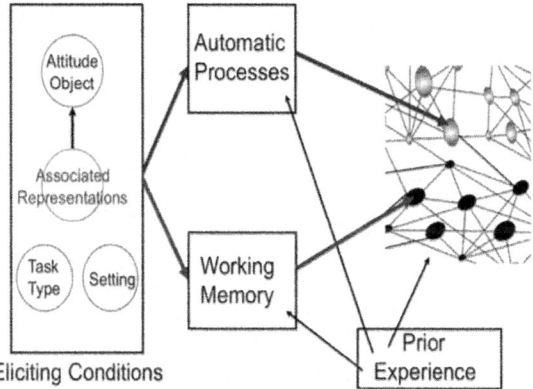

Figure 8.2 Outline of an Attitudinal Setting, Feature, and Procedural Pathway
for a Regard Response
Adapted from Bassili and Brown 2005: 554.

It is important to consider carefully the bottom of the triangle of Figure 8.1:
"Beliefs about and attitudes towards languages, varieties and speakers," for
that is the source for the nature of the response. This is a major consideration in
the context of awareness, for it allows for further exploration of the conscious-
nonconscious distinction, and I will explore the following questions about this
repository: (1) How is it structured? (2) How do the stimuli (i.e. the things
"noticed" in Figure 8.1) interact with it? and (3) How are regard responses
formed from its output?

I borrow from cognitive social psychology in Figure 8.2 to further detail
how a perceiver begins to process the *attitude object* in terms of:

(A) the *elicitation conditions* it has been presented in (please note "Associated
    Representations");
(B) the perceiver's procedural capacities;
(C) the perceiver's pre-existing knowledge; and
(D) the perceiver's underlying conceptual structure, shown in Figure 8.4 as a
    "connectionist model" (e.g. McClelland and Rumelhart 1986).

Processing takes place within a subset of the network called the "attitudinal
cognitorium" (Rosenberg 1968) which has all the features of neural networks.
Figure 8.3 shows that some items are strong (1), some weak (2); some
connections are strong (3), some weak (4); some items are not connected at
all (5), and those connections between others are inhibited (6).

Once regard elements in the cognitorium are collected, it might seem that a
response is ready to emerge, either an implicit one (Figure 8.4) or an explicit
one (Figure 8.5).

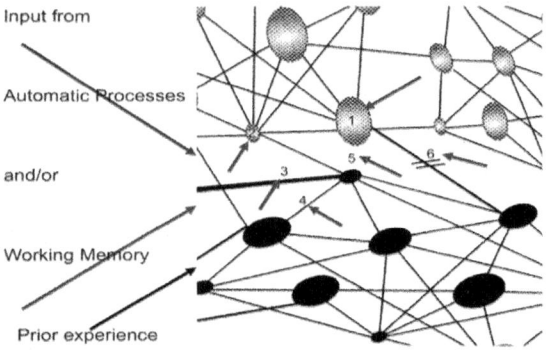

Figure 8.3 The Internal Structure of a Regard Cognitorium, i.e. the Nodes and Pathways in a Connectionist Network
Modified from Bassili and Brown 2005: 554.

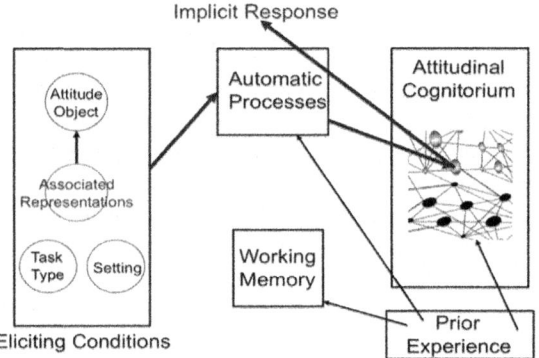

Figure 8.4 The Emergence of an Implicit Regard Response
Modified from Bassili and Brown 2005: 554.

This distinction between implicit and explicit responses is an oversimplification, implying that the response is the exclusive result of one or the other process, but the cognitorium is usually activated by input from both automatic processes and working memory, and each type is weighted. In Figure 8.6, the automatic processes are strongest throughout (thicker arrows), suggesting primarily nonconscious activity, but the arrows could have been of opposite (or perhaps even equal) thicknesses. Note, however, that the "Response" is a result of the variously weighted inputs from both procedural outcomes.

There are further complications. In Figure 8.7, "Working memory" (i.e. conscious processing) has provided a prior experience in which a response about to be made on the basis of implicit input might be criticized for being rude, racist, impolite, etc.... A now weightier explicit pathway emerges from

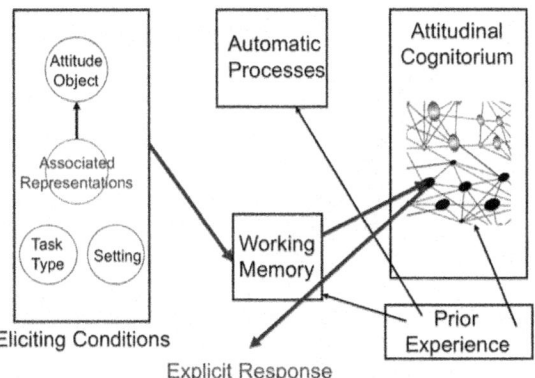

Figure 8.5 The Emergence of an Explicit Regard Response
Modified from Bassili and Brown 2005: 554.

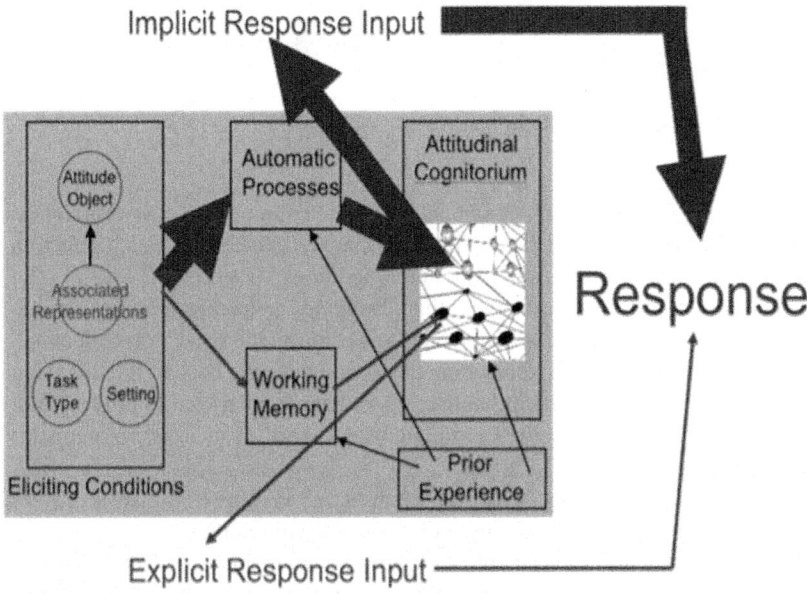

Figure 8.6 Weighted Inputs in the Emergence of an Essentially Implicit
Regard Response
Modified from Bassili and Brown 2005: 554.

working memory and reformulates the input, giving greater weight in the response to conscious activity.

This excursion into the cognitive shape and workings of the bottom line of Figure 8.1 allows a tweak here and there of that representation.

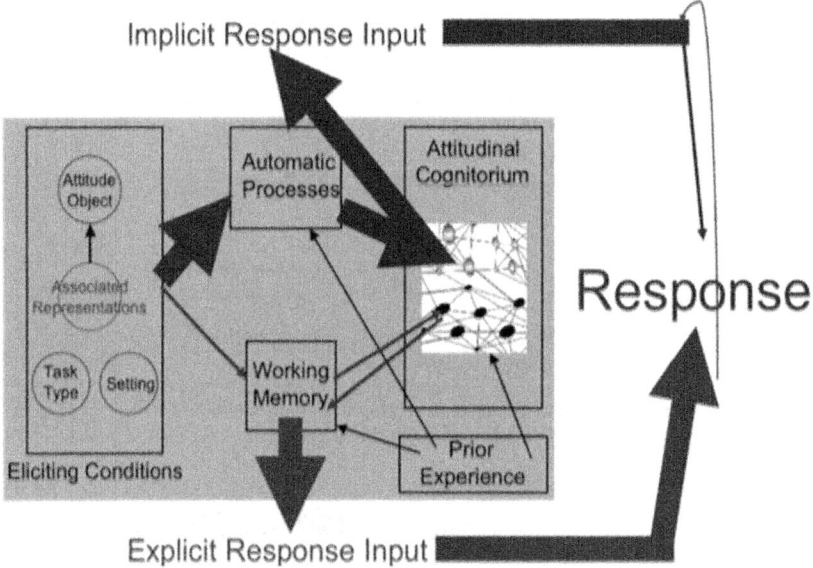

Figure 8.7 A "Weight Change" in the Emergence of a Regard Response
Modified from Bassili and Brown 2005: 554.

(1) After "noticing" and "classification," the "imbuing" process takes place as a result of the details of the cognitorium that are selected, and such selection is very much dependent on the "eliciting conditions" (Figures 8.3 to 8.7). The arrow of Figure 8.1 might suggest that "imbuing" takes place before (and is input to) the cognitorium; a better representation might show "classification" going to the cognitorium and bringing the imbuing details back to the linguistic object, but the entire processing outline given here is not meant to be temporal/ linear in a neurological sense, although recent work in neurosociolinguistics (Loudermilk, 2015; Staum Casasanto 2012) and various implicit design measures (e.g. Campbell-Kibler 2010, 2012; Pantos and Perkins 2013; Rosseel *et al.* 2014) seem to bring us increasingly closer to mental realities.

(2) Once the very specific set of regard characteristics is selected for that contextual experience, they become the conscious and nonconscious resources (characterized as the "Implicit" and "Explicit Response Input" in Figures 8.6 and 8.7) for the eventual regard response. This is the procedural operation that is shown between the bottom text of Figure 8.1 and the text just above it (i.e. "b' Cognitive states and processes that guide b").

The remainder of this chapter tries to marshal evidence for the likelihood of the procedural pathways outlined above, not least in the direction of suggesting that regard responses based on attitude, belief, and ideology are likely to be non-uniform (and even apparently contradictory).

### Some Evidence

Now I dare show you in Figure 8.8 a (partial) cognitorium.[11] It contains some (and I believe the principal ones) of the beliefs and stereotypes a Michigander might have at the ready after they classify a linguistic event as "Southern."

This cognitorium (or something like it) is an essential background for the contradictory regard responses that southeastern Michiganders have to "Southern." Figure 8.9 shows their responses when asked to rank the fifty US states (and New York City and Washington, DC) on a scale of 1 to 10 for language "pleasantness." Michigan (together with Illinois, Minnesota, Colorado, and Washington) is highest-rated, and one of the most typical "Southern" states, Alabama, is (together with New York City) rated lowest.

Compare this low rating of the South for "pleasantness" to the results shown in Table 8.2 from a semantic differential presentation of speech areas of the United States (not voices) to similar Michigan respondents.

Table 8.2 shows, using labels derived in a pre-study from similar respondents, that in this study the "pleasant" elements of the South do not fare so badly. In fact, the South outstrips the North (i.e. Michigan and a small area around it) for the concepts "casual," "friendly," "down-to-earth," and "polite," surely important components of "pleasantness." On the other hand, the low ratings for Southern pleasantness are also easy to find in the Figure 8.8 cognitorium. Southerners can be "prejudiced," "violent," and "hypocritical," all decidedly unpleasant traits.

I will not speculate why a task that asked respondents to rate the states for pleasantness resulted in such a bad score for the South and such a good one for Michigan and a few other non-Southern states, while a "silent" semantic differential task that asked similar respondents to rate locally derived attributes for speech regions resulted in ratings for the South that were even better than those for the Michigan area in just the attributes that one would associate with "pleasantness." I will, however, state the obvious: Cognitoria are so complex and even internally contradictory that only a slight difference in a task (or the

---

[11] WARNING! Professional driver on a closed course. Do not try this at home! Although it may seem that one might make up such an exemplary cognitorium on the basis of personal experience and intuition, that is not what has been done here, but I cannot survey the experimental and ethnographic work on Michigan respondent regard structures on which this representation is based that Nancy Niedzielski and I (and many of my former students) have carried out over the years. The references will guide any interested reader who seeks the details, and the parallel between a cognitorium that is related to a specific concept and an *indexical field* (Eckert 2008) should be obvious.

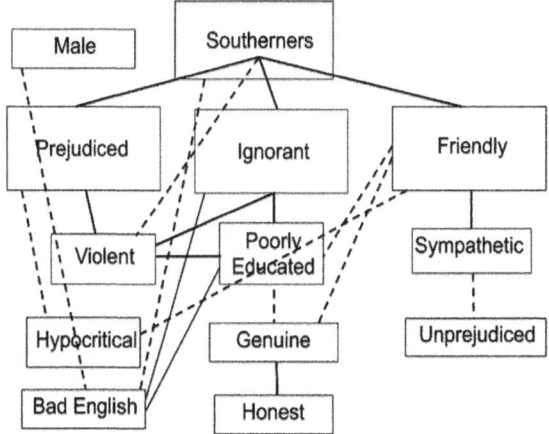

Figure 8.8 A Southeastern Michigan Cognitorium for Concepts Associated with "Southern"
Expanded from Preston 2010b: 18.

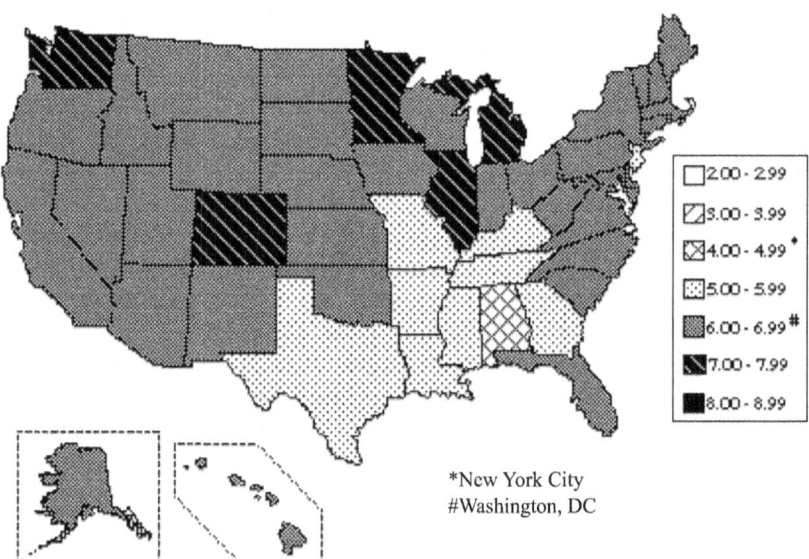

*New York City
#Washington, DC

Figure 8.9 Southeastern Michigan Ratings for the Fifty US States, New York City, and Washington, DC for Pleasantness
1 = least pleasant, 10 = most pleasant
(Preston 1996b: 312).

Table 8.2 *Ratings for the North (the Local Area) and the South for Twelve Traits by Southeastern Michigan Respondents on a 1-to-6 Scale (Preston 1999b: 366)*

| South | | | North | | |
|---|---|---|---|---|---|
| Rank | Attribute | Mean | Rank | Attribute | Mean |
| 1 | Casual | 4.66 | 1 | No drawl | 5.11 |
| 2 | Friendly | 4.58 | 2 | No twang | 5.07 |
| 3 | Down-to-earth | 4.54 | 3 | Normal | 4.94 |
| 4 | Polite | 4.20 | 4 | Smart | 4.53 |
| 5 | Not nasal | 4.09 | 5 | Good English | 4.41 |
| | | * | 6 | Down-to-earth | 4.19 |
| 6 | Normal [Abnormal] | ‡3.22 | 7 | Fast | 4.12 |
| 7 | Smart [Dumb] | ‡3.04 | 8 | Educated | 4.09 |
| 8 | No twang [Twang] | ‡2.96 | 9.5 | Friendly | 4.00 |
| 9 | Good English [Bad Eng.] | ‡2.86 | 9.5 | Polite | 4.00 |
| 10 | Educated [Uneducated] | ‡2.72 | 11 | Not nasal | 3.94 |
| 11 | Fast [Slow] | #‡2.42 | 12 | Casual | 3.53 |
| 12 | No drawl [Drawl] | ‡2.22 | | | |

*Key:* * the only significant ($p < 0.05$) break between two adjacent scores (determined by an analysis-of-variance with a Tukey comparison of means);
‡ values below 3.5 (which indicate the opposite polarity, shown in brackets);
# the only scores significantly different for gender ($p < 0.05$, determined by a series of t-tests).

"eliciting conditions") may activate different beliefs and attitudes. Any report of regard responses to linguistic stimuli of any sort should speak of "an" attitude, not, as is all too often the case, "the" attitude.

Some things that are not so obvious and offer opportunities for future research involve at least the following:

What consistency is there even when respondents and eliciting conditions are held fairly constant? In Preston 1985, for example, a histogram for ratings of New York City language correctness by southern Indiana respondents shows a clearly bimodal distribution, one masked by the average score; the interpretation seems clear.

> One group of informants [sic] (the high raters ...) were, no doubt, responding to the stereotypes of the area's dominance in the arts, finance, fashion, culture, and other areas. A second group (the low raters ...) responded, however, to negative caricatures of the area (Preston 1985: 397).

These empirical data reveal rather directly the existence of conflicting beliefs about New York City's speakers; it would be a stretch of the imagination to assume that the population contained just such a proportion of those who held negative and positive beliefs; it is much more likely that in spite of the identical character of the task, different parts of the cognitorium were activated in different respondents. One might suggest that ordinary statistical procedures should accompany any such study, but they are often not used or are given the interpretation that such variable results are noise. I believe that any language regard study must be prepared for variability, just as all sociolinguistic production studies are, and that they should seek such variability directly by carefully manipulating and controlling the elicitation environments, just as production studies do. Luckily, just such practices in the study of regard have begun to emerge, focusing in the case of this volume on awareness and control and in another on variability in regard responses (Prikhodkine and Preston 2015).

### Conclusion

These advances in experimental and ethnographic approaches to the collection and interpretation of regard data may not, however, satisfy sociolinguists who want to know how such findings interact with their main concern: language variation and change. Although it is comforting to know that the leaders of the field have long regarded the *evaluation* problem as central (Weinreich *et al.* 1968), their characterization of it was minimally programmatic and suggested a sort of simple categorality that does not seem to hold in the light of more recent work.

The theory of language change must establish empirically the subjective correlates of the several layers and variables in a heterogeneous structure. Such subjective correlates of evaluations cannot be deduced from the place of the variables within linguistic structure. Furthermore, the level of social awareness is a major property of linguistic change which must be determined directly. Subjective correlates of change are more categorical in nature than the changing pattern of behavior: their investigation deepens our understanding of the ways in which discrete categorization is imposed on the continuous process of change (Weinreich *et al.* 1968: 186).

Although I believe much of this volume rather directly addresses the importance of regard studies to variation and change, I want to conclude by examining one of the most direct and far-reaching claims about this importance that directly hinges on awareness and evaluative regard. In Kristiansen's work in Denmark (e.g. 2009), when respondents from several locales throughout the country were asked to name which variety of Danish they liked best, they unfailingly named their own variety. When presented with actual speech samples in a verbal guise format, however, they preferred Modern Copenhagen speech for solidarity factors (cool, nice, etc. . . . – called "dynamism" in Kristiansen's account) over their own varieties and Conservative Copenhagen area speech for standardness characteristics (intelligent, goal-directed, etc. . . . – Kristiansen's "superiority")

(188). Linguistic change all over Denmark, however, shows change in the direction of Modern Copenhagen speech, a variety preferred only when offered in a guise format, one which Kristiansen labels nonconscious and declares to be the guiding regard principle for linguistic change.

In contrast, Michiganders do not prefer their own speech for pleasantness in some regard tasks, but do in others, and, as shown in Niedzielski's work (1999, summarized above) do not even hear it correctly. Although they clearly prefer their own in conscious, overt evaluations (Preston 1996b) for both what Kristiansen would call *superiority* ("correctness") and *dynamism* ("pleasantness"), in a semantic differential task (without speech samples), their own speech is regarded as superior for correctness, but not so highly for pleasantness ones (Preston 1999b). Most Michiganders are, however, like Danes, moving in a single direction – in this case towards the NCVS, but it is not at all clear that only nonconscious preferences are driving them. The Danes like Modern Copenhagen speech best, especially along pleasantness dimensions, when given a verbal guise test, and that is the direction in which Danish change moves. The Michiganders actually prefer non-local speech for pleasantness when presented with a semantic differential that refers only to areas, but their own speech is not at all influenced by the areas they prefer. They consciously prefer their own speech, the direction of change, but are unable to note the details of it, referring instead to older, conservative norms or imagined media or other norms as the facts of their own local speech (Preston 2011, 2015).[12]

To conclude, I think we need much more information about language regard in Denmark, Michigan, and everywhere else in the world before we can complete folk cognitoria that will provide the essential background to the social psychological work that attracts some for its own value, but also provides a basis for interpretive subtlety to those who seek explanatory and enabling characteristics of the ebb and flow of variation and change. To achieve this, we must, first, recognize the variability of beliefs and attitudes, many, but not all, based on the distinction between conscious and nonconscious processes, and, second, we must devise increasingly subtle techniques for teasing them out.

REFERENCES

Albarracín, Dolores, Johnson, Blair T., and Zanna, Mark P. (eds.). 2005. *The Handbook of Attitudes*. Malwah, NJ and London: Lawrence Erlbaum Associates.

---

[12] Not exactly the same tests were given in Southeastern Michigan and all over Denmark, but in both sites relatively conscious and nonconscious data were gathered, allowing at least some comparisons and certainly justifying a need to know more.

Alim, H. Sami and Smitherman, Geneva. 2012. *Articulate while Black*. New York: Oxford University Press.

Bassili, John N. and Brown, Rick D. 2005. Implicit and explicit attitudes: research, challenges, and theory, in Dolores Albarracín, Blair T. Johnson, and Mark P. Zanna (eds.), *The Handbook of Attitudes*, pp. 543–74. Mahwah, NJ: Lawrence Erlbaum Associates.

Bright, William (ed.). 1971. *Sociolinguistics*. The Hague: Mouton.

Büld, Heinrich. 1939. *Sprache und Volkstum im nördlichen Westfalen: Sprachgrenzen und Sprachbewegungen in der Volksmeinung*. Emsdetten: H. & G. Lechte.

Campbell-Kibler, Kathryn. 2010. New directions in sociolinguistic cognition. *University of Pennsylvania Working Papers in Linguistics* 15(2):31–9. http://repository.upenn.edu/pwpl/vol15/iss2/5.
    2012. The Implicit Association Test and sociolinguistic meaning. *Lingua* 122(7):53–63.

Clopper, Cynthia, Hay, Jennifer, and Plichta, Bartłomiej. 2011. Experimental speech perception and perceptual dialectology, in Marianna Di Paolo and Malcah Yaeger-Dror (eds.), *Sociophonetics: A Student's Guide*, pp. 149–62. London and New York: Routledge.

Cross, Jeremy. 2002. "Noticing" in SLA: Is it a valid concept? *TESL-EJ* 6(3), retrieved from http://tesl-ej.org/ej23/fromed.html. 8 February 2014.

Devine, Patricia G. 1989. Stereotypes and prejudice: Their automatic and controlled components. *Journal of Personality and Social Psychology* 56:5–18.

Dovidio, J. F., Kawakami, K., Johnson, C., Johnson, B., and Howard, A. 1997. The nature of prejudice: Automatic and controlled processes. *Journal of Experimental Social Psychology* 33:510–40.

Eckert, Penelope. 2008. Variation and the indexical field. *Journal of Sociolinguistics* 12(4):453–76.

Fazio, R. H., Jackson, J. R., Dunton, B. C., and Williams, C. J. 1995. Variability in automatic activation as an unobtrusive measure of racial attitudes: A bonafide pipeline? *Journal of Personality and Social Psychology* 69:1013–27.

Graff, David, Labov, William, and Harris, Wendell A. 1986. Testing listeners' reactions to phonological markers of ethnic identity: A new method for sociolinguistic research, in David Sankoff (ed.), *Diversity and Diachrony*, Current Issues in Linguistic Theory 53, pp. 45–58. Amsterdam and Philadelphia, PA: John Benjamins.

Hoenigswald, Henry. 1966. A proposal for the study of folk-linguistics, in William Bright (ed.), *Sociolinguistics*, pp. 16–26. The Hague: Mouton.

Hymes, Dell. 1971. Response to Hoenigswald, in William Bright (ed.), *Sociolinguistics*, p. 26. The Hague: Mouton.

Kristiansen, Tore. 2009. The macro-level social meanings of late-modern Danish accents. *Acta Linguistica Hafniensia* 41:167–92.

Labov, William, Ash, Sharon, and Boberg, Charles. 2006. *The Atlas of North American English: Phonetics, Phonology, and Sound Change: A Multimedia Reference Tool*. Berlin: Walter de Gruyter.

Labov, William. 1972. *Sociolinguistic Patterns*. Philadelphia, PA: University of Pennsylvania Press.

Lippi-Green, Rosina. 1997. *English with an Accent*. London: Routledge.

Loudermilk, Brandon. 2015. Implicit attitudes and the perception of sociolinguistic variation, in Alexei Prikhodkine and Dennis R. Preston (eds.), *Language Attitudes: Variability, Processes and Outcomes*. Amsterdam and Philadelphia, PA: John Benjamins, pp. 137–156.

McClelland, J. L. and Rumelhart, D. E. 1986. A distributed model of human learning and memory, in J. L. McClelland and D. E. Rumelhart (eds.), *Parallel Distributed Processing: Explorations in the Microstructure of Cognition*, Vol. 2, pp. 170–215. Cambridge MA: MIT Press.

Milroy, Lesley and Preston, Dennis R. (guest eds.). 1999. *Journal of Language and Social Psychology* 18(1) (Special Issue: Attitudes, perceptions, and linguistic features).

Milroy, James and Milroy, Lesley. 1999. *Authority in Language*. London: Routledge.

Niedzielski, Nancy. 1999. The effect of social information on the perception of sociolinguistic variables, in Milroy, Lesley and Preston, Dennis R. (guest eds.). *Journal of Language and Social Psychology* 18(1):62–85.

Niedzielski, Nancy and Preston, Dennis R. 1997. Family values, in S. Eliasson and Ernst Håkon Jahr (eds.), *Language and Its Ecology: Essays in Memory of Einar Haugen*, pp. 131–59. Berlin: Mouton de Gruyter.

2000. *Folk Linguistics*. Berlin and New York: Mouton de Gruyter.

2003. *Folk Linguistics* (rev. pbk edn.) Berlin and New York: Mouton de Gruyter.

2009. Folk linguistics, in Nik Coupland and Adam Jaworski (eds.), *The New Sociolinguistics Reader*, pp. 356–373. Houndsmills, UK: Palgrave Macmillan.

Pantos, Andrew J. and Perkins, Andrew W. 2013. Measuring implicit and explicit attitudes toward foreign accented speech, *Journal of Language and Social Psychology* 32(1):3–20.

Pasquale, Michael and Preston, Dennis R. 2013. The folk linguistics of language teaching and learning, in K. Drozdział-Szelest and M. Pawlak (eds.), *Psycholinguistic and Sociolinguistic Perspectives on Second Language Learning and Teaching*, pp. 1–11. Berlin and Heidelberg: Springer.

Plichta, Bartłomiej. 2004. Interdisciplinary perspectives on the Northern Cities Chain Shift. Unpublished doctoral dissertation. Michigan State University.

Polle, Freidrich. 1889. *Wie denkt das Volk über die Sprache? Gemeinverständliche Beiträge zur Beanwortung dieser Frage*. Leipzig: Teubner.

Potter, Jonathan and Wetherell, Margaret. 1987. *Discourse and Social Psychology: Beyond Attitudes and Behaviour*. London: Sage.

Preston, Dennis R. 1982. Perceptual dialectology: Mental maps of United States dialects from a Hawaiian perspective, in D. R. Preston (ed.), *Working Papers in Linguistics* (University of Hawai'i Linguistics Department) 14 (2):5–49.

1985. Southern Indiana perceptions of "correct" and "pleasant" speech, in Henry J. Warkentyne (ed.), *Methods V/Méthodes V: Papers from the Fifth International Conference on Methods in Dialectology*, pp. 387–411. Victoria, BC: Department of Linguistics, University of Victoria.

1993. The uses of folk linguistics. *International Journal of Applied Linguistics* 3(2):181–259.

1994. Content-oriented discourse analysis & folk linguistics. *Language Sciences* 16(2):285–330.

1996a. "Whaddayaknow?": The modes of folk linguistic awareness. *Language Awareness* 5(1):40–74.

1996b. Where the worst English is spoken, in Edgar Schneider (ed.), *Focus on the USA*, pp. 297–360. Amsterdam: John Benjamins.

1998. Why we need to know what real people think about language. *The Centennial Review* XLII(2):255–84.

1999a. Discourse interaction and content: A test case. *SKY Journal of Linguistics* 12:145–75.

(ed.) 1999b. *Perceptual Dialectology*, Vol. I. Amsterdam: John Benjamins.

2005. What is folk linguistics? Why should you care? *Lingua Posnaniensis* 47:143–62.

2010a. Methods in (applied) folk linguistics: Getting into the minds of the folk. *AILA Review* 24:15–39.

2010b. Variation in language regard, in E. Zeigler, P. Gilles, and J. Scharloth (eds.), *Variatio delectat: Empirische Evidenzen und theoretische Passungen sprachlicher Variation* (für Klaus J. Mattheier zum 65. Geburtstag), pp. 7–27. Frankfurt am Main: Peter Lang.

2011. The power of language regard – Discrimination, classification, comprehension, and production, in Proceedings of the conference on Production, Perception, Attitude. Leuven, 2–3 April 2009. *Dialectologia* (Special Issue II, Dirk Speelman, Stefan Grondelaers, and John Nerbonne (eds.)):9–33. www.publicacions.ub.es/revistes/dialectologiaSP2011/.

2015. Variation in language regard, in Alexei Prikhodkine and Dennis R. Preston (eds.), *Language Attitudes: Variability, Processes and Outcomes*. Amsterdam and Philadelphia, PA: John Benjamins, pp. 3–36.

Prikhodkine, Alexei and Preston, Dennis R. (eds.). 2015. *Language Attitudes: Variability, Processes and Outcomes*. Amsterdam and Philadelphia, PA: John Benjamins.

Rosenberg, Milton J. 1968. Hedonism, inauthenticity, and other goads toward expansion of a consistency theory, in R. P. Abelson, E. Aronson, W. J. McGuire, T. M. Newcomb, M. J. Rosenberg, and P. H. Tanenbaum (eds.), *Theories of Cognitive Consistency*, pp. 279–349. Chicago, IL: Rand-McNally.

Rosseel, Laura, Geeraerts, Dirk, and Speelman, Dirk. 2014. Auditory affective priming: Exploring new methods to measure attitudes to language varieties, a paper presented to the International Conference on Methods in Dialectology, Groningen, the Netherlands, 15 August.

Rubin, Donald L. 1992. Nonlanguage factors affecting undergraduates' judgments on nonnative English speaking teaching assistants. *Research in Higher Education* 33(4):511–31.

Schmidt, Richard. 1995. Consciousness and foreign language learning: A tutorial on the role of attention and awareness, in Richard Schmidt (ed.), *Attention and Awareness in Foreign Language Teaching and Learning (Technical Report No. 9)*, pp. 1–64. Honolulu: University of Hawai'i at Manoa.

Sibata, Takesi. 1971. Kotoba no kihan ishiki. *Gengo Seikatsu* 236:14–21, May (Special Issue: Words that bother us). (The quotation and page reference are taken from the translation 'Consciousness of language norms,' Chapter 22 in

T. Kunihiro, Fumio Inoue, and Daniel Long (eds.), 1999, *Takesi Sibata: Sociolinguistics in Japanese Contexts*, pp. 373–79. Berlin: Mouton de Gruyter).

Silverstein, Michael. 1981. The limits of awareness, Sociolinguistic working paper no. 84. Austin, TX: Southwest Educational Development Laboratory.

2003. Indexical order and the dialectics of sociolinguistic life. *Language & Communication* 23:193–229.

Staum Casasanto, Laura. 2012. I trust you implicitly ... but not explicitly! How to get language attitudes without asking. A paper presented to the International Symposium 'Variation of Language Attitudes: Mechanisms and Stakes.' Lausanne, April.

Trudgill, Peter. 1986. *Dialects in Contact*. Oxford, UK: Blackwell.

Twilfer, Daniela. 2010. *Dialektgrenzen im Kopf: Der westfälische Sprachraum aus volkslinguistischer Perspektive* (Westfälische Beiträge zur niederdeutschen Philologie 13). Gütersloh: Verlag für Regionalgeschichte.

Weinreich, Uriel, Labov, William, and Herzog, Marvin I. 1968. Empirical foundations for a theory of linguistic change, in Winfred F. Lehmann and Yakov Malkiel (eds.), *Directions for Historical Linguistics*, pp. 95–188. Austin and London: University of Texas Press.

Wilton-Franklin, Antje and Stegu, Martin (issue eds.). 2010. *AILA Review 24*. Amsterdam: John Benjamins.

# 9    Silence as Control: Shame and Self-Consciousness in Sociolinguistic Positioning

*Anna M. Babel*[*]

## Introduction

In this chapter, I show that speakers actively resist using certain styles of language (which they may or may not control) based on a perception that those styles do not match their own positioning as social actors. Through a discussion of the way in which speakers develop and present these values through their explicit speech and actions, I argue that both *awareness* and *control* are rooted in large-scale systems of social meaning that can be manifested in multiple ways. In the sense that I examine it in this chapter, "awareness" can be observed as part of a style or stance that interacts with deeper societal structures of power and control, as well as through overt comments about language practice and in the use of particular variables, as it has more often been studied. Arguably, the former, broader sense is the more salient type of awareness for speakers, and the level at which power and positioning are negotiated most explicitly. Because of the complex nature of awareness, this process not only involves linguistic features, but is also bound up with questions of culture and political stances, ways of knowing, and attitudes that are connected to the full complex system of cultural signs in which language participates.

## Literature Review

Language interacts with deeper societal structures of practice and power, as has been shown repeatedly in research on sociolinguistics and related disciplines (Foucault 1980; Bourdieu 1991; Urban 1996; Eckert and Wegner 2005). Research on language ideologies has also amply demonstrated that language is connected to powerful political and cultural forces (Silverstein 1979; Woolard

[*] I would like to express my very sincere thanks to Barbara Johnstone, Kathryn Campbell-Kibler, and Lauren Squires for their helpful comments on a previous version of this chapter. Thanks also to John Rickford for his perceptive and challenging discussion of our LSA panel in 2013. This research was supported in part by an NSF Graduate Research Fellowship, by the Freiburg Institute for Advanced Studies, by the University of Michigan, and by the Ohio State University.

1998; Irvine and Gal 2000; Choksi and Meek, this volume). Even in his earliest sociolinguistic studies, Labov showed convincingly that ways of speaking are influenced by attitudes about language that are tied to economic and material circumstances, and that individuals have substantial latitude in the way they position themselves with respect to these systems of power and privilege. To take a pair of classic examples, Labov's Martha's Vineyarders were interested in *resisting* the prestige and economic status of wealthy mainland varieties by presenting themselves as locals (Labov 1972). In a case study in New York City, Labov described Nathan B, who does not use or, apparently, perceive the difference between the prestige variant [θ] and the low-status [d] despite his high level of education and upper-middle-class background (Labov 2006: 157–60). Labov noted that although Nathan B was asked to take speech classes in order to gain an academic appointment, he declined to do so. While Nathan B is often framed as "deviant" or an "outlier" in the academic literature, we can also see his linguistic behavior as a way of exercising his ability to resist societal norms. As briefly illustrated by this pair of classic examples, both individuals and groups use language to express their resistence to or conformity with particular societal norms (see also Eckert 2000).

Labov's Vernacular Principle states that the "vernacular," a style of speech of which we are least aware, is the "truest," least self-conscious, and most relaxed – the least controlled (Labov 1972, 2006). (See Carmichael, this volume, for a discussion of the Vernacular Principle.) Thus, awareness, control, and authenticity are linked from the very beginning of the sociolinguistic literature. While by Labov's definition less "natural" than the vernacular, a speaker's ability to modify their speech based on context has been taken as evidence of their capacity for style-shifting (Rickford and McNair-Knox 1994; Eckert and Rickford 2001; Johnstone 2005). In some contexts, style-shifting can even be considered artificial; Schilling-Estes describes style-shifting as performance or "putting on" a dialect (1998). Whether natural or artificial, linguists have considered an active command of particular sociolinguistic features (more often phonetic/ phonological than grammatical) as proof of a speaker's control of sociolinguistic variation.

Labov attempts to capture the role of awareness – perception – of sociolinguistic variables through his well-known three-way classification of indicator/ marker/stereotype (1972: 178–9). Indicators are variables that are socially stratified, but of which people are unaware; markers are socially and stylistically stratified and people show some level of awareness through attempts to control them; and stereotypes are explicitly discussed and associated with particular social groups (but may not be in active use in the community). This schema, however, is notoriously slippery; it is very difficult to find clear-cut examples of features that fit neatly into one of the three categories. This may be due in part to the choice to begin with *linguistic variables* rather than *language attitudes*. Particular sociolinguistic variables may or may not be accessible to people for explicit discussion, although they often have strong opinions about styles of speech or social groups that they associate with a set of linguistic features. The shift from the study of variables to the study of attitudes is laid out by Preston (1996, this volume; see also Choksi and Meek, this volume).

In the literature that attempts to capture what makes us aware of particular sociolinguistic variables, the relationship between "linguistic" and "social" factors is highly fraught. A plethora of studies on the theoretical concept of *salience* ultimately fail to distinguish between purely linguistic and purely social factors in recognizing language (Auer *et al.* 1998; Rácz 2013; see also Preston this volume, Choksi and Meek, this volume, for discussion). Silverstein (1981) argues that linguistic criteria for recognizing language are linked to sociopragmatics and to other cognitive mechanisms; however, even Silverstein fails to capture the importance of social norms in producing and discussing language. One of his central examples concerns the repetition of an uncomplimentary augmentative form, which the speaker subsequently insists she has not used and does not recognize. What, if not societal norms and interpersonal relationships, would result in this kind of reaction?

No subfield of linguistics has done more to complicate the relationship between social and linguistic factors than sociophonetics. Sociophonetic studies have demonstrated that awareness of sociolinguistic variables is related to the perception of social categories on the part of the listener (Niedzielski 1999; Hay *et al.* 2006). This observation, made through experimental techniques, takes the discussion away from status of a *particular linguistic variable*, based largely on structural characteristics, and moves it towards *beliefs held by listeners*. However, there are limitations to sociophonetic research. Because of its focus on perception, this literature addresses awareness in a very precise way, but does not address control (see McGowan, this volume, for an exception to this generalization). Much like early variationist studies, the vast majority of this literature describes college students (largely middle-class, white, and monolingual) in Anglophone North America and New Zealand. Therefore, these scholars can take for granted the readers' background knowledge of the varieties they describe – a body of cultural knowledge that should not be taken lightly, and which must be made explicit when discussing cultural situations that are not as familiar to academic readers who often share these demographic characteristics.

The picture is further complicated because both "awareness" and "control" have multiple overlapping senses or levels. Scholars in different subdisciplines are not always measuring the same thing when they discuss awareness and control (see Campbell-Kibler, this volume). In part, this is due to the fact that at a cognitive level, it seems that there is more than one type of awareness to consider (Campbell-Kibler 2010, this volume; Labov *et al.* 2011; Drager and Kirtley this volume). Awareness of linguistic features can – indeed must – be measured on multiple dimensions and on multiple scales (Preston 1996). It has also been shown that perception (awareness) does not equal production (control). Johnstone and Kiesling give evidence that the speakers who are most aware of "Pittsburghese" features are those who do not use them, and vice versa (2008). This point is reinforced by Nycz: Even very high awareness may not lead to change, while absence of awareness does not preclude it (this volume, p. 76). Squires (this volume) argues that there is a distinction between *perceiving* and *noticing*, distinguisting between implicit and explicit knowledge of variation (p. 83); see also Preston, this volume, on noticing (p. 186).

One of the most difficult challenges faced by scholars is how to understand awareness and control through – or in spite of – this great complexity of factors. The main goal of this chapter is to examine the larger social and cultural environment in which awareness and control are embedded, and through this to gain a better understanding of how speakers use the social and linguistic material available to them in order to position themselves as social actors. In order to do this, I want to take a step back and think about what scholars have considered "proof" of awareness and control in their work. Throughout the literature reviewed above, we can make a generalization that evidence of awareness and control is found in one of three ways: (1) through experimental methods that measure perception, as in sociophonetics; (2) through a speaker's demonstrated use of a variable over different contexts, as in variationist sociolinguistics; and (3) through the ability to discuss language explicitly, as in the study of language ideologies and "folk" linguistics (Niedzielski and Preston 2003). However, in order to fully understand awareness and control, we must be able to give a detailed account of the integration of social systems with linguistic practice and positioning. In order to address this question, I examine a case that goes in the opposite direction; a case in which speakers *refuse* or *resist* the use of a particular style of speech. Rickford (1985) demonstrates that in any social situation, there are multiple competing systems of value at work. Given this fact, how might we think of evidence that comes from the *absence* of speech or from *refusal* to participate in a particular context?

I frame this question through a discussion of the literature on silence. In scholarly work that uses largely qualitative methods, scholars have conclusively demonstrated that silence is not just an absence of speech, and certainly not an absence of meaning (Maltz 1985; Tannen and Saville-Troike 1985; Jaworski 1993; Jaworski 1997; Kurzon 2007b; Ephratt 2011; Kurzon 2011). In order to be socially meaningful, however, silence must be placed in a sociolinguistic context (Basso 1970; Kurzon 2007b). Once placed in a social context, silence can be intersubjective (Pagis 2010) – a form of communication – and intertextual (Kurzon 2007a). As in the case studies that I present, silence is often gendered and may represent resistance to social structures (Gal 1989; Fivush 2010). Kurzon argues that silence can be "metaphorical," in Lakoff's sense, when it concerns not an absence of speech, but rather silence on a particular topic, or off-the-record speech (2011). Whether silence is literal or metaphorical, however, it participates in a system of cultural norms and expressions.

Importantly, the practice of silence may or may not reveal a lack of control – both in the sense of being able to shift styles or perform different types of speech, and in the sense of using silence to exert or resist power rooted in hegemonic social structures. For this reason, measures of control that consider only linguistic performance and omit resistance and refusal may miss types of awareness that occur at a more complex level of social structure than the individual sociolinguistic variable. In the study of awareness and control to date, speakers' *performance* of features or the demonstrated ability to *recognize* them has been taken as the best way to measure awareness. In the study of silence, on the other hand, awareness of linguistic and social norms leads speakers to use silence – that is, the *avoidance* of particular topics, variables, linguistic forms, or speech itself – as a meaningful social resource. I argue that this avoidance can constitute evidence of not just awareness, but also of social positioning – a type of control. This broader societal sense of control complements and encompasses the more specific sense, in which speakers control particular features of a style or register of speech.

## Data 1: Ethnographic Evidence

### General Background

The data for this chapter come from my fieldwork in a contact zone of central Bolivia, located in the triangle between Cochabamba, Sucre, and La Paz (see Map 9.1). The town where I work, Iscamayo,[1] is a medium-sized town of several thousand inhabitants, located on a main road between two major cities. It is located in the Santa Cruz valleys, in an area where there is a high degree of Quechua-Spanish contact influence. Quechua contact features are commonly used as socially meaningful linguistic markers, even by Spanish-dominant speakers. I have participated in this community as a researcher, a family member and friend, and a development worker since 2002. I use my long-term relationship with this community to engage in deep ethnographic fieldwork. The present analysis comes from the observations I have made over the twelve years of my participation in the community, and in particular from a series of recordings made in 2008, which were made with the intention of

---

[1] Personal and place names are pseudonyms, unless they concern major cities or public figures acting in a public role.

Map 9.1 Bolivia

describing the occurrence of contact features across three types of situations: conversations, interviews, and meetings (see Babel 2011). In this following section, I discuss the use – and disuse – of the speech genre known as *oratoria* "oratory" in meetings and other types of events, such as interviews.

### Meetings and Oratory

In the Santa Cruz valleys of Bolivia, community meetings, and thus community representation, are the domain of the wealthy, the educated, the literate,

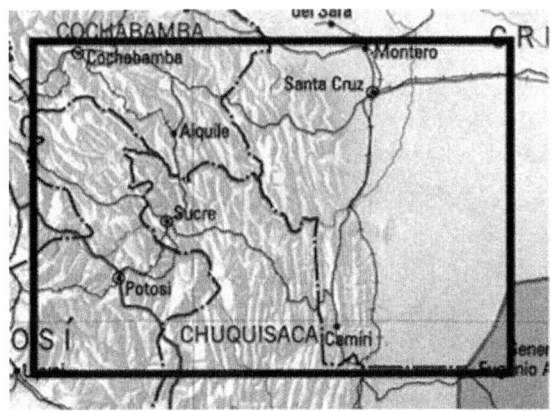

Map 9.2 Central Bolivia

and the oratorically skilled. In this area, as in much of Latin America, speakers are expected to use a named genre of speech, *oratoria* 'oratory' in formal, on-the-record situations such as public meetings. A pamphlet that I bought on this topic emphasized fluency, naturalness, and finding one's own voice; but in my observations of public meetings, I found that another important aspect of oratory involved the command of a flowery oral genre including learned and technical vocabulary. People were implicitly and explicitly evaluated on their oratorical skill when they engaged in public speech, and oratory was taught in schools. Self-improvement pamphlets teaching people how to improve their oratory were sold by hucksters on public buses, together with tracts on nutrition and religion. Formal oratory was not the only type of language that was used in meetings, nor were good orators the only people to speak in meetings, but they were generally felt to be an important ingredient in establishing a meeting context.

Women from rural areas were often reluctant to enter these settings as speakers because they felt ashamed of their own poverty, ignorance, and illiteracy; or, not exclusively, they expressed scorn for the way in which the meetings were organized and run because they were ineffective and often corrupt. Many of these women identified with a traditional value system, which emphasized personal ties, hard work, and generosity as the primary criteria on which a person was judged. On these measures, they were well-respected members of their community. In contrast, under the "modern" system of values, they were judged as lacking personal wealth, education, and social mobility (cf. Hill 1995).

The division between "speaker(s)" and "audience member(s)" was visible in the physical organization of meetings as well as in the type of speech and speakers that participated in them. In the formal community meeting, the canonical context for the use of oratory, speakers – often wealthy and male – sat or stood facing the audience. Speech was strictly regimented, with the use of *la palabra* (literally 'the word') as a formalized method of taking or ceding the floor.[2] While the rules of order were not always strictly adhered to, it was generally felt that a "good" meeting involved orderly turn-taking and following the agenda. In one unruly meeting I observed, an audience member accused those present of "buzzing like a swarm of bees" because they would not adhere to the one-speaker-on-the-floor format. Meeting speech was "on-the-record" both figuratively and literally – it was recorded in the minutes, or *libro de actas*, kept by the meeting secretary, and formed a part of the permanent record of the organization.

However, on-the-record speech was not the only kind of speech that went on at meetings. Women who identified with a traditional value system might sit towards the back of the audience and whisper to each other, or hang over the edges of the room – at windows and doors – and occasionally throw out comments that might generate a laugh or be picked up by other participants in the official, on-record speech. These off-the-record contributions were sometimes in Quechua, which was never used on the floor; when made in Spanish, they were much more likely to contain Quechua contact features (which were especially humorous in this context) than were the on-the-record contributions.

Women's meetings – organizations that are specifically targeted to women, such as the Mother's Club or agricultural groups that work with small-scale domestic production – were organized differently from canonical meetings. While presiding officers were seated in an area reserved for the *mesa directiva* "board of directors" at the head of the room, in the absence of outside observers there was usually general private conversation rather than official, on-the-record speech. People sat near their friends and made their opinions known by facial expressions, gaze, and comments thrown out on the floor, or muttered under their breath without formal turn-taking or use of *la palabra*. When women did speak to the group, they often covered their mouths or giggled as if embarrassed or shy. Decisions tended to be made among blocs of friends or relatives *before* they were discussed in the meeting. Rather than focusing on the formal structure of the meeting event, the emphasis of these clubs was on projects and deeds: cooking, knitting, raising livestock, planning trips, and organizing or participating in community events. While some women did speak in the more formal community meetings, they were generally wealthy or well-educated, and they were in a small minority among the

---

[2] The phrase *la palabra* is used to request the floor in formal meetings; this is a common practice throughout Spanish-speaking countries. I am not certain what cultural history or system of meeting rules this may be derived from.

speakers. Women's meetings were less prestigious and considered less important than the formal community meetings.

### Ethnographic Evidence of Resistance

In the data that I present here, women demonstrated their awareness of social expectations related to language by controlling their participation in events such as the meetings described above, as well as in formal, structured interviews that I attempted to carry out in the community. These interviews are similar to meetings, in that they were understood by my participants as a situation in which a demonstration of education and erudition was required. As I discuss in more detail below, most of my female friends avoided them at all costs. At a superficial level, it appeared that women were not participants in interviews and meetings, yet they *did* participate in ways of their own choosing, and they exerted considerable control over the outcome of the projects they were asked to participate in. The following ethnographic vignettes illustrate they ways in which women's silence could mask their very real participation in these social contexts and the power that they held over the outcomes. This control is – to me – evidence that women are not simply "opting out" of oratorical contexts; rather, they are shaping their roles in development projects through alternative types of positioning and participation. However, these modes of engagement with social categories and expectations largely preclude the use of sociolinguistic features that would qualify as evidence of "control" as it has been traditionally considered in sociolinguistics.

### Vignette 1: San Antonio

I'm sitting in a neighborhood meeting in *Barrio San Antonio*, a poorer neighborhood on the periphery of town, settled mostly by recent migrants. An outsider, an engineer from the city of Cochabamba, is running the meeting. I am seated on a little stage with the community leaders, all older men; the engineer paces back and forth in front of us. Facing us are rows of chairs. On these chairs sit a couple of dozen community members, mostly men. Women, especially women wearing *pollera*, are squatting around the edges of the room or hanging on the open windows.[3] Trying to involve them in the conversation, the engineer, who has been speaking in Spanish, turns and addresses them in Quechua. "Haku!" he says. *Come here!* "Ima sutiyki?" *What's your name?* They giggle and hide their faces and blush, refusing to answer.

---

[3] The *pollera* is a knee-length gathered skirt that indexes a woman of indigenous roots who participates in the modern economy. Women who wear *pollera* are often, but not always, Quechua-Spanish bilinguals.

*Vignette 2: Town Hall*

I'm in a meeting in the Town Hall, in the center of town, at the center of the local power structure. I'm sitting about halfway back in the inevitable rows of chairs. The room is full, with perhaps sixty people present, some standing at the back. My sister-in-law is seated next to me, my mother-in-law on the other side. It's a meeting about the construction of state-financed housing with disaster funding from the national government. All those present have signed loans for property in the construction zone. As the treasurer goes over *rendición de cuentas*, giving a budgetary report, my sister-in-law keeps up a steady commentary on the proceedings in my ear, behind her hand. I can barely hear her and can't understand her at all, although she giggles raucously at intervals. Even though I have my recorder on my lap, it picks up virtually nothing of her speech. Back at home, she and my mother-in-law discuss the proceedings with interest, indicating their agreement or (more often) scornful disregard of the concrete steps that they are being asked to take, and worrying over the time and money that they are asked to contribute to the project.

*Vignette 3: Barrio Nuevo*

I'm in a meeting in *Barrio Nuevo*, an established neighborhood outside the center of town. Another engineer is present, explaining about a program run by the electrical company to plant trees in the area (Iscamayo is very arid and trees do not grow naturally). The company offers to provide the trees for free; the community members are responsible for planting, watering, and tending them. The men at the front of the room make elegant speeches about the importance of the project and the beauty of the trees that will grow. A bold, cheerful woman, sitting to one side, is giggling noisily with the women to either side, her eyes shining. Finally, she interjects, speaking to the room. *¿Y si se k'ajlla?* 'And if it splits?' she asks, using a Quechua word, wondering if she will be held responsible if the trees fail to thrive. The room breaks up in laughter. The engineer ignores her and continues with his presentation.

*Vignette 4: Mother's Club*

I'm in a Mother's Club meeting in a small town just outside of the urban area, where the women's group is discussing an upcoming trip to a neighboring town. After we discuss the difficulties of finding appropriate transportation, the president calls for a vote on whether to go through with the trip, but the women just sit there and whisper with each other. Finally, the president stands up and walks around the room, looking at each woman in turn and asking whether she can come. Answers range from a shy yet daringly direct *Ya* 'Okay' to *No sé todavía* 'I'm not sure yet' (this is a polite indirection, implying "no"). A few women make sour faces and state directly *No se va a poder* 'I can't make it,' expressing not only their unwillingness to go, but also, perhaps, disapproval of the trip. Few of the responses are completely audible on the recordings I make of the meeting. I write in my field notes that this method seems to be barely more effective than calling for a vote.

### Discussion of Recording in the Field

The encounters described in the ethnographic vignettes are typical of my experiences recording women in community meetings. Their input was both invisible – inaudible – and yet key to the workings of the development projects that I observed and participated in. I wondered if the engineer in Vignette 1 realized how insulting his code-switch was, and how rude it was to speak to someone in Quechua in the words he chose, as if addressing a child. I wondered whether the second engineer, in Vignette 3, realized that the woman who giggled and asked him about what would happen if a tree were broken would veto her family's participation in the project that evening at home. I saw how the content of the public meeting in Vignette 2 was discussed and how decisions were made among family in a private setting following the meeting, and I later understood that most of the issues that were discussed in the meeting in Vignette 4 had already been determined through private conversations and in personal networks before the meeting was held.

When I was ready to do language ideologies interviews, I was confident that I would be able to find participants who were willing to talk to me. I selected households at random, using the water utility's list of members, and used my in-laws' formidable web of contacts to get introductions. One woman seemed pleased and intrigued to meet me, but when we set an appointment to meet for a recording, she was not at home. This happened three times. One time, visiting unannounced, I caught her at home with a friend and they talked on record, nervously, for about two minutes. Then they suddenly discovered they had an urgent errand they had to attend to. Finally, I gave up.

Another time, I asked a friend of mine to wear a recorder around her neck. She took it off after about thirty seconds, saying she was worried it would swing into the pot where lunch was cooking and get ruined. On yet another day, I recorded three older women. They professed complete ignorance and amazement about the workings of my little recording gadget. At the time, cell phones and digital audio players were not common in town. None of the women was familiar with technology. At most, they had completed a few years of formal schooling, and had spent their lives cooking, cleaning, raising children, and tending livestock. I left the recorder running while I went out to buy some sodas, hoping they would forget about it, and me. When I got back, it had been switched off, and nobody could tell me how it had happened.

Other women promised to give me an interview, but only when their husbands were present. Then they let their husbands talk to me while they ran back and forth making lunch and serving us sweet fruit juice. In one case, I interviewed a man who I knew only through his wife, who sold chicken from her house. When I asked to interview her, and she immediately declined and offered to introduce me to her husband, who spoke with me not only willingly and at length but with great assurance and authority. "What kind of work do you do?" I asked, a question on my list. "I'm a teacher," he told me. "My wife is a housewife." I knew from other consultants that because he was completely blind, he had not worked as a teacher for at least twenty years, and indeed could not walk out of the house without his wife's arm to guide him.

In my recordings and transcripts, women were both elusive and pervasive. Seldom could I get someone to sit down and chat with me while the recorder was running unless I shared a truly intimate relationship with them (for this reason, many of my recordings are of close family members and friends). When I asked for interviews, I was told that I should speak to someone who was a "real Iscamayeño," a term that refers to a person who was born in the town and whose family has lived there a long time, but which also has racial overtones; I was told I should interview someone who knew how to speak good Spanish, not the inferior, mixed-up variety that most of my consultants said they spoke.

Slowly, I learned what was obvious from the beginning – public speaking was not seen as a feminine skill. Marina, one of the few women who served as a community representative, emphasized to me that she was always terrible at declamation contests in school.

> I've never liked it, you know, speaking, making speeches. At school I never could do it. When they ma-, made me stand up to present . . . that was my greatest fear. I *hated* it. I got up there and didn't know what to say.[4]

And yet this public silence did not equal powerlessness or voicelessness – not in the least. Marina was an active and well-regarded member of the Town Council for two three-year terms before retiring from public service. She told me that given her lack of formal education, she hadn't been sure she would like being a community representative, but that once she had tried it *no lo hallaba tan difícil* 'I didn't find it so hard.' Marina said these words with dry humor, as if sharing an inside joke with me, clearly disdainful of the incompetence and

---

[4] No sé, nunca no me ha gustado, digamos, así, hablar, discursear. En la escuela nunca no sabía yo. Cuando me sa-, sacaban a exponer, no ve, sacan así a uno, nnnno, yo era, mi terror era eso. No me gust-*a*-ba. Salía y no sabía qué iba a decir.

corruption for which Bolivian politicians – mostly educated men with high social status – are well known. I found that women were frequently the driving force behind major development projects; without their participation and consent, any project was doomed. Their participation was off-record, expressed through the feminine genres of *chisme* 'gossip,' frank conversations among intimates, shades of expression, and remarks made at the outskirts of the meeting and passed on to the floor.

Indeed, many of the women I worked with were quite actively engaged in establishing the limits of their willingness to participate, both in development projects and in taking the floor in community meetings. Several women expressed to me in private that they felt ashamed, *pasaba vergüenza*, when attention was called to them in public. I have no doubt that this was true. Yet, over time, I came to see their refusal to engage in these contexts not just as a lack of ability, but as a way of rejecting the value system of a public sphere in which they were treated as less than full participants because of their lack of schooling, illiteracy, poverty, and discomfort with speaking in the elegant, flowery language associated with *oratoria*. Instead, they turned to their kitchens, children, livestock, and fields, where value was assigned primarily on hard work, reliability, generosity, and participation in kin and community networks of exchange. When called on to participate in formal contexts, they did so on their own terms and in their own ways, as the ethnographic data that I present in this chapter indicates.

Women's ability to use formal oratorical styles is in some sense beyond the point. The point is that they are *aware* of the genre of interviews and community meetings which call for the linguistic style of *oratoria* – a type of speech that includes not only statistical distributions of linguistic features, but also bodily habitus, the willingness to call attention to oneself, and the nerve and daring to go on-record and risk being harshly judged. The choice to engage or not to engage in these sociolinguistic contexts is one of a variety of methods that women use to position themselves as a certain type of person, but it is important to recognize that their resistance and refusal to engage in oratorical contexts does not in the least exclude them from participation in community decision-making and projects. As such, the choice to remain silent – or to speak off-the-record – is a powerful form of social action that women use to control the way they position themselves and the way they are perceived in the community.

## Data 2: Case Studies

Women who orient to the traditional value system resisted being placed in situations in which they might be expected to use oratory, a genre of speech that they might not control. Moving from the larger sense of social control to the more specific sense of sociolinguistic control or style-shifting, how can we differentiate between a lack of control of a particular speech style and a refusal to employ a register which one may in fact control? In this section, I turn to specific analysis of the linguistic patterns of two speakers, both women who orient to a traditional value system, who are pushed into formal speech situations. While they are similar in their positioning as traditional women who resist being placed in a context in which a formal genre of speech is expected, they have different ways of adapting to the speech situation in which they find themselves.

### Prima

Prima was about 60 years old at the time of recording and had four adult children, all enrolled in the university or university graduates. She was of *alteña* 'rural highland' background, and regularly returned to the highlands for seasonal crop sowing and harvest. Her husband was a successful farmer who owned valuable land close to the center of town, and their home, which was built of cement with finished floors and walls, was located on a desirable lot near the center of town. In addition, Prima owned a vacant lot a little further from the center, where she raised chickens for family consumption. Prima wore a straight skirt, not *pollera*, and neither spoke nor understood Quechua, although her older sister wore *pollera*. She was very reluctant to attend meetings and several times commented to me that she was not the meeting "type."

Prima participated in my recordings in two contexts. The first was a language ideologies interview at which her husband was also present, while the second was a more relaxed interview about kitchen practices. The latter interview served as a pre-condition for receiving a rebuilt stove from a nongovernmental development organization I worked with. Because of the subject matter, this interview dealt with a topic about which women, especially rural women who cooked on wood-burning stoves, felt they had special expertise. While it was difficult to impossible to get women to participate in the language ideologies interviews (Prima participated only because I was renting a room in her home and she found it difficult to avoid me), they participated willingly and even enthusiastically in the kitchen practices interviews.

In the following quantitative analysis, I examine the distribution of a set of linguistic features in Spanish in Prima's language ideologies interview versus in her kitchen interview. The features are arranged in order of their occurrence in meetings versus conversational contexts across the entire corpus of transcribed recordings from my 2008 fieldwork, totaling 480 minutes (see Figure 9.1). I chose many of these features because they are cases of semantic convergence with Quechua (see Table 9.1); two (*o sea* and *lo que*) are not contact-related, but are notably more frequent in more formal speech contexts.

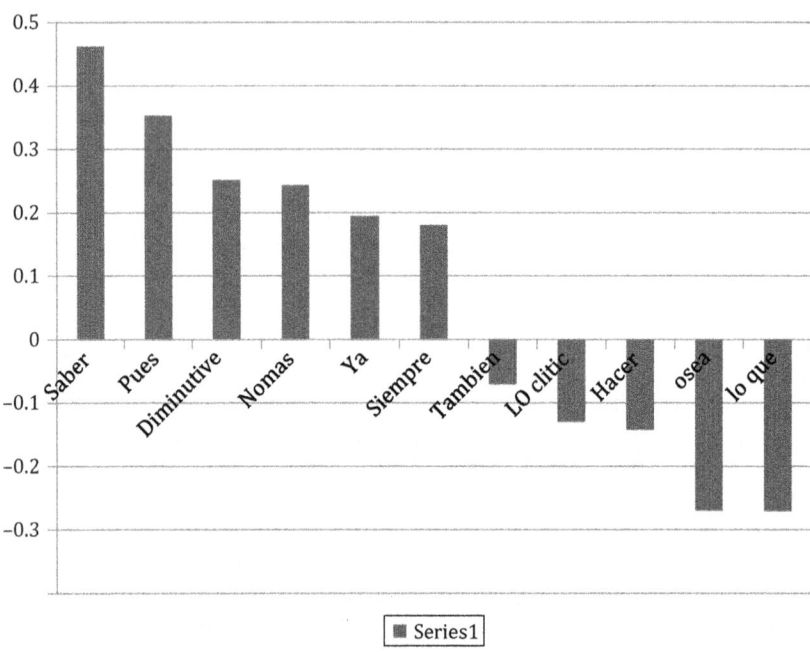

Figure 9.1 Features in Order of Formality
(Least Formal to Most Formal)

While all these words are Spanish, the use of many of the words most common in informal contexts are related to Quechua influence, as discussed in more detail in the works cited in Table 9.1. At the far right of Figure 9.1 are the features most likely to appear in meetings, the Spanish discourse markers *o sea* "that is" and *lo que* "what [complementizer]," which are common in formal genres of speech across the Spanish-speaking world. The latter words are by far most common in formal types of contexts.

Figure 9.1 illustrates the likelihood that features will occur in conversations, contexts in which people tend to orient to ideas of tradition and intimacy (represented by positive values on the chart), versus the likelihood that they will occur in meetings, contexts in which people tend to orient towards formal, modern ideas (represented by negative values on the chart). The chart is ordered based on the difference between the distribution of features over meetings and conversations in the entire corpus. That is, if 64 percent of occurrences of *pues* are in conversations, versus 17 percent in meetings, then *pues* receives an index of 0.47.

In Figure 9.2, Prima's incidence of contact features in the less formal, traditionally oriented kitchen interview is marked with dark gray bars, while

Table 9.1 *Informal-Formal Discourse Features*

| Feature | Gloss | References |
|---------|-------|-----------|
| *saber* as habitual marker (cf. *soler*) | to be accustomed to | Pfänder (2002: 235–6) |
| *pues* | so | Mendoza (2008: 228), Calvo Pérez (2000: 98–100), Escobar (2000: 136–7), Pfänder (2009: 126–30) |
| *-ito, -ita* | Diminutive morphology | Escobar (2012: 81) |
| *nomás* | just | Mendoza (2008: 228), Calvo Pérez (2000: 100–2), Escobar (2000: 137), and Pfänder (2009: 130–3) |
| *ya* | already | Cerrón-Palomino (2003: 250–1), Calvo Pérez (2000: 80–96), Escobar (2000: 138), and Pfänder (2009: 118–21) |
| *siempre* | always, entirely | Mendoza (2008: 228), Calvo Pérez (2000: 77–80), and Pfänder (2009: 124–6) |
| *también* | also | Cerrón-Palomino (2003: 246–8), Calvo Pérez (2000: 90–4), Escobar (2000: 137), and Pfänder (2009: 134–5) |
| *hacer* as causative marker | caused to | Escobar (2000: 128) |
| *o sea* | that is | Not contact-related |
| *lo que* | what/which + complementizer | Not contact-related |

her incidence of contact features in the more formal language ideologies interview is marked with light gray bars. Therefore, one would expect the DARK bars, for informal contexts, to be higher on the left and lower on the right, and the LIGHT bars, for formal contexts, to follow the opposite pattern.

The scale of the graph is based on the number of occurrences of a particular feature divided by the number of words in the section of transcript in question and multiplied by 1,000. Where no bar is present, the word did not occur in this transcript. While these charts are useful for visualization purposes, the small number of data points precludes statistical analysis.[5]

Impressionistically, it seems that Prima follows the general patterns of distribution of contact features, using more formal features in the light gray language ideologies interview and more informal features in the dark gray

---

[5] I offer this quantitative analysis as one of several types of evidence, including the ethnographic material in the previous section, the conversations I had with my consultants, impressions based on my participation in the situations I describe, and the transcription excerpts that I present below. I believe that these figures are of value despite their lack of statistical significance because they contribute an overview of the data that, for reasons of space, I cannot present through the transcripts alone.

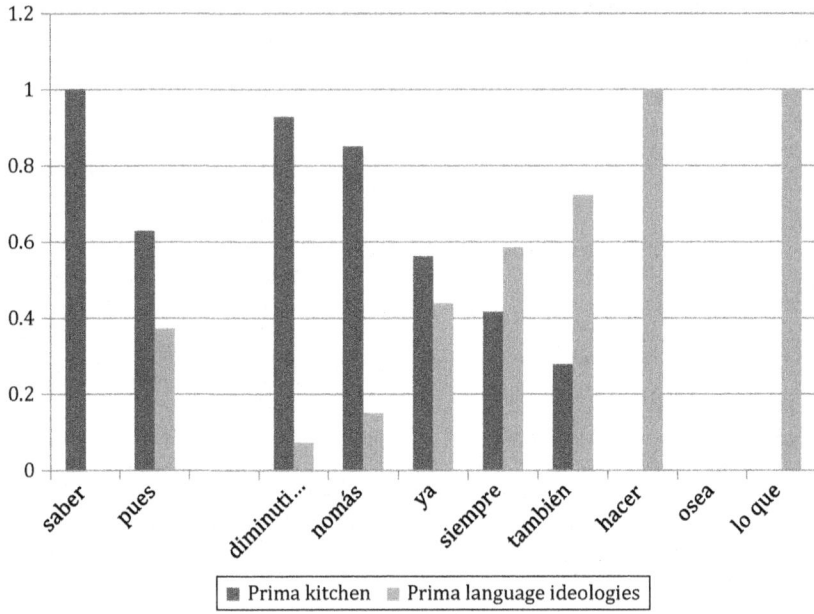

Figure 9.2 Prima Kitchen Interview vs. Language Ideologies Interview

kitchen interview. This impression concords with my observations of her speech in the two contexts. The following transcriptions give a further illustration of the differences that I observed. In Transcript 1, taken from my language ideologies interview, Prima is on her best linguistic behavior, talking about her hope that her children would study English. (N, in Turn 11, is her husband.)

## Transcript 1

P (Prima), A (Anna), N (Nicolás, Prima's husband)

1. P: **En cambio** yo harto h̲e deseado que mi hija antes entre a estudiar ingl̲és.
2. A: Mhm
3. P: También, Nelly, Nestor, y **así como que**, allá. Si hay, no ve, para llevar, puro ingles, no ve?
4. A: Hay
5. P: Hay, pues, pa salir y, de, profesora de inglés están, no ve?
6. A: Sí, sí, sí. Hay eso.

1. P: **On the other hand**, I always wished that my daughter would study English.
2. A: Mm-hmm
3. P: Also, Nelly, Nestor, and **so on**, over there. There is, isn't there, to study, just English, right?
4. A: There is.
5. P: There is, to graduate and, be an English teacher they're there, right?
6. A: Yes, yes, yes. There is that.

7. P: Y, ellos, no han tenido interés. Igual el Henry. Ha hecho dos, tres meses, parece, inglés,

8. A: Mhm

9. P: Y de ahí lo ha dejado **también**. Porque ya **también**, no podía alcanzar, si,

10. A: M, sí.

11. N: M

12. P: Yy, lo ha dejado así. Y, es bien es saber [el in]. De los dos.

13. A: A ha

14. P: Entender.

7. P: And they, weren't interested. Henry was the same. He did two, three months, I think, of English,

8. A: Mm-hmm

9. P: And then he stopped **too**. Because at that point, he couldn't [afford], and,

10. A: Mm, yes.

11. N: M

12. P: And, so he just stopped. And, it's good to know [En-]. Both.

13. A: Uh-huh

14. P: To understand.

In Transcript 1, Prima used formal-sounding phrases such as *en cambio* "on the other hand" and *así como que* "such that" (Turns 1, 3); she also used *también* twice in Turn 9. As noted in Babel (2011), this contact feature is used and over-used when speakers are trying to establish a formal register. Prima was clearly monitoring her speech; she was fairly disfluent, she corrected herself in Turn 12, and phrased her statements as questions in Turns 3 and 5. In the first line, Prima's *e* vowel was slightly raised (boldface and underlined), a telltale and highly salient Quechua contact feature. Later in the conversation she asked me, *Usted va a pasar clases alll, a su idioma de Usted, o no?* "Will you [formal] be teaching classes innnn, in your [formal] language, or not?" The use of the formal person *Usted*, which she rarely used with me in more casual settings, is one more sign of a formal style of speech; she drew attention to this by using the explicit pronoun twice in this short sentence (Spanish does not require explicit pronouns). Prima certainly didn't need to use the formal pronoun with me, a much younger woman and a renter in her house; rather, by doing so, she cast herself as a polite and educated person in an effort to live up to the interview context.

Prima varied her use of contact features to fit different situations. For example, in Transcript 2 below, taken from our more relaxed kitchen practices interview, she made suggestions about how to improve the cooking stove that she obtained from an NGO.

### Transcript 2

P (Prima), A (Anna)

1. P: Y yo decía, **Anita, sabís** que decía?

2. A: Mhm

3. P: Que si no hubiera tenido el ladrillo, **fuera** solamente el **fierro**,

1. P: I was thinking, **Anita, you know** what I was thinking?

2. A: Uh-huh?

3. P: What if it didn't have the brick, if it **were** just the **metal** [ring].

4. A: Mhm

5. P: Eso más bien quería yo Anna decir. Que tenga solamente ese **fierro**, y tenía las **patitas**, que no tenga el ladrillo para que, tenga más **campito** adentro! Si **asicito** es el **campito**!

6. A: Mm, ya ya ya ya.

7. P: No ve? Mientras más campito, más **pon̲imos leñita** y más bracea, más calda va.

4. A: Uh-huh

5. P: That's what I was thinking, instead, Anna. That it should just have the **metal** [ring], and the **feet**, and not the brick so that it, has more **space** inside! It's this **tiny**, that **space**!

6. A: Mm, yeah, yeah, yeah.

7. P: Right? When there's more space, we **put** more **wood** and it burns better, it heats more.

I interviewed Prima in the role of a representative of the NGO, running through a cooking-practices questionnaire with her. In Transcript 2, Prima responded to the question, "How could the stove be improved?" Although Prima had a number of serious complaints about the stoves, she was worried that direct criticisms might be offensive or place me in a difficult position. She invoked our close relationship through intimate forms of address (the *vos* conjugation of the verb *sabís*, the diminutive *Anita*) and through a pronounced $\varphi^w$ in the words *fuera* and *fierro* (in boldface, Turns 3 and 5). Both these features are closely linked to rural female speakers from the countryside. She used the raised-vowel form of *sabés [sabís]* "you know" and *ponemos [pon̲imos]* "we know" (Turns 1 and 7, in boldface). She also used negative politeness strategies (cf. Brown and Levinson 1987), focusing on the fact that it's "just me" that is giving this advice, using subjunctive verb forms in Turn 3, and a proliferation of diminutives (*patitas* "little feet," Turn 5; *campito* "little space," Turn 5, 6; and *leñita* "little sticks," Turn 7).

In Transcript 1, Prima sounded somewhat uncomfortable and disfluent, but she did produce a formal-sounding style of speech. In Transcript 2, on the other hand, she sounded quite at home, using contact features dexterously to maintain a polite and friendly relationship while giving constructive criticism. Prima used these features to index a close personal relationship, one that for her was rooted in tradition and in traditional values of respect and politeness.

We learn from these data that Prima could, in fact, modify her style of speech when she was obligated to participate in a context that she perceived as being more formal. While she was reluctant to participate in these contexts, this reluctance masked an ability to control a more formal genre of speech. Refusal to engage in formal speech situations does not equal a lack of control in the sociolinguistic sense.

### Juana

Juana, the second speaker, was in her early 50s at the time of recording and had six children ranging from elementary-school age to early 30s. Juana and Prima were next-door neighbors and were both originally from the highlands surrounding Iscamayo. Juana, like Prima, wore a straight skirt rather than *pollera*. While Juana regularly attended meetings, such as the Parent-Teacher Organization, the Mother's Club, and other community organizations, she seldom made public statements on the floor, limiting her participation to private comments and off-the-record conversation.

Juana maintained a dense network of social connections in the area, treating families from the surrounding rural areas with respect and affection. People characterized Juana favorably as friendly, kind, and generous, as well as hardworking and unpretentious. Juana was well known in town as a hard worker and a dependable person in a pinch. She frequently worked for wealthy Iscamayo matrons, taking care of their children, washing clothes, or assisting with food preparation for large social events. Her knowledge of the families of Iscamayo was encyclopedic. These characteristics – a hard worker with a "dense, multiplex" social network (cf. Milroy and Milroy 1992) – are one of the premiere expressions of value within the "traditional" system.

In my quantitative analysis, I examine an instance in which she assisted me with an interview with another individual – an older woman from the country-side who could be considered a peer of Juana's. I compare this to a meeting in which she discussed the stove project with an audience of people who were interested in acquiring a stove. In the latter context, she was visibly and audibly nervous, in contrast to the former, in which she acted as an expert in guiding the conversation.

As in Prima's data above, one would expect the DARK bars, for informal contexts, to be higher on the left and lower on the right, and the LIGHT bars, for formal contexts, to follow the opposite pattern. The scale of the graph is based on the number of occurrences of a particular feature divided by the number of words in the section of transcript in question and multiplied by 1,000. As above, the small number of data points precludes statistical analysis.

Juana's use of linguistic variables was not as consistent as Prima's. While she used the features at the extreme left (*pues*) and extreme right (*o sea, lo que*) of the graph as would be expected, the intermediate features show variation that is inconsistent with general patterns of use. This quantitative analysis suggests that Juana employed a less formal register in the meeting context than did Prima in the language ideologies interview.

It is tempting to characterize Juana's performance through a deficit model. She does not control a formal register; she is not aware of the conventions of oratory; she has less ability to style-shift than does Prima. Indeed, a community insider with whom I discussed this data questioned whether Juana "has a meeting voice." Yet this is at best a partial truth. Juana's use of language in the meeting is more agentive than this view would suggest.

This impression is borne out by a close examination of the meeting transcript, which is reproduced in part in Transcript 3. As is evident at first glance,

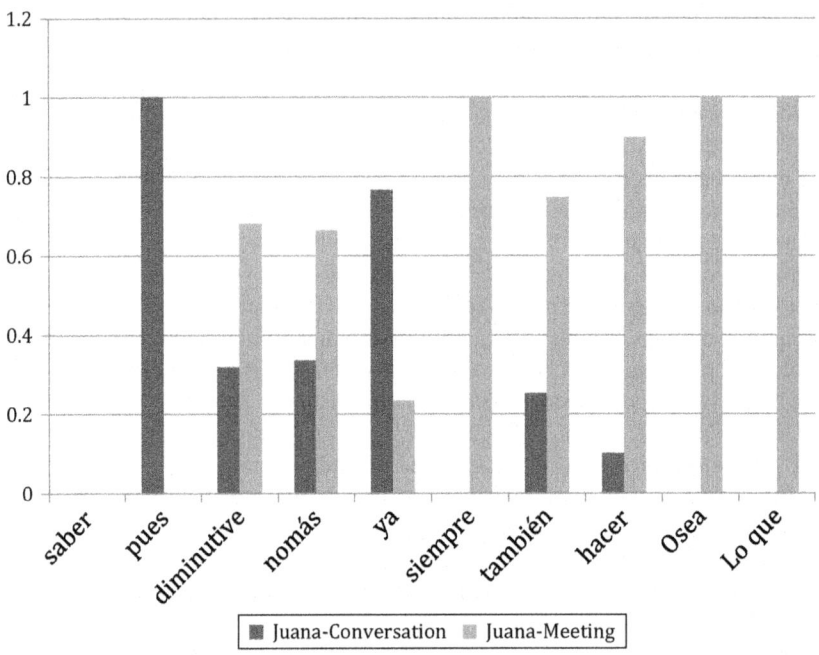

Figure 9.3 Juana Conversation vs. Juana Meeting

the first speaker, Enrique, employs an oratorical style with high-flown vocabulary that is essentially a monologue; Juana's turns, on the other hand, are short and conversational.

### Transcript 3

J (Juana), E (Enrique), F (Froilán)

1. E: Increíble pero fue así. Y en ahí pude yo tam'ien, apr-, digamos, aprovechar de lo que hicieron, digamos, el, preparado un, como unn, todos los, los que iban, iban mirando [la realidad]. Tenía bienn el sabor, entonces. Y hoy, en otra ocasion también, volví a , volvieron a hacer, en otro lugar, igual. Vi pero que en realidad, estas cocinas son, especialmente para aquellas personas que, quieren, poca [..]dad. Yo en, en mi casa, la mayoría, casi la mayoría de los días es que [pruebo] para diez personas. Pero algunas

1. E: It's incredible but that's how it was. And in that I could appr-, let's say, take advantage of what they made, let's say, the, preparation of a, like umm, everyone who went, was seeing the reality of it. It had a gooood flavor, then. And now, on another occasion also, I returned, they returned to do it, in another place, the same again. I saw thus that in reality, these stoves are, specially made for those people who want little [. . .]. I, in my home, mostly, most days it's that I [serve] for ten people. But some days,

veces, doce. Peroo, en todo ese tiempo, me he dado cuenta que en realidad, para que funcione bien estas cocinas, tienen que ser unas leñas que tengan peso. Y así tiene la leña peso, y funciona bien. Puede hacer hervir para más. Yo confío bien en este. Lo único [. . .] es por un lado, [. . .] ha hecho coser. Eso es.

2. F: Eeeso.

[10-second pause]

3. J: <laugh>

4. J: Bueno, en lo de las cocinas a leña, yo veo que muy económicas son. O sea, uno se trae su leña, y, si quiere, si quiere hacer las cositas rápido, y bueno, el cosito es pequeño, pue, para poner leña.

5. F: Así ha de ser, ha de ser.

6. J: Y, uno agarra, s-, le pone una, pedacito así pequeño también por arriba, y, y eso arde como si estuviera apurándose con su, con un, así tronco.

7. F: Mm

8. J: Arde bien.

9. F: Baa

10. J: Y hace cocer su comida rápido.

11. F: Baa

12. J: Yo, cuando no tengo gas, es directo a la, ahí a la cocina. Rápido arde, hasta que mis hijos se van a la escuela, y [hasta que vuelven Uds] yo vengo tarde de allá,

13. F: Hm

14. J: Y, hago cocer mote, hago cocer, cualquier cosa

15. F: Baa

16. J: es como si tuviera uno con esas otras leñitas, digamos, cocinitas a leña si.

17. F: Baa

18. J: Solamente hay que estar continuoo apurándole.

19. F: Aa

20. J: Pero si es leña buena, como dice Enrique, si es fina la leña,

21. F: Más calda tiene.

22. J: Sí. Sigue ardiendo, le apuro otra vez, y aparte que no junta mucha ceniza si.

23. F: Hmm.

twelve. Buuut, in all this time, I've realized that in reality, in order for these stoves to work well, one has to use the firewood that has good weight. And so when the firewood is heavy, it works well. It can even make it boil for more [people]. I trust this [stove] well. The only [. . .] is on the one hand [. . .] made it cook. That's all.

2. F: Thaaat's it.

[10-second pause]

3. J: <laugh>

4. J: Well, in terms of the wood stoves, I find them very economical. That is, one brings one's firewood, and if one wants, if one wants to do things quickly, well, the thingy is small, you see, to put firewood in.

5. F: Must be so, must be.

6. J: And, one grabs it, a-, one puts a little bitty piece on top, too, and, and it burns as if it were being hurried with its, with a, like a big log.

7. F: Mmmm

8. J: It burns well.

9. F: Huuuh

10. J: And it cooks one's food quickly.

11. F: Huuuh

12. J: I, when I don't have gas, I go directly to this stove. It burns quickly, and by the time my children leave for school, and [by the time you come home] I come back late from over there,

13. F: Hmm

14. J: And, I cook boiled corn, I cook, anything

15. F: Huuuh

16. J: it's as if one had one with those other pieces of firewood, that is, wood stoves.

17. F: Huuuh

18. J: Only you have to be there feeding the fire all the time.

19. F: Aaah

20. J: But if the wood is good, as Enrique says, if the firewood is good quality,

21. F: It burns hotter.

22. J: Yes. It keeps burning, I hurry it up a little, and also it's true that it doesn't produce too much ash.

23. F: Hmmm

The meeting began with general chatter (not shown in this segment of the transcript). I was demonstrating some stoves to a few people who had come to see them, while Juana and another community member, Enrique, chatted with their neighbors. Both Juana and Enrique had been using the stoves for more than a year and were present at my invitation to act as experts in discussing the stoves with potential users. After I made a few remarks, I ceded the floor to Enrique, who gave a fairly florid speech filled with oratorical flourishes and dramatic prosodic features. Enrique's turns were long and he addressed the audience with considerable confidence. Enrique's last turn is reproduced in Turn 1 in Transcript 3.

At this point, I turned to Juana. My recollection of the moment is that she gave me a wide-eyed stare, silently but expressively performing surprise at being asked to take the floor and unwillingness to do so. There is a full 10 seconds of silence on the recording as this exchange takes place. But she eventually stood up and exchanged places with Enrique, beginning to speak with a short, nervous laugh.

In her first turns (Lines 4 and 6), Juana stumbled a bit, using the generic subject *uno* 'one' and vocabulary such as 'economical' and *o sea* 'that is,' one of the most common discourse markers in oratorical style. With the support of an elderly man in the audience, however, she soon found her stride. This man, whom I refer to by the pseudonym Froilán, was a lifelong agricultural laborer from the countryside. He responded with frequent positive minimal feedback to Juana's discussion, at one point finishing a sentence for her (Line 21). As she continued to address the audience, Juana began to speak to them as if to a group of friends, addressing them directly as *Usted(es)*, the polite form of "you," which is an appropriate address term for ritual kin and between adults who are not intimates. She began to appeal to shared knowledge: the familiar rhythm of sending children off to school, cooking soup in the morning for the afternoon meal. Although she referred to the man who spoke before her simply as "Enrique" in Line 20, she later referred to two women from the community using the honorific *Doña* (not reproduced in this section of the transcript). As she continued speaking, Froilán's contributions overlapped with hers more and more, and her turns became shorter as his became longer, until the speech became a discussion. After a few minutes, another audience member and I also began contributing observations.

Over the course of this 10-minute recording, Juana shifted the genre of the meeting event to something more like a testimonial. The testimonial is a familiar genre, widely heard on radio advertisements, in which *comadres* and *compadres* 'ritual co-parents' address each other in exaggerated country accents, using polite address forms such as *Usted* "you [formal]" and *Doñ(a)*, an honorific address form. Like stigmatized dialects in other areas in the world, such as the American South, these features are intended to convey artless sincerity, sometimes humor, and above all, reliable recommendations. While Juana's discussion is not precisely the same type of performance as these radio advertisements, it fits within the model of a friendly conversation between people of similar social status and backgrounds. Ultimately, her "speech" became a four-way conversation between herself, Froilán, me, and the other audience member.

Juana did not demonstrate the ability to style-shift that Prima did in Transcripts 1 and 2. However, while we have no positive evidence of her sociolinguistic control of the genre of oratory, she did demonstrate a great deal of control over the situation through her ability to shift the style of the discourse setting from oratory to testimonial. This situational control is a sign of her own dexterity in adapting to the situation in which she found herself, positioning herself not as an expert, but as a neighbor and friend. Juana's initial resistance to being pressed into an oratorical role also expressed her positioning within the traditional value system.

### Discussion

Both Prima and Juana, in their different ways, fit into the category of the traditional woman from the countryside. Both resisted participating in formal settings in which oratorical types of speech might be expected. However, they had different ways of adapting to these situations when they were forced into them. Prima largely replicated the general sociolinguistic patterns of oratorical features used by speakers at meetings – an ability that would have been invisible had she not been forced to participate in this context. Juana, on the other hand, continued to employ informal types of speech. Rather than conform to a set of norms that she might not fully control, she styled her contribution as a testimonial. Seen this way, Juana was an active participant in constructing a context in which she felt comfortable participating.

Given my observations of and conversations with these women, as well as others who shared their positioning, I suggest that this reluctance and refusal should not be interpreted as a sign of lack of control in either the sociolinguistic or the broader societal sense. Prima clearly demonstrated an ability to shift styles in the two situations examined here. Juana, despite her apparent lack of a "meeting voice," demonstrated considerable ability to shape speech events, both in guiding the conversation she participated in and in casting her participation in the meeting as a testimonial. Reluctance and refusal, far from demonstrating a lack of competence, are part of a conspicuous orientation to a traditional value system in which women are not denigrated for their relative lack of formal education and oratorical ability, but rather fulfill an important role as hard workers and valuable members of kin and ritual social networks.

## Conclusion

The data that I examine in this chapter show that *awareness* of a particular style or genre of discourse as part of a larger social system leads speakers to *control* their participation in situations in which they would be expected to employ particular sociolinguistic features. In doing so, I consider (at least) two types of control: control in the sense in which it has been used in previous work in sociolinguistics, that is, the use of sociolinguistic variables over different social contexts; and control in the broader sense of negotiating one's participation in a social situation. Likewise, awareness is multifaceted: speakers may or may not be aware of particular variables, but they are certainly aware of the existence of expectations regarding language use by particular speakers in particular situations. At this level, both awareness and control are related to larger-scale social systems of power and privilege. This broader sense of awareness and control has not been examined seriously or explicitly enough in the existing literature, although it has sometimes been assumed or referenced. Even when examined in isolation, sociolinguistic variables act as part of a complex semiotic web of features, each with its own set of associations that affects the way in which people use and understand them in particular social contexts.

I frame this argument with reference to the literature on silence, which scholars have argued must be considered in relation to speech and social context: Prima's and Juana's practices of resistance are recognizable *only* in relation to sociolinguistic norms at the community level. These norms are locally constructed and produced through forms of practice. Factors such as gender, class, and social standing are all relevant in the use and interpretation of particular instances of silence or indirection. The refusal to use the oratorical genre where it is expected is itself a form of resistance. People can demonstrate control, then, not only through the use of particular patterns of features, but also through resistance to general community norms or through refusal to speak.

Awareness and control function at multiple levels of recognition and at multiple cognitive levels, as demonstrated by Campbell-Kibler (this volume). However, when we consider these levels, we also must attend to the way in which language users understand social norms and position themselves with respect to social groups. Preston invokes Dell Hymes in suggesting that we should be able to "cut across" these different levels of consciousness by moving beyond a conscious-unconscious dichotomy and focusing on the "common ground" of the complexity of social attitudes (this volume, p. 183). I argue in this chapter that we must be sensitive to the many different ways in which people can express or respond to these attitudes. Speakers' production may or may not constitute strong evidence that they control (or don't control) a particular set of features. The ability to control features is not the same as the choice to use them; and the choice to avoid a particular style or set of features is not the same as a lack of control.

In addition to evidence of speakers' control of particular sociolinguistic variables, we must also consider the role of power and resistance in shaping speakers' strategies and participation in social situations such as the meetings and interviews I discuss. When the women who I describe in this chapter are called upon to produce public, on-the-record discourse, they actively resist the "oratorical" role, producing speech that positions them according to an alternative system of value. However, this resistance may mask an ability to produce linguistic forms that conform to the conventions of formal or oratorical speech, and it certainly is not indicative of a lack of control in the larger social sense. Therefore, we must be careful not to characterize non-conformity to sociolinguistic norms as a "lack" of control. Reluctance and refusal constitute a different kind of monitoring and self-control, perhaps more difficult to measure and quantify, but just as real as on-the-record speech.

## REFERENCES

Auer, Peter, Barden, Birgit, and Grosskopf, Beate. 1998. Subjective and objective parameters determining "salience" in long-term dialect accommodation. *Journal of Sociolinguistics* 2:163–87.

Babel, Anna M. 2011. Why don't all contact features act alike? Contact features as enregistered features. *Journal of Language Contact* 4:56–91.

Basso, Keith. 1970. "To give up on words": Silence in Western Apache culture. *Southwestern Journal of Anthropology* 26:213–30.

Bourdieu, Pierre. 1991. *Language and Symbolic Power*. Cambridge, MA: Harvard University Press.

Brown, Penelope and Levinson, Stephen C. 1987. *Politeness: Some Universals in Language Usage*. Cambridge University Press.

Calvo Pérez, Julio. 2000. Partículas en el castellano andino, in J. Calvo Pérez (ed.), *Teoría y práctica del contacto: el español en América en el candelero*, pp. 73–112. Madrid: Iberoamericana and Vervuert.

Campbell-Kibler, Kathryn. 2010. New directions in sociolinguistic cognition. University of Pennsylvania Working Papers in Linguistics 15.

Cerrón-Palomino, Rodolfo. 2003. *Castellano andino: Aspectos sociolingüísticos, pedagógicos y gramaticales*. Lima: Pontificia Universidad Católica del Perú.

Eckert, Penelope. 2000. *Linguistic Variation as Social Practice: The Linguistic Construction of Identity in Belten High*. Oxford, UK: Blackwell.

Eckert, Penelope and Rickford, John R. 2001. *Style and Sociolinguistic Variation*. Cambridge University Press.

Eckert, Penny and Wegner, Etienne. 2005. What is the role of power in sociolinguistic variation? *Journal of Sociolinguistics* 9:582–9.

Ephratt, Michal. 2011. Linguistic, paralinguistic and extralinguistic speech and silence. *Journal of Pragmatics* 43:2286–307.

Escobar, Anna María. 2000. *Contacto social y lingüístico: El español en contacto con el quechua en el Perú*. Lima: Pontificia Universidad Católica del Perú.

2012. Spanish in contact with Amerindian languages, in J. I. Hualde, A. Olarrea, and E. O'Rourke (eds.), *The Handbook of Hispanic Linguistics*, pp. 65–88. Malden, MA: Wiley-Blackwell.

Fivush, Robyn. 2010. Speaking silence: The social construction of silence in autobiographical and cultural narratives. *Memory* 18:88–98.

Foucault, Michel. 1980. *Truth and Power. Power/Knowledge*, pp. 109–33. New York: Pantheon.

Gal, Susan. 1989. Between speech and silence: The problematics of research on language and gender. *IPrA Papers in Pragmatics* 3:1–38.

Hay, Jennifer, Warren, Paul, and Drager, Katie. 2006. Factors influencing speech perception in the context of a merger-in-progress. *Journal of Phonetics* 34:458–84.

Hill, Jane H. 1995. The Voices of Don Gabriel, in D. Tedlock and B. Mannheim (eds.), *The Dialogic Emergence of Culture*, pp. 97–147. Urbana, IL: University of Illinois Press.

Irvine, Judith T. and Gal, Susan. 2000. Language ideology and linguistic differentiation, in P. Kroskrity (ed.), *Regimes of Language*, pp. 35–83. Santa Fe, NM: School of American Research Press.

Jaworski, Adam. 1993. *The Power of Silence: Social and Pragmatic Perspectives Newbury Park*, Newbury Park, CA: Sage Publications.

(ed.) 1997. *Silence: Interdisciplinary Perspectives*. Berlin: Mouton de Gruyter.

Johnstone, Barbara. 2005. Style, and the linguistic individual: A sociolinguistic approach to voice, in Alexandra Jaffe (ed.), *Stance: Sociolinguistic Perspectives*, New York: Oxford University Press.

Johnstone, Barbara and Kiesling, Scott F. 2008. Indexicality and experience: Exploring the meanings of /aw/-monophthongization in Pittsburgh. *Journal of Sociolinguistics* 12:5–33.

Kurzon, Dennis. 2007a. Peters Edition v. Batt: The intertextuality of silence. *International Journal for the Semiotics of Law – Revue internationale de Sémiotique juridique* 20:285–303.

2007b. Towards a typology of silence. *Journal of Pragmatics* 39:1673–88.

2011. On Silence. *Journal of Pragmatics* 43:2275–7.

Labov, William. 1972. *Sociolinguistic Patterns*. Philadelphia, PA: University of Pennsylvania Press.

2006. *The Social Stratification of English in New York City*. Cambridge University Press.

Labov, William, Ash, Sharon, Ravindranath, Maya, Weldon, Tracey, Baranowski, Maciej, and Nagy, Naomi. 2011. Properties of the sociolinguistic monitor1. *Journal of Sociolinguistics* 15:431–63.

Maltz, Daniel. 1985. Joyful noise and reverent silence: The significance of noise in Pentecostal worship, in D. Tannen and M. Saville-Troike (eds.), *Perspectives on Silence*. Norwood, NJ: Ablex.

Mendoza, José G. 2008. *Bolivia. El español en América: Contactos lingüísticos en Hispanoamérica*, pp. 213–36. Barcelona: Editorial Ariel.

Milroy, Lesley and Milroy, James. 1992. Social network and social class: Toward an integrated sociolinguistic model. *Language in Society* 21:1–26.

Niedzielski, Nancy. 1999. The effect of social information on the perception of sociolinguistic variables. *Journal of Language and Social Psychology* 18:62–85.

Niedzielski, Nancy A. and Preston, Dennis Richard. 2003. *Folk Linguistics*. Berlin and New York: Walter de Gruyter.

Pagis, Michal. 2010. Producing intersubjectivity in silence: An ethnographic study of meditation practice. *Ethnography* 11:309–28.

Pfänder, Stefan. 2002. Contacto y cambio lingüístico en Cochabamba (Bolivia), in N. Díaz, R. Ludwig, and S. Pfänder (eds.), *La Romanía americana. Procesos lingüísticos en situaciones de contacto*, pp. 219–54. Madrid: Iberoamericana and Vervuert.

2009. *Gramática Mestiza La Paz*. Bolivia: Instituto Boliviano de Lexicografía.

Preston, Dennis. 1996. Whaddayaknow: The modes of folk linguistic awareness. *Language Awareness* 5:40–74.

Rácz, Péter. 2013. *Salience in Sociolinguistics: A Quantitative Approach*. Berlin: De Gruyter.

Rickford, John R. 1985. Standard and non-standard language attitudes in a creole continuum, in Nessa Wolfson and Joan Manes (eds.), *Language of Inequality*, Vol. 36, pp. 145–60. Berlin: Walter de Gruyter.

Rickford, John R. and McNair-Knox, Faye. 1994. Addressee- and topic-influenced style shift: A quantitative sociolinguistic study, in D. Biber and E. Finegan (eds.), *Sociolinguistic Perspectives on Register*, pp. 235–76. New York: Oxford University Press.

Schilling-Estes, Natalie. 1998. Investigating "self-conscious" speech: The performance register in Ocracoke English. *Language in Society* 27:53–83.

Silverstein, Michael. 1979. Language structure and linguistic ideology, in P. R. Clyne, W. F. Hanks, and C. L. Hofbauer (eds.), *The Elements: A Parasession on Linguistic Units and Levels*, pp. 193–95. Chicago, IL: Chicago Linguistic Society.

1981. The limits of awareness. *Texas Working Papers in Linguistics* 84:1–30.

Tannen, Deborah and Saville-Troike, Muriel. (eds.) 1985. *Perspectives on Silence*. Norwood, NJ: Ablex.

Urban, Greg. 1996. Entextualization, replication, and power, in M. Silverstein and G. Urban (eds.), *Natural Histories of Discourse*, pp. 21–44. Chicago, IL: University of Chicago Press.

Woolard, Kathryn. 1998. Language Ideology as a Field of Inquiry, in B. Schieffelin, K. Woolard, and P. Kroskrity (eds.), *Language Ideologies: Practice and Theory*, pp. 3–47. New York: Oxford University Press.

# 10 Theorizing Salience: Orthographic Practice and the Enfigurement of Minority Languages

*Nishaant Choksi and Barbra A. Meek*[*]

## Introduction

A favorite pedagogical exercise of Meek's when teaching about representations of American Indians and Alaska Natives is an optical illusion (by Winson; www.optical-illusionist.com/illusions/eskimo-face-illusion#comments) that she projects onto a screen and asks the students to identify.

Some see an American Indian man with an extraordinarily large proboscis, raven black hair, an earring, and slitty eyes. Some find an Eskimo walking away, in a fur-trimmed parka and mukluks. Others discover both; others, neither. Those students who discern neither image often hail from another continent, but those raised in the United States and Canada easily treat the image as depicting an indigenous North American figure. Obviously there is a salience to the image and to the arrangement of features, though ambivalent, that encourages these mutual interpretations (readings). That is, these readings are socially mediated, as indicated by the distributions of readers and non-readers, those students who "see" the indigenous character and those who do not. The visual manifestation(s) and bivalency of the imagery is rendered interpretable because of its ideological resonance. The social-ideological domain through which it circulates (and is in part created) informs our reading of the image, rendering the two images salient. Similarly, linguistic practices inform and are informed by social-ideological domains, rendering certain interpretive aspects salient and obscuring others. Salience, then, is a process whereby the (strategic) use of socio-culturally inflected elements *enfigures* representations (utterances, texts, images, performances), investing and

[*] We would like to thank Anna Babel and Kathryn Campbell-Kibler for inviting us to participate in this project and for their provocative feedback on earlier drafts. We are equally indebted to the anonymous reviewer and to participants of the University of Michigan Linguistic Laboratory, who provided critical yet encouraging comments. We are also grateful for the research support we've received from the following organizations: Wenner-Gren, the Woodrow Wilson Foundation, the National Endowment for the Humanities, Fulbright-Hays, the America-Scandinavia Foundation, and the University of Michigan. Any mistaken or uninterpretable enfiguring of evidence, salience, or obscurity are our own doing.

Figure 10.1 Indian Eskimo Illusion
Image credit: public domain; www.optical-illusionist.com/illusions/eskimo-face-illusion

constraining them with a certain provenance that will elicit an interpretation.[1] It is a coming-into-being of enfigurement. It is not necessarily awareness, and neither the producer nor the perceiver-interpreter necessarily control or have detailed knowledge about the elements involved in the enfiguring of a representation.

Salience is the semiotic, socially constituted dynamic within linguistic practice that affects the individual-centered processes of the "reflective" (controlled, metapragmatic awareness) and the "reflexive" (automatic, perceived or "felt" difference) (see Drager and Kirtley, this volume). That is, salience is a social-culturally entangled and constitutive aspect of a process of representation, where part of what is representable may be cognitively derived and the other part may be socio-culturally derived. A range of linguistic phenomena, from acquisition to literacy, demonstrate and participate in this process. Our focus here will be on projects developing conventions for representing

---

[1] By "enfigure," we draw on Goffman's notion of "figure" such that what is being circumscribed sociolinguistically is a character or characterization of a type of person. This phrase is analogous to Agha's use of enregisterment and Brigg's and Bauman's uses of entextualization, indicating the making into and marking of some formation as a register and/or text. In our case, "enfigure" refers to the making into and marking of a type of person or a persona, the process of personifying some form in and through practice.

indigenous minority languages. The first case derives from Meek's research in the Yukon Territory, Canada, showing how the representational strategies used in different domains of aboriginal language revitalization brought into relief certain expectations and disagreements. The second case comes from Choksi's work in India with an *adivasi* (a generic term meaning "original inhabitant") group, and focuses on the plethora of representational forms and their distillation across different domains of practice. Once developed, these styles of representation have the potential to circulate and become standardized. Through standardization, they become the taken-for-granted norms of representation. The Yukon case illustrates this goal of language standardization as the aboriginal languages took shape through entextualization and the desire to establish unique orthographic conventions for each of the eight territorially recognized aboriginal languages. These representations instantiate certain phonological and social differences that in return mediate the everyday expectations of language learners, teachers, and observers. The Indian case describes how the enfigurement of one phonetic feature in particular has come to provide an identical basis for competing claims of authority for proponents of multiple competing orthographic systems, refracting ideologies of unity and difference.

## *Salience: Linguistic Anthropological Approaches*

Although important in sociolinguistics, linguistic anthropology, and related disciplines, the concept of salience has been subject to multiple and often conflicting theorizations. For instance, Auer *et al.* (1998) suggest that the sociolinguistic literature has a conflicted view of salience, describing the concept as both "objective," that is, as a property of linguistic form, and "subjective," that is, as subject to speakers' attitudes. In their own work on dialectic accommodation, they suggest that it is the "subjective" criteria, such as style switching, representation in writing, or stereotyping which brings certain linguistic features into the speaker's awareness, thus sheltering the feature from accommodation to other linguistic varieties. Recent approaches such as Preston (this volume) have attempted to rethink older concepts of salience (such as in Trudgill 1986), arguing that rather than thinking of salience along a subjective/objective binary, one should examine how forms come to be noticed both consciously and unconsciously as part of a wider "folk linguistic theory" (Preston 1996).

Linguistic anthropologists have considered the relationship between salience and awareness by considering the semiotic processes through which speakers relate linguistic forms to wider social and cultural ideologies of language and language use. Instead of focusing on subjective or objective characteristics, linguistic anthropologists instead consider under what conditions speakers can articulate sociolinguistic difference, and how these articulations, both grounded

in the grammatical organization of the language as well as the socially conditioned organization of communicative practice, become either subject to conflict, debate, and political dispute, or how they serve to inform commonsensical,
often unchallenged assumptions about languages and their speakers (cf. Agha
2007; Irvine and Gal 2000).

Questions of salience in the linguistic anthropological literature have usually
been encompassed by explorations in how speakers come to be "aware" of
certain forms and not others. For instance, the contrast between "subjective"
speaker-centered accounts of language and "objective" linguistic accounts is
the subject of Silverstein's 1981 essay, "The limits of awareness." He argues
that "meaning" does not reside in the referential content of a particular
utterance, but in the pragmatic considerations that render a particular linguistic
form subject to metalinguistic awareness. For instance, when certain linguistic
features presuppose relationships that are beyond the speech event, such as the
difference between "ordinary" and "mother-in-law" vocabulary in the Australian language Djirbal or honorific use in Indonesia, the contrasting features
find articulation by native speakers through metapragmatic discourse. Such
patterns contrast with Silverstein's own field experience with Wasco-Wishram
speakers, where the phonetic gradations between augmentative, neutral, and
diminutive nominal forms, though easily manipulated by speakers, were not
subject to metapragmatic awareness. This is because, as Silverstein argues,
these features created relationships as part of the speech event itself rather than
being presupposed. Silverstein suggests at the end of his essay that "the salient
aspect of the social fact is meaning; the central manifestation of meaning is
pragmatic and metapragmatic speech, and the most obvious feature of pragmatic speech is reference. We are now beginning to see the error in trying to
investigate the salient by projection from the obvious" (1981: 21). Salience is
not always obvious nor is it equivalent to awareness. Rather, salience emerges
as part of a process of creation, creating a relationship between linguistic
elements and socio-cultural phenomena.

Critical to a linguistic anthropological conception of salience is Bauman and
Briggs's (1990) discussion of "entextualization," and its related processes of
decontextualization and recontextualization. As entextualized forms circulate
through different domains of practice, speakers arrange these forms in a
dialectical relation with their existing ideological commitments. Stylistic or
generic elements that maintain links across different texts guide individual
interpretations (of relatedness or similarity) without necessarily resulting
in individual articulations (or awareness) of the links that allow for these
intertextual connections. Unlike the concept of awareness where there is an
available metapragmatic commentary, salience assumes a more tacit juncturing
of everyday phenomena. In summary, salience, in sociolinguistic terms, is the
semiotic process by which a figure takes shape through particular linguistic

flourishes (such as in the way in which the Hollywood Injun English enfigures a character as American Indian and socializes an audience to recognize this enfigurement thusly; cf. Meek 2006).

## Form and Interpretation: Designing a Language in the Yukon

Our first case from Meek's fieldwork in the Yukon Territory (Canada) attends to salience in relation to aboriginal language revitalization projects. Such projects amplify individual awareness of linguistic form and practice in that they emphasize language documentation and evaluations of linguistic knowledge. They are explicit projects of representation, and thus "reflexive activities" (Agha 2007). At the same time that awareness of linguistic form is heightened in these activities, certain elements gather increasing salience. That is, those elements that are salient in multiple ways (cognitively, socially, culturally, etc.) will be more likely to be enfigured as a language in these cases. However, different participants with different life experiences and expectations will have different ideas about and practices for enfiguring a language.

While the documentation of aboriginal peoples in North America has been a mainstay of European colonization, identifying and mapping populations to specific regions, efforts to document aboriginal languages have been more intermittent. In the Yukon Territory, Canada, early linguistic documentation happened primarily through efforts to preserve aboriginal narratives (e.g. Teit and Boas 1898). Even as late as the 1970s and 1980s, attention to aboriginal language practices happened through the guise of narrative, and often in a standard style of English, thus fueling the pervasive aboriginal tale of theft and abandonment by non-local researchers. Concerted efforts to document aboriginal languages and analyze grammatical structure emerged alongside nationwide efforts to empower First Nations and territorial efforts to negotiate land claims.

As the civil rights movement took shape in the United States, its aboriginal counterpart emerged in Canada. Spearheaded by the Assembly of First Nations, aboriginal peoples began to demand equal treatment and compensation by the Canadian Government. At the same time, Francophone communities were also demanding recognition of and support for their language needs.[2] Eventually,

---

[2] The majority of Canadian legislation regarding language focuses on French and English. Initiated by a study on Canadian bilingualism and biculturalism in the late 1950s, incoming Premier Trudeau established Canada's Official Languages Act in 1969 and then incorporated language policy into the 1982 Canadian Charter of Rights and Freedoms, sections 16 through 23, making up the first part of the Canadian Constitution. The effect of this legislation was twofold. It placed French on equal (constitutional and institutional) footing with English, and it mandated minority language education rights. That is, it demanded the provision of funding for minority

the Canadian Government instituted an official language policy, recognizing both English and French, established initially in 1969 under then Prime Minister Pierre Trudeau and then revised in 1988 to accommodate the Constitution Act of 1982, which made explicit reference to language policy and practice for Ottawa, New Brunswick, and Quebec. The Yukon Territorial Government and the Council of Yukon Indians (now Council of Yukon First Nations (CYFN)) saw the impending amendments as an opportunity to negotiate their own official languages policy with the Canadian government and approved the Yukon Official Languages Act in 1988:[3]

(3) The Yukon recognizes the significance of aboriginal languages in the Yukon and wishes to take appropriate measures to preserve, develop, and enhance those languages in the Yukon. S.Y. 1988, c. 13, s. 1.

(3) Le Yukon reconnaît l'importance des langues autochtones au Yukon et souhaite prendre les mesures nécessaires pour maintenir et valoriser ces langues au Yukon, et en favoriser le développement. L.Y. 1988, ch. 13, art. 1

Both the nationwide and territorial discourses incorporated a recognition of and concern for the plight of aboriginal languages (Hinton and Meek, forthcoming; Meek 2009). Funding accompanied this concern, resulting in an initial five years of support from the federal government and renewable thereafter for the documentation of aboriginal languages in the Yukon Territory and the development of programming for aboriginal language education, including teacher training. Language, and languages, became a salient figure in the formatting of minority and aboriginal politics, bringing into the design aboriginal languages while at the same time obscuring to some extent emerging Aboriginal-English dialects and English more generally.[4]

### Regimentation of Form: YNLC and Textual Production

The first attempts at institutional documentation by the territorial government and CYFN happened through the Yukon Native Languages Centre, or YNLC. Initially a program, the Centre's establishment in 1985 coincided with initiatives to change national language legislation and recognize multiculturalism as an important dimension of the conceptualization of the Canadian nation-state.

---

language education, from training teachers to developing curriculum materials, within the provinces and territories.

[3] See www.gov.yk.ca/legislation/acts/languages.pdf.

[4] This is not intended to suggest that the majority language, English, was ever threatened by the political resurgence of minority languages. It is simply to point out that discursively English and English language competence were backgrounded in the legislation and aboriginal proclamations regarding aboriginal rights, languages, and education during a time when the Canadian Government was attempting to terminate Indian status as an answer to aboriginal poverty.

These bureaucratic changes eventually included the commitment of federal funds for language documentation, preservation, and revitalization for the Yukon's First Nations. Under the direction of a MIT-trained linguist, the Centre was responsible for shepherding the emerging aboriginal language programs in the territory's public schools. The model for language reflected in the Centre's discourse, practices, and mission suggest an underlying formal linguistic model, a model that would guide the orthographic conventions developed to represent the territory's eight aboriginal languages.

The Centre remains active today, developing new materials (such as audio books, online language lessons), publicizing aboriginal language activities and accomplishments, supporting the Native Language Instructor Program, and expanding as a resource for indigenous language research and development. As its website notes, "[t]oday the Centre staff is actively teaching, document-ing, and promoting Yukon Native languages."[5] It houses a significant amount of linguistic data (texts, recordings) and documentation of the territory's aboriginal languages. It has also produced a range of texts, available through its website, for learning and teaching the territory's aboriginal languages. According to its website, "[t]hese [materials] include a curriculum guide; language lesson booklets and audio CDs / tapes, and interactive computer CDs; dictionaries and reference materials; story booklets; and games and teaching aids. YNLC continues to expand its website to include more screen and audio materials." Notably, while texts appear to make up the majority of the Centre's efforts, recording and orality are emphasized in the Centre's discourse about the creation of these texts and in their pedagogical orientation.

In the Centre's discussion of the creation of the texts and lessons, it emphasizes that the staff "begin with sound," recording a fluent speaker and then "YNLC linguists ... prepare the transcriptions of the recorded sentences. Note that we do not proceed from the written to the spoken as is usual with similar projects, but do the reverse. *The fluent speaker is the model.*"[6] The Centre continues by pointing out the necessity of having the highest possible sound quality for these recordings, in order "to accurately reproduce *the subtle phonetic distinctions which are critically important.*"[7] While such subtle phonetic distinctions might certainly be important in general, and most cer-tainly to a linguist documenting an endangered language, never once did a speaker or teacher of any of these aboriginal languages bemoan the loss of these phonetic elements in either a learner's speech or in their non-representation in the teaching materials and texts. Although salient to many (at least as dialect differences; see Meek 2007), awareness and metalinguistic

---

[5] See www.ynlc.ca/ynlc/index.html.
[6] See www.ynlc.ca/materials/audio_lessons.html. Emphasis added.     [7] Emphasis added.

commentary enfigured these languages in relation to the experiences and expectations of the linguists managing these projects.

A similar discourse appears with respect to the site's discussion of the production of the Native Language Audio Story Books. The Centre emphasizes orality and "local ways of speaking;" "[s]ound is a useful tool for teaching and learning any language. But sound is even more useful for native language teaching where the emphasis, especially in earlier grades, is on oral rather than written language."[8] The site also points out that the story books produced by YNLC are not simply translations of English (or even French) printed materials. Instead,

[a] YNLC story book begins with a set of black and white picture pages. The author composes a story in her own language to match the pictures, and on each page she writes the text corresponding to the picture. When the native language text is complete, the author provides an English translation. Next, the author's voice is recorded, sentence by sentence, onto the computer. The voice recordings and the native language text are then combined with colour pictures into the first draft of the audio story book. At this stage *the linguists can verify that the native language text is spelled correctly* by playing the voice recordings, and they can confirm that the English translation is accurate. Then the book is posted to the web. If a print version is desired, it is made after the audio version is finished.[9]

Unsurprisingly, expertise for oral production resides with fluent Native language speakers and expertise for textual production resides with linguists. Thus, the enfigurement of the territory's aboriginal languages reflects the presuppositions and experiences of university-trained linguists (Meek included) and not necessarily those of fluent Native speakers.

In addition to audio story books and language lessons, the Centre produces materials that specifically target the acquisition of literacy skills, referred to as listening exercises, and these are used in the YNLC's literacy workshops to help students (language teachers and interested others) discern the sound-symbol correspondences. "A typical exercise has three parts: a short list of common words which contrast the sounds; a series of sentences containing one or more of the target sounds; and a sheet with pictures for each of the sentences."[10] The exercises focus on differences between similar sounds (in terms of place of articulation, but differing in manner), such as <tl> and <tl'> or <t> and <t'>. Vowel sounds were contrasted primarily in relation to length and nasality, with occasional exercises focused on tone. These exercises are intended to socialize the novice writer into a representational scheme designed for aboriginal languages, a scheme that highlights the sound differences within and across languages.

---

[8] See www.ynlc.ca/materials/story_books.html.     [9] Ibid., emphasis added.
[10] See www.ynlc.ca/materials/highs/literacy.html.

*Interpretation of Form: Learning and Representing*
*the Kaska Language*

Literacy exercises were part of Kaska language revitalization from the beginning, facilitating the creation of texts, curriculum materials, and the training
of teachers for public school instruction. They were also a regular component
of the language workshops that Meek helped organize and run from 1998 to
2000. While elders either demonstrated the pronunciation of the sounds or
worked on their beading, the other workshop participants engaged in the
exercises, diligently concentrating on what they heard and how to represent
the sound on the worksheet. On one occasion, however, the focus was on
providing Meek with practice writing and listening, socializing her into appropriate interactional norms and expectations. This meant that Meek stood at the
white board and wrote what she heard while each person in the room read
out the sentences. Additionally, as linguists, there was interest in documenting
the various dialects, especially the one with the interdental fricatives. The
enfigurement of Kaska at these literacy events was not only to socialize all
of the participants into certain orthographic norms, it was to learn these norms
in relation to the particular varieties of Kaska spoken in the community.

The enfigurement of Kaska in the public elementary school classroom
rendered this orthographic component salient in slightly different ways
towards different ends. For younger grades (kindergarten through second),
the literacy exercise emphasized pronunciation, such as demonstrating the
difference between "l" and barred or Indian "l" ([l] and its voiceless counterpart). However, rather than having students write the sounds on a piece of
paper, they were asked to point to the appropriate letter displayed, using a yard
stick.[11] In the fourth-grade classroom, this routine played out differently in that
we began to focus on sound-morpheme correspondences rather than exclusively sound-phoneme relationships. For example, the verb forms for "X feels
Y" offered an opportunity to transform a salient pattern into an explicit,
patterned awareness of pronominal form. The teacher pronounced the verb
words, such as <sesdlí'> (*I feel cold*), the students suggested spellings of her
utterance, and then the teacher contrasted that form with a similar one,
<sendlí'> (*you feel cold*) and so forth. In this way, a salient grammatical
pattern for the teacher became an overt one and part of the students' awareness
of Kaska grammar. Pedagogically, the teacher explained that she tried to
design her teaching "based on words the children can produce." In practice,
her students seemed to be able to produce a wide range of words and sounds,
including novel verb forms that they had never seen, written, or perhaps even

---

[11]    The teacher noted that "Native kids appeared to be better" at identifying the differences than the
non-Native students. They also appeared to be more proficient at reproducing the sounds.

heard prior to those lessons. In the classroom with younger language users and/or novice learners, this model of language emphasized sound over text, enfiguring the Kaska language as pedagogically different from English and French, the model of language that guided other instruction. In student discourse, this difference underscored students' decisions to switch from Kaska to French, prompting explanations such as "they're not coming anymore because they say that French gives them a better education and prepares them better for high school." The differences in pedagogical styles and norms between these language classes were clearly salient to some students, if not explicitly identifiable discursively.

In order for aboriginal language literacy to occur and to a lesser extent classroom instruction, orthographic conventions were needed. One of the first steps towards textual production in the Yukon was the creation of orthographies with which to depict the various aboriginal languages. To that end, the Centre developed eight distinct orthographies, one for each of the eight territorially recognized aboriginal languages.[12] The forms of the letters are based on Roman script, with sounds aligning somewhat with the conventions of the International Phonetic Alphabet (IPA). For example, the symbol <a> is usually pronounced [a] and not [æ], and <i> is often articulated as [i] in the First Nations' orthographies. These symbols do not correspond with typical English spelling conventions, those that most First Nations individuals acquired in school and use in their daily lives. That is, the sound [i] is not represented as <ee> or <ea> and the sound [æ] is not represented as <a>, as in <cat>. Instead, it is symbolized by an <e> with a straight line over it. And [u] appears as <u> with a straight line over the top, whereas in other aboriginal languages the symbol <u> (or <u> with an umlaut) indicates [schwa]. However, certain distinctions and styles of representation salient to the linguist may not be as transparent or parse-able to the non-linguist.

During workshops and in interviews with teachers, learners, and elders, people often complained that these specialized symbols were cumbersome, especially the diacritics. In part, their frustration with the orthographic conventions managed by YNLC reflected the fact that these practices diverged from their own intuitive orthographic habits, habits derived from their experiences with English. At the workshop where we developed the Kaska alphabet book (Meek *et al.* 2002), the women with whom Meek worked decided to modify some of the representational elements in order to make the text "more accessible" and "more readable." Plus, as one of them put it, "[they] already

---

[12] The eight languages are: Tlingit, Northern Tutchone, Southern Tutchone, Han, Kaska, Tahlan, Tagish, and Gwich'in. On a logo developed by the former Aboriginal Language Services to symbolize aboriginal language revitalization in the Yukon, each language is represented encircling in translation the phrase "We Are Our Language" (see Meek 2010: 131).

know the tones so why would [they] have to mark them?" A few years later, when Meek was visiting one of these women at her office, she leafed through a copy of the book only to discover that it had been marked up with bars over "u's" and other similar "corrections" – the diacritics that had been removed had been re-added. Could it be that the linguists at the Centre who managed and corrected orthographic representations in their own texts had altered this one? Regardless of the answer, the women's attempt to eliminate elements that were salient to them had re-materialized. While aboriginal language revital-ization in the Yukon has in part been an attempt to re-enfranchise First Nations peoples, it remains at the same time a national project invested in modern, dominant conventions of linguistic representation salient and sanctioned institutionally.

Another complicating feature is the unique representational form of the different orthographies. Captured succinctly in the Yukon Territory's logo for aboriginal languages, each language and accompanying language commu-nities have their own style of orthographic representation (see footnote 11). YNLC's website also demarcates the languages and groups of speakers in this way, together with guidelines for using each orthography in their language lesson booklets. (The alphabetic charts for representing each of the eight recognized languages can be found through the website's "Language" link that takes users to a list of the eight languages and links to PDFs of the alphabets for each language.[13])

Some of the linguistic differences rendered orthographically are already salient to language users, if not part of their discourse about linguistic differ-ences. For example, Northern Tutchone has grammatical high tone, while Southern Tutchone has grammatical low tone. Northern Tutchone speakers remarked on this difference as well as deploying it to personify different characters in oral narrative performances. In contrast, other orthographic differences are not as well motivated. For example, to represent an unstressed vowel, schwa, orthographic conventions vary – an "a" with an umlaut in one case versus a bare "a" versus a bare "u." This variability – especially in relation to the use of an elaborate system of diacritics – inhibits comprehensibility across languages (and dialects) and inhibits usage of the orthography and writing more generally. It also deviates from the writing system already known to those who read and write – the English alphabet. Across the board, Kaska speakers and learners indicated that they would prefer a representational system that coincided with their current writing habits. The one exception was an elder who asked Meek to develop a syllabary for representing Kaska, analogous to the syllabic systems used for Inuit (Inuktitut) and Cree. The

---

[13]  See www.ynlc.ca/languages/index.html.

rationale for this request suggested an alignment with other First Nations and their writing traditions in counter-alignment to the nation-state and a traumatic colonial history epitomized for many by residential schooling and its association with the Roman alphabet.

Another challenge raised by orthographic representation concerns dialects and their recognition. While dialects are certainly salient and socially significant, the conceptual predisposition to orthographically recognize group differences aggravates contestations over linguistic representations in texts and pedagogical materials and confrontations around pedagogy and teaching. Kaska parents and grandparents were concerned that their child or grandchild would learn the "wrong" dialect in school, or not learn their own dialect. This concern related to their awareness of dialects and their association of dialects with matrilines (Meek 2010). That is, dialect differences were part of the enfigurement of familial belonging in this community. These concerns over dialect differences, however, did not extend to English or French. Similarly, another parent thought that the then preschool teacher "[was] going to teach the children Cree," an indirect resolution to the dialect dilemma that obscures the variability within Cree itself. Thus, the linguistic variation within Kaska became indexical of and enfigured familial belonging, which then mediated the language's representation on the page.

This complexity heightens the recognition of difference across languages (and First Nations) and to some extent discourages written communication across aboriginal languages and First Nations. Given the trauma of residential schooling, whether directly as physical abuse or indirectly through neglect and isolation, where literacy skills were mandated, the practice itself is already a fraught one for many First Nations individuals. The added orthographic complexity intended to represent features iconic of dialect differences begins to mask the mutual intelligibility of these languages, and these forms. Salience of one kind – intelligibility – is swapped for salience of another kind – sociolinguistic difference.

### Saliencies of Sound and Saliencies of Script: The Case of Santali

Similar to the discussion of orthographies and language construction in the Yukon, in eastern India among *adivasi* communities, sociolinguistic difference does not arise from any substantive difference in the phonetic form of the features, but rather in their visual properties as orthographically instantiated within a script. Thus, what is considered a salient phonetic difference between languages or even within a given language, may in fact result from the differential ideological associations attached to the multiple script systems in use, and how orthographic practice and ideologies of script enfigure both evaluations of correct "pronunciation" and speakers' political commitments.

In order to illustrate this, we draw on the rich and politically fraught linguistic and graphic milieu of eastern India, focusing especially on the graphic practices of Santali-speakers, with and among whom Choksi has conducted research since 2009. Santali is spoken throughout the eastern Indian states of Assam, Bihar, Jharkhand, Orissa, and West Bengal, as well as in Bangladesh and Nepal. It is classified as a Munda language of the Austro-Asiatic family, and like speakers of most Munda languages in India, Santali speakers are considered *adivasis* (indigenous people, or in India, scheduled tribe) by the Indian Government. Most Santals are bilingual in at least one or more of the dominant Indo-European languages (Bengali, Hindi, Oriya, Assamese, etc.), in addition to often knowing other Munda languages spoken in the area.

Santali was first written down by missionaries in the late nineteenth century. The first printed book in Santali was a song collection documented by American missionary Jeremiah Phillips in 1845 and published in a modified Eastern Brahmi (Bengali) script. In 1863, drawing on the work of German linguist Karl Lepisus, Norwegian missionaries L. O. Skrefsrud and P. O. Bodding created a modified Roman orthography to represent Santali, and they later began a Santali-language printing press, publishing numerous grammars, dictionaries, and story and song collections, as well as a Santali-language Bible.

Following Indian independence in 1947, India was divided into federal states on linguistic grounds, and each territory had an official language to be represented in a single, official script. For instance, the official language of West Bengal was Bengali in Eastern Brahmi script, while for Orissa it was Oriya in the Utkal script. Bihar (and later Jharkhand) were to adopt Hindi as their state language in the Devanagari script. Santals, who mostly resided in the forest and hill areas far outside urban centers, found themselves on multiple sides of the borders of these newly created entities. As a result of literacy programs, Santals learned to read and write in the script of their respective territory. Santals then modified the respective state scripts (Eastern Brahmi, Utkal, or Devanagari) with some diacritics in order to write their own language in those scripts.

Right before and after Indian independence, there was a movement in the *adivasi* areas of Bengal, Orissa, and Bihar for a separate *adivasi*-majority state called "Jharkhand." The state was eventually not recognized in the initial federal organization in independent India; however, the movement spurred on new social movements among various *adivasi* groups around language and cultural assertion. As part of this movement, a Santali schoolteacher, poet, and dramatist, Raghunath Murmu, developed his own script for Santali known as "Ol-Chiki" or "writing-symbol." In addition, Murmu also wrote a grammar (*Ronod*) justifying the use of the script as, he argued, it better represented the sounds of the Santali language than any of the existing scripts in use at the time, including the Roman orthography. The Ol-Chiki script became popular, especially among the southern Santali speaking areas of Orissa, southern Jharkhand, and southeastern West Bengal.

Because Santals had a tightly knit social and ritual system that resisted incorporation into the Hindu caste-hierarchy, they were targeted for missionary evangelization in the nineteenth century. As in many contexts, language became a primary site of missionary activity. When missionaries first encountered and began describing Santali, they immediately noticed its phonetic and morphological differences from the neighboring dominant Indo-Aryan languages. Santals themselves have a distinction between their own speech, what they called *hoŗ roŗ*, or speech of "men" and *diku roŗ*, or speech of "foreigners." Yet, the distinction was more a recursive differentiation between an already existing social distinction between *hoŗ* and *diku*, and differed, as Banerjee (1999) notes, in different times and places. Thus, the distinction between "Santali" and "Bengali" or other Indo-Aryan languages at the level of phoneme was most likely a product of missionary intervention.

### Enfiguring Sounds and Persons: The Case of the Santali /ə/

In this section, we discuss how certain phonetic elements have become metapragmatically salient, acting recursively to signal differentiation at multiple social levels. We argue that it is through the process of writing, and socialization into a missionary-derived ideology of isomorphism, that the Santali language requires a unique "script" in order to adequately grasp the phonetic system that has in fact rendered these elements salient. Yet, the salience of these phonetic elements is foregrounded not by continuities with missionary practice, but rather by the discontinuities and conflicts which have arisen as Santali-language literacy increases within a multilingual and multiscriptural milieu in which issues of script, language, and representation continue to exist on a contested political terrain.

One particular vowel, the mid-central vowel /ə/, illustrates this complexity. According to Anderson (2007: 11), the /ə/ in Santali either can exist as an "allophone of /a/ or phoneme of limited distribution /ə/ in both Northern and Southern Santali dialects." Indeed, during Choksi's fieldwork, he heard examples of both [a] and [ə] in free variation, but also, in certain words, as clear phonemic contrast. The /ə/ in Santali, however, although transcribed by linguists such as Anderson as a mid-central vowel, is slightly higher than the /ə/ in Indo-European languages such as Hindi. Thus, it is perhaps closer to the close-mid central vowel, transcribed in Vietnamese (also in the Austroasiatic language family) as /əː/ (Brunelle 2014: 94). In either case, it remains distinct from the Hindi /ə/, as well as the eastern Indo-European languages such as Bengali, Oriya, and Assamese, which do not have /ə/ at all.

While the phoneme is not exceedingly common, it nevertheless occupies a pre-eminent position in debates around Santali script and language. This likely has to do with the way in which it came to be recognized as a salient element of distinction, both in the entextualization of Santali grammar and in the creation of the Santali script. In what was perhaps the first grammar of Santali, Jeremiah Phillips's *An Introduction to the Sántál Language* (1852), which was written in Eastern Brahmi (Bengali) characters, the phonetic distinction is not made within the orthography at all. The only thing "peculiar" to Santali mentioned by Phillips in his opening section is the "half-formed guttural sounds" (3), or word-final glottal stops. As far as vowels, Phillips's description follows closely the vowel paradigm of Bengali.

It was later, during the development of the Roman script, that the /ə/ vowel was specifically encoded within the script through the use of diacritical marks. The Norwegian missionary P. O. Bodding, who was one of the most influential and prolific documenters of Santali grammar, justifies the use of Roman script in his material because, he suggests, the Bengali and Devanagari characters "do not lend themselves easily to diacritical marks" (1922: 3). Diacritical marks, moreover, are necessary, according to Bodding, because "the lack of them is the cause of much uncertainty and wrong pronunciation, specifically with foreigners, both when reading and speaking the language" (5). Thus, the Roman script facilitated what Bodding believed to be "correct" pronunciation specifically for *foreigners* (most likely foreign missionaries).

However, for Bodding, the enthusiasm with which Santals learned to write their language in the Roman script also justified its use. Bodding writes:

Santals have a mind much directed towards concrete and special subjects. To distinguish in writing between the different sounds is therefore something in accordance with their mental character. We have very little trouble in teaching them to write correctly, when they use our system. A better proof of its soundness is not needed (1922: 5).

Bodding's statement above reveals a double ideological move that occurred during the period of socialization into the Roman script. On the one hand, we see that an ideology of "correctness," which Bodding mentions in relation to acquisition by foreigners, was also simultaneously applied to the training of Santali speakers. On the other hand, the "correct writing system," in the case of the modified Roman script, corresponded not only with Santali sounds, but also enfigured the Santali "mental character." Thus, sound, script, and the collective psychological character of a group were all merged, Bodding claims, in Santals's adoption of the Roman-Santali script. That is, whether or not Santali speakers were aware of their intellectual proclivity towards the Roman-Santali script, the script's adoption renders salient a system of representation that emphasizes sound differences, and correlates that system with the unique psycho-cultural characteristics of a Santal person.

Bodding's activity was mainly in the northern Santali-speaking region of the Santal Parganas (in what is present-day Dumka district, Jharkhand), but the Roman writing system was adopted by all the major missions in the Santali-speaking region in an agreement brokered by Bodding in 1905.[14] Within the script, the /ə/ was clearly marked as part of what Bodding called the "resultant" vowels. Resultants were marked with a dot (.) diacritic below the vowel, what in Santali is called a *tudək'*. Bodding says that in Santali, "all the 'ordinary vowels' may be resultant ... in writing we use the dot only with a [ə] sometimes with o when it is demanded by necessity and seldom with e" (1922: 2). The [a] vowel as it is written in Roman script, the only regularly marked "resultant" in the Roman script, actually stood in for several concomitant sounds. It "seems to be a modified high-back narrow ... mid-back narrow ... or a modified low-mixed narrow. a thus represents several sounds" (1922: 13). The [a] therefore represents, like any grapheme, a range of phonetic variation in addition to being allophonic with [a] in many cases. Thus, only through orthography does the [a] come to stand for a distinct sound segment.

As Santals became trained, Bodding noted, to write "correct" speech, they also became trained to notice certain distinctions. Missionaries and literate Santals underscored these distinctions as *unique* to the Santali language, as well as the Santali "mental character." The intertextual linkages between script, particular sounds, and a unique language and culture were part of a broader missionary agenda to foment a national identity among the Santals as distinct from Hinduism in order to promote evangelization and build an independent national church (Carrin-Bouez 1986). Script, and in particular the diacritics utilized in orthography and the sounds associated with those diacritics, became foregrounded in literacy socialization as a salient feature of differentiation. They not only iconized the Santali people and language (*hoɾ*as opposed to the *diku* or non-Santal), but they also recursively iconized "correct" language and script over all the other script systems in current use (such as the Devanagari or Bengali scripts).

The use of Roman script was limited in numerous ways. Roman-script presses were only available at a few missions, while by the mid twentieth century Brahmi-script presses were widely available. Also, increased access to public education meant that Santals were becoming literate in the Indo-Aryan languages and Brahmi script, and thus Brahmi-script literacy far outpaced literacy in Roman. Finally, Roman script, because it was developed and propagated in a missionary context, was associated with evangelization.[15]

---

[14] MS Fol 1686, 9:6, Santalia archive, National Library, Oslo.
[15] Thus, Roman script is often associated with Christian Santals, although non-Christian Santali speakers, particularly in north Jharkhand and northern West Bengal, use it as well.

Table 10.1 /ə/ [or /əː/] in Santali Orthographic Systems

| Script | Symbol | |
|---|---|---|
| Roman | a̧ | "Resultant" (Bodding 1922: 2) |
| Devanagari | आ | Modified from आ /a/ |
| Eastern Brahmi | আঁ | Modified from Bengali অ+ৌ /au/ |
| Ol-Chiki | ᱚ. | *gəhlə tudək'* (Murmu 2005: 8) |

Yet, even though Devanagari and Eastern Brahmi scripts were adopted, the saliency of certain phonetic features that were first encoded in the Roman script remained the same. Even though Brahmi-script Santali was never taught in a formal setting, both the Eastern Brahmi and Devanagari scripts were modified with diacritics or elements that do not exist in Bengali or Hindi respectively to represent the "resultant vowel" encoded in the Roman script a̧ (see Table 10.1).

For a non-standard script, this modification remains remarkably consistent, spreading mostly through contact with published material, including pamphlets, books, posters, etc.

Despite the widespread use of Brahmi scripts for writing Santali, Raghunath Murmu and other supporters of Ol-Chiki script argued that none of Bengali, Devanagari, or Roman adequately represented the Santali phonetic repertoire, and a separate script was necessary (Zide 1999). The script was also seen as integral to larger Santali aspirations for separate statehood and was popularized in song and drama (Lotz 2007). In the post-independence period, Murmu founded an organization known as ASECA (Adivasi Socio-Educational Association) in order to promote the use of Ol-Chiki in Santali-speaking areas. As Murmu notes in his grammar (2005: 8), part of Ol-Chiki's innovaton is the accuracy in which it represents Santali vowels, in particular the /ə/. Murmu represented this vowel through the creation of what in the Ol-Chiki system is called the *gəhlə tudək'* , a diacritic (.) attached to the Ol-Chiki grapheme /a/ ᱚ to make ᱚ. /ə/. Consequently, although the script replaces the graphic set with new characters, it maintains and underscores aspects of phonetic segmentation that are salient to the very claims of autonomy that underlie the script's creation in the first place. Moreover, in the Ol-Chiki system the diacritic is given an actual name and explanation within the orthographic system, which heightens its salience as a point of differentiation. For Ol-Chiki advocates, therefore, no longer does the vowel itself, as segmented out in script, signify differentiation and "correct" speech, but rather it is the specific use of the named *gəhlə tudək'* diacritic within Ol-Chiki, over and above other means of signification. Thus, the *gəhlə tudək'* once again, within the ideology of Ol-Chiki script, re-enfigures a unique representation of the Santali language/culture.

Throughout Choksi's interviews, Ol-Chiki advocates and ASECA members consistently emphasized the importance of the *gəhlə tudək'* as both central to the Santali language and simultaneously a unique innovation of Ol-Chiki script. During initial interviews with a former general secretary of ASECA West Bengal, one of the first things he mentioned about Ol-Chiki script in relation to Eastern Brahmi or Devanagari was the *gəhlə tudək'*. He said that no other script provides accurate pronunciation of the /ə/ vowel. When Choksi asked him whether the Eastern Brahmi-Santali convention to write the /ə/ with a modified "ou-kar" (see Table 10.1) represents the sound equally well, the former secretary responded by saying, in English, that this representation was "against the rules of Bengali grammar and therefore not accepted by linguists." In his formulation, the Eastern Brahmi script enfigured "Bengali" grammar as well as "Bengali" persons (i.e. non-Santals), and because the writing of the /ə/ in Eastern Brahmi did not correspond to conventional Bengali orthography, it was not correct. "Correct" grammar and pronunciation requires, in this view, a unique orthographic convention which foregrounds not only the vowel sound, but also the various semiotic elements (ideological and intertextual) that render this vowel sound salient.

The *gəhlə tudək'* is seen by Ol-Chiki advocates as not only representing Santali sounds, but also promoting a version of correct speech that enfigures a distinct notion of Santali language and culture. This is highlighted by the fact that some Ol-Chiki advocates, such as one of Raghunath Murmu's close colleagues who has devoted most of his life to the promotion of the script, argue that the *gəhlə tudək'* is being lost in some regions. For instance, he reported that in some regions of West Bengal, instead of *dəl* "lentil soup," they say *dail*. This is because, he suggested, of the "Hindi" influence in the region (in standard Hindi, it is pronounced *dal*). He went on to say that one has to preserve and maintain "tradition," and this is why the Ol-Chiki script, and the innovation of the *gəhlə tudək'*, is so important. He emphasized that this is "our own" pronunciation and for that we need "our own" script to maintain that tradition. However, the very emphasis on the distinction of the *gəhlə tudək'*, as the advocate's discourse makes clear, obscures the widespread phonetic diversity practised in everyday speech throughout the Santali-speaking area.

Indeed, in Ol-Chiki classes attended by Choksi, other students, who were all native speakers, sometimes pronounced words written with the *gəhlə tudək'* with [a] sounds. This is likely because the phoneme, as noted above, in everyday speech or in some dialects has tended towards /a/. Yet, the pronunciation was corrected by the teachers, in part because learning to pronounce the *gəhlə tudək'* correctly was part of learning to read Ol-Chiki script. Thus, the salience of the *gəhlə tudək'* sound was socialized in and through the learning of Ol-Chiki, which is perhaps why it inspired such passion in Ol-Chiki advocates. The relevance and adequacy of the script rested on its claims to uniquely map onto a whole set of distinctions that have been circulating since Santali was put into writing a century ago, and thus innovations like the *gəhlə tudək'*, which may not be as relevant in everyday speech, have to be emphasized at the moment of learning. This was illustrated by the fact that as we were studying the *gəhlə tudək'* in class, one of the Ol-Chiki teachers mentioned that sometimes ASECA members go too far, placing the *gəhlə tudək'* on words which are correctly pronounced without it.[16]

At the same time that Ol-Chiki advocates justify the uniqueness of their script by appealing to the /ə/, Roman script advocates justify the uniqueness of their script through an identical discourse. As Choksi was talking to an editor of a Catholic Santali-language journal that employs the Roman script, the editor mentioned that in his area of the Santal Parganas (northern Jharkhand) there was a movement to promote the Ol-Chiki script. However, he said that he believes that Ol-Chiki is clearly defective, because it does not adequately represent the /ə/. This is because, he argues, Ol-Chiki developed in the southern Santali speaking areas, where they speak a mixed language and do not routinely pronounce the /ə/, and now they want to impose their style upon Santali speakers in the Santal Parganas where /ə/ is routinely pronounced. In addition, he added, the Ol-Chiki movement is explicitly anti-Christian, and they are trying to exclude Christians through the medium of script.

While it is doubtful that the editor knows how to read Ol-Chiki, as the *gəhlə tudək'* is a central feature of the script, the sound has become salient for him at a number of levels. The phonetic feature enfigures regional differentiation (northern versus southern Santali), where northern Santali, the language recorded by Bodding, is often seen as more "original" or "superior" to the dialects of the southern region from where Ol-Chiki originated. Finally, the feature also refracts a distinction between Christian and non-Christian Santals. Hence, supporters of different script systems can make *identical* linguistic arguments about an *identical* phonetic feature, but still believe their positions to be diametrically opposed to one another. The phonetic-graphemic feature thus is not salient as an abstract linguistic feature, but acts as a metonym of an entire orthographic system that in turn enfigures claim to distinction and uniqueness, rendering, in the name of language, certain sets of speakers, regions, and histories salient, while obscuring others. This claim to both unity (of form, speakers, script, and code) and differentiation (between scripts, speakers, regions, etc.), made by advocates of both Roman and Ol-Chiki, is built on long-standing ideological distinctions between *hoɽ* and *diku* and its recursive manifestations, such as "correct" and "incorrect." Consequently, the claims to uniqueness rely on the

---

[16] The notion that ASECA was trying to promote the use of the *gəhlə* by expanding its use was one encountered by Choksi elsewhere as well.

presence of multiple systems. Conflict and opposition within a multiscrip-tural milieu ensure that features such as the /ə/ remain salient.

### Discussion: Salience and Obscurity

In the previous sections, we outlined the relationship between ideology, salience, and linguistic and orthographic form. Both cases involved indigenous-language minorities who have been subject to a history of colon-ization and marginalization (in the form of British imperialism), and who recently have been involved in projects to create new orthographies for their languages. The Kaska case examined differences and similarities in the ways in which Kaska language users and more formally trained linguists crafted and standardized an orthography for Kaska, and how such representational pro-cesses mediate and conflict with everyday expectations. The second case involved the history of orthographic practice among speakers of Santali, an indigenous Austro-Asiatic language spoken in eastern India. In both cases, we showed how a small segment of grammar and usage, when crafted into the socially contested field of orthographic practice, became salient icons of much larger social, political, and historical debates taking place within these two indigenous communities.

Our cases are not unique; they coincide with other documented situations in which speakers, through orthographic practices, render certain linguistic seg-ments both salient and obscure. For instance, in describing a writing and literacy program among the Tolowa, a Native American community from the Pacific Northwest, Collins and Blot suggest that the "question of textual form, whether to use Unifon or IPA, had implications for claims to identity, that is, affiliations with different families and claims to tribal identity. These questions brought into a play a politics of tribal recognition and academic authority, of powers desired and feared in practices of writing and styles of representation" (2003: 14). Consequently, the absence of standardization and ideological regimentation and the diversity of the ways in which linguistic segments are crafted in orthographic form foregrounds those segments in ways that other discursive domains may not have foregrounded them.

Thus, the "phonetic component" of language becomes "salient" not simply due to disputes over pronunciation. Rather, the form of representation (i.e. how a character is shaped and what orthographic system is used) also becomes subject to discussion and dispute (also see Bender 2002; Mitchell and Webster 2011; Schieffelin and Doucet 1998; see also, Cahill and Rice 2014). While the Tolowa debate may ostensibly be over phonetic value, the phonetic value only becomes salient in metapragmatic discourse as it is intertextually aligned with orthographic form, family and tribal affiliation, the politics of tribal recognition, and a linguistic academic discourse which privileges a "faithful" representation of sound. At the same time, as Collins and Blot also note, the alignment between social categories and linguistic form as a process of entextualization necessarily leaves out, or obscures, the multiplicity of divergent ideologies to which that form may have been aligned, rendering an orthography or orthographic character ideologically contested within a given community of practice.

Thus, in tracking the creation of orthographies, both among aboriginal communities in the Yukon, Canada, and among an *adivasi* community in eastern India, we have outlined conditions under which speakers became aware of linguistic form as well as the processes by which these particular grammatical forms assume sociolinguistic salience. This has involved, as the Yukon case suggests, the entwining of different discourses, which have intertextually connected emergent orthographies to official Western ethnolinguistic ideologies of nation and ethnic difference, while at the same time signifying First Nation movements for sovereignty and autonomy. Similarly, among Santali speakers, /ə/ has come to enfigure, through missionary discourses and post-independence political mobilization, ethnic difference and sociolinguistic unity among proponents of multiple script systems.

When discussions of linguistic form enter into metapragmatic discourse, and are mobilized in political practice, these forms garner a new set of meanings, anchored through intertextuality and more particular semiotic processes such as fractal recursivity and iconization (Irvine and Gal 2000). As long as speakers are aware not only of difference in form, but also anchor these differences within a larger sociopolitical field of difference, we suggest, these forms will continue to remain sociolinguistically salient. However, we note as well that practices, forms, and ideologies may become jointly sedimented in standardized repertoires such as orthographies, and differences may no longer be seized upon. For instance, the equation of orthography with groupness, or the phonetic foundation of orthographic systems in both the Yukon and eastern India, have obscured other relevant vectors of difference that could have potentially informed the sociopolitical field. In the case of Santali, the seeming agreement of the entextualization of /ə/ within different Santali scripts has obscured the significant and important differences in everyday pronunciation upon which speakers could also have drawn to assert both difference and unity. For the Kaska language, competing orthographic representations (as in "corrections") constrain salience, shifting into focus a salient pattern that matters to one audience (the linguists), but not the other (Kaska language speakers and teachers). Salience is limited by social experiences, expectations, evaluations, and context, the elements that allow for connections to be made or obscured. Yet salience constrains dimensions of awareness and obscurity immanent in processes of sociolinguistic enfigurement at the very moment of its emergence.

### Conclusion: Salience and Awareness

Is salience about production or is it about perception? For us, it is about (establishing) the relationship between the two. Although Labov's "monitor" model and Silverstein's metalinguistic model suggest that salience is primarily about perception (listener awareness), Preston's levels and McGowan's degrees of awareness (as discursive availability, accuracy, detail) and (speaker) control, together with Briggs and Bauman's model of entextualization, suggest that (sociolinguistic) salience happens in relation to both perception and production. Salience emerges through the discursive mediation of performance (production) and the habitual attenuation of interpretation (comprehension/ perception) from exposure or experience in everyday life (cf. Drager and Kirtley, this volume). Salience becomes artifactualized in the reflexive adjustments made by interlocutors in relation to the interactional project and their investment in that project, that is, in relation to the socio-cultural context (such as individual biographies, national politics, cultural heritage, and social differences). In our case, we focused on the creation and implementation of orthographies for minority languages, revealing how (con)textual salience provoked reflexivity and awareness of linguistic form beyond the form itself. Both cases show how linguistic representations influenced and were influenced by the models of language into and through which people had already been socialized, alongside the political-economic context of their creation. These cases were useful for investigating salience and awareness because they were "reflexive" activities (Agha 2007), "activities in which communicative signs [were] used to typify other perceivable signs" (Agha 2007: 16), i.e. orthographic form to typify linguistic form. And, as Campbell-Kibler notes, "through these activities, reflexive models are produced, transmitted, and altered, and through these models speakers and listeners make social sense of their own and others' linguistic (or human) behavior. Such activity is as much a part of sociolinguistic behavior as the utterance of sociolinguistically variable forms itself" (this volume; p. 130).

Thus, salience, as a kind of indexical process, connects production and perception. It is the process by which an utterance or other linguistic gesture evokes an interpretation (perception of a linguistic performance or utterance) through the use of particular linguistic elements under particular socio-cultural conditions, rendering the linguistic gesture sufficiently meaningful. Of course, this process can be far more precarious, resulting in unintended connections (and interpretations), as well as obscuring others. For example, Drager 2011 shows how experience influences interpretation differently. Participants from different generations listened to speech samples. Older subjects "heard" a difference between speech samples from older speakers and those from younger speakers, while younger subjects did not. While overt awareness of differences may be minimal, if at all, the paths through which relevant activation takes place may be more routinized and established in long-term memory of older listeners than for younger listeners (Drager and Kirtley, this volume). Memory and routinization (or socialization) participate in the management of salience. Similarly, McGowan (this volume) provides evidence showing how in production several (non-Chinese-speaking) actors' performances of Mandarin-Chinese-accented English demonstrated "[a] surprising availability and control of a range of features which shared many features in common either with reported features of authentic L1 Mandarin-accented English or with aspects of authentic alternations" (p. 55). While they were unaware of their own "authentic" linguistic maneuvers, they were able to present an interpretable "Asian" character for an English-speaking audience. Their grammatical knowledge, together with their training as actors and participants in US society, rendered their linguistic characterizations readable as "Asian" (although not necessarily as "Mandarin Chinese"). In our exploration of orthographic development, linguistic and social dimensions proved relevant and salient to these projects of typification. Through the enfigurement of two different minority languages, particular features of these languages were recruited to signify particular social differences, while others were obscured in order to heighten (or diminish) the various aspects of difference that were being invested in by the parties involved in these projects of entextualization. For the Kaska case, one administrative goal was to mark Kaska (the language and its speakers) as socially and politically distinct. This marking happened in part through the development of particular orthographic conventions. For Santali, political distinction was also entailed in the development and use of orthographic conventions, although in this case, a range of scripts was used across different contexts to index and assert a Santali presence within the social and linguistic landscape. The salience of these linguistic practices became emblematized orthographically and strategically placed textually in order to raise political awareness.

In summary, salience is that which is susceptible to being noticed by a particular kind of interpreter or subject who is set to notice and not merely as a property of perception or of language or of memory (of cognition). This susceptibility is also or mutually a result of the social-cultural context within which some (linguistic) form is constituted, uttered, and performed (the situation that sets up the noticing). Expectations mediated by socializing practices can render certain features or dimensions more salient than others. The everyday (built and natural) environment mediates perception, thus socializing individuals into certain (expected) patterns, aesthetics, styles, and arrangements. Language is similarly influenced by discourses and ideologies relating linguistic practice and form to socio-cultural differences and patterns (by group or heritage or politics, etc.). Everyday experiences and expectations also influence memory, viewed as socialization into linguistic, social, and cultural routines throughout a lifetime. Salience emerges in tandem with these cognitive domains and socialization. However, salience shifts into awareness at moments of disjuncture – whether as perceived difference (Squires, this volume), as ideological and interactional dissonance (Meek 2010), or as orthographic disagreement. Such unexpected moments, remarkable events, or unique experiences affect salience in that they can be, and are, the catalysts for transforming that which is salient into something that can be artifactualized, typified, categorized, and leveraged for other projects, future investments, and social-linguistic change.

## REFERENCES

Agha, A. 2007. *Language and Social Relations*. New York: Cambridge University Press.
Anderson, Gregory D. S. 2007. *The Munda Verb: Typological Perspectives*. Berlin: Mouton de Gruyter.
Auer, P., Barden, B., and Grosskopf, B., 1998. Subjective and objective parameters determining "salience" in long-term dialect accommodation. *Journal of Sociolinguistics* 2:163–87.
Banerjee, Prathama. 1999. Historic acts? Santal rebellion and the temporality of practice. *Studies in History* 15(2):209–46.
Bauman, Richard and Briggs, Charles L. 1990. Poetics and performance as critical perspectives on language and social life. *Annual Review of Anthropology* 19:59–88.
Bender, M. 2002. From "easy phonetics" to the syllabary: An orthographic division of labor in Cherokee language education. *Anthropology & Education Quarterly* 33:90–117.
Bodding, P. O. 1922. *Materials for a Santali Grammar I: Mostly Phonetic*. Dumka, India: Santal Mission of the Northern Churches.
Brunelle, Marc. 2014. Vietnamese (Tieng Viet), in Paul Sidwell and Jenny Mathias (eds.), *The Handbook of Austroasiatic Languages*, Vol. 1, pp. 909–46. Leiden: Brill.
Cahill, Michael and Rice, Keren (eds.). 2014. *Developing Orthographies for Unwritten Languages*. Dallas, TX: SIL International.
Carrin-Bouez, Marine. 1986. De la langue au discours : Une dialectique du repli et de la modernisation dans une minorité tribale de l'Inde. *Langage et Société* 35(1):67–91.
Collins, James and Blot, Richard K. 2003. *Literacy and Literacies: Texts, Power, and Identity*. Cambridge, UK and New York: Cambridge University Press.
Drager, Katie. 2011. Speaker age and vowel perception. *Language and Speech* 54(1):99–121.
Hinton, Leanne and Meek, Barbra. Forthcoming. Language revitalization: Canada and U.S., in S. M. Coronel-Molina and T. L. McCarty (eds.), *The Handbook of Indigenous Language Revitalization in the Americas*. New York: Routledge.
Irvine, Judy and Gal, Susan. 2000. Language ideology and linguistic differentiation, in Paul V. Kroskrity (ed.), *Regimes of Language: Ideologies, Polities, and Identities*,

pp. 35–83. Santa Fe, NM and Oxford, UK: School of American Research Press and J. Currey.

Lotz, Barbara. 2007. Casting a glorious past: Loss and recovery of the Ol-Chiki Script, in Angelika Malinar (ed.), *Time in India: Concepts and Practices*, pp. 235–62. New Delhi: Manohar.

Meek, Barbra A. 2006. And the Injun goes how!: Representations of American Indian English in (white) public space. *Language in Society* 35(1):93–128.

2007. Respecting the language of elders: Ideological shift and linguistic discontinuity in a Northern Athapascan community. *Journal of Linguistic Anthropology* 17(1):23–43.

2009. Language ideology and aboriginal language revitalization in the Yukon, in Paul V. Kroskrity and Margaret C. Field (eds.), *Native American Language Ideologies: Beliefs, Practices, and Struggles in Indian Country*. Tucson, AZ: University of Arizona Press.

2010. *We Are Our Language*. Tucson, AZ: University of Arizona Press.

Meek, Barbra A., Jules, Leda, Skidmore, Marie, and Magun, Aggie. 2002. *Kaska Alphabet Book*. Whitehorse, YT (Canada): Queen's Printer.

Mitchell, B. and Webster, A. K., 2011. "We don't know what we become:" Navajo ethnopoetics and an expressive feature in a poem by Rex Lee Jim. *Anthropological Linguistics* 53:259–86.

Murmu, Raghunath. 2005. *Ronod*. Jhargram, West Bengal: Marsal Bamber.

Phillips, J. 1852. *An Introduction to the Sántál Language; Consisting of a Grammar, Reading Lessons, and a Vocabulary*. Calcutta: Calcutta Schoolbook Society.

Preston, Dennis. 1996. Whaddayaknow?: The modes of folk linguistic awareness 1. *Language Awareness* 5:40–74.

Schieffelin, Bambi B. and Doucet, Rachelle Charlier. 1994. The "real" Haitian Creole: Ideology, metalinguistics, and orthographic choice. *American Ethnologist* 21(1):176–200.

Silverstein, Michael. 1981. The limits of awareness, Sociolinguistic Working Paper no. 84, pp. 1–16. Austin, TX: Southwest Educational Development Laboratory.

Teit, James Alexander, and Boas, Franz. 1898. Traditions of the Thompson River Indians of British Columbia ... collected and annotated, in Franz Boas (ed.), *Memoirs of the American Folklore Society*, Vol. 6. New York: Houghton, Mifflin & Co.

Trudgill, P. 1986. *Dialects in Contact*. New York: Blackwell.

Zide, Norman. 1999. Three Munda scripts. *Linguistics of the Tibeto-Burman Area* 22(2):199–232.

# 11 Sociolinguistic Agency and the Gendered Voice: Metalinguistic Negotiations of Vocal Masculinization among Female-to-Male Transgender Speakers

*Lal Zimman*

### Introduction: Agency and Transgender Voices

In both sociocultural linguistics and contemporary transgender politics, there is a strong connection between agency, power, and ideology. Sociolinguists have, since the field's earliest days, recognized that speakers have control over at least some aspects of their linguistic practices, and that understanding linguistic variation depends in part on researchers' ability to tap into these aspects of awareness and agency, as the contributions to this volume make especially clear (particularly Campbell-Kibler, Carmichael, and Babel). Ideology figured prominently in the theorization of sociolinguistic agency from the field's inception, with a "standard language ideology" (per Lippi-Green 1997) driving people towards more standard speech in contexts of greater awareness or, alternatively, away from that standard as an expression of resistance. One question as yet unexplored is how ideologies about sociolinguistic agency itself might be taken up by speakers as a ground on which to constitute certain kinds of subjectivities. In contrast to the normalization of awareness and control to be found in much sociolinguistic literature, the practice of self-consciously shifting the gendered characteristics of the voice takes on a decidedly different ideological valence in some transgender communities. In the analysis to follow, two perspectives on transgender people's control over the gendered characteristics of their voices are examined in order to call attention to the variable ways in which agency can be constructed, the ideological implications of those constructs, and the importance of considering these ideologies when producing accounts of speakers' awareness and control over their sociolinguistic practices.

In transgender communities, agency is a complex and multifaceted issue. Like lesbian and gay activists, trans people often make sense of their gender identities as innate and even biological in origin, in contrast to normative discourses that frame a gender role transition as an unnecessary, even indulgent, deviation from the natural order. This stance, which disavows the ability to choose one's internally felt gender identity, works to legitimize trans people's social positionalities through an intertextual relationship with other discourses of authenticity and recasts a gender role transition as a means of realizing an inevitable inner truth. At the same time, however, agency is of critical importance in the discourses about self-definition and bodily self-determination that dominate trans communities in contemporary North American contexts (contrast Besnier 2003, for instance). That is, a core socio-political goal of many trans communities in the United States has been to secure individuals' freedom to choose what kinds of gendered body modifications they might wish to pursue and to name the identity categories to which they most authentically belong. This tension, between rejecting control over one's sexual or gender identity and claiming freedom to act in a particular framework of culture and power (Ahearn 2001), provides the ideological backdrop for the discourses analyzed in this chapter.

In order to better explicate these ideologies, I investigate the construction of linguistic agency found in transgender speakers' ethnographically situated discourses and contrast them with those that appear in academic literature on trans people's voices. Although studying the speech of trans people has promised unique insights for sociocultural linguists, most research on transgender voices to date has been carried out by speech pathologists who have a less reflexive and more scientifically oriented perspective on gender and sex. The discourses that occur in this body of literature reflect and reinforce hegemonic cultural ideologies about the inauthenticity of trans people's self-defined gender identities, while simultaneously homogenizing the speech of "women" and "men" as macro categories. As I explore in detail below, research on trans voices often has the effect of naturalizing the speech and gender presentations of non-trans (or *cis*[1]) women and men, while delegitimizing and pathologizing those of trans speakers. This is accomplished in part by portraying trans people as individuals who are working against their biology in order to imitate the purportedly naturally feminine or masculine voices of cis women or men, respectively. This naturalization erases the tremendous variability that exists in the gendered practices of cis women and men on the bases of class, ethnoracial identity, culture of origin, sexuality, or disability, to name a few. Furthermore, the idea that trans people might have their own ideas about how they would like to sound, might not want to change their voices at all, or might achieve a voice that allows them to "pass" without any special conscious effort is rarely acknowledged. In the case of trans men (i.e. female-to-male trans people), who appear in only a small portion of studies carried out on trans voices, testosterone tends to be emphasized as the primary means of achieving

---

[1] *Cis* ("on the same side") is the Latin antonym of *trans* ("across"), and is widely used by trans people in order to name the unmarked identities of people who identify with the gender category to which they were assigned at birth. The words *cisgender* and *cissexual* are also in use.

a male voice, although a few more recent studies (particularly van Borsel *et al.* 2000; Adler and van Borsel 2006) have suggested that trans men should seek speech therapy despite the effects of hormone therapy.

Clearly, there are a number of both popular and academic discourses about trans people and their voices that facilitate the assumption that their transition process is driven primarily by individual, agentive choices about how to control their speech and behavior in order to conform to norms for their "new" gender. And, indeed, this kind of self-conscious effort does characterize the experience of some trans individuals. However, my research on the voices of female-to-male transgender speakers highlights a rather different perspective, in which trans people who make use of testosterone orient to self-conscious vocal masculinization as far less desirable than passively allowing hormonal changes to deliver a deeper, more masculine voice. In the metalinguistic discourse analyzed in this chapter, the potential to exercise agency over the gendered characteristics of the voice is consistently disavowed. As the final section of this chapter underscores, this rejection is crucial in producing an account of the sociolinguistic styles found in transmasculine[2] communities. Furthermore, it highlights the complex ways in which power and hegemony factor into linguistic awareness and control.

While transmasculine speakers' construction of sociolinguistic agency may at times appear contradictory, a closer examination reveals a parallel between these speakers' discourses about sociolinguistic control and ideologies about personal agency over gender identity and the body. Even as their metalinguistic commentary contests broad transphobic cultural ideologies, however, other problematic ideologies are implicated in their stead as the practice of changing the gendered characteristics of one's voice is ascribed a negative political and moral value. Specifically, lack of awareness and control is equated with naturalness and authenticity, while the exercise of control is linked to artifice and assimilation.

This chapter, then, concerns the shifting roles played by agency, awareness, and control in the negotiation of gender and the voice among trans men and others on the transmasculine identity spectrum. Much as Silverstein (1985) describes, the metalinguistic commentary I analyze here demonstrates how ideologies exert an influence over what he calls the "structural realm" – i.e. linguistic patterns of which speakers may not be consciously aware. The trans speakers discussed here show relatively little awareness of the linguistic

---

[2] As of the time of this fieldwork, *Transmasculine* was an umbrella label that could be applied to anyone who was assigned female at birth but who did not self-identify as a woman, although not everyone fitting this description self-identified with this term (see Zimman 2012 for more on its problematics). In addition to self-identified men, the label *transmasculine* can also include genderqueer, non-binary, and gender non-conforming individuals who employ a masculine mode of self-presentation.

characteristics that are said to distinguish women's and men's voices, but they are far more sensitive to the socio-indexical (pragmatic, for Silverstein) meanings attached to the practice of self-conscious masculinization itself. These ideologies about the undesirability of linguistic control become the means through which agency is exercised on the structural level of sociophonetic style despite these speakers overtly constructing themselves as lacking or rejecting agency over their voices. Agency, from this perspective, is not about an internal sense of intentionality, but is rather the product of discursive practices that bring speakers' subjectivities into existence (e.g. Butler 1990). Silverstein focuses on the ways in which ideology can be a means of exercising linguistic agency, but the present analysis suggests that exercising agency can itself be a tool for ideological work, and that claims on or disavowals of awareness and control may be critically important in our explanations of social and linguistic practice. In the case of the present analysis, the way in which trans speakers' distance themselves from self-conscious linguistic masculinization provides both an explanation and a legitimation for the non-normatively masculine phonetic characteristics that are evident in many transmasculine people's speech.

The substance of this chapter begins by characterizing speech pathologists' investigations of trans voices over the last four decades as a means of illustrating some of the discourses about gender against which trans men's negotiations of agency are positioned. Next, examples of transmasculine people's discourses about the voice come from metalinguistic commentary recorded in interviews and conversations with participants in a two-year ethnographic study on fifteen transmasculine individuals in the San Francisco Bay Area during the early stages of testosterone therapy. This corpus of interviews is supplemented by lists of advice known as *passing tips* that circulate in online communities for trans men. Such commentary, I argue, works to both reflect and partially constitute trans people's local ideologies that divide an individual's embodiment from a more authentic inner self. The focus of my analysis is on the potential contradictions that emerge as trans men simultaneously claim certain kinds of agency while disavowing others, highlighting some of the ways in which agency appears to work through "fragmented subjectivities," in Ahearn's (2000: 13) terms. In resolving these tensions, my goal is to highlight the depth and complexity of speakers' own engagement with linguistic agency and the necessity of examining that engagement as part of our sociocultural linguistic analyses. Agentive intentionality is not something that can be observed or measured directly, nor should the experience of agency be equated with speakers' explicit claims about their intentions. What we can observe, alongside the linguistic reflexes of awareness and control, is the way in which language users produce an understanding of agency that has real implications for their linguistic practices; it is on this issue that I conclude with a summary of these speakers' gendered phonetic styles and the connection between those styles and the ideologies analyzed here. This form of constructed agency is not only exercised over language, but also constituted through language, which serves as a means of doing ideological work with importance that extends beyond the realm of sociolinguistic practice.

### Trans People and Sociolinguistic Control in the Speech Pathology Literature

One domain in which we can see the ideology that transgender people must actively attempt to control their gendered presentations – and particularly their speech – is the research carried out by speech-language pathologists, which remains the largest body of work on the voices of trans people. I have presented more extensive analysis of this literature in other spaces (Zimman 2012), wherein I focused on approximately twenty publications from journals and books on speech-language pathology and the speech sciences between 1977 and 2011 (including Bralley *et al.* 1978; Mount and Salmon 1988; Spencer 1988; Wolfe *et al.* 1990; Günzburger 1995; McFadden *et al.* 1998; Gelfer 1999; van Borsel *et al.* 2000; Gelfer and Schofield 2000; Dacakis 2002; Gelfer and Mikos 2005; Adler and van Borsel 2006; Davies and Goldberg 2006; T'Sjoen *et al.* 2006; Owen and Hancock 2011). In this section, I focus on three of the ideologies I have identified in this body of work that are particularly relevant to the present discussion of agency and sociolinguistic control: the naturalization of gender differences in the voice; the assumption that trans people need agentive interventions to change and control their "natural" voices; and the assumption that trans people want to sound like women or men who embody gender- and heteronormativity – a notion that is itself always inflected by race, class, and other lenses of subjectivity. Although the quotes I'll use as exemplars may seem extreme or antiquated, the speech pathology literature shows movement away from these discourses only within the last handful of years, while the existing body of work continues to inform both researchers and clinicians who work with trans speakers. Furthermore, these ideologies are simply one instantiation of the wide-spread denaturalization and delegitimation of trans people's gender identities that continues despite significant gains trans activists have seen in the past few decades. It is worth noting that trans women are the focus of the great majority of the speech-language pathology literature, while trans men's voices have only recently been the subject of similar investigations. As pathologists' discourses concerning trans women have spread to the emerging literature on trans men's voices, ideological clashes become apparent between the language ideologies taken up by researchers and those expressed by transmasculine speakers. Often, these tensions center around the role of agency and control in shaping the gendered characteristics of trans voices. Like speech scientists, transmasculine people who make use of testosterone often naturalize the male voice as a product of hormonal sex, but may also reject the notion that they should put effort into living up to the ideals of cis masculinity. Although the few studies of trans men's voices that have been published suggest that members of this group could "benefit" from speech therapy (van Borsel *et al.* 2000; Adler and van Borsel 2006), the ideological schisms I identify in this section and the next indicate that awareness and control over the gendered voice is conceptualized quite differently by speech-language pathologists on the one hand and trans-masculine individuals who make use of testosterone on the other.

As in much research on gender differentiation in the voice, there is a strong tendency in the speech pathology literature to frame the gendered voice as a product of biological differences between the sexes, despite the extensive evidence that gendered phonetic traits emerge during childhood language socialization (e.g. Sachs 1975) and may vary within gender groups as much as between them (e.g. Stuart-Smith 2007). Testosterone is known to affect the larynges of trans men, creating an often dramatic drop in vocal pitch (van Borsel *et al.* 2000; Damrose 2009; Papp 2011; Zimman 2012), but studies of trans women's voices emphasize that feminizing hormone therapy does not raise trans women's pitch, leading to conclusions like Wolfe *et al.*'s: "the natural voice pitch of the male-to-female transsexual remains at a lower level, completely at odds with a new female role, unless change is attempted" (1990: 43). Gelfer and Mikos (2005) claim that "[a]cquiring the voice characteristics of the reassigned gender is a particular challenge for male-to-female transgendered persons, because the vocal mechanism in most cases has attained adult male dimensions, and it is not affected by the administration of female hormones" (545). Notably, it does not appear that this claim has been empirically verified. Even as estrogen is assumed to have no effect on trans women's voices, phoneticians studying cis women's voices have claimed (perhaps speciously) that estrogen contributes to greater articulatory precision among women as compared to men (Whiteside *et al.* 2004; Wadnerkar *et al.* 2006).

Based on an understanding of trans women as having male voices by nature, authors in this body of work assume that trans speakers need help overcoming their "natural voices" in order to achieve "female-like speech" (Spencer 1988). A dichotomy is thus constructed between biologically determined gender differences, which give us our "natural voices," and self-consciously chosen speaking styles that can to some extent mask those natural characteristics. At the same time, the idea of "female-like speech" is homogenized, erasing the variability found among cis women's voices across communities. Spencer claims that "speech changes which result in a 'female-sounding' voice represent deliberate acquisition of specific behaviors rather than the effects of hormone therapy" (1988: 40). The notion that trans women might sound female without explicit instruction is not usually considered (although Gelfer

(1999) gives credence to the possibility), which may be in part because trans people fitting this description are unlikely to seek out speech therapy. But trans women who have little difficulty producing normatively feminine voices are erased from the research, reinforcing the idea that trans women are naturally masculine and must exert control over that natural state in order to achieve something that resembles the natural femininity of cis women, who need not put in any effort to sound "female-like."

A final ideological position evident in the speech pathology literature is the assumption that trans speakers want to sound like stereotypically straight, gender-normative cis people who also embody white, middle-class, American femininity (or, when applicable, masculinity). When Gelfer refers to successful trans women clients as speaking with an "acceptable" female voice (1999: 1) and Spencer describes the more feminine-sounding trans women in her study as having "more adequate speech patterns" (1988: 39), it is against that highly privileged – and not necessarily reality-based – norm that trans women are being compared. This is true if only because scholars' and speech therapists' knowledge about gendered characteristics in the voice is informed by studies that often use college students as representatives of "women" and "men" in general. But this assumption is intensified by lack of acknowledgement that, for example, some trans women may prefer to be read as lesbians and/or masculine women, as women of color, as older women, or as working class women. In fact, even where trans women suggest they might have different goals, the insistence on gender normativity may persist; Spencer remarks with wonder that all of her clients were satisfied with their voices despite the fact that not all were perceived as female speakers in decontextualized experimental contexts. She concludes that the trans women who are perceived as men must be mistaken about how they sound: "subjective clients reports of the adequacy of the speech product may not be valid" (1988: 40).

Trans women remain the primary focus of this research on trans voices – based in part on the demand for speech therapy from this group – but speech researchers who have recently begun to look at trans men's voices have argued that this group could similarly profit from speech therapy because their voices may continue to diverge from normative expectations for linguistic masculinity – expectations that are not necessarily embodied even by straight cis men. Such arguments, it should be noted, exist in an economically symbiotic relationship with speech therapy practitioners: researchers have the power to legitimize speech therapists' services with the argument that a segment of the population "needs" speech therapy, while demand for speech therapists' services in turn justifies the funding of speech pathology research.

Despite the weight of these arguments, trans men on testosterone are often in a position to resist the idea that they require speech therapy or other means of controlling and consciously changing the gendered characteristics of their voices. As the remainder of this chapter demonstrates, this reluctance is driven in large part by trans men's conflicting relationship with agency over their bodies versus agency over their gender presentations.

Speech-language pathology may in some ways seem a world apart from sociocultural linguistics, but I shine a light on this literature because sociocultural linguistic research on trans people's voices risks the same kind of problematic assumptions about speaker agency if we are not careful to situate our claims about agentive sociolinguistic practices in both locally grounded and broader sociocultural context.

## Agency in Transmasculine Discourses about the Gendered Voice

Turning to metalinguistic commentary from transmasculine participants in my ethnographic fieldwork, a different set of ideologies about sociolinguistic control is evident – one that ultimately informs their sociolinguistic practices on a finer level. The overarching theme in this commentary is one of rejecting the idea that vocal masculinization can or should be achieved through self-awareness and control over gendered elements of the voice rather than hormone therapy. On the few occasions that my participants did acknowledge making these kinds of attempts, it was framed as something they had done in the past, before testosterone provided them with a deeper, male-sounding voice, and generally with little success. Of course, starting hormone therapy involves certain kinds of agentive choices, often driven specifically by the desire for a lower voice. Yet the speakers I put into focus do not talk about the influence of testosterone on their voices in terms of personal agency, but rather tend to present it as a matter of biological determination that is, for the most part, out of their hands. As I will argue later in this section, the apparent paradox in making strong claims over certain kinds of agency while simultaneously rejecting others can be understood as part of a broader ideological separation between sexual embodiment and an internally felt and self-defined gender identity that is central to contemporary formulations of trans identity. Importantly, though, other familiar ideologies are simultaneously engaged in this talk, including the naturalization of vocal pitch as determined by hormonal sex, the valorization of bio-medical interventions over behavioral changes, and the idea that femininity is achieved through artifice, while masculinity is characterized by an absence of effort.

There are three primary themes through which transmasculine speakers problematize and reject self-conscious masculinization of their voices: the effects of testosterone on the voice, the high value placed on authenticity, and political objections to linguistic assimilation.

As noted, trans men's voices are known to drop in pitch when testosterone therapy is administered, and members of this group tend not to seek out speech therapy in part for this reason. Because testosterone is a mainstay of female-to-male medical transition, the received wisdom is that trans men do not need speech therapy in order to sound male. In his review of "transgender and language," Kulick (1999) argues that this assumption – that trans women need speech therapy while trans men do not – reflects and perpetuates the naturalization of masculine speaking styles and the treatment of femininity as artificial and achieved only through careful training. Since Kulick's publication (though probably not because of it), speech-language pathologists have conducted a handful of studies on trans men's voices and have also begun to question the assumed primacy of testosterone-fuelled changes (most overtly van Borsel *et al.* 2000 and Adler and van Borsel 2006). Transmasculine people making use of testosterone, however, continue to emphasize the effects of hormone therapy on the voice.

Important to this discussion is the idea of *passing*, or being perceived as a member of one's self-identified gender, which has a central and yet highly problematized status in many trans communities. On the one hand, trans people who are not perceived in the way they would like often talk about *passing* as a goal or express frustration at their inability to *pass*. Since most of my participants were early in their transitions when I started recording them and were thus still negotiating the extent to which they were perceived as men, the term was not uncommon in their conversations. At the same time, when participants in my study talked about passing, they often signaled their awareness of the problems with the term – for example, by gesturing scare quotes with their fingers – as well as in some cases overtly objecting to the notion that they should strive to pass. The main objection to the word *passing* in this context is that it usually refers to people who are perceived as members of a group to which they do not, in reality, belong. For instance, one might say that people of color at times *pass as white* despite not being white or that gays and lesbians may similarly *pass as straight* despite not being straight. To say that a trans person *passes as a (wo)man* suggests that trans men are not really men and trans women are not really women, only mistakenly perceived as such. Despite objections over the word itself, it is of great importance for many transmasculine people – especially those who have not (or not yet) seen dramatic physical masculinization from hormones – to manage their gender presentations. Indeed, for my participants, the choice to go on testosterone was motivated by a desire to be read as male at least some of the time in their everyday lives. Many also invoked an internal sense of what they feel their body should be like (see Prosser 1998; Salamon 2010 for more on this idea), but the social perceptions of others was an important factor for everyone in my study. Notably, this complex and problematized view of passing is absent from the speech pathology literature.

Because of the interest transmasculine people may have in shaping their self-presentation in order to "pass" as men, a genre of texts known as *passing tips* has developed for circulation in online trans communities. This information is then further disseminated within local communities. One website, "The FTM Passing Tips Site,"[3] which contains advice that I encountered in near identical form in online spaces for trans men in the 1990s, features advice on a range of topics from clothing and haircuts to swimming and negotiating men's restrooms. Some example tips from this site include the following:

- If you live in a cosmopolitan area where there are a lot of butch lesbians then it's going to be much more difficult for you to pass. One way to help distinguish yourself from them is to dress more conservatively – you might want to leave the leather motorcycle jacket at home for a while.
- All-over crewcuts are also problematic because they emphasize the shape and size of one's skull and are therefore feminizing (look at Sinead O' Connor).
- Footwear can be a real problem if you have small feet, although you do save money if you can wear boys' athletic shoes.

In contrast to passing tips with detailed advice about clothing, haircuts, different methods for binding (i.e. flattening one's chest) or packing (i.e. creating a bulge in the crotch of one's pants), relatively little guidance is available on vocal masculinization. This paucity also stands in stark contrast with the both informal and commercial guidance available to trans women for vocal feminization. Like many of the passing tips on this site, the single sentence under the "voice" section is phrased in terms of generalities about how women and men behave. It reads:

- Women tend to use an upward inflection at the end of their sentences, while men tend to speak in more of a monotone.

Despite the importance of vocal pitch, it is not treated as something that can or should be consciously manipulated the way that the use of rising versus falling or flat intonation might be. In fact, the only other reference made to gender differences in the voice in this document of approximately 6,000 words is an insistence that testosterone is "the only safe and effective way" to achieve a lower-pitched voice:

- The only safe and effective way to lower your voice, masculinize your body, and grow facial hair is to take testosterone under the care of a doctor. Any other way is ineffective and potentially hazardous to your health.

In this way, the voice is framed differently from other semiotic indexes of gender, such as bodily hexis (Bourdieu 1984), how much a person talks, or

---

[3] Retrieved from www.ftmpassingtips.com on April 10, 2012.

what they talk about. Advice on "body language" is fairly common, with the same website asserting: "Women tend to be less obtrusive, while men tend to take up more space. If you watch commuters on a bus, women tend to sit with their legs crossed and their arms drawn in, and men tend to sit with their legs apart and their arms out." Other websites[4] suggest being less talkative, not smiling as much, and avoiding "gossip" in order to pass. Yet, the overall emphasis in transmasculine discourses on linguistic masculinization is on physiological changes brought about by testosterone, such that the voice is listed in conjunction with body hair and the general notion of a masculinized body. Another site goes as far as to instruct trans people not to intentionally adopt a lower pitch range, warning that:

- Deepening your voice on the phone is fine and may be a good idea if you're on the high side, but don't try to deepen it when having a conversation in person. You can see it in a person's face when they're trying to change their voice.[5]

The foregoing discussion of electronically mediated passing tips that circulate within and across trans communities – of which participants in my fieldwork were almost universally aware – leads into the first language ideology taken up by the trans men whose metalinguistic commentary are the focus of the remainder of this section: the idea that testosterone will "take care of . . . pretty much everything," as Mack puts it in Excerpt 1 (lines 9 to 10). Notably, Mack's formulation casts testosterone as the grammatical subject and thematic agent in the process of "taking care of" voice masculinization, grammatically encoding what Duranti (2004) calls the "chain of causality" from testosterone to the voice through strategic manipulations of syntactic structure.

And, indeed, changes in vocal pitch documented for these speakers by Zimman (2012), as well as similar findings for other trans populations like those studied by Papp (2011), support the conclusion that testosterone generally does help speakers move from a pitch range considered typical for women into a range considered typical for men. One of the speakers in this study, whom I call Mack, characterizes the way in which trans men typically see the effect of testosterone. Mack is a 46-year-old, white, straight-identified[6] trans man who grew up in the Bay Area and works as a bus driver for a private charter company. During one of our conversations in his home in the southern outskirts of San Francisco, Mack was telling me about some of his

---

[4] E.g. www.tssupport.org/Tips/FTM, www.t-vox.org/index.php?title=FTM_passing_tips, and www.wikihow.com/Pass-As-a-Male-%28For-FTMs%29 retrieved on April 10, 2012.

[5] Retrieved from www.t-vox.org/index.php?title=FTM_passing_tips on April 10, 2012.

[6] That is to say, Mack not only exclusively dated women, but also saw his attraction to them as heterosexual, as did several other participants in this study, even as others who were attracted exclusively to women described those attractions as *queer*.

transfeminine friends and how hard many of them work in order to be recognized as women. In Excerpt 1, I ask him whether he thinks trans men tend to put in as much effort into masculinizing their appearance and behavior. Significantly, Mack has been frustrated with the relatively slow speed at which his own voice has changed, yet maintains confidence that testosterone will eventually do for him what it has done for other trans men he knows.

**Excerpt 1, Mack (at 49 Weeks on Testosterone)**

| | | |
|---|---|---|
| 01 | M: | Yeah, she was really successful. And, but she was a really hard worker on |
| 02 | | everything. She was really committed to really really movin' through the |
| 03 | | world as female and not being clocked? |
| 04 | LZ: | Mhm. |
| 05 | M: | Y'know? |
| 06 | LZ: | Do you think that trans guys in general are as committed t- to like, kind |
| 07 | | of, doing everything possible to, |
| 08 | M: | In my experience, the trans guys and the trans women I've met, I'd say |
| 09 | | no, because guys know that testosterone's gonna eventually take care of |
| 10 | | everyth- pretty much everything.= |
| 11 | LZ: | =[Right. |
| 12 | M: | [I myself have been lazy on some things because it's very easy to just |
| 13 | | go, well yeah, but in a year it's gonna be gone anyway,= |
| 14 | LZ: | R[ight. |
| 15 | M: | [=y'know, in a year my voice is gonna be deep anyway,= |
| 16 | LZ: | Mhm. |
| 17 | M: | =y'know. So I think, my experience has been that trans women work a lot |
| 18 | | harder. |

My own observations support Mack's claim that trans men are by and large confident that testosterone will masculinize their voices to the extent that they see little reason to gain awareness and control that might lead to more normatively masculine speech. It is partly for this reason that trans men and other transmasculine people do not often talk about purported differences between men's and women's voices – seemingly rejecting awareness as well as control – aside from pitch and the related feature of intonational patterns. In contrast with the few resources on voice masculinization, trans women have a larger body of knowledge on which to draw, including books and other guides produced by trans women themselves (e.g. James 2012, nd; also Laing 1989), which call attention to markers like voice quality, resonance, and particular segments linked to gender (e.g. /s/). However, the important fact here is not simply that trans men's hormonal regimens affect the voice in ways that trans women's do not. The more significant point is that even Mack, with his still relatively high-pitched voice, subscribes to the ideology that self-conscious masculinization is both unnecessary and, as the next examples will show, undesirable for transmasculine people on testosterone.

The power of testosterone to bring about changes in the voice is not the only reason transmasculine people on testosterone give for their rejection of agentive linguistic masculinization. The second language ideology expressed by the participants in this study centers around the idea that linguistic self-monitoring is contrary to the ultimate goal of a gender role transition: to express an authentic self that is naturally masculine and/or male. Accordingly, when I asked my participants whether they would consider putting in effort to speak in a more masculine way, I was told by several individuals that constant self-monitoring would undermine their desire to more fully express what they feel as an authentic sense of self. Some of these trans speakers felt it was completely unnecessary to alter their speech, gesture, clothing, or any other aspect of their gender expression because they were already quite normatively masculine. Adam, for example, is a 38-year-old, white, queer-identified trans man who grew up in the New York City suburbs and works as a program director for an LGBT youth organization. He is the only speaker in this study whose voice was occasionally perceived as male even before testosterone, which is a relatively unusual experience among trans men. Adam told me that his self-presentation had been masculine for decades by the time he decided to transition medically, and that he never felt that masculinity required effort; it was always the prospect of subduing his masculinity that presented the bigger challenge. His transition-related anxieties centered less around whether he would be perceived as a man and more around losing his status as a visibly queer person as he began to blend in with straight cis men. But even among the participants in my study whose gender presentations and voices were less typically masculine than Adam's, it was typical to emphasize the value of authentic self-expression over normative masculinity.

When my participants did talk about trying to masculinize their voices, it was always framed as something they did at the beginning of their transitions, before their voices changed from testosterone. It was also often framed as unconscious or unsuccessful, each of which distances the speaker from the notion that they have achieved masculinity only through an active imitation of non-trans men. I had a conversation on this topic about halfway through my year of recording Kyle, a 24-year-old queer trans man who grew up in the Bay Area and was working at a camp for children and pre-teens. During an afternoon we spent chatting in my San Francisco apartment, Kyle told me about "subconscious" attempts he had made in the past to "squash" his natural effeminacy (Excerpt 2, lines 02–05). His efforts were motivated by wanting to be seen as male (line 06), but now that he found himself increasingly achieving that goal, he reports becoming more open to reincorporating femininity into his gender expression, for instance by wearing makeup and hot-pants (i.e. very short shorts) to go dancing at a club. The dialogue in Excerpt 2 comes from a conversation about the concern Kyle shares with Adam: that his affiliation with local queer communities will become invisible now that he is being seen as a man and losing his status as a visibly gender non-conforming person. He relates his self-ascribed effeminacy back to this issue of visibility in lines 09 to 11, in which he refers to a conversation he had with his partner, a femme woman who has also struggled with maintaining visibility as a queer-identified person.

**Excerpt 2, Kyle (at 32 Weeks on Testosterone)**

```
01   K:    I have this, like, tendency, like, where like I think I'm naturally would describe
02         myself as like kind of faggy or like an effeminate man.
03   LZ:   Mhm.
04   K:    But as I'm transitioning I've like, not consciously, but subconsciously
05         kind of like squashed a little of that natural, like, expression. Because
06         I'm [like, "I really want to pass, I really want to be seen as male."=
07   LZ:        [Mm. Mhm.
08   K:    =Um, that conversation has kind of come around that, where she's like,
09         actually, like, it's kinda great that that's who you are, because that's
10         going to be something that, uh, is going to help you be identified as
11         visibly [queer and you're worried about what is that going to look like.
12   LZ:           [Mm.
```

In this context, Kyle situates himself as the agent of these shifts away from femininity in his speaking style and other forms of gendered expression, yet he also mitigates the intentionality behind that agency by pointing out that the change has not come about "consciously, but subconsciously" (line 04). Now that testosterone has changed Kyle's body to the extent that he achieves equal footing with non-trans men when it comes to the so-called secondary sex characteristics, there is room for his "natural," authentic effeminacy to come to the surface.

Another participant who talked about trying to speak in a more masculine way towards the start of his transition was Dave, whose commentary illustrates the ways in which trans men who are not stereotypically masculine may draw on other elements of their identities as authorization for ostensibly feminine speech characteristics. Dave is a 23-year-old white, queer trans man from an upper-middle-class Bay Area family, and an artist who was unemployed during most of the duration of my fieldwork. Like Kyle, Dave feels more comfortable expressing femininity than he did before he was consistently perceived as a man, particularly because it fits with his identity as a fem queer man.[7] As Dave puts it in Excerpt 3, "now that I read completely as male, [...]

---

[7] In Dave's case, a person who is attracted to a range of gender identities and who presents himself in a more feminine style than is normatively permitted of men even as he self-identifies as a man (rather than, say, positioning himself outside of the gender binary).

I'm just gonna sound like a faggot, it's fine" (lines 09-10). This selection comes from our final meeting, in which I asked him to reflect back on the ways his voice has changed, or not changed, during his transition so far.

### Excerpt 3, Dave (at 112 Weeks on Testosterone)

| | | |
|---|---|---|
| LZ: | Do you think anything other than your pitch has changed, as your voice | 01 |
| | has changed (.) since (.) transitioning? | 02 |
| D: | I tried to swoop less, when I was early in transition. Like, I very much | 03 |
| | tried to sound like, more modulated masculine and have less of like the sort | 04 |
| | of queeny voice? | 05 |
| LZ: | Mhm. | 06 |
| D: | I very consciously tried to do that and failed a lot 'cause I would forget. | 07 |
| | Um. But I've definitely stopped doing that now that I read completely as | 08 |
| | male, cause now I'm like fu:ck I'm just gonna sound like a faggot, it's | 09 |
| | fine. Who cares? | 10 |

Unlike Kyle, Dave does not take any steps towards softening his agentive responsibility for "very consciously tr[ying]" to "swoop less." However, he also suggests that it was not realistically possible for him to limit his swoopiness given that his attempts to decrease his pitch range or intonational variability were unsuccessful. Dave distances himself from the person he was before he "read completely as male" and emphasizes that he "definitely stopped" monitoring his prosody the way he used to once he had the security of being recognized as a man.

Dave has also developed an overtly political perspective on the passing tips I mentioned above, which he told me about during one of our earlier meetings. As he sees it, the crux of both passing tips and speech therapy is the idea that a person should change themselves in order to meet others' expectations about how men and women look, act, and sound. When I asked Dave whether he thought people could be successful in self-monitoring their speech – given that Dave told me his own attempts to "swoop less" did not succeed – he told me that he thinks people can be successful, but that "their success is something that [he] find[s] repulsive" (Excerpt 4, lines 03–04). Because he identifies strongly both as a man and as a fem, Dave is especially concerned with making space for male-identified people whose voices fall well outside of the expectations for heteronormative cis masculinity.

### Excerpt 4, Dave (at 67 Weeks on Testosterone)

| | | |
|---|---|---|
| LZ: | Do you think the passing tips, like about voice, like "talk in a monotone" | 01 |
| | or whatever, that people are successful, or can be successful in doing that? | 02 |
| D: | I think they can, if they're that determined. Um, but their success is | 03 |
| | something I find repulsive, so. Like I'm in favor of them reading correctly | 04 |
| | as male and having that privilege and not that pressure in their life and | 05 |
| | I'm like mmm no. Not that way. Somebody has to fight the fight for men | 06 |
| | with flamboyant voices. | 07 |

Dave's comment exemplifies the contradiction with which I am concerned: he wants trans men to have what he calls the "privilege" of being perceived as men, if that is their goal, but he doesn't want that end to be achieved through limiting their self-expression or assimilating to hetero- and gender-normative standards for appropriate masculinity. The least problematic option left for linguistic masculinization, from this perspective, is testosterone.

### Agentive Tensions

As I mentioned in the introduction to this chapter, even as the participants in my fieldwork rejected agentive masculinization of their voices, they also valued agency in a number of ways that are central to their communities' formulations of trans identity. One of these is in the elevation of self-identified gender category as the ultimate determiner of how an individual's gender should be understood. What determines that a person is truly a man, in such a framework, is the mere fact that he defines himself as one. This emphasis on self-identification runs against dominant cultural discourses about gender and sex, which depend on external authorities (e.g. scientists, doctors, or religious figures) to define what makes a person female or male. It also runs against many academic theories of identity in that gender is seen as a matter of individual self-determination rather than being relational and co-constructed (e.g. Bucholtz and Hall 2004, 2005). Agency is also highly valued in trans communities in discussions of bodily autonomy and access to medical technologies available for the re-shaping of sexed embodiment, which have historically had to be approved by gate-keeping professionals (Speer and Parsons 2006). Contrary to clinical expectations that a gender role transition must follow a linear set path of hormones and surgery, trans communities have spent decades advocating for the opportunity to pick and choose which aspects of a medical transition fit each individual's needs, if any.

Going on testosterone is thus clearly understood as a matter of free choice, but the ensuing pitch changes are not framed as agentive shifts in the same way that conscious stylistic changes are. Although this separation of biology and style may seem intuitive, what is most striking is the fact that, for these speakers, even the choice to begin testosterone therapy somehow avoids the threat to authenticity posed by speech therapy. One could easily make the same argument about testosterone that these trans speakers make about agentive style-shifting. Clearly, hormone therapy is as much a tool of potential assimilation as stylistic changes are, and transmasculine people who opt not to make use of hormone therapy may invoke their desire not to change who they are, how they look, or how they speak just so that others will perceive them as legitimately male, extending Dave's critique about trying to "swoop less" (Excerpt 3, line 03).

To understand this potential tension, we need to take into account the ways in which discourses of trans identity separate biological sex from the internal, authentic self (see Valentine 2007 for additional history). In these discourses, a person's "true" gender transcends their biology, which is what makes it possible for people categorized as biologically female to see their self-identification as male as the more authentic representation of who they are (or vice versa). Particularly instructive here is a final quote from Kam, a 30-year-old white, genderqueer, trans boy[8] from working class Cincinnati who was a graduate student and maintained a distinctly non-normative blend of femininity and masculinity. He also strongly resisted the pull to compromise his self-expression in order to "pass" as male, for instance foregoing chest binding despite the fact that this choice made it more likely that he would be perceived as a woman. Like Dave, Kam recognized that his speaking style was far from the masculine norm because of his pitch range and variability, which was amplified by his frequent use of falsetto voice quality; also like Dave, Kam had no interest in changing this aspect of his self-presentation. When I asked him how much his voice had changed after just five weeks on testosterone, he told me that it's difficult to tell because he gets excited about his voice being lower, which leads him to start "squealing" out of happiness and brings his pitch back up. The talk from Excerpt 5 is what followed.

**Excerpt 5, Kam (at 5 Weeks on Testosterone)**

| | | |
|---|---|---|
| K: | Um, but, yeah. I feel like it's dropped just a tiny bit. | 01 |
| LZ: | Mhm. Do you still try to, like, control- like, y'know, keep it in the lower | 02 |
| | part of your range? or do you just kind of let it do its own thing. | 03 |
| K: | It's:- in some spaces and at some times I'll find myself doing it, and I'm | 04 |
| | like, "^oh, what am I doing that for?^" And I'm like, ohh. I think I'm really, | 05 |
| | just, actually have always had like, a deeper register like when I'm just | 06 |
| | like having normal conversation and just like talking or whatever, but like | 07 |
| | when I'm ^excited,^ or when I'm like, whatever, like, my voice is much | 08 |
| | much higher? | 09 |
| LZ: | Mhm. | 10 |
| K: | Um. Like, someone I am close to, like, described it as like, never: bothering or | 11 |
| | caring to learn male patterns of speech? ((laugh)) | 12 |
| LZ: | Uh-huh ((laugh)) (xxx) yeah. | 13 |
| K: | I mean he's, been on T for like 10 years, just about, and he still- his | 14 |
| | voice is low, but his like, on the phone he gets taken as female, um, all | 15 |
| | the time because he never, he= | 16 |
| LZ: | Yeah. | 17 |
| K: | =Claims that he's never bothered to learn or care ((laugh)) | 18 |
| LZ: | Right, [yeah, (totally). | 19 |

---

[8] Several of the participants in this study describe themselves as genderqueer, or neither strictly female nor male, and among this group *boy* was sometimes preferred to *man* as an identity label.

| | | |
|---|---|---|
| 20 | K: | [About how guys talk- or whatever. |
| 21 | LZ: | [Yeah                    [Yeah |
| 22 | K: | [So he gets excited and [like, I'm like I feel like that will also be true |
| 23 | | of me.= |
| 24 | LZ: | Mhm. |
| 25 | K: | =Like, I'm not- I'm, I'm just so like, I'm a giggly, bubbly, like, squealy |
| 26 | | type of person? ((laugh)) |

Kam describes himself as unconcerned with shifting his intonation patterns to the point that, when he notices himself constraining the way he speaks, he asks himself "what am I doing that for?" (line 05), indicating that he questions his motivations for style-shifting towards more typically masculine patterns. Moreover, he asks this question of himself with falsetto voice quality, suggesting that his internal monologue incorporates this aspect of his voice. Repeating the word *squeal* to refer to his own voice for the second time in just a few moments, Kam says that he's just a "giggly, bubbly, like, squealy type of person" (lines 25–6) and that he doesn't see that changing. In so doing, he iconically links his linguistic style to his characterization of himself as an individual. Despite these facts, Kam does not enact this kind of resistance when it comes to changing his voice with testosterone; in fact, he had told me only a few minutes earlier that his sole reason for going on hormones was to change his voice. Based on his account, this decision to go on testosterone did not conflict with his intent to maintain his gender presentation, which he also described as "femmey" and "faggy."

There is a critical qualitative difference for transmasculine people on testosterone, then, between agentively choosing to modify the body and agentively choosing to modify other forms of semiotic self-presentation. Yet, this apparent contradiction can be made sense of in terms of the separation that trans discourses of identity draw between the body and the authentic self.

Because the vocal changes that come with testosterone therapy are understood as physiological in nature, they do not inhibit expression of one's true, inner self, just as transmasculine people see their pre-transition, ostensibly "female" bodies as separable from their internally felt masculine identities. Instead, testosterone simply gives transmasculine people access to a physiological baseline that is comparable with what non-trans men have – almost as if this happens through an accident of nature rather than being precipitated by a conscious decision. Once they can make use of a male-sounding pitch range, transmasculine speakers position themselves as free to avoid changing the stylistic elements of their speech and to thereby continue expressing what they experience as an authentic self, while also tapping into the importance non-trans people typically place on gendered embodiment, including the voice, in the attribution of gender.

Although the ideologies I have described are aimed at unseating transphobic representations of trans people's inauthenticity, they carry with them a dark side in the form of implicit ideologies that these speakers would be unlikely to overtly endorse. Importantly, the split I have identified between body and mind is not enough to account for the ideologies about agency I have discussed. Transfeminine people, after all, create a similar division between embodied sexual characteristics and self-defined gender, yet they tend to have a very different perspective on making self-conscious vocal changes. This is where additional levels of ideology that are not particular to the context of trans identity come into play.

First, the naturalization of masculinity, discussed above, grants these speakers license to construct their genders as effortless even as many trans women are comfortable acknowledging that a degree of effort is put into producing their femininity. Regardless of whether there is an actual difference in the self-conscious behavioral changes made by trans men as compared to trans women, the cultural context provides men with both greater means for constructing their gender as effortless and the demand that they take advantage of these means if they want to authenticate their masculinity.

Second, even as transmasculine speakers challenge the idea that someone with a deep voice must take on all of the stylistic elements normatively associated with masculinity, they also reinforce a perspective on gender differentiation in the voice that is dependent primarily on biology. The ideologies naturalize sexual embodiment despite the investment trans communities have in contesting this naturalization (Zimman 2014). It also creates a system of stratification among trans people; that is, if exposure to testosterone is the most important aspect of whether a voice should be considered female or male, trans women would be understood as having naturally male voices, while the voices of trans men who are not on testosterone would be considered female. In this hierarchy, transmasculine people on testosterone would be uniquely positioned among trans people as possessing a match between vocal sex and gender identity.

Trans people are often the focus of scrutiny over the authenticity of their gender presentations and identities. On the one hand, trans people face delegitimation or violence when they fail to live up to normative expectations for the self-identified gender category. At the same time, trans people who do live up to those expectations may be criticized for being excessively normative and hence reinforcing harmful gender stereotypes. The discourses analyzed in this chapter are one way in which speakers work to balance these demands, while also laying claim on the limited forms of embodied gender privilege to which they have access.

### Ideology into Practice

A summary of the sociolinguistic styles employed by the speakers I have been discussing is now warranted as a means of exploring how ideologies about agency shape sociolinguistic practice. The sociophonetic arm of this project was focused on documenting change in the voices of the fifteen participants during their first and/or second year on testosterone. As would be expected, all of these speakers saw a decrease in vocal pitch, although to different extents and at different rates of change. A few speakers never reached a normative male pitch range during the time I recorded them; Mack from Excerpt 1 is one example of a speaker whose mean pitch decreased only from approximately 220 to 200 Hz over the course of the year. However, most dropped to an average well below 140 Hz. Much more variability was found, however, in articulatory indices of gender like the spectral qualities of /s/. Zimman (2012, 2015) describes the enormous variability in the mean frequencies of /s/, with these fifteen speakers covering the entire range typically reported for American English-speaking men and the entire range typically reported for their female counterparts (i.e. as low as 4,500 Hz and as high as 10,000 Hz; see Flipsen 1999). While some speakers did undergo statistically significant changes in their articulation of /s/, most did not. Among those who did see some change, a few actually shifted upwards, away from the norm for men, which aligns with speaker self-reports about being more comfortable expressing femininity as their pitch settled into a male-sounding range. The speakers with the lowest pitch voices in the study, including Dave from Excerpts 3 and 4 (with an average below 115 Hz), also had among the highest mean frequency ranges for /s/ (averaging above 9,000 Hz). Indeed, in interviews and ethnographic inter- actions with nearly 100 transmasculine people in three metropolitan areas in the United States over the last ten years, I have found it not at all uncommon for trans people on testosterone to have low-pitched voices paired with articu- latory characteristics commonly associated with femininity or gay male iden- tities (see Zimman 2013 for more on perceived gayness among trans men).

One potential interpretation of these facts is that transmasculine speakers really don't need to change features of their voice other than pitch in order to be perceived as men on the basis of their voices. However, early results from a perceptual pilot study using modified guises of these participants' read speech suggest that both formant frequencies and /s/ contribute significantly to how low a speaker's mean pitch needs to be in order for their voice to be perceived as male in an experimental context. That is, a speaker with a very high frequency /s/ will need to have a lower mean pitch to be perceived as male than another speaker who has a lower frequency /s/. Another potential inter- pretation of these facts is that trans men are not very good at masculinizing their voices and may be more successful with this process if they worked with a speech therapist. However, once we take into account the rejections of sociolinguistic agency articulated in the discourse presented above, a third explanation emerges in which ideology and sociolinguistic style align. These speakers' ideologies about sociolinguistic agency are for this reason an essential part of understanding why they employ the particular combinations of sociophonetic features they do. In rejecting control over their voices, trans people on testosterone construct styles that both index an ideological stance and constitute a particular kind of subjectivity invested with moral and political value. Here, stylistic practice and ideology mirror and mutually reinforce one another. Regardless of these speakers' potential ability to control their voices – a question that is worth exploring further in its own right – the agency they claim for themselves is limited.

### Conclusion

The discourse analyzed in this chapter highlights the complex ways in which ideology, power, and hegemony factor into sociolinguistic awareness and control. Silverstein (1985) proposes that the effect of ideology on structure (i.e. linguistic forms) is one way agency is exercised over language. People need not be explicitly aware of the linguistic details of a change in the formal realm – which in this case stands in for the gendered elements of the voice – in order to exercise power and control over that change. Rather than explicit linguistic awareness, agency is realized through ideologically motivated shifts in the indexical realm, which by extension has an effect on linguistic forms themselves. For transmasculine speakers, ideologies about hormonal sex and gendered authenticity assign particular indexical meanings to the practice of shifting towards gender-based linguistic norms, which then work to shape the actual styles found among trans speakers. Paradoxically, ideologies about the undesirability of linguistic control become the means through which agency is exercised on the structural level of sociophonetic style, even as these speakers overtly constructing themselves as lacking or refusing agency over their voices.

Silverstein focuses on the ways in which ideology can be a means of exercising linguistic agency, but my own analysis suggests that the construction of agency itself is a tool for ideological work, and that claims on or disavowals of awareness and control may be of great importantance for our explanations of social and linguistic practice. While power is often gained through claims on agency, for these speakers it is through the disavowal of sociolinguistic agency that they contest transphobic ideologies about the voice. This is not to say, however, that the discourse analyzed is wholly subversive. Even as they challenge transphobic ideologies about gendered authenticity, they simultaneously lay claim on certain forms of male privilege and reinscribe the naturalization of hormonal effects on the voice in ways that are derived directly from cis-normative systems of oppression and inequality.

A final lesson to be taken from these speakers' complex and at times seemingly contradictory engagements with agency and control is that these notions are sociocultural constructs that carry weighty implications for systems of power. This point is of particular importance for sociocultural linguists who hope to understand how speakers exercise sociolinguistic agency because it demands that we consider our field's ideologies about awareness and control and how our speakers' perspectives might be erased in our analyses in favor of our own. Rather than assuming we know what agency means for our speakers, we could learn a great deal by pairing our sociolinguistic analyses of awareness and control with closer attention to the discourses within which these practices take place. Such attention will challenge linguists to confront the inherent complexity of agency itself much in the way anthropologists have done – to recognize it not as a psychological property of the individual, but as a culturally grounded, ideological experience at the core of what it means to be a speaking subject.

### Transcription Conventions

| [ | overlapping speech |
| (( )) | non-linguistic action (e.g. laughter, coughing) |
| = | latching speech (i.e. continued from previous line with no pause) |
| (.) | brief pause |
| (word) | uncertainty regarding transcription |
| (xxx) | indecipherable speech |
| ^word^ | falsetto voice quality |
| "word" | stylized reported speech |
| ? | rising intonation |
| , | continuing intonation |
| . | falling intonation |
| : | lengthened phone |

## REFERENCES

Adler, Richard K. and van Borsel, John. 2006. Female-to-male considerations, in Richard K. Adler, Sandy Hirsch, and Michelle Mordaunt (eds.), *Voice and Communication Therapy for the Transgender/Transsexual Client*, pp. 139–67. San Diego, CA: Plural Publishing.

Ahearn, Laura M. 2000. Agency. *Journal of Linguistic Anthropology* 9(1–2): 12–15.

2001. Language and agency. *Annual Review of Anthropology* 30:109–37.

Besnier, Niko. 2003. Crossing genders, mixing languages: The linguistic construction of transgenderism in Tonga, in Janet Holmes and Miriam Meyerhoff (eds.), *The Handbook of Language and Gender*, pp. 279–301. Malden, MA and Oxford, UK: Blackwell.

van Borsel, John, de Cuypere, Griet, Rubens, Robert, and Destaerke, B. 2000. Voice problems in female-to-male transsexuals. *International Journal of Language & Communication Disorders* 35(3):427–42.

Bourdieu, Pierre. 1984. *Distinction: A Social Critique of the Judgment of Taste.*
   New York and London: Routledge.
Bralley, Ralph C., Bull, Glen L., Gore, Cheryl Harris, and Edgerton, Milton T. 1978.
   Evaluation of vocal pitch in male transsexuals. *Journal of Communication
   Disorders* 11(5):443–9.
Bucholtz, Mary and Hall, Kira. 2004. Theorizing identity in language and sexuality
   research. *Language in Society* 33(4):469–516.
   2005. Identity and interaction: A sociocultural linguistic approach. *Discourse Studies*
   7(4–5):585–614.
Butler, Judith. 1990. *Gender Trouble: Feminism and the Subversion of Identity.*
   New York and London: Routledge.
Dacakis, Georgia. 2002. The role of voice therapy in male-to-female transsexuals. *Head
   & Neck Surgery* 10(3):173–7.
Damrose, Edward J. 2009. Quantifying the impact of androgen therapy on the female
   larynx. *Auris, Nasus, Larynx* 36(1):110–12.
Davies, Shelagh and Goldberg, Joshua M. 2006. Clinical aspects of transgender speech
   feminization and masculinization. *International Journal of Transgenderism*
   9(3–4):167–96.
Duranti, Alessandro. 2004. Agency in language, in Alessandro Duranti (ed.),
   *A Companion to Linguistic Anthropology*, pp. 451–473. Malden, MA:
   Blackwell.
Flipsen Jr., Peter, Shrilberg, Lawrence, Weismer, Gary, Karlsson, Heather, and
   McSweeny, Jane. 1999. Acoustic characteristics of /s/ in adolescents. *Journal of
   Speech, Language, and Hearing Research* 42(3):663–77.
Gelfer, Marylou Pausewang. 1999. Voice therapy for the male-to-female
   transgendered client. *American Journal of Speech-Language Pathology*
   8(3):201–8.
Gelfer, Marylou Pausewang and Mikos, Victoria A. 2005. The relative contributions of
   speaking fundamental frequency and formant frequencies to gender identification
   based on isolated vowels. *Journal of Voice* 19(4):544–54.
Gelfer, Marylou Pausewang and Schofield, Kevin J. 2000. Comparison of acoustic and
   perceptual measures of voice in male-to-female transsexuals perceived as female
   versus those perceived as male. *Journal of Voice* 14(1):22–33.
Günzburger, Deborah. 1995. Acoustic and perceptual implications of the transsexual
   voice. *Archives of Sexual Behavior* 24(3):399–407.
James, Andrea. 2012. Transsexual voice resources [webpage]. www.tsroadmap.com/
   voice/transsexual-voice.html.
Kulick, Don. 1999. Transgender and language. *GLQ: A Journal of Lesbian and Gay
   Studies* 5(4):605–22.
Laing, Alison. 1989. *Speaking as a Woman: A Guide for Those Who Desire to
   Communicate in a More Feminine Manner.* King of Prussia, PA: Creative Design
   Services.
Lippi-Green, Rosina. 1997. *English with an Accent: Language, Ideology, and
   Discrimination in the United States.* New York: Routledge.
McFadden, Dennis, Pasanen, Edward G., and Callaway, Narriman Lee. 1998. Changes
   in otoacoustic emissions in a transsexual male during treatment with estrogen.
   *Journal of the Acoustical Society of America* 104(3):1555–8.

Mount, Kay H. and Salmon, Shirley J. 1988. Changing the vocal characteristics of a postoperative transsexual patient: A longitudinal study. *Journal of Communication Disorders* 21(3):229–38.

Owen, Kelly and Hancock, Adrienne B. 2011. The role of self- and listener perceptions of femininity in voice therapy. *International Journal of Transgenderism* 12(4): 272–84.

Papp, Viktória. 2011. The female-to-male transsexual voice: Physiology vs. performance in production. PhD dissertation. Houston, TX: Rice University.

Prosser, Jay. 1998. *Second Skins: The Body Narratives of Transsexuality*. New York: Columbia University Press.

Sachs, Jacqueline. 1975. Cues to the identification of sex in children's speech, in Barrie Thorne and Nancy Henley (eds.), *Language and Sex: Difference and Dominance*, pp. 152–71. Newbury, MA: Newbury House Publishers.

Salamon, Gayle. 2010. *Assuming a Body: Transgender and Rhetorics of Materiality*. New York: Columbia University Press.

Silverstein, Michael. 1985. Language and the culture of gender: At the intersection of structure, usage, and ideology, in Elizabeth Mertz and Richard J. Parmentier (eds.), *Semiotic Mediation: Sociocultural and Psychological Perspectives*, pp. 219–59. London: Academic Press.

Speer, Susan A. and Parsons, Ceri. 2006. Gatekeeping gender: Some features of the use of hypothetical questions in the psychiatric assessment of transsexual patients. *Discourse & Society* 17(6):785–812.

Spencer, Linda E. 1988. Speech characteristics of male-to-female transsexuals: A perceptual and acoustic study. *Folia Phoniatrica et Logopaedica* 40(1):31–42.

Stuart-Smith, Jane. 2007. Empirical evidence for gendered speech production: /s/ in Glaswegian, in Jennifer Cole and José Ignacio Hualde (eds.), *Laboratory Phonology 9*, pp. 65–86. New York: Mouton de Gruyter.

T'Sjoen, Guy, Moerman, Mieke, Van Borsel, John, Feyen, Els, Rubens, Robert, Monstrey, Stanislas, Hoebeke, Piet, De Sutter, Petra, and De Cuypere, Griet. 2006. Impact of voice in transsexuals. *International Journal of Transgenderism* 9(1):1–7.

Valentine, David. 2007. *Imagining Transgender: An Ethnography of a Category*. Durham, NC: Duke University Press.

Wadnerkar, Meghana B., Cowell, Patricia E., and Whiteside, Sandra P. 2006. Speech across the menstrual cycle: A replication and extension study. *Neuroscience Letters* 408(1):21–4.

Whiteside, Sandra P., Hanson, Anna, and Cowell, Patricia E. 2004. Hormones and temporal components of speech: Sex differences and effect of menstrual cyclicity on speech. *Neuroscience Letters* 367:44–7.

Wolfe, Virginia I., Ratusnik, David L., Smith, Furman H., and Northrop, Gretajo. 1990. Intonation and fundamental frequency in male-to-female transsexuals. *Journal of Speech and Hearing Disorders* 55(1):43–50.

Zimman, Lal. 2012. Voices in transition: Testosterone, transmasculinity, and the gendered voice among female-to-male transgender people. PhD dissertation. Boulder, CO: Department of Linguistics, University of Colorado.

  2013. Hegemonic masculinity and the variability of gay-sounding speech: The perceived sexuality of transgender men. *Journal of Language & Sexuality* 2(1):5–43.

2014. The discursive construction of sex: Remaking and reclaiming the gendered body in talk about genitals among trans men, in Lal Zimman, Jenny Davis, and Joshua Raclaw (eds.), *Queer Excursions: Retheorizing Binaries in Language, Gender, and Sexuality*, pp. 13–34. New York: Oxford University Press.

2015. Transmasculinity and the voice: Gender assignment, identity, and presentation, in Tommaso Milani (ed.), *Language and Masculinities: Performances, Intersections, Dislocations*, pp. 197–219. New York: Routledge.

# Index

Lightning Source UK Ltd.
Milton Keynes UK
UKOW05n0615200517
301633UK00007B/108/P